THE MONTANANS' FISHING GUIDE

Volume I: Montana Waters West of Continental Divide

by Dick Konizeski

Edited and Revised by
BILL ARCHIE AND MICHELE ARCHIE

Mountain Press Publishing Company
Missoula, Montana
1998

Library of Congress Cataloging-in-Publication Data

Konizeski, Richard L., 1917-
    The Montanans' fishing guide / by Dick Konizeski. —5th ed.
      p.   cm.
    Contents: v. 1. Montana waters west of Continental Divide /
edited and revised by Bill Archie and Michele Archie
     ISBN 0-87842-371-0 (alk. paper : v. 1)
    1. Fishing—Montana—Guidebooks.   2. Montana—Guidebooks.
I. Archie, Bill, 1942-   . II. Archie, Michele. III. Title.
SH517.K64   1998
799.1'1'09786—DC21   97-51573
                                          CIP

PRINTED IN THE UNITED STATES OF AMERICA

Mountain Press Publishing Company
P.O. Box 2399 • Missoula, MT 59806
Ph. 406-728-1900 • Fax 406-728-1635

This book is dedicated to the preservation of our wilderness heritage.

ENJOY IT

CHERISH IT

PROTECT IT

Contents

Publisher's Note

I still have my first copy of Dick Konizeski's *Montanans' Fishing Guide,* purchased back when I was in high school. Its pages are dog-eared and its cover worn smooth and dulled with years of use. There are a number of loose pages in the Bitterroot section. I remember poring over references to lakes and mountain valleys, looking at photographs of drainages I wished to ascend. This book wasn't just a seasonal guide either. My friends and I would study it all year—scouting, daydreaming, and planning. Funny part is, I was not an avid fisherman back then. Oh, I fished some, but more likely I could be found climbing a peak in the Missions, cross-country skiing, or backpacking into new territory.

I took my old copy off the shelf the other night as I was thinking about writing these few words to introduce the first revision of *The Montanans' Fishing Guide* in over a dozen years. It was like greeting an old friend I hadn't seen in a long time. The bond was still there, but we'd both seen some changes with the passing of the years. Konizeski self-published the first edition of the *Fishing Guide* in 1963, long before self-publishing was in vogue. Originally, all the waters in the state were contained in a single volume. The earliest edition I have in my office is the second self-published edition, bearing the date 1965–1966. Konizeski had marked it up for a future revision, so there are marginal notes throughout, and the price was a whopping $1.95. The green cover with a yellow border proclaims it to be "the original and only *Montanan's Fishing Guide,*" that it "tells where to go and how to get 'em," and that it "belongs in every tackle box."

Dick Konizeski worked in the forestry department at the University of Montana when he wrote the book. He retired in 1979 and settled in Port Townsend, Washington, where I've heard he now explores larger waters aboard a wooden sailboat. Mountain Press purchased the rights to the *Fishing Guide* when Konizeski left Montana. The first Mountain Press edition was published in September 1970 in two volumes, the first covering the waters west of the Continental Divide and the second the waters east of the divide. My own tattered copy is actually volume one of a second Mountain

Press edition, published in June 1974. The western volume underwent a complete revision, edited by Dale Burk, in about 1982. The eastern volume was revised around the same time by Jim Derleth.

I can only imagine what an effort it must have been to categorize and track all the information that eventually became the first *Montanans' Fishing Guide*. In the foreword to the 1965 edition, Konizeski states that the book was the result of eight years of research. He refers to himself as "editor" rather than "author." He goes on to say that while he investigated more than nine thousand lakes and streams, he listed only those with fishing potential. Many people joked about Konizeski suffering to visit and fish each lake and stream personally. Quips aside, Konizeski had complex state fishery records to dig up, field people from assorted agencies to interview, maps to scrutinize, details to ponder, and all those various Rock Creeks and Fish Creeks in different drainages to sort out and keep straight. And all done precomputer, with notes probably kept on index cards and later transcribed via manual typewriter into a manuscript. It was for Konizeski a labor of love. The result was a remarkable reference, not just for fishermen (back then that's what they were called, regardless of gender), but for backpackers, hikers, hunters, and outdoorsmen.

Now, thanks to the tireless devotion of father-daughter team Bill and Michele Archie, a new edition of this tried-and-true classic is before you. The book's evolution is, as it's always been, the cooperative effort of many public-spirited and conservation-minded individuals and agencies from across the state. So, take it and go. Fish, hike, hunt, climb—enjoy the outdoors!

As for me, I look forward to getting reacquainted with my old friend. My two kids are old enough now that I can start showing them some of the country I rambled through when I was younger, and there is a lot of country for us yet to explore.

John Rimel
Publisher

Acknowledgments

Since its first publication in 1963, Dick Konizeski's *Montanans' Fishing Guide* for west of the Continental Divide has helped anglers enjoy western Montana's varied and rich fisheries. Over the years, his book has pointed people toward places they wanted to explore and enjoy but weren't sure how to find or what to expect when they got there. Now, thirty-plus years later, we are pleased to offer this updated version of a time-honored anglers' guide to Montana's western waters.

Updating this guide was a time-consuming task that could not have been done without the help of many people. Dick Konizeski put in thousands of miles on the trail and endless hours fishing when he surveyed the lakes and streams the first time around, and in putting together the original descriptions, he relied on the enthusiastic cooperation of various state and federal agencies, and a host of fishing folk from Montana and out of state. In revising the guide, we went back to those same agencies and a new set of anglers for information that would help us provide accurate and up-to-date descriptions of fisheries and access.

Without the help of two of our family members, Anne and Paul Archie, this book wouldn't have made it to press—at least not on time! And special thanks to Janet Decker–Hess and John Fraley of Montana Fish, Wildlife and Parks, and Joe DosSantos of the Confederated Salish and Kootenai Tribes, for going the extra mile to give us the information and contacts we needed.

We'd also like to thank the people who shared their knowledge about each of the major rivers described in the introduction of each section. Thanks also to the various local photographers, archivist Dan Gard at the U.S. Forest Service, the Ravalli County Museum, Glacier National Park, and Montana Fish, Wildlife and Parks for contributing the photos that lend visual images to the written descriptions.

Introduction

Montana is a vacationer's paradise truly at the crown of the continent. Here, headwaters flow to three great oceans: the Pacific via the Clark Fork of the Columbia drainage west of the Continental Divide; the Atlantic through the Missouri drainage east of the divide; and north to Hudson Bay via the Belly River in Canada. Within this area is some of the nation's truly great trout water, wild and free-flowing rivers and pristine alpine lakes, along with true wilderness in sufficient abundance to spark the imagination of those who want solitude along with their fishing. For those who don't mind being nearer to civilization, many of Montana's streams and lakes are easily accessible by road. Some of them—like the Clark Fork River and Flathead Lake—are adjacent to major highways.

Variety of both fishing water and species is the rule rather than the exception here. Home to native westslope cutthroat and bull trout, and to brown and rainbow trout introduced over one hundred years ago, Montana's trout fisheries are known nationwide. Mackinaw (lake trout) are commonly caught in places like Whitefish Lake and Flathead Lake. Western Montana also boasts both largemouth and smallmouth bass, northern pike, sturgeon, grayling, golden trout, brook trout, sunfish, whitefish, and kokanee salmon.

Mix this variety with a paradise of forested mountains and valleys and canyons where willow-thatched meander patterns trace streams and rivers, and you have fishing potential supreme. Enhancing the natural beauty is the wildlife, which can often be seen while fishing: elk, mule deer and whitetails, bighorn sheep, mountain goats, wolverine, grizzly and black bears, moose, geese, ducks, lynx, bobcats, and mountain lions, as well as coyotes and, in a few really wild places, wolves that are reinhabiting parts of their former range.

The two volumes of *The Montanans' Fishing Guide* (East and West) are your passport to these incredibly diverse fishing waters. This volume, for west of the Continental Divide, is loaded with information that can help you choose the right lake, stream, or reservoir for the sort of fishing you want to enjoy.

Three major watersheds comprise the fishing resource of these great drainages in western Montana: the Clark Fork of the Columbia, the

Flathead, and the Kootenai river systems. And in each there are subdrainages that, in themselves, are substantial and highly popular fishing areas. The entries in this guide are organized into ten major drainages, with a separate section on the waters of Glacier National Park.

Each entry contains a description of the body of water, information about access and the fishery, and often some little tidbits about the area. To help you find your way on a map, there's a legal description consisting of township, range, and section numbers. The index at the back of the book can help you locate bodies of water by name. We use ratings of fishing potential that range from poor to excellent, with various grades in between. These ratings are formulated based on the experience of local experts, creel census data, and fishery studies. They're not meant to be the last word on fishery quality, but they do give an indication of the success a visiting angler might expect to enjoy.

This guide is intended to help you learn about and enjoy the tremendous array of fishing possibilities west of the Continental Divide in Montana. From relaxation by the remote waters of Glacier National Park's backcountry to the quest for big rainbows through the ice at Georgetown Lake, this book can only point you in the right direction. It guides you toward fishing potential unequaled anywhere. From there it's up to you.

Catch and release. —Bill Archie

Fishing Montana in the 1990s and Beyond

Over time, fishing in Montana has become a different experience from what it was when *The Montanans' Fishing Guide* was originally written. A former bass lake is now managed for trophy rainbows. A logging road crosses the stream that you once reached by cross-country trek. "Catch-and-release" is a common practice. Travel restrictions on some forest roads aim to protect stream habitat. New fishing regulations are helping to rebuild fish populations where they had declined. Private land often changes hands, and more and more "No Trespassing" signs are sprouting up on fenceposts in some areas.

As Montana's population and popularity grow, more of us seek the enjoyment of being in this beautiful country. With added pressures on fisheries and the countryside, we all need to remember how to enjoy the outdoors while treating it kindly.

Here are some factors that are changing the face of fishing in western Montana.

Emphasis on native and wild fisheries. In the 1970s, Montana almost completely stopped stocking hatchery-raised fish in rivers and streams. The management emphasis now is on wild, naturally reproducing trout. This means that Montana does not manage streams as "put and take" fisheries as do many other states. Most of the hatchery trout are stocked in lakes and reservoirs. Especially for backcountry lakes that are stocked, the emphasis is shifting to native westslope cutthroat.

Western Montana's two native species of trout—cutthroat and bull trout—are considered by the state to be species of special concern. This means that special efforts are under way to protect the two species. For example, most waters in the Blackfoot River drainage and many in the Flathead River drainage are catch-and-release fishing only for cutthroat. Bull trout populations have declined so much that Montana Fish, Wildlife and Parks has closed all waters in western Montana (except Swan Lake) to fishing for bull trout. The agency has also increased education efforts and enforcement patrols in areas where cutthroat and bull trout are found, and is assisting in stream restoration projects designed to improve habitat.

Bucket biology. Illegal introductions of fish wreak havoc on lake and river fisheries and are costly—and often impossible—to undo. Species such as perch, walleye, sunfish, northern pike, and different kinds of bait fish are popular with so-called "bucket biologists," whose clandestine activities pose a threat to native species that can't compete. It's not difficult to come up with a long list of lakes whose trout fisheries have been ruined by hordes of stunted yellow perch or sunfish.

In 1995, the Montana legislature passed a law making it illegal to transport live fish from one body of water to another, and for anglers to possess live fish away from the body of water in which they were taken. This law was meant to reduce illegal introductions of fish. If you see someone breaking this law, help protect our fisheries and report them. Fisheries managers need to know about new threats as soon as possible in order to try to reduce the damage. Also, don't move insects from one body of water to another, and don't release aquarium fish or bait fish.

Whirling disease. In 1994, whirling disease was detected in rainbow trout from Montana's Madison River drainage. Since then, it has been found in fish in other drainages, both east and west of the Continental Divide. Whirling disease can be fatal for trout and salmon.

As of 1997, trout infected with whirling disease have been found in three of western Montana's major river drainages: the Blackfoot, the Clark Fork upstream of the Bitterroot, and the Flathead below the South Fork. Tests performed in 1996 showed that twelve individual waters in the Clark Fork above the Bitterroot were infected.

Interestingly, the 1996 testing in western Montana turned up two isolated pockets of infection surrounded by uninfected waters. These pockets are in Cottonwood Creek in the Blackfoot drainage and in the East Fork of Rock Creek in the Upper Clark Fork drainage (near Missoula). Isolated infections raise questions about how the disease is spreading from water to water. Researchers do know that whirling disease is transmitted by a tiny parasite that can survive in live fish, dead fish, water, riverbed mud, and dried riverbed mud. Until further research establishes the actual means of transmission, it pays to be cautious.

Montana Fish, Wildlife and Parks urges everyone to follow these guidelines for preventing the spread of whirling disease:

1) **Do** remove all mud and aquatic plants from your vehicle, boat, anchor, trailer and axles, waders, boots, and fishing gear **before** departing the fishing access site or boat dock.
2) **Do** dry your boat and equipment between river trips.
3) **Don't** transport fish from one body of water to another.
4) **Don't** dispose of fish entrails, skeletal parts, or other by-products in any body of water.
5) **Don't** collect sculpins (also known as bullheads) or use sculpins as bait.
6) **Don't** use parts of trout, salmon, or whitefish for bait.

Habitat protection and improvement. State and federal land managers, nonprofit groups, and private landowners are taking steps to protect and improve fish habitat. These measures include water leases to maintain in-stream flows key to fish spawning and survival, and stream restoration projects. Montana Fish, Wildlife and Parks has completed forty-two stream restoration projects since its River Restoration Program began in 1989, and more are in the works. And in 1996 the Future Fisheries Improvement Program began funding projects aimed at restoring and enhancing habitat for wild fish populations in lakes, rivers, and streams.

Increasing fishing opportunities. Montana Fish, Wildlife and Parks is taking the lead in creating more and better opportunities for people to fish. Accessibility has been improved for people with disabilities; examples include special fishing-access sites and Fishing Without Barriers Day on Flathead Lake. Youth Angler Education courses give young people skills and knowledge in angling, ethics, aquatic ecology, and water safety. And Fish, Wildlife and Parks continues to expand and improve its network of public fishing-access sites.

Increasing fishing pressure. As more and more people hit the water to enjoy fishing in western Montana, it's especially important to keep our impact to a minimum and to respect others who are enjoying this beautiful country.

One way to do that is to follow fishing regulations and to keep only the fish that you will eat. If you do it right, catch-and-release can help keep fish populations up. Montana Fish, Wildlife and Parks offers the following tips for successfully releasing fish:

1) Use artificial lures to reduce wounding of fish.
2) Use single, barbless hooks.
3) Play the fish rapidly—not to exhaustion.
4) Keep the fish in the water as much as possible and wet your hands before handling the fish.
5) Hold the fish horizontally with both hands.
6) Do not squeeze the fish or its gills.
7) If deeply hooked, cut the line far down the throat.
8) Hold the fish upright facing upstream until it can swim.
9) Release the fish in quiet water near where it was hooked.

Whether you drive up to a lake or hike in 13 miles, it's important to leave no signs that you were there. That way, others can enjoy their fishing experience as much as you did. Make sure you pack out your garbage, avoid polluting the water, dispose of human waste properly, and camp and have fires in designated areas. Montana Fish, Wildlife and Parks has several publications that explain how to minimize your impact, and there are some excellent books on the subject.

If you're using streams, remember that Montana's Stream Access Law gives you access between ordinary high-water marks. Please respect the rights of private landowners and, by all means, ask first before you cross private land. Also, be aware of restrictions on motorized watercraft in certain waters. A listing of boat and motor restrictions is provided in the Montana fishing regulations booklet.

One of the cardinal rules of fishing is to make sure your actions don't affect someone else who's out there trying to enjoy the water. As more people use Montana's waters for recreation, it's important to treat everyone the way you would like to be treated.

Finding Your Way Around Western Montana

Two types of maps were of immeasurable value in preparing this book, and you will probably find them useful, too, as you attempt to navigate the roads, trails, and off-trail wilds of western Montana. The first type is a U.S. Forest Service forest visitor map, and the second type is a topographic map. Here's a bit of detail about each of these types of maps:

The U.S. Forest Service makes available *forest visitor maps* for each of the National Forests in western Montana. The maps are large and easy to read, generally printed at a scale of $\frac{1}{2}$ inch per mile. Each map shows roads, trails, streams, lakes, recreation sites, land ownerships, and major points of interest on the National Forest lands and surrounding private holdings. Most of these maps include fairly comprehensive listings of road closures and vehicle restrictions as well, but since the status of forest roads changes over time, it makes sense to check locally about roads you are interested in traveling.

To obtain Forest Service maps, write or call the information assistant at the USDA Forest Service Northern Region headquarters for a listing of available maps and an order form. Or visit a local National Forest or ranger district office for maps of the surrounding area. (Contact information for Northern Region and National Forest headquarters follows.) Forest Service maps may also be available in local general stores and outdoor-supplies stores.

High-quality *topographic maps* are available from two sources. The U.S. Forest Service prints topographic maps of each wilderness area in western Montana. These maps are available from Forest Service regional and forest headquarters. The more common source of topographic maps is the U.S. Geological Survey, which produces maps that cover most of the area described in this guide. Topographic maps show the general configuration of the terrain, as well as lakes and streams, roads and trails, cities and towns, Forest Service installations, etc. Many outdoor and sporting goods stores sell these maps, some libraries have collections that you can photocopy, or you can write to the U.S. Geological Survey for an index to topographic maps for Montana and an order form (see the address below).

Another source of maps is the *Montana Atlas and Gazeteer*, published by DeLorme Mapping and widely available in bookstores, outdoor stores, and convenience stores. This collection of maps can help you locate many of the streams and lakes in this guide and may help get you in the general vicinity of some of the less well known spots. While it does cover all of the landscape of western Montana, this gazeteer has some drawbacks: it does not provide as comprehensive a guide to the landscape as do Forest Service maps, and while it includes topographic lines, they're often difficult to decipher.

Both forest visitor and topographic maps include township, range, and section numbers that you can use in conjunction with the information in this book to quickly locate a particular body of water on the map. Township, range, and section numbers are used in describing a location for legal purposes: township numbers run north and south (up and down) along the sides of the map; range numbers run east and west (horizontally) along the top and bottom of the map; and section numbers are shown on the body of the map. After each entry in this book, you'll find a series of numbers in brackets, such as [T30N R27W S16]. The first number is the Township number, and it is followed by either N for north or S for south. The second number designates the Range, and the W or E that follows it stands for west or east. The third number designates the Section. For those of you unfamiliar with using these markings, the process is simple. First find the township number along the side, and the range number along the top or bottom. In the area where they intersect on the body of the map, look for the appropriate section number.

Moving bodies of water such as streams and rivers are not easily located by a single set of township, range, and section numbers. This book conforms to the standard convention of locating the mouth of the stream or river (that is, where it empties into the next largest body of water).

What Maps Can't Tell You

Forest visitor maps provide enormous quantities of useful information—it's no wonder that most people who spend much time outdoors in western Montana have a collection of them, all in various stages of falling apart! But there are certain things that even these maps can't tell you that might affect your ability to fish where you'd like. Two of these are changes in land ownership and management, and the condition of roads and trails.

As private land changes hands, your ability to access lakes and streams across that land may also change. In areas such as the Bitterroot Valley (and many other rapidly developing parts of western Montana), where large tracts of land have been subdivided and many other large holdings have been sold and sometimes taken out of agricultural production, many anglers experience increasing difficulty gaining access to areas where permission was once easily granted. It behooves the angler to be respectful of fences and "No Trespassing" signs, and not to assume that access across private land will always be granted. On the other hand, it doesn't hurt to ask!

A specific type of land transfer to watch in the coming years is the sale of Plum Creek Timber Company lands to smaller private owners and developers. Plum Creek owns vast acreage in western Montana and has begun to evaluate which of those holdings the company should keep as timberlands and which are more suitable for other purposes. The sale of Plum Creek lands has already begun to change access to lakes in western Montana, particularly in the Thompson Lakes area, and on the Bitterroot, Island, and Ashley Lakes west of Kalispell. Large amounts of land have been sold already, are on the market, or are earmarked for sale by Plum Creek, and much of this land is either along lakeshores or in areas that control access to the water. Forest visitor maps are not revised often enough to include accurate information about these changes in land ownership, and the implications for fishing access may be tremendous.

Forest visitor maps also cannot illustrate the condition of roads or trails, and these conditions might have a significant impact on your ability to get where you're going. Here's an example: Between Phillipsburg and Deer Lodge is a mountain range known as the Flint Creek Range. These mountains are surrounded by a lot of agricultural land that is dry, dry, dry. That's why many of the lakes in the Flint Creek Range are actually reservoirs—impoundments that were built years ago to help provide a reliable source of water to the farms and ranches in the valleys below. Many of the roads in this part of the country originated either as jeep tracks to high-up mining claims or as construction roads for the dams that hold these lakes in place. Lots of them are not maintained for regular use because there's really no reason to do so. If one of the dams is in need of repair, the same bulldozer that's going to do the work on the dam can also fix the road as it goes in. Reading a map is not going to tell you whether a road is in great shape or barely passable. This book provides some information about general road conditions, but nothing takes the place of experience. If you're concerned about a particular road, check with the Forest Service ranger district before you head out on your fishing expedition. If you're the more adventurous sort, by all means, go exploring. But know the limitations of your vehicle—it's no fun to break down miles from town!

Sources of Maps and Other Information

For information about maps, road or trail conditions, area closures, current license fees, regulations, and the like, the government agencies in charge of managing wildlife and public lands are excellent sources. Here are some that you might contact.

Confederated Salish and
Kootenai Tribes
Natural Resources Department
P.O. Box 278
Pablo, MT 59855
406-675-2700

Glacier National Park
Park Headquarters
West Glacier, MT 59936
406-888-5441

Montana Fish, Wildlife & Parks
Region 1 Headquarters
490 N. Meridian Road
Kalispell, MT 59901
406-752-5501
24–hour recorded information:
406-257-4630

Montana Fish, Wildlife & Parks
Region 2 Headquarters
3201 Spurgin Road
Missoula, MT 59801
406-542-5500

USDA Forest Service—
Northern Region
P.O. Box 7669
Missoula, MT 59807
406-329-3511

USDA Forest Service—
Bitterroot National Forest
1801 North First Street
Hamilton, MT 59840
406-363-7117

USDA Forest Service—
Deerlodge National Forest
400 North Main Street
P.O. Box 400
Butte, MT 59703
406-496-3400

USDA Forest Service—
Flathead National Forest
1935 Third Ave. East
Kalispell, MT 59901
406-755-5401

USDA Forest Service—
Helena National Forest
Federal Building, 301 South Park
Drawer 10014, Room 334
Helena, MT 59626
406-449-5201

USDA Forest Service—
Kootenai National Forest
506 U.S. Highway 2 West
Libby, MT 59923
406-293-6211

USDA Forest Service
Lolo National Forest
Bldg. 24, Fort Missoula
Missoula, MT 59801
406-329-3750

U.S. Geological Survey
Map Distribution
USGS Map Sales
P.O. Box 25286,
Federal Center, Bldg. 810
Denver, CO 80225
FAX 303-202-4693

Montana Game Fish

The following pages reproduce fish paintings
by wildlife artist Ron Jenkins.

BROOK TROUT. Range up to 9 pounds; are distinguished by variable dark brown-to-olive-to-scarlet red (in some alpine lakes) color, round red spots with blue margins on the sides, wavy lines across the back, and white margins along the ventral fins.

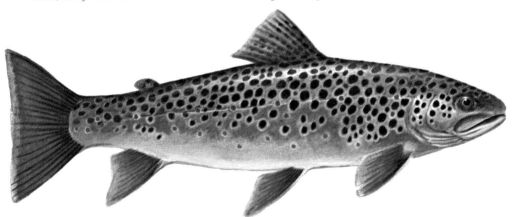

BROWN or GERMAN BROWN or LOCH LEVEN TROUT. Range up to about 20 pounds and are common to 5 pounds; are distinguished by yellowish brown color, relatively large dark spots on the back, and a few red spots (sometimes with a narrow bluish band) on the sides.

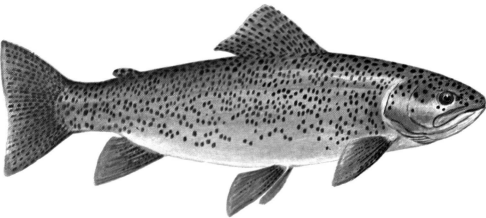

RAINBOW TROUT. Range up to 20 pounds and are common to 5 pounds; are distinguished by usually light sides and somewhat darker back with numerous irregularly shaped spots and a broad red band along the midline of each side. They frequently cross with cutthroat, spawning progeny that are difficult to identify.

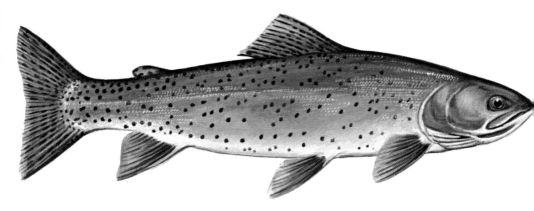

CUTTHROAT TROUT. Range up to 15 pounds but are generally under 12 inches long in the small headwaters of most Montana drainages, up to 5 pounds in many lakes; are distinguished by a dark red or orange slash along the bottom of each jaw, and numerous dark spots on the posterior parts of the body.

GOLDEN TROUT. Generally average less than 1½ pounds; are distinguished by the beautiful coloration, generally yellowish color with bright carmine strips along the belly from the throat to the anal fin, small scales.

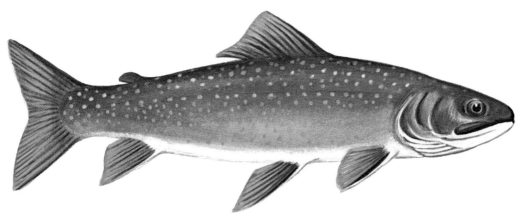

BULL TROUT or DOLLY VARDEN. Range up to 30 pounds and are common to 15 pounds; are distinguished by a large mouth, olive color with round orange to yellowish spots on the sides, and a white border on the ventral fins; are generally more slender than the brook trout.

ARCTIC GRAYLING. *Mostly average between 6 and 12 inches but range up to 2 pounds or 20 inches; are distinguished by a large, beautifully colored dorsal fin, large eyes, small mouth, grayish silver color, and irregularly shaped black dots.*

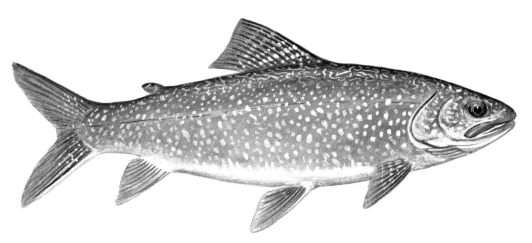

LAKE or MACKINAW TROUT. *Range up to 40 pounds, are common to 15 pounds; are distinguished by a light or greenish gray color, many irregular light spots on the sides and back, large mouth, and deeply forked caudal fin.*

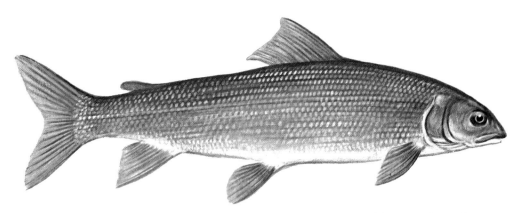

WHITEFISH. *Range up to 5 pounds or 24 inches; are distinguished by a small mouth, silvery sides and belly, and olive drab back.*

COHO or SILVER SALMON. The seagoing variety ranges up to 30 pounds or so. You shouldn't expect to catch one here, since experiments with introducing them to Montana waters failed years ago.

KOKANEE or SOCKEYE SALMON. Range up to 5 pounds but average between 12 and 14 inches; are distinguished by dark greenish color on the back, silver on the sides and belly, the anal fin shorter than the base line, small teeth. The mature males are a bloody red with no spots and a hooked nose.

STURGEON. Several species are found in Montana; some range up to several hundred pounds. They are distinguished by a flat belly, ventrally located mouth, cartilaginous nobby plates along the sides and back, and four barbels (or whiskers) directly in front of the mouth.

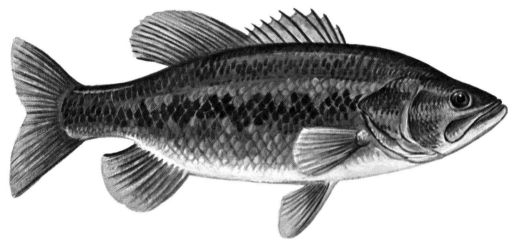

LARGEMOUTH BASS. Range up to 14 pounds; are distinguished by the dark, metallic green back and greenish yellow sides, a broken, dark greenish band from the eye to the caudal fin, a large mouth that extends to well behind the eye in adults, and large scales.

SMALLMOUTH BASS. Range up to 4 pounds but average around 1½ to 2½ pounds; are usually distinguished from largemouth bass by a shorter jaw that ends below the reddish eye and a dorsal fin that is only lightly notched.

YELLOW PERCH. Are reported up to 21 inches but mostly range between 5 and 15 inches; are distinguished by a deep greenish back, with indentations extending down the yellowish sides, and a dirty white belly, coarse scales, an arched back, and head with a more or less concave profile.

NORTHERN PIKE. Range up to 27 pounds but average between 3 and 8 pounds; are distinguished by a long narrow body and equally elongated head, with a deep mouth and large vicious teeth, forked tail, and dirty greenish yellow mottled body.

WALLEYE. *The average angler cannot tell these from sauger. Both are large members of the perch family; the average size creeled is 12 to 14 inches. Walleye and sauger are common in the reservoirs and large rivers in the eastern part of the state.*

SUNFISH or PUMPKINSEEDS. *Green sunfish and bluegills have both been introduced into Montana. Mostly about the size of your hand (4 to 6 inches long), flat-bodied with coarse, iridescent scales.*

PADDLEFISH or SPOON-BILLED CATFISH. *Are usually from 2 to 4 feet long (reportedly two in the 120–pound class have been taken in Montana); are distinguished by smooth and very large gill slits.*

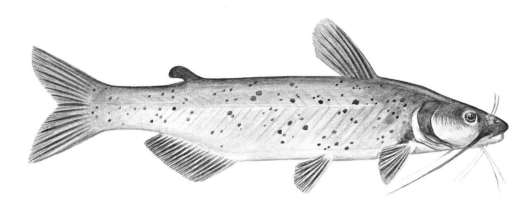

CHANNEL CAT. Hard-looking but good eating; distinguished by a slender, smooth-skinned body with a small head, whiskers on the chin, spines on the dorsal and pectoral fins, a long anal fin, and a forked tail; bluish to greenish gray on top and white below; ranges up to 30 pounds or so in the lower Missouri, Yellowstone, and Musselshell Rivers.

BULLHEAD. With a black body, smooth skin. Weighs up to maybe 5 pounds, big head, wide mouth with whiskers, and more-or-less square tail; looks plenty attractive in a frying pan.

LING. You take one horrified look, scream, and throw your rod and all into the drink: that, my friend, was a ling—a gruesome-looking half-brother to the seagoing cod, but more closely resembling the slippery eel. Many claim its flesh is as toothsome as its looks are revolting.

Palisades near entry to Como Lake. —Courtesy U.S. Forest Service

The Historic Bitterroot River

From its lofty birthplace in the snow-capped peaks of the Bitterroot and Sapphire mountains, the Bitterroot River delivers cold, gin-clear water to a thirsty valley. Since the 1800s the Bitterroot has slaked the demands of irrigators, loggers, and sportfishers. In the years when log drives rumbled down the creeks and the main river, native westslope cutthroat, bull trout, and mountain whitefish tantalized anglers with their wariness and hard fighting, much the same as they do today.

Over the years, demands on the river have changed. Many family farms and ranches have been subdivided for rural residences, and the log drives have ended. But fishers continue to turn to the river for recreation and a good meal of fresh fish. In 1910, the *Western News* said, "Nothing draws so well these warm days as the Bitterroot River. Fishermen line the shores almost daily and Sunday sees everyone but the baseball fans out." Since these early days, brown, rainbow, and brook trout have been added to the river's fare, along with the largemouth bass that lurk in the depths of the lower river and its sloughs.

While demands on the river have changed, so has interest in the river. The "new breed" of Bitterrooter has a keen interest in the way the water is managed, the way the land is used, and the way the fish and wildlife are managed. Competing interests often must find creative compromises. For example, through a series of meetings and negotiations between irrigators and recreational river users, water is sent downstream during the irrigation season from Painted Rocks Reservoir, on the West Fork, to provide instream flow through a section that formerly went nearly dry. This cooperative arrangement benefits fish, anglers, canoeists, and other recreational users. It also fosters better understanding between people who value the river from totally different points of interest. This understanding is critical to the health of the river ecosystem. John Muir, world-famous naturalist, said it best: "When you try to pick anything out of the universe, you find it hitched to everything else."

In its 800-foot descent from the confluence of its east and west forks, the Bitterroot meanders approximately 85 miles, in a northerly direction, to join the Clark Fork of the Columbia near Missoula. The river has a variety of braided and single channels throughout its course. It is characterized by beautiful riffles, runs, extremely deep holes, and logjams.

The diatom-slickened cobbles, which make up the streambed, make wading to the best-looking fishing holes tricky.

From the rugged Bitterroot Mountains on the river's west side, a multitude of creeks provide the river with most of its water. Before they leave the mountains, these streams provide excellent fishing for pan-size trout, but they're heavily tapped for irrigation once they enter the main valley. The Sapphire Mountains, rimming the east side of the valley, are much drier than the western ranges, harboring only a handful of trout streams.

Floating has become a very popular pastime on the river. On a summer day, you can find many people in an assortment of floating craft plying the excellent rafting water. Novice rowers must beware of the sharp bends, steep, fast riffles, and logjams that can make the heart race and the grip tighten on the oars.

Wildlife abounds along the Bitterroot, secure in the cottonwood and pine groves with the heavy undergrowth of rose, willow, and alder. Waterfowl and trout are abundant in the spring creeks, which rise in the bottomlands and meander along the river, finally contributing their cool water to the main stream.

The Bitterroot River, with its clear water, majestic mountains, hard-fighting trout, and mild climate, provides a recreational setting that is hard to beat.

Dennis L. Workman
Regional Fisheries Manager
Montana Fish, Wildlife and Parks

Lee Metcalf National Wildlife Refuge. —Courtesy Ravalli County Museum, Ernst Peterson Collection

AICHELE LAKE. See Sheafman Lakes.

AMBROSE CREEK. A small stream flowing west into Threemile Creek, a few miles north of Stevensville. The lower reaches are used entirely for irrigation, and there's little or no access. But the upper reaches are followed by road through mostly private land for 7 miles, and they're heavily fished for small cutthroat. [T9N R19W S6]

BAILEY LAKE. A high alpine lake at the head of Lost Horse Creek, reached by foot trail 1½ miles west of the Lost Horse road from the USFS guard station. Bailey Lake covers about 12 acres and drops off gradually to a maximum depth of 32 feet at the northwest end. It provides fair fishing for cutts that have been stocked here since 1988, plus maybe some rainbow-cutthroat hybrids from way-back rainbow plants. [T4N R23W S6]

BAKER CREEK. This small stream flows for 4 miles from Baker Lake to the West Fork of the Bitterroot River, 6 river miles south of Conner. The lower mile is fair fishing for small cutthroat and occasional bull trout. [T1N R21W S3]

BAKER LAKE. From US 93 take the West Fork (of the Bitterroot) highway south, 1 mile past the Trapper Creek Guard Station; then take a gravel road northwest for 2½ miles to Pierce Creek, where you bear off to the right, onto a muchly switchbacked logging road, for 6½ miles to Baker Point; from there take a rough hunters' trail north for another 1½ miles to the lake. This is a small 9-acre, 52-foot-deep lake, in sparsely timbered alpine country, just below Trapper Peak. It is seldom fished (probably because of its isolation), but it can produce good catches of 7- to 11-inch Yellowstone cutthroat. [T2N R21W S31]

BASS CREEK. Drains Bass Lake, flowing 12 miles eastward to the Bitterroot River, 5 miles north of Stevensville. The lower few miles are used mostly for irrigation and are on private land. Inside the National Forest boundary, 8 miles of trail lead into the Selway-Bitterroot Wilderness and eventually to Bass Lake. This trail is popular with everyone from day hikers to packers, with its campground, stock ramp, and plentiful parking at the trailhead. The creek is poor to fair fishing for small cutthroat, brook trout, and a few rainbows. An occasional bull trout hangs out in the upper reaches. [T9N R20W S3]

Main falls of Bass Creek.
—Courtesy U.S. Forest Service

BASS LAKE. This irrigation impoundment is reached via the Bass Creek trail, going west 8 miles past the end of the Bass Creek road. At its peak, Bass Lake is 140 feet deep (here's one that doesn't freeze out) and covers 100 acres, in an alpine area that is rocky and brushy, with a little scrub timber. The Department of Fish, Wildlife and Parks air-dropped rainbow into the lake in the summers of 1967 and 1978, and in 1984 the lake was stocked with westslope cutthroat fry. Bass is good fishing for fat fish. [T10N R21W S30]

BEAR CREEK. Flows eastward, from the junction of its north and south forks for 9 miles, through a deeply glaciated canyon, to the Bitterroot River, 2 miles south of Victor. The lower 4 miles are on private land and used for irrigation, but the upper reaches, followed by a good trail, are heavily fished for small cutthroat and brook trout, with an occasional rainbow thrown in. [T7N R20W S7]

BEAR CREEK. A small stream, about 6 miles long, that flows south to Lolo Creek, 12 river miles west of the town of Lolo. It's followed by rough gravel road for a few miles, and it's good fishing in early season for small cutthroat and brookies. [T12N R22W S26]

BEAR (or BEAR CREEK) LAKE. A beautiful cirque lake in sparsely timbered to rocky country at the headwaters of the North Fork of Bear

Across Bass Lake from South Lolo Pass. —Courtesy U.S. Forest Service

Creek, in the Selway-Bitterroot Wilderness west of the town of Victor. It's reached by following the Bear Creek trail for about 3 miles from the trailhead to the confluence of the north and south forks. Follow the trail along the North Fork a couple of miles to the confluence with the Middle Fork, then continue along the North Fork a couple more miles upstream on an old, unmaintained trail to the lake. Bear Lake covers about 20 acres, with perhaps 3 acres in aquatic vegetation and a maximum depth of 30 feet. You'd best go for the scenery. It used to be good fishing for 10- to 14-inch brook trout but it is reported to be barren now, maybe because of the old abandoned dam at the outlet. [T8N R22W S21]

BEAR RUN CREEK. A very small tributary of Miller Creek, containing a few small cutthroat and brookies. A fine kids' fishing stream, followed closely by road for most of its length. [T12N R19W S26]

BEAVER CREEK. A small tributary of Big Creek, in the Selway-Bitterroot Wilderness, west of Stevensville. It's crossed by the Big Creek trail 2 miles east of Big Creek Lake. Beaver is excellent fishing for small cutthroat. [T9N R22W S36]

Bear Creek at trail crossing. —Courtesy U.S. Forest Service

BEAVER CREEK. A short stream, about 5 miles long, flows to the West Fork of the Bitterroot south of Conner, 12 river miles south of Painted Rocks Lake. It is followed by a gravel road for its entire length, and it's good fishing—especially in the numerous beaver dams—for small cutthroat and brook trout. There may be some small bull trout here, too, so be careful to properly identify and release them. [T3S R22W S33]

BEAVERTAIL CREEK. A small, eastward-flowing tributary of the West Fork of the Bitterroot River. Reach it at the mouth via the West Fork road, 2 miles south of the West Fork Ranger Station. Followed by a gravel road, it's fair fishing for small cutthroat and brookies 1½ miles above the mouth. [T1N R22W S36]

BIG CREEK. A clear, wadable stream that drains Big Creek Lake, flowing eastward for 16 miles, to join the Bitterroot River about 5 miles south of Stevensville. The lower few miles are dewatered for irrigation; the upper reaches are followed (not too closely) by trail, and they're good fishing, mostly for 6- to 10-inch cutthroat, with a few rainbows and brookies. There's a declining resident population of bull trout in the canyon reaches. At the trailhead, there's a campground with a stock ramp and lots of parking. [T8N R20W S8]

BIG CREEK, South Fork. A small stream about 6 miles long, the outlet of South Fork and Pearl lakes in the Selway-Bitterroot Wilderness. Take the Big Creek trail 9 river miles west, to the mouth of the South Fork, and follow the trail south to headwaters. The South Fork is good fishing for small rainbow, cutthroat, and brook trout, but it would be worth the trip just for the scenery. [T9N R22W S35]

BIG CREEK LAKES. Take the Big Creek trail 9 miles west, all the way to the northern end of Big Creek Lakes, then another couple of miles to the southern end. The trail is heavily used and well maintained, running through conifer cover at the bottom of a rock-walled glacial canyon. The lakes—which are separate only during low water in late summer and fall—receive heavy use, so respect the occasional campsite closures, so that vegetation can recover. Together, Big Creek Lakes cover about 240 acres and have a maximum depth of over 100 feet. They are overpopulated with 12- to 16-inch rainbow and cutthroat, plus a few lunkers that will go to 3 or 4 pounds. Fishing is generally excellent for both species, each of which tends to occupy different areas. The lakes were last planted in 1977. [T9N R22W S34]

BITTERROOT IRRIGATION DITCH (or HEDGE DITCH). A large ditch along the east side of the valley that flows only during the summer months, and it's paralleled by a maintenance road for much of the valley's length. It is excellent fishing in spots for brook and rainbow trout that range up to 5 pounds. There is an extended northern pike and whitefish season here between Hamilton and Bunkhouse Bridge, so check current regulations. [T4N R21W S11]

Big Creek Lake from Pearl Lake Pass. —Courtesy U.S. Forest Service

East Fork of the Bitterrroot River near campground.
—Courtesy U.S. Forest Service

BITTERROOT RIVER, Burnt Fork. A beautiful, easily waded stream flowing from Burnt Fork Lake for 30 miles, through the Sapphire Mountains, to join the Bitterroot River about 1 mile north of Stevensville. It's paralleled by road and trail to headwaters. The Burnt Fork is excellent fishing, with many pools and eddies for small cutthroat in the upper reaches; add in rainbows, brook trout, and whitefish below. Watch for a few bulls below, especially in the fall. [T8N R19W S11]

BITTERROOT RIVER, East Fork. Crossed by US 93 at Sula, the East Fork is followed by a good gravel road and trail for about 42 miles to headwaters. The upper reaches flow through conifer- and brush-covered canyons; the lower reaches are in pastureland. The East Fork is a clear, easily fished stream, fair in summer for 10- to 12-inch cutthroat and lesser numbers of brook, brown, and rainbow trout. In winter months, the best fishing is for whitefish that range up to 15 inches. You might bump into some bull trout here, especially in the upper reaches, and especially in the fall. Permission from landowners is required along the lower reaches. There has been a lot of habitat destruction in the lower portion, where highway construction really damaged fishing, and in the middle, because of stream straightening and channelization by agricultural operators. Special creel limits apply here, and there is an extended season for whitefish. Check current regulations. [T2N R20E S7]

BITTERROOT RIVER, Nez Perce Fork. A large, clear tributary of the West Fork of the Bitterroot River, it's followed by a good road for 20 miles, from mouth to headwaters. It's all on National Forest land, except for a few miles in the lower reaches. An easily fished stream with many beaver dams in the upper reaches, it contains mostly 8- to 11-inch cutthroat, rainbow, and brook trout, along with bulls and browns in the right season. [T1N R22W S25]

BITTERROOT RIVER, West Fork. A beautiful, clear, easily fished stream, about 50 miles long from its mouth at Conner to its head at the Montana-Idaho border. It's followed the entire way by paved and gravel roads. There are numerous beaver dams in the area between Buck and Ditch creeks and in the upper headwaters. The West Fork is quite heavily fished, but it produces good catches of rainbow, cutthroat, and whitefish, plus a few brook trout. An occasional bull trout and brown trout round out the roster of species. Use has increased in recent years; the fish population is affected by the drawdown of Painted Rocks. The West Fork was planted in the late '70s with catchable rainbow, to help reestablish the fishery. [T2N R20W S7]

West Fork of the Bitterroot River. —Courtesy Ravalli County Museum, Ernst Peterson Collection

BLODGETT CREEK. A clear, wadable stream flows from Blodgett Lake for about 18 miles due east, through forested mountains, to the Bitterroot River, a couple of miles north of Hamilton. The lower few miles are dewatered for irrigation; the upper reaches are followed by road, ending in a public campground, and a long trail that stays close to the creek and offers plenty of campsites. The upper reaches are generally good fishing for small cutthroat and brookies, with some rainbows in the lower, more heavily fished sections. In the fall, bull trout spawn here, but fewer and fewer each year. [T6N 20W S6]

BLODGETT LAKE. A small lake at the head of an exquisitely beautiful canyon—one of the most outstanding wilderness vistas in the country.

Blodgett Canyon. —Courtesy U.S. Forest Service

Take the long hike up the Blodgett Creek trail, into the Selway-Bitterroot Wilderness, and on to the lake. Blodgett was last planted in 1984; it's good fishing for westslope cutthroat trout. [T6N R23W S27]

BLUE JOINT CREEK. A clear, dashing inlet of Painted Rocks Lake, about 22 miles long. Take a Forest Service road 6½ miles west from the West Fork road off US 93, going around the north end of Painted Rocks Lake; you can follow a trail west some 12 miles to headwaters. It's an excellent and easy-to-fish mountain stream for cutthroats from 8 to 14 inches, along with a few brookies and whitefish. You might find some bull trout here as well. [T2S R22W S4]

BOULDER CREEK. A beautiful tributary of the Bitterroot River, crossed at the mouth by the West Fork highway and followed by a road going north to a USFS campground a mile upstream. From the campground, a good trail follows the drainage—if not always the creek—west for 11 miles, to headwaters at Boulder Lake. An easily fished stream in a deeply glaciated canyon, it's excellent for small red-bellied, green-backed cutthroat. There's an occasional bull below the falls. [T1N R21W S20]

BOULDER LAKE. A high alpine lake in sparsely timbered, glaciated country north of Bare Peak. Take a good trail 10 miles west from the end of the Boulder Creek road. This is a deep lake, about 20 acres, with an 8-foot dam at the outlet; it's spotty and only poor to fair fishing for 7- to 17-inch cutthroat. It was last planted in 1969. [T1N R23W S1]

BRYAN LAKE. This lake sits at the headwaters of the Middle Fork of Bear Creek, in the Selway Bitterroot Wilderness west of the town of Victor. Reach it by following the Bear Creek trail 3 miles to the North Fork, up the North Fork a little over two miles, and finally up the Middle Fork another few miles to the lake (that's about 8½ miles altogether). Bryan Lake sits at about 6,700 feet above sea level, covers about 20 acres, averages 20 feet deep, and has a fair amount of aquatic vegetation around the upper end. It was planted with rainbow in the 1930s, and the last report says the few descendents will average a pound or better and are in excellent condition. [T8N R22W S29]

BUCK CREEK. Flows from Buck Lake for about 4 miles to the East Fork of the Bitterroot River. Take the East Fork road 16 miles east from Sula to the East Fork Ranger Station, then go 2 miles south on the Little East Fork road to the Anaconda-Pintlar Wilderness boundary, and from there follow a good trail east for 4½ miles to the mouth of the creek, at Kurtz Flats. The fishing is good for small cutthroat trout. [T2N R16W S19]

BURNT FORK BITTERROOT RIVER. See Bitterroot River, Burnt Fork.

BURNT FORK LAKE. Take a good gravel road 6 miles south up the Burnt Fork Creek from Squaw Peak, and then follow a poor trail 7 miles to the lake; or take a USFS trail 5 miles east from the end of the Willow Creek road. Burnt Fork lies in heavily timbered limestone terrain, covering about 30 acres. It's dammed, and it has a water-level fluctuation of about 20 feet, in accordance with irrigation requirements. Heavily fished, it's excellent for 7- to 12-inch cutthroat and some small rainbow trout. There are small bull trout here as well. [T6N R18W S3]

BUTTE CREEK, West Fork. See West Fork Butte Creek.

BUTTERFLY CREEK. A small stream, about 3 miles long, flowing to Willow Creek 2 miles east of the Butterfly Guard Station. It's followed by a dirt road for about 1 mile. This stream was once good fishing for small cutthroat and rainbow, but due to logging operations is now only fair. It was planted with rainbow in the 1950s. [T6N R19W S10]

CALF CREEK. A very small tributary of Willow Creek, about 1½ miles west of the Butterfly Guard Station. There is no trail, but it is fair fishing for about 1 mile above the mouth for small cutthroat and rainbow trout. [T6N R19W S12]

CAMAS CREEK. A small, eastward-flowing tributary of the Bitterroot River, 8 miles south of Hamilton. The lower 3 miles are used for irrigation and are private; the upper reaches are fair fishing for small cutthroat, rainbow, and brook trout. The trail along the drainage stays high up, following the creek only for about a mile below Lower Camas Lake. Take the Lost Horse county road 2 miles to the Camas Lake/Lost Horse Observation Point road, and go north for 6 steep, rough miles to the trailhead. [T5N R21W S25]

CAMAS LAKES. These two lakes are a mile apart in the Camas Creek drainage. Upper Camas is 15 acres and 54 feet deep, while Lower Camas covers 7 acres and is 17 feet at its deepest. The lower lake is reached on a good trail, suitable for hikers and horses, going about 2½ miles west from the trailhead. You'll need to leave the pack animals at one of the two campsites at the lower lake, using your own two hooves to carry you over boulder fields and up to Upper Camas. Lower Camas Lake is overpopulated with wee little cutthroats. Upper Camas offers a little better fishing, for lots of little cutts and an occasional lunker. Partway up between Lower and Upper Camas are a couple of adjoining shallow (unnamed) ponds, which freeze out each winter but are usually restocked annually by migrants from above and below. [T5N R22W S25]

CAMERON CREEK. An open meadowland stream that flows for 9 miles to the East Fork of the Bitterroot River at Sula. The stream flows mostly

Lower Camas Lake. —Courtesy Michele Archie

through posted private land, so ask before you fish. It's pretty much all accessible by county and private roads, and has fair to good fishing for 6- to 10-inch cutthroat and brook trout. Depending on the season, you might also run into spawning browns, bulls, and rainbows. [T1N R19W S17]

CAMP CREEK. A small tributary of the East Fork of the Bitterroot River, paralleled by US 93 for 7 miles from Sula to Lost Trail Resort. Although the stream runs through private land, permission to fish is readily available. It is excellent fishing for 6- to 10- inch cutthroat and brookies, plus an occasional brown trout. [T1N R19W S17]

CAMP CREEK, East Fork. Joins the West Fork near Lost Trail Resort, 7 miles south of Sula on US 93. It's paralleled by the highway and logging roads for much of its 4½-mile length. A small stream with lots of nice holes, it's good fishing for small cutthroat and brook trout. [T1S R19W S16]

CAMP CREEK, West Fork. A 4-mile-long tributary of Camp Creek, it joins the main stream a mile north of Lost Trail Hot Springs Resort on US 93. The lower reaches are largely accessible by logging roads. The fishing is good for pan-size cutthroat and brook trout. [T1S R19W S16]

CANYON CREEK. The outlet of Canyon Lake, it flows eastward for about 7 miles to the Bitterroot River at Hamilton. The lower 3 miles are dewatered for irrigation, and you can't get permission to fish them anyway. The upper reaches are followed by a good trail that takes off from the end of a USFS road, where there's fair fishing for 6- to 8- inch cutthroat trout. [T6N R21W S26]

CANYON LAKES. Three lakes in high (elevation around 7,300 feet) glaciated country. The middle lake is the only reliable fishing, planted last with westslope cutts in 1990. It is reached by trail 3½ miles west and a couple of thousand feet in elevation, from the end of the Canyon Creek road. Canyon is about 45 acres, deep, and dammed, with as much as 20 feet of water-level fluctuation. Nevertheless, it's good fishing for cutts that range from 8 to 12 inches in length. [T6N R22W S27]

CAPITAN (or EL CAPITAN) LAKE. Fifteen acres, deep, and around 6,500 feet in elevation, Capitan lies in a deeply glaciated but heavily timbered mountain region. Take the Rock Creek trail west for 8 miles past Lake Como, then a hunters' trail south for 5 miles up El Capitan Creek to the shore. The lake used to be barren, but it has plenty of feed; it was stocked with golden trout in 1963, but they didn't take. Capitan was planted with westslope cutthroat trout in 1968 and periodically since then—last in 1990. The cutts do pretty well here, but El Capitan is getting a lot more fishing pressure now than in previous years. It's good elk country, too. There's lots of grass for the horses, and a beautiful campsite. [T3N R23W S16]

CAPRI LAKE. You'll probably need to look at a Forest Service map to help you make sense of the directions to this 4-acre lake in heavily timbered country southwest of Sula, at the headwaters of Fault Creek. Follow the Warm Springs Creek trail south for 11 miles to its junction with the Overwhich Falls trail. Proceed west a short distance to the junction with USFS trail 400, which skirts Pass Lake and follows Fault Creek northwest to Capri Lake. The last ¼ mile is through undergrowth—no trail here. There are several other ways to reach trail 400, none of which are particularly straightforward! Capri is mostly very shallow, but it gets deep at the lower end, with lots of lily pads around the margins. The spawning grounds are inadequate here but at last report, there was fair fishing for 8- to 10-inchers, left over from old cutthroat plants in 1967 and 1979. It hasn't been planted since, and the fishing is sure to have dropped off accordingly. [T1S R20W S20]

CARLTON CREEK. Crossed near the mouth by US 93, 3 miles north of Florence. There's no trail. The outlet of Carlton Lake, the creek flows for 5 miles down a steep, timbered, brushy canyon, and then for 3 miles along the Bitterroot Valley, where it is dewatered for irrigation. Permission to fish is available on the lower, private reaches, where the fishing is

Carlton Lake.
—Courtesy U.S.
Forest Service

marginal for cutthroats and brookies. Inside the National Forest, look for cutts, brookies, and maybe a bull trout or two. [T11N R20W S26]

CARLTON LAKE. You used to be able to drive right up to this one, but the road was closed years ago, and now it's washed out, so you can't even take your ORV. Take heart, though; it's a beautiful 4-mile hike on a good trail, which takes off from a switchback at the end of the Mormon Peak road south of Lolo, headed south and west. The trail climbs through subalpine fir into whitebark pine and subalpine larch on Carlton Ridge. From the ridge, the trail drops down to the lake, which sits ½ mile east of Lolo Peak, at 7,700 feet above sea level. The lake is 40 acres and 30 feet deep, in a rocky, sparsely timbered glacial cirque. Fishing can be good for small to medium-size cutts and rainbows. [T11N R21W S27]

CEDAR CREEK. A very small and equally steep tributary of the South Fork of Lolo Creek, about 3 miles upstream. There is no trail, but if you look for holes in the lower ½ mile, you may be able to find a few small cutthroats hiding out. Take the walk anyway: the creek is aptly named. [T11N R21W S7]

CHAFFIN CREEK. Crossed near the mouth by US 93, 4 miles south of Darby, the creek is followed by gravel road and trail for 8-plus miles to

Chaffin Lake, west of Sugarloaf Peak. If you hope to see the trailhead, stay to the right of the fork that's about 3 miles from the start of the Chaffin Creek road. A wrong turn will lead you toward Trapper Creek. Chaffin Creek, inside the National Forest boundary, is a clear mountain stream flowing through timbered, brushy country; it's fair fishing for small cutthroat and some brook trout. [T3N R21W S36]

CHAFFIN LAKE. The westernmost of three glacial lakes beneath Sugarloaf Peak, Chaffin is just upstream from Tamarack Lake. Take a good trail 8-plus miles west from the end of the Chaffin Creek road, off US 93. This 10-acre lake was last stocked with cutts in 1990, but fishing reports are scarce. Stop by if you're at Tamarack Lake and check it out. [T2N R22W S9]

CHARITY (or SNOW) LAKE. This third in the Faith-Hope-Charity chain of lakes is barren. The last section of trail to the lake is closed to motorized vehicles year-round. [T3N R17W S7]

CHICKEN CREEK. A small, clear stream flowing eastward for about 8 miles from the crest of Razorback Mountain to the West Fork of the Bitterroot River. It's crossed at the mouth by the West Fork road, 2½ miles south of Alta. A poor hunters' trail follows the creek a few miles upstream. There are lots of little cutthroat and rainbows here, about the right size for camp fare. [T3S R22W S9]

CHRANDAL CREEK. A very small and steep tributary of Hughes Creek, reached at the mouth by a gravel road 3½ miles east of Alta. There's rough road and trail access to the lower couple of miles. Chrandal is a brushy stream, but it's good fishing for small cutts. [T3S R21W S6]

CHRISTISEN CREEK. Short, small, and steep, Christisen Creek flows to the West Fork of the Bitterroot River 8 miles south of Conner. It's crossed at the mouth by the West Fork road. It's fair fishing there for pan-size cutthroat and rainbow trout. [T1N R21W S8]

CLAREMONT CREEK. A small tributary of the Burnt Fork, Claremont is reached at the mouth by the Middle Burnt Fork road, going 8 miles east from Stevensville. The creek is followed for about ¼ mile upstream by a poor dirt road. It is somewhat polluted by overgrazing, but there's still fair fishing near the mouth for small rainbow and cutthroat trout. [T8N R19W S11]

CLIFFORD CREEK. Take the East Fork road off US 93 for 16 miles east from Sula to the guard station, then follow the Little East Fork road for 2 miles to the Anaconda-Pintlar Wilderness boundary. Hit the trail 3½ miles farther to the creek's mouth, then follow the trail upstream (north) for another couple of miles, before the trail heads away from the creek to the Lick Creek Saddle. Clifford, a small tributary of the East Fork, flows through a heavily timbered, brushy valley. It's good for 6- to 8-inch cut-throat trout. [T2N R16W S19]

COAL CREEK. Take the West Fork road south from Conner and follow it past Painted Rocks Lake about a mile. A small, rapid, snow-fed stream in steep, timbered mountains, it is followed by logging roads for much of its length. Fishery researchers noticed some old sedimentation problems in the lower reaches, as well as some dewatering during the fall. But there are still plenty of little cutts of up to 8 inches. [T2S R22W S10]

COMO LAKE. At the mouth of Rock Creek Canyon, 15 miles southwest of Hamilton. Take a county road 4 miles west off US 93. Como is a large (1,000 acres) irrigation reservoir, with about 50 feet of drawdown and a maximum depth of 100 feet at the lowest water level. It lies in a beautiful glaciated canyon and is flanked to the south and east by remnants of great lateral and terminal moraines. It was poisoned in 1960 and stocked with rainbow, and it's fair fishing now (for 12-inch to 2-pound trout) for vacationers at the public campground north of the dam. It is stocked every year with rainbow trout and hatchery brood stock. A hikers' trail takes you along the north side to an unimproved campground above some falls at the head of the lake. This is undoubtedly one of the most beautiful lakes in western Montana when it is full, prior to the irrigation

Como Lake. —Courtesy U.S. Forest Service

season, and the ugliest when it is drawn down, during the height of the recreation season. It is also heavily used for waterskiing when it's full. [T4N R21W S32]

CRYSTAL LAKE. A small (8 acres) glaciated lake reached by steep trail ½ mile west of Boulder Lake, in high, sparsely wooded talus slope country. This high lake (at 7,700 feet elevation) drops off steeply on one side to a maximum depth of about 30 feet, but slopes gradually down the other side from mossy, grassy, rubble-covered banks. Reportedly good fishing now for 14- to 16-inchers, it was planted with cutthroat last in 1977. [T1N R22W S6]

DALY CREEK. From Hamilton, take Montana 38 east 17 miles to the mouth of Daly Creek. Just north of the Black Bear campground, follow the road for 16 miles along the north side, and a few hundred feet above the creek you'll see Daly's headwaters at Skalkaho Pass. This is a small, clear stream with many rapids, flowing through a deep, heavily timbered canyon; it's good habitat and fun fishing for small cutthroats. Watch for bull trout here as well. [T5N R19W S24]

DEER CREEK. Flows eastward to the West Fork of the Bitterroot River, across the river from the West Fork road, 2½ miles south of Alta. It's followed by a good trail for 14 miles to headwaters. A high mountain stream in timbered country, it is good fishing for 7- to 9-inch cutthroat in the numerous beaver dams along its length. [T3S R22W S9]

DICK CREEK. There is road access to within ¼ mile of much of its length. But only the lower reaches (within about ½ mile of its mouth at the South Fork of Lolo Creek) are worth fishing. It's a bit of a bushwhack, so you'll have to ask yourself whether the 6-inch cutthroat you're likely to catch are worth it. [T11N R21W S13]

DIVIDE CREEK. Take the Sleeping Child Creek trail southeast for 5 miles past the hot springs to the mouth of this creek. Head east on the trail that leads to its headwaters, which are near Coyote Meadows. Divide is a small, clear mountain stream that rises to about 7,000 feet and descends to less than 5,400 feet in 7 miles. It contains fair numbers of pan-size cutthroat trout and is easily fished—a good kids' creek. Make sure the kids know what a bull trout looks like, though, since there's a resident population here, and these fish will need to be released. [T4N R19W S28]

DOLLAR LAKE. Take the Boulder Creek trail west for 12 miles to Turbid Lake, then climb down (way down) ¼ mile. Dollar Lake is about 5 acres, in steep, rocky country, with a few trees around the shore. It is only about 20 feet deep with gradual drop-offs, and, in view of its elevation

(7,200 feet), it seems like it should freeze out, but it provides the best fishing of the entire Boulder Lake group for 10- to 12-inch cutthroat. It is seldom fished—it's just too hard to get there. [T1N R22W S6]

DUFFY LAKE. A small (18-acre) lake at 7,300 feet in elevation, in a cirque at the head of Sweeney Creek. From near the end of the county road at the mouth of Sweeney Canyon, west off US 93 just south of Florence, take a logging road for 6 miles up the north ridge, then a foot trail 7 miles west, going past Peterson Lake. In timbered, steep, and rocky country just east of the crest of the Bitterroot Range, Duffy Lake is mostly under 30 feet deep and mud bottomed. The remains of an old dam are still present at its outlet. It offers only poor fishing for a few rainbows. [T10N R21W S9]

EAST FORK BITTERROOT RIVER. See Bitterroot River, East Fork.

EAST FORK CAMP CREEK. See Camp Creek, East Fork.

EAST FORK GRAVE CREEK. See under Grave Creek.

EAST FORK LOLO CREEK. See Lolo Creek, East Fork.

EAST FORK PIQUETT CREEK. See Piquett Creek, East Fork.

EASTMAN CREEK. There's no road or trail access to this very small creek that enters Willow Creek about 8 miles east of Corvallis. You might find fair fishing for about a mile above the mouth for pan-size cutthroat and brook trout that have migrated from Willow Creek. [T6N R19W S9]

EIGHTMILE CREEK. Take the Eastside highway going east from Florence for 2 miles, across the Bitterroot River, then turn left (north) at the T; turn right (east) onto the Eightmile road and follow it for 12 miles to the headwaters of Eightmile Creek. This clear little mountain stream flows through timber and brush and is impounded by numerous beaver dams. The lower reaches go dry due to irrigation. The ponds are good early-season fishing for small cutthroat and brook trout. Eightmile flows through mostly private land, and it can be hard to get permission to fish. [T10N R20W S12]

EL CAPITAN LAKE. See Capitan Lake.

ELK LAKE. Reached by USFS trail up Rock Creek, 12 miles west of Como Lake, Elk Lake occupies part of a steep-walled, glaciated canyon in heavily wooded country. It is very deep, covers about 20 acres, and has a moderate amount of aquatic vegetation around the shore. The lake, whose name suggests the quarry of the hunters who frequent the lake in the fall, has limited spawning grounds and hasn't been stocked since 1952. The fishing is fair. [T4N R23W S34]

Faith Lake. —Courtesy Michele Archie

FAITH (or SPUD) LAKE. A tiny (2-acre) lake, deep, with boggy shores, in heavily timbered country at the head of Moose Creek. Take the good trail to Fish Lake north 7 miles from the trailhead, off the Martin Creek logging road. There's been lots of trail reconstruction, and the last part of the trail is now closed to motorized vehicles. Faith Lake was planted with cutthroat years ago and their progeny (mostly 6- to 11-inchers) do a real good job of supporting moderate-to-heavy fishing pressure now. [T3N R17W S17]

FISH LAKE. A high (elevation 7,500 feet) mountain lake in heavily timbered country, east of Darby. Take a newly reconstructed USFS trail 6 miles north from the Fish Lake trailhead, off the Martin Creek logging road. The trails in this area have been rebuilt and rerouted, so watch the new trail signs. Only hikers and horses are allowed on the trail to Fish Lake. This shallow lake covers about 4 acres, including its boggy shores. There can be good fishing for 6- to 10-inch cutthroat. [T3N R17W S17]

FISH LAKE. A high lake that sits about 6,500 feet up, near the crest of the Bitterroot Range in the Selway-Bitterroot Wilderness, northwest of Darby. Reach it from the Lost Horse Creek road, either by a good horse trail that starts 6 miles west of US 93, then go 12 miles up South Lost Horse Creek; or take an equally good trail 6 miles southeast from the end of the Lost Horse road, over Bear Lake Pass. Fish is a fair-size lake (about 50 acres), deep at the upper end and shallow below, in heavily timbered mountains. The fishing is fair for 6- to 12-inch rainbow. [T4N R23W S16]

FLAT ROCK CREEK. A very small, clear mountain stream, reached at the mouth by the Burnt Fork road, 16 miles east out of Stevensville; it's followed by logging road for 2 miles to the forks. Flat Rock is good fishing for small cutthroat and rainbow trout, migrating from the Burnt Fork. [T7N R18W S5]

FOOL HEN LAKE. See Willow Lake.

FRED BURR CREEK. Go 3 miles south of Victor on US 93, turn west on the Bear Creek road for 5 miles, to the mouth of Fred Burr Canyon, and continue (if you get permission at the nearby ranch house) west on a private access road for 6 miles, to the Fred Burr Reservoir. Follow a trail past the reservoir for 10 miles, bearing south into the Selway-Bitterroot Wilderness and to the head of the creek at Fred Burr Lake. This is a rapidly flowing stream in a timbered and very brushy canyon, bounded by sheer rock walls that in some places rise almost vertically 200 feet above the creek. Once inside the National Forest boundary, the stream is excellent fishing for small cutthroat, plus a few rainbow and brook trout. [T7N R20W S18]

GARRARD LAKE. See Sheafman Lakes.

GASH CREEK. The lower 3 miles of this creek flow through open pastureland, the upper 6 miles through a heavily wooded, glacial canyon. It is reached by county road, 5 miles southwest from Victor. Parts of the creek are accessible by road and trail—to say that the road and trail "follow" the creek is an overstatement. This is a small, steep, snow- and rain-fed stream that was planted years ago, and it's reported to be fair fishing along the lower reaches for small cutthroat and rainbow trout. [T8N R21W S35]

GIRD CREEK. This Willow Creek tributary is about 19 miles long. The lower couple of miles are dewatered for irrigation, and there are about 8 or 9 miles of road access to the upper reaches, through the timber and park land of the Sapphire Mountains, east of Hamilton. A small stream that is generally only poor fishing, Gird contains a few 10- to 20-inch rainbow, brook, and brown trout—with a rare resident bull trout to boot. [T6N R20W S4]

GLEASON LAKE (or JONES RESERVOIR). Follow the Willow Creek road, a good gravel road, east for 15 miles from the mouth of the canyon; this will take you to within a bit more than a mile (but what a mile!) of the lakeshore, 1 mile east of Palisade Mountain. Gleason is a small lake at 16 acres, mostly less than 30 feet deep, with a 16-foot irrigation dam and as much as 15 feet of water-level fluctuation. The bottom is mud, there's lots of aquatic vegetation, and the fishing used to be good for nice fat rainbow, but they've been done in by hordes of shiners. The lake is now planted with westslope cutthroat trout, last in 1990. [T6N R18W S6]

GOAT LAKE. A cirque lake of about 5 acres, in timber and park country, a few miles south of Como Peaks in the Selway-Bitterroot Wilderness. Take the Tin Cup Creek trail about 6 miles, going west from the trailhead at the canyon mouth; from there, take a steep foot trail 2½ miles north. Goat is a fairly shallow lake with boggy margins, the remains of an abandoned dam at the outlet, and places to camp. Planted with cutthroat years ago, it's excellent fishing now for small (6- to 8-inch) trout. [T3N R22W S29]

GOLD CREEK. Take the Burnt Fork road 14 miles east from Stevensville to the Gold Creek campground, then follow a good trail south for 7 miles to the stream's headwaters on Willow Mountain. In good game country, it's fair fishing for camp-size cutthroat trout, along with some brookies. There are a few resident bull trout hanging around. [T7N R19W S1]

GRANITE CREEK. Take US 12 to the creek's mouth, near Lolo Hot Springs. Granite is followed by logging roads (subject to seasonal closures) upstream 8 miles, to headwaters. Numerous beaver ponds in the lower reaches provide fair fishing for pan-size cutthroat. You might also hook into a rainbow or brook trout. The North Fork is a very small stream that is crossed at the mouth by the Granite Creek logging road and followed by road and nonmotorized-vehicle trail to its headwaters. In its lower reaches, there are occasional pools that contain a few 6- to 8-inch cutthroat. [T11N R23W S7]

GRAVE CREEK. From Lolo, take US 12 west 16 miles to the Grave Creek-Petty Creek road, which follows the creek north for most of its 7-mile length before dropping over into the Petty Creek drainage. A slow-flowing, marshy stream in heavily timbered mountains, Grave contains some small cutthroat, brookies, and rainbows, but it's not much of a fishing stream. The East Fork is a short, small stream that flows into Grave Creek 2 miles above its mouth, and it's good early-season fishing in the lower reaches for pan-size cutthroat. [T12N R22W S20]

HAACKE CREEK. A small tributary of the Burnt Fork, it is reached at the mouth by the Burnt Fork road, 10 miles east from Stevensville. There's a short trail along the first ½ mile or so, but it's on private land. There is fair fishing for a few miles upstream, for small rainbow and a few cut-throat trout. [T8N R19W S13]

HAUF LAKE. A 12-acre lake situated high (elevation 7,100 feet) above the deeply glaciated canyon of Mill Creek, in timbered, rocky country. From the Mill Creek trailhead, take the trail about 6 miles west, then follow a very poor foot trail 1 mile south to Hauf Lake, which is 2,200 feet up from the bottom of the canyon. The lake is fairly deep, dammed at the outlet, and has as much as 18 feet of water-level fluctuation in accordance with irrigation demand. Last stocked in 1990, it's fair fishing for cutthroat that reportedly average about 1 pound, but they're seldom shown a hook. This is good mountain goat country. [T6N R22W S10]

HAYES CREEK. A very small stream, flowing eastward for 6 miles from the flanks of the Bitterroot Mountains to the Bitterroot River near Charlos Heights. The lower reaches, which are mostly dewatered for irrigation, are followed by county roads and heavily fished by children for small cutthroat and brook trout. [T4N R21W S2]

HAYES CREEK. Crossed near the mouth by US 93, 6 miles south of Missoula, this small stream provides some fair kids' fishing in the middle reaches for small cutthroat trout. There's gravel-road access up to the National Forest boundary, and a trail to the headwaters. [T12N R20W S10]

HIDDEN LAKE. A small lake, covering 14 acres, east of Connor and about ½ mile southwest of West Pintlar Peak, in heavily timbered country. Take the Little East Fork road, southeast off the East Fork road off US 93, for 2 miles, to the Anaconda-Pintlar Wilderness boundary; then follow a good USFS trail up the river, going east for 11 miles past the guard station. Hidden Lake is quite deep, with lots of boulders around the margins, and it's home to cutts and rainbows from earlier plantings. [T2N R16W S12]

HIDDEN LAKE. True to its name, Hidden Lake is hard to find. Covering 10 acres, at about 6,900 feet in elevation, the lake occupies a small cirque on the south side of, and 2,200 feet above, Big Creek Canyon, 6 miles above Big Creek's mouth, west of Stevensville. To reach it, take the Big Creek trail to barren Glen Lake and follow the Big Creek-Sweathouse divide cross-country for 2 miles northwest, to a vantage point about 700 feet above the shore, and from there it's a steep scramble down. This lake is seldom fished, and then only by a stray angler (in the know), for the basketful of half-pound rainbow and cutts you can catch when you hit it right. At other times, you can go away skunked. [T8N R22W S11]

HIGH LAKE. High Lake is 39 acres, with an 85-foot maximum depth at low water, a 25-foot dam at the outlet with a consequent 20-foot water-level fluctuation, and an elevation of 7,100 feet. Take the Blodgett Creek trail, northwest of Hamilton, 4 miles west past the mouth of the canyon; then take a poor goat trail south up the rocky canyon wall for 2 miles, climbing 1,400 feet to the lake. You may see mountain goats along your way, and wish you were one of them—the trail isn't very easy to follow. High Lake was stocked with rainbow years ago, but recent fishing reports are few and far between. The rare person who makes it into High Lake doesn't talk much about the fishing after they make it back out to civilization. [T6N R22W S21]

HOLLOMAN CREEK. There are about 3 miles of fishing water in this small tributary of Miller Creek. It is crossed at the mouth by the Miller Creek road, and it's followed by good gravel road for most of its length. If you stay away from the mouth, which is on posted, private land, you might catch some small cutthroat. [T11N R18W S18]

HOPE LAKE. Hope Lake covers 10 acres and has a maximum depth of 50 feet, with steep drop-offs all around, some large boulders, and a few lilies along the edges, elevation 7,500 feet. The lake can be reached from the campground at Mussigbrod Lake, at the end of the Plimpton Creek road, off USFS road 3, west of Wisdom: from the campground, take a fair USFS trail north for 8 miles, passing into the Anaconda-Pintlar Wilderness and up to the Continental Divide. Head 1½ miles east along the Divide, and finally another mile north to the shore. Note well: This last mile is closed to all but foot travel. The surrounding country is very steep and rocky, but heavily wooded, with conifers growing right down to the water. A fisherman's report, cited here, was that the fishing is good now for 18- to 20-inchers and he really enjoyed the solitude. This lake was last planted in 1981, with rainbow. [T1N R16W S9]

HOPE (or LEGEND) LAKE. The second in the Faith-Hope-Charity string of lakes in the Sapphire Mountains northeast of Sula. Hope is about 7 miles north along the Fish Lake trailhead, off the Martin Creek road— the last mile or so of trail is closed to motorized vehicles. Hope covers a couple of acres and gets deep quick. It is mostly forested around the edges, but a boulder slope and a grassy area along one shoreline offer some good casting opportunities. It's got pan-size cutts in it, but sometimes you can't tell they're there. [T3N R17W S18]

HOWARD CREEK. A small stream flowing to Lolo Creek opposite the old Lolo Ranger Station. A USFS dirt road provides seasonal access along the stream's 8-mile length. The first mile is poor to fair fishing for 6- to 8-inch brook, cutthroat, rainbow, and an occasional brown trout. [T12N R23W S25]

HOWARD'S LAKE (or MARY'S FROG POND). Two acres, maximum depth 35 feet, immediate shore boggy and marshy, set in heavily timbered mountains. About 10 miles west of Lolo on US 12, head south on the USFS road toward Elk Meadows. About 9 miles from the highway, look hard off to the right for a poor, unmarked trail that pitches over the steep edge about ¼ mile west to the lake. Howard's was discovered and stocked in the 1960s. It is not shown on most maps. It now provides good fishing for 10- to 18-inch rainbow—with lots of mosquitoes and a few cutthroat. It's too small to stand much fishing pressure—and too hard to find to get much. [T11N R22W S15]

HUGHES CREEK. Take the West Fork road off US 93 going 4 miles south of Painted Rocks Lake, to the mouth of Hughes Creek. Follow a poor gravel road for 12 miles upstream (west) through steep, timbered mountains, and continue on a USFS trail for 6 miles, almost to headwaters. A rapidly flowing, snow-fed creek, Hughes is easily fished for good catches of 6- to 10-inch cutthroat, some brookies, and an occasional bull trout. [T2S R22W S34]

JACK THE RIPPER CREEK. Continue west on a good trail from the end of the Blue Joint Creek road for 6 miles, to the mouth of Jack the Ripper. Although there's no maintained trail, you can follow the stream 3 miles to headwaters. This is a real pretty little snow-fed stream, with good fishing in its lower reaches for small cutthroat. [T2S R23W S8]

JOHNSON CREEK. From Painted Rocks Lake, take the West Fork road south for 12 miles, to the mouth of Johnson Creek; from there you can take an unmaintained foot trail upstream for a couple of miles. Johnson Creek is a very small, clear stream that is fishable for about 1½ miles above the mouth for small cutthroat and rainbow. [T3S R22W S33]

JONES RESERVOIR. See Gleason Lake.

KELLY LAKE. A small lake of about 10 acres, about 2 miles west of West Pintlar Peak in heavily timbered country. Take the Little East Fork road for 2 miles to the Anaconda-Pintlar Wilderness boundary, then continue east on a good USFS trail up the East Fork of the Bitterroot, about 11 miles past the guard station. Or come at Kelly Lake from the north, up the Copper Creek drainage, or along the Middle Fork of Rock Creek and over Bitterroot Pass. Fishing reports are scarce, which suggests that you might not see anyone else while you're checking it out. [T2N R16W S12]

KENCK LAKE. See Sears Lake.

KERLEE LAKE. About 6 miles southwest from the Tin Cup Creek trailhead, look for an unmarked path that heads across the creek and to the north. It's a steep and poorly marked climb that takes you, in a mile or so, to the lake, in a small cirque on the southern, alpine slopes of Como Peaks. Kerlee is a small lake (37 acres) and quite shallow, although it doesn't freeze out. It's been planted with cutthroat, last in 1990. It can be excellent fishing, although recent reports suggest that the fish are small. [T3N R22W S29]

KIDNEY LAKE. Go to Lower Camas Lake, hoof it around to the south side, and hike up the little inlet 440 yards south, and 500 feet straight up to Kidney Lake. Or watch for the blaze marking an old trail, about ¼ mile east of Lower Camas. The trail peters out after an old hunting camp, but it points you in the direction of a sane way up to the lake. Kidney Lake is almost two lakes, covering 12 acres within a 16-foot maximum depth, and it's fair fishing for small cutts. It was last stocked in 1990. [T5N R22W S36]

KNAACK LAKE. See Sheafman Lakes.

KOOTENAI CREEK. This clear, snow- and lake-fed outlet of the three Kootenai Lakes flows due east, through a deep, rock-walled, timber- and brush-covered glacial canyon, for 9 miles to the Bitterroot Valley, and then across farmland to the river. It is crossed near the mouth by US 93 just northwest of Stevensville, and is followed by a good trail from the mouth of the canyon to headwaters. The lower reaches (below the canyon) are sometimes completely dewatered for irrigation, although you might get permission to fish if you ask. Within the canyon, it is a beautiful stream with many boulders, holes, and riffles containing lots of 6- to 8-inch cutthroat and rainbow-cutthroat hybrids, as well as some rainbows and brookies (from South Kootenai Lake). Keep an eye out for small resident bull trout as well. [T9N R20W S21]

KOOTENAI LAKES. See Middle, North, and South Kootenai Lakes.

LAPPI LAKE. A 10-acre lake with a maximum depth of over 40 feet and an elevation of 6,900 feet. Lappi occupies a small, subalpine cirque on the south side of, and 1,100 feet above, Bass Creek Canyon. Take the Bass Creek trail west for 5 miles past the Charles Waters Memorial Campground at the mouth of the canyon, and then a very poor foot trail, around ledges and over rocks, up the steep, clifflike side of the canyon, south for 1 mile to the lakeshore. Once you get there, you're in for a surprise—it's barren. [T9N R21W S4]

LARRY CREEK. Not much of a stream—small, steep, and about 4 miles long—when the lower reaches are not dewatered for irrigation, and when

Kootenai Falls.
—Courtesy U.S.
Forest Service

the upper reaches don't dry up. It's crossed by a county road 3 miles south of Florence, and it produces a few small cutthroat for the local kids. [T10N R20W S23]

LAVENE CREEK. A very small tributary (about 2½ miles long) of the West Fork of the Bitterroot River. It's crossed at the mouth by the West Fork road, about 8 miles south of Conner. There's no trail, but there's a logging road, about 4 miles long, from the West Fork road that gets you into the head of it—the only problem is, there's no fishing up there. Stick to the lower reaches, near the mouth, for fair fishing for small cutthroat and rainbow trout. [T1N R21W S17]

LEGEND LAKE. See Hope Lake.

LITTLE BLUE JOINT CREEK. A clear, snow-fed tributary of Blue Joint Creek. It's paralleled by a USFS road along a rocky, timbered canyon for a few miles, and then by a trail for 2 miles to headwaters. This small creek is good fishing for a couple of miles above the mouth for 8-inch cutts, with a few rainbows and brookies thrown in. [T2S R22W S4]

LITTLE BOULDER CREEK. A clear, dashing, and small inlet of Painted Rocks Lake, crossed at the mouth by the West Fork road, then followed along the north side by a USFS logging road for 1½ miles, and finally by a trail for 3 miles to headwaters. The lower reaches are fair fishing for small (pan-size) cutthroat and brook trout. [T1S R22W S26]

LITTLE BURNT FORK CREEK. A wee small tributary of the Burnt Fork, crossed by the Burnt Fork trail at the mouth, about 2½ miles north of Burnt Fork Lake. It's not much of a stream but does provide fair fishing along the lower reaches for camp-fare cutthroat. [T7N R18W S35]

LITTLE ROCK CREEK. This creek drains three unnamed cirque lakes between El Capitan and Como peaks, flowing for 2 miles to Little Rock Creek Lake, and from there 4 miles to Como Lake. Take the Como Lake road around the south side of the lake, then go up a steep and rough road to the Little Rock Creek trailhead. The trail reaches Little Rock Lake in 6½ miles, but it doesn't follow the creek very closely for most of that distance. Nonetheless, this is a pretty little stream, and it's good fishing for cutts ranging up to 10 inches. [T4N R22W S36]

LITTLE ROCK CREEK LAKE. Reach as described under Little Rock Creek above. The lake is about 24 acres, shallow (although it doesn't freeze out), and boggy around the margins, and it contains lots of feed. It was planted years ago with cutthroat. The fish are all about 10 to 12 inches long now, providing excellent fishing for the very few stray hunters (it's almost never hit for fishing alone) who find their way to the lake. This is real good elk country. [T3N R22W S9]

LITTLE WEST FORK CREEK. A dashing, snow-fed tributary of the West Fork of the Bitterroot River, crossed at the mouth by the West Fork road, 4½ miles south of the West Fork Ranger Station. There's some road access to the lower reaches, which are excellent fishing for small cutthroat, as well as some brookies and rainbow. There's no trail. [T1N R22W S32]

LOCKWOOD LAKE. A 10-acre, 15- to 20-foot deep cirque lake at the headwaters of Mill Creek, in the Selway-Bitterroot Wilderness. It's reached by a fair trail from Mill Creek Lake, and it's barren. [T7N R22W S36]

LOLO CREEK. A good-size mountain stream flowing for 30 miles from Lolo Pass to the Bitterroot River at the town of Lolo, and followed the whole way by US 12. The upper reaches are timbered, the lower reaches are pasture and farmland. An easily and heavily fished stream, it produces good summer catches of 8- to 14-inch rainbow, cutthroat, and brookies, plus a fall spawning run of brown trout. It's a popular creek for whitefish in the winter. [T11N R20W S1]

LOLO CREEK, East Fork. It flows into Lolo Creek about a mile south of Lolo Hot Springs on US 12. It's followed by a gravel road for 9 miles to headwaters. A clear mountain stream that contains some small cutthroat, brook trout, and whitefish, it is generally only poor to fair fishing. [T11N R23W S18]

LOLO CREEK, South Fork. From Lolo, take US 12 west for 10 miles, just past the Woodman School, then head south on USFS road 451. Follow the signs to the South Fork trailhead a few miles along, then take the good USFS trail to headwaters. There are about 10 miles of fishing water, to the Meadow Creek junction. The lower couple of miles (below the trailhead) are on posted, private land, so ask before you fish. The stream's good for 6- to 14-inch cutthroat and an occasional small brook trout. Watch for little bull trout here—easy to confuse with brookies, they must be released if you catch one. [T12N R21W S29]

LOLO CREEK, West Fork. It's paralleled by US 12 from its mouth at Lolo Hot Springs for 7 miles to its headwaters at Lolo Pass. This small stream is heavily fished for fair early- to middle-season catches of 10- to 12-inch cutthroat, with the possibility of catching just about any other kind of trout, too. [T11N R23W S7]

West Fork of Lolo Creek. —Courtesy U.S. Forest Service

LOST HORSE CREEK. The outlet of Twin Lakes, as well as Tenmile and Twelvemile Lakes, Lost Horse flows for 20 miles down a deeply glaciated, brush- and timber-covered canyon to the Bitterroot River, 10 miles south of Hamilton. It's crossed by US 93 near the mouth, then followed by a gravel road to headwaters. Since the road is progressively rougher as it heads toward the Bitterroot divide, towing a trailer is not recommended. Lost Horse Creek is heavily fished—as you can tell from the large numbers of pullouts along the road—for fair to good catches of 7- to 9-inch cutthroat and rainbows, along with a few brook and bull trout. North Lost Horse is a very small stream, flowing southeast to Lost Horse Creek. It's followed upstream by a poor trail (if you can find it) to headwaters, but only the lower half mile is worth fishing—little trout in little pools. [T4N R21W S11]

LOST HORSE CREEK, South. The outlet of Fish Lake, this stream flows for 9 miles, down a heavily forested, glaciated canyon, to the main Lost Horse Creek. There it is reached by a good road going west 5 miles from Charlos Heights. The stream is followed to the lake by a USFS trail, and,

Lost Horse Creek. —Courtesy Michele Archie

while it's good fishing for 7- to 9-inch cutthroat, it's mostly passed up for the lake. [T4N R22W S12]

LOST HORSE LAKE. This lake is 67 acres and deep, with boggy shores, in timbered mountains, at the headwaters of South Lost Horse Creek. Lost Horse Lake can be reached by a hunters' trail going 3 miles southeast from Fish Lake. This wilderness lake was planted in the 1940s with cutthroat, which provide excellent fishing for the few anglers who make the trip. [T4N R23W S23]

LYMAN CREEK. A very small tributary of Cameron Creek that runs through state land, in timbered and logged mountains, north of Sula. Lyman Creek is seldom fished—there's no trail—but it's fair here and there for pan-size cutthroat and brook trout. [T2N R19W S22]

MARTIN CREEK. This creek flows, through heavily timbered mountains, for 15 miles to the East Fork of the Bitterroot River. A lot of the drainage was burned in the Sleeping Child fire in the 1960s, so it's a good place to see regeneration in action. Martin Creek is followed by a logging road upstream for about 3 miles, and from there on in it's crosscountry for several miles northwest, to an upper logging road that takes you to headwaters. There's a Forest Service campground about a mile above Martin's confluence with the East Fork. About 11 miles of fishable water produce good catches of 6- to 10-inch cutthroat, if you're willing to hike between holes. Watch for small bull trout in the upper reaches. [T2N R17W S17]

MARY'S FROG POND. See Howard's Lake.

MCCLAIN CREEK. A very small, steep stream flowing to the Bitterroot River, 5 miles south of Lolo. It's a tiny stream on private land, and even if you get permission to fish it, you won't hook up with much more than a few brookies and cutts, sized to match the creek. [T11N R20W S23]

MEADOW CREEK. Take a good gravel road south for 7 miles from the East Fork road off US 93, 13 miles east of Sula. From there, a gated road follows the stream for another mile and a half, just about to headwaters. A brushy, beaver-dammed stream in timbered mountains, it's seldom fished but does contain some small cutthroat, especially in the lower reaches. There may be some bull trout here, too. [T2N R18W S24]

MEADOW CREEK. Only a couple of miles long and not really a fishing stream, it does contain a few small cutthroat for ½ mile above its junction with the South Fork of Lolo Creek, west of Florence. Access this one from the South Fork trail. [T11N R21W S31]

Middle Kootenai Lake near Idaho line. —Courtesy U.S. Forest Service

MIDDLE KOOTENAI LAKE. This 15-acre lake is mostly 15 to 30 feet deep, in heavily timbered mountains at the head of Kootenai Creek. Reach it via 10 miles of good horse trail going west from the end of the county road at the mouth of the canyon. This lake was planted with golden trout in the late 50s, but there aren't any left. [T9N R22W S11]

MILL CREEK. Take US 12 for 8 miles southwest of Lolo to the mouth of Mill Creek. Take a logging road and trail upstream for about 2½ miles of occasional access. It's a small stream, but it's fished quite a bit for fair catches of 6- to 8-inch cutthroat and brook trout. [T12N R21W S34]

MILL CREEK. The outlet of Mill, Lockwood, Sears, and Hauf Lakes, Mill Creek flows through a steep, rocky canyon, in heavy timber and brush, for 15 miles, then for another 1½ miles, through pasture and farmland, to its confluence with Fred Burr Creek. The mouth of the canyon is reached from US 93 at Woodside, going west on a county road that ends at the trailhead, which is replete with picnic area and stock ramp. The stream is followed closely by 12 miles of good trail to head-waters. Its upper reaches are fair fishing for small rainbows and cutts, the lower reaches for brookies, browns, and rainbows. [T7N R20W S19]

MILL LAKE. Take the Mill Creek trail, reached as described above, 12 miles west to this mountain lake, which covers a few dozen acres and is dammed at the outlet. The fishing is no great shakes, but you'll hook into some cutthroat here. [T6N R23W S1]

MILLER CREEK. A small stream about 14 miles long, it flows to the Bitterroot River, 5 miles south of Missoula. The lower reaches can be completely dewatered for irrigation; the upper reaches flow through timbered mountains and pastureland. Miller Creek is followed by road along its entire length, through mostly private land, much of which is developed. Once this stream was heavily fished. Now access is limited, but you may get permission to fish if you ask. The fishing is fair for brook trout and cutts. [T12N R20W S15]

MINE CREEK. A small stream, about 5 miles long, that flows to Hughes Creek on the side opposite the road, 8 miles east of Alta. Followed by a logging road for about 3 miles above the mouth, it's generally fair to good fishing for 8- to 10-inch cutthroat, and it's excellent fishing in some large beaver ponds a mile above the mouth. [T3S R21W S3]

MOOSE CREEK. A high mountain stream, the outlet of Faith, Hope, Charity, and Fish Lakes, it flows for 9 miles, through heavy timber, to the East Fork of the Bitterroot River, at the East Fork Guard Station. It's followed by logging road about 3 miles upstream from its confluence with Martin Creek, and then by 3 miles of trail, and cross-country another few miles to headwaters. A few people fish it for 6- to 12-inch cutthroat. You might also hook up with a resident bull trout. If you do, land it quickly and release it. [T2N R17W S16]

MUD CREEK. A real small tributary of the West Fork of the Bitterroot River, crossed at the mouth by the West Fork road, a mile north of Painted Rocks Lake. There is no trail here, but the creek is clear, fast, and fair fishing near the mouth for pan-size rainbow and cutthroat trout. The lower reaches of this creek are on private land, so ask permission before you fish. [T1S R22W S23]

NELSON LAKE. This lake covers 35 acres, with a maximum depth of about 30 feet, and it's dammed—with 10-foot fluctuations of water level. Nelson Lake occupies a barren alpine cirque 2 miles southeast of Bare Peak. From the north side of the Nez Perce highway, 4 miles south of the West Fork Ranger Station, take the Gemmel Creek road north to the end, then follow 4 miles of steep trail almost to the lake. About 2 miles from the trailhead, a footpath takes off to the right. Follow this footpath to the lake, otherwise you're looking at a steep 1-mile downhill hike to the lake, from an overlook point on a nearby ridge. Nelson used to be good fishing and was very popular for skinny cutthroat trout, but they don't reproduce well here, and now the fishing is only fair for 8- to 12-inchers. [T1N R22W S17]

NEZ PERCE FORK BITTERROOT RIVER. See Bitterroot River, Nez Perce Fork.

NORTH FORK GRANITE CREEK. See under Granite Creek.

NORTH FORK SWEENEY CREEK. See Sweeney Creek, North Fork.

NORTH FORK TRAPPER CREEK. See Trapper Creek, North Fork.

NORTH KOOTENAI LAKE. About 15 acres, and deep, in a rockbound cirque at the headwaters of Kootenai Creek, the lake is reached by trail 11 miles west from the mouth of the canyon. It's surrounded by steep slopes of timber, brush, and rock. There's flat terrain and plenty of space to camp at the head and the outlet. This is a beautiful lake, and it's fair fishing (when they bite) for beautiful silvery rainbow that'll run up to 4 pounds. [T9N R22W S11]

NORTH (or NORTH FORK) LOST HORSE CREEK. See under Lost Horse Creek.

O'BRIEN CREEK. This small stream flows for 10 miles through timber above and hayfields below to the Bitterroot River just across the Maclay Bridge from the Target Range area of west Missoula. It's followed upstream

North Kootenai Lake.
—Courtesy Michele Archie

by a gravel road for much of its length, mostly through private land. The lower reaches are generally dewatered for irrigation but, if you get permission to fish, the middle and upper reaches offer a limited amount of fair fishing for pan-size cutthroat and brook trout. A good creek for kids. [T13N R20W S24]

ONE HORSE CREEK. Flows for 5 miles from One Horse Lakes, through a brush-floored, rock-walled canyon, to the Bitterroot Valley, and then to the river near Florence. Access is limited, but some fishing is allowed. The lower reaches are mostly dewatered for irrigation; the upper reaches—to which there is no road or trail access—are fair fishing for small cutthroat, and maybe some brookies. [T10N R20W S14]

ONE HORSE LAKES. There are three of them, but only the southernmost contains fish. It is about 15 acres, with a mud bottom and a moderate amount of aquatic vegetation around the shore, and it's not more than 20 to 25 feet deep anywhere. There's a trail into the One Horse Lakes Basin that runs south for a couple of miles from Carlton Lake. The fishing is good for small rainbow trout. [T11N R21W S33]

OVERWHICH CREEK. This one is better known for the game hunting in the area than for its fishing. It flows through conifer-covered mountains for 20 miles to the West Fork of the Bitterroot River, 1 mile south of Painted Rocks Lake. It's followed by road and trail to headwaters. The fishing is excellent for small cutthroat, from the mouth to some high (about 75 feet) falls 14 miles upstream. [T2S R22W S10]

PAINTED ROCKS LAKE (or WEST FORK BITTERROOT RESER-VOIR). About 4 miles long by ½ mile wide, mostly good and deep, in a heavily wooded canyon. It's followed clear around on the south side by the West Fork road. Painted Rocks Lake has had its share of hard times due to excessive drawdown, but there seem to be a few hardy ones of just about every kind of trout and whitefish that hang on. There is a good campground at the upper end, and, despite the relative scarcity of fish, it's a pretty reservoir when full, which unfortunately is mostly before the recreation season. Also, it's a nice drive, and there are lots of good creeks and small mountain lakes in the vicinity. The dam was rebuilt and the outlet structure repaired in the spring of 1967. It was stocked with cutts almost every year from 1975 to 1984, and it can be good fishing in the early season. [T1S R18E S26]

PASS LAKE. Stop off on your way to Capri Lake from the Warm Springs Creek trail, or from the Porcupine Saddle trailhead near the Indian Creek campground. Pass Lake is about a mile east of Capri. Stocked with cutts in 1952, it still provides marginal fishing. [T1S R20W S28]

PEARL LAKE. Take the Big Creek trail for 9 miles west from the mouth of the canyon, then the South Fork trail south for 6 miles to the South Fork Lake, and finally an unmaintained elk and mountain goat trail north for ½ mile to the lakeshore, in a beautiful alpine setting. Stop by, if you're in the neighborhood, for some fair cutthroat fishing in this deep 10-acre lake. [T8N R22W S17]

PETERSON LAKE. Take a logging road from the north side of the Sweeney Creek Canyon, off US 93 just south of Florence, for 6 miles of switchbacks that are rough and steep in places. From the trailhead, follow 5 miles of mostly good but climbing trail, to the lakeshore. Peterson covers about 30 acres, is shallow (up to about 20 feet deep) with a muddy bottom, and is overpopulated with 6- to 11-inch rainbow (mostly 6-inch) that are reportedly caught two at a time. This one ought to be hit harder, so some of these little ones could grow up. It's tough casting, except at the inlet. [T10N R21W S10]

PIERCE CREEK. A very small stream flowing to the West Fork of the Bitterroot River, about 5 miles south of Conner. It supports a few small cutthroat and rainbow in the first mile above the mouth, and it's fair early-season fishing. There's some access by gravel road. [T2N R21W S34]

PIQUETT CREEK. Take the West Fork road 7 miles south of Conner, and then take a logging road that's off the east side of the road south for

Pearl Lake.
—Courtesy U.S.
Forest Service

54

5 miles; a trail will take you 10 miles upstream to headwaters. A clear, easily fished mountain creek in heavily timbered country, it's followed by gravel road and trail to its headwaters at Piquett Lake. The fishing is good for 6- to 8-inch cutthroats and brookies, with a very occasional rainbow or brown trout. [T1N R21W S3]

PIQUETT CREEK, East Fork. Take the West Fork road for 7 miles south of Conner, then turn south on a logging road off the east side of the road and go for 1½ miles to the mouth of this stream. You can head on upstream on a logging road for another 3 miles, finally fighting your way up the bottom for another 4 miles to headwaters. It's a clear, snow-fed stream in timber and brush; the lower reaches—to which the logging road provides limited access—contain a good population of small rainbow and cutthroat trout. [T1N R21W S3]

PIQUETT LAKE. It's 6½ acres and about 20 feet deep with steep drop-offs all around, in a sparsely timbered alpine cirque, with barren talus slopes above. Piquett Lake is reached by trail up the Little Boulder Creek drainage, up Piquett Creek, or from one of several other directions. Last planted in 1983, it has very spotty—but sometimes fair to good—fishing for small cutthroat. [T1S R21W S21]

PORCUPINE CREEK. Take the Warm Springs Creek trail 7½ miles south to the mouth of Porcupine Creek, or come at it from the Porcupine Saddle trail. There's a trail along the lower mile and a half of this very small mountain stream. It's fair kids' fishing for 5- to 7-inch cutthroat trout. [T1S R20W S15]

RAILROAD CREEK. Take Montana 38 east from US 93 and go just past the Black Bear campground, then turn off the main road to follow Skalkaho Creek south a couple of miles, to the mouth of Railroad Creek. The lower 3 or 4 miles of this stream are followed by logging road and then by trail. This is a small stream, the lower reaches of which provide poor fishing for small (6- to 7-inch) cutthroat. [T5N R18W S29]

REIMEL CREEK. This little stream flows to the East Fork of the Bitterroot River a couple of miles east of Sula, and it's followed by trail 8 miles south to headwaters. The lower 2 miles are poor fishing for small cutthroat and brook trout. [T1N R19W S16]

RIPPLE LAKE. A shallow, 7½-acre lake, with muskeg margins in heavy timber just west of West Pintlar Peak in the Anaconda Pintlar Wilderness. Heading east from the East Fork of the Bitterroot trailhead, 2 miles southeast of the East Fork Guard Station, the lake is a good 11 miles back. It originally contained only cutthroat but was planted with rainbow in 1959. It's slow fishing for 8- to 12-inchers of both species, and a few that'll hit maybe 4 or 5 pounds. [T2N R16W S11]

ROARING LION CREEK. From the mouth of Roaring Lion Canyon (reached by county roads 5 miles southwest of Hamilton), continue west for 3½ miles on a USFS access road to a big parking area at the trailhead. There are 8 miles of well-maintained trail from there that follow the stream pretty closely. Below the canyon, the stream can be completely dewatered for irrigation, but the upper reaches are excellent fishing for eatin'-size cutthroat. A good place to take a beginner. [T5N R21W S1]

ROCK CREEK. Crossed at the mouth by US 93, 4 miles north of Darby, it's followed by a county road a few miles to Como Lake. Trails skirt Como Lake to the north and south (the south trail is for stock, the north trail is for hikers only), meeting at the head of the lake. From there, follow some 14 miles of trail west past Elk Lake to Rock Creek's headwaters, near the Montana-Idaho state line. In the upper sections, small to midsize cutthroat provide most of the action, while below Como Lake there's some early-season fishing for 8- to 10-inch rainbows. The lower reaches are completely dewatered for irrigation. [T4N R21W S23]

ROMBO CREEK. A very small tributary of the West Fork of the Bitterroot River, crossed at the mouth by the West Fork road, 4 miles south of the ranger station. It is no better than poor fishing in the lower reaches for small cutthroat trout. [T1S R22W S22]

RYE CREEK. About 16 miles long, flowing through steep, timbered mountains to the Bitterroot River 3 miles north of Conner, Rye Creek is crossed at the mouth by US 93 a few miles south of Darby, and it's followed by county road and a good USFS road practically to headwaters. It doesn't run much water and is only poor to fair fishing for pan-size cutthroat and brook trout, as well as a few whitefish. [T3N R21W S36]

SAGE HEN LAKE. See Willow Lake.

SALT CREEK. A very small tributary of the West Fork of the Bitterroot River, reached at the mouth by the West Fork highway, 5½ miles south of the Alta Guard Station. There's no road or trail access, but Salt Creek is fair fishing for the first couple of miles above the mouth for 7- to 8-inch cutthroats. [T3S R22W S28]

SAWMILL CREEK. This small tributary of the Burnt Fork is reached at the mouth by the Burnt Fork road, near Squaw Peak. It's fair fishing for small (pan-size) rainbow and cutthroat, in the lower reaches only. There's about a mile of fishable water, accessible from a gravel road, but it's mostly on private land—ask first. [T8N R19W S13]

SAWTOOTH CREEK. It's crossed near its mouth by US 93, 1½ miles south of Hamilton. The lower reaches are all fouled up for irrigation, but the upper reaches flow for 10 miles down a beautiful, glaciated canyon, and they're followed pretty closely the entire distance by a USFS trail, accessed from the Roaring Lion Road, going west from US 93. The trail starts out good but isn't well maintained along the upstream portions. At the trailhead, southwest of Hamilton on the Roaring Lion road, you'll find plenty of parking and a stock ramp, a big change from the days when you had to side-hill it around from Roaring Lion Creek because of restricted access. It's worth the trip just for the scenery, but the fishing is fair too, for small (6- to 7-inch) cutthroat and some rainbow. [T6N R21W S35]

SEARS (or KENCK) LAKE. About 20 acres, with a 20-foot maximum depth, this lake has considerable aquatic growth around the upper end. It is reached by a very poor foot trail going north 1½ miles from the main Mill Creek trail (west of Woodside), at a point about 8 miles west of the mouth of the canyon. Sears was stocked many years ago with rainbow, and then with cutthroat. However, there is very little inflow during the summer months, and it is drawn so very low for irrigation that the lake was apparently barren for some time. But Montana Fish, Wildlife and Parks stocked it with cutts again as recently as 1990, so it might be worth an exploratory visit. [T6N R22W S5]

SHAROTT CREEK. A small stream crossed at the mouth by US 93 a mile west of Stevensville. There's limited road access to the lower reaches and an unmaintained foot trail that follows the stream 5 miles west to headwaters, below St. Mary's Peak. There is fair fishing here for 6- to 7-inch rainbow and cutthroat in the lower reaches only, since it's very steep and rocky above. [T9N R20W S28]

SHEAFMAN CREEK. This stream is crossed at the mouth by US 93, 4½ miles south of Victor, and within the National Forest it is followed (sort of) by trail west for 6 miles to Garrard Lake. It's a steep stream in the upper reaches, which flow through a deeply glaciated, timbered canyon; the lower reaches (within the Bitterroot Valley) are mostly dewatered for irrigation. It sometimes goes dry the whole length except for some good pools in the upper reaches, wherein a few 8- to 10-inch cutthroat manage to survive. [T7N R20W S18]

SHEAFMAN (or GARRARD, AICHELE, AND KNAACK) LAKES. These three lakes are close together in the headwaters of Sheafman Creek, but only Garrard, the easternmost one, has fish. It is reached by a steep but well-constructed trail 6 miles west from the trailhead, at the mouth of Sheafman Canyon, in beautiful scenic country. Garrard is about 6 acres,

15 feet deep, and held up by an old dam that hasn't been used in years. There's not much inflow or outflow during the summer, and the lake is fair fishing for 8- to 12-inch cutthroat. [T7N R22W S33]

SHEEPHEAD CREEK. Sheephead Creek is crossed at its mouth by the Nez Perce highway, 11 miles southwest of the West Fork Ranger Station, and it's followed along the north side by something of a trail northwest for 6 miles to headwaters. The trailhead is near the Fales Flat campground. Sheephead Creek is an easily fished stream (good for kids) for 6- to 9-inch cutthroat trout. [T1S R23W S16]

SHELF LAKE. A high (elevation 7,600 feet) alpine lake, about 11 acres, with a maximum depth of 20 feet, in a sparsely timbered, talus-slope locale. It's reached by trail going northwest up the Boulder Creek drainage (off the West Fork road), or by a steep climb ¼ mile down the talus slope from Piquett Lake. The fishing is fair to good for 10- to 14-inch cutthroat, last stocked there in 1983. [T1S R21W S22]

Skalkaho Falls.
—Courtesy U.S. Forest Service

SIGNAL CREEK. Take the Burnt Fork trail southeast from Stevensville to the mouth of this creek, in Boulder Basin; a trail follows it southwest. The lower 2 miles above the mouth are fair fishing for camp-size cutthroat and rainbow. The upper reaches are too steep for fish. [T7N R18W S23]

SILVERTHORN CREEK. A wee small tributary of McCalla Creek, just southwest of Stevensville. There's limited access by road or trail, except to the mouth, and it's mostly on private land. This one is fair kids' fishing in the lower reaches for small cutthroat and rainbow. [T9N R20W S33]

SKALKAHO CREEK. An easily accessible, easily fished stream, closely followed by Montana 38, a logging road, and a trail for 14 miles, from its mouth, 3 miles south of Hamilton, eastward to its headwaters in the Sapphire Mountains. The lower 5 miles can be almost completely dewatered for irrigation. The upper reaches, which flow through beautiful and largely unspoiled country, support a cutthroat fishery and provide good fishing for 10- to 12-inchers, plus some brookies and a few big browns. Watch for bull trout here, especially in the fall. Below Daly Creek, look for lots of rainbow and whitefish, too. Lots of rattlesnakes here! [T5N R21W S1]

SLATE CREEK. A small, wadable inlet of Painted Rocks Lake that flows into the lake at the Slate Creek campground. The lower couple of miles are accessible by gravel road. It's pretty small for fishing, but it does support lots of small cutthroat. [T2S R22W S2]

SLEEPING CHILD CREEK. Take US 93 south from Hamilton for 2½ miles, to the Skalkaho junction, then continue due south on a county road for another 2½ miles to the mouth of Sleeping Child; from there, follow the road eastward for 7 miles, almost to the hot springs, from which point you can hike up a good USFS trail southeast for several miles to headwaters. Sleeping Child is a heavily and easily fished stream that produces a little bit of everything, including brookies, cutts, rainbows, whitefish, and fall-spawning brown trout below. Don't forget to ask permission to fish the private lands along the lower parts of the stream. Above, look for the cutthroat to grow more abundant, and some resident bull trout. [T5N R21W S25]

SLOCUM CREEK. A very small tributary of the Burnt Fork of the Bitterroot River, crossed at the mouth by a county road 7 miles east of Stevensville. Slocum Creek flows through heavily grazed pastureland and becomes quite warm in summer, but nonetheless it's a fair kids' stream for small rainbow and cutthroat trout. [T8N R19W S4]

SMITH CREEK. This tiny tributary of Sweathouse Creek is reached by a good gravel road, 2 miles west out of Victor. It's on private land, but kids who get permission can have fun fishing the lower couple of miles for small cutthroat and rainbow. [T8N R21W S35]

SNOW LAKE. See Charity Lake.

SODA SPRINGS CREEK. Take the Nez Perce road 4 miles west from the West Fork Ranger Station to Little West Fork Creek, then a USFS logging road west for 1½ miles, to the mouth of Soda Springs Creek. There's not much parking or anything else at the trailhead. The rough and often boggy trail follows the stream for about 5 miles of fair fishing for small cutthroat trout. [T1N R22W S32]

SOUTH FORK BIG CREEK. See Big Creek, South Fork.

SOUTH FORK BIG CREEK LAKE. This lake, 40 acres and deep, has considerable aquatic vegetation. This cirque lake, in timber and park country, is reached by a poor, unmaintained trail, 4 miles south from a point on the Big Creek trail that's about 1 mile east of Big Creek Lake. South Fork Lake used to be good fishing for 8- to 12- inch rainbow, but excessive fluctuation of the water level (due to leakage from an old, abandoned dam) wiped them out. There are some rumors that there are still descendants of a 1977 stocking of westslope cutts hanging around. [T8N R22W S17]

SOUTH FORK LAKES. No two ways about it, you have to bushwhack to these lakes at the headwaters of the South Fork of Lolo Creek. Go in either west from the South Fork trail, or east from the South Fork of Spruce Creek, on the Idaho side. Once you get there, you'll find lots of little cutts to keep you busy. [T10N R22W S35]

SOUTH FORK LOLO CREEK. See Lolo Creek, South Fork.

SOUTH KOOTENAI LAKE. It's 50 acres and mostly less than 20 feet deep, with brushy margins and talus along the northwest side. South Kootenai Lake lies in a heavily wooded cirque, reached by a good trail up Kootenai Creek, 11 miles west of the mouth of the canyon, northwest of Stevensville. It is overpopulated with tiny brookies—10 inches is a monster—that provide excellent fishing for even the rankest neophyte. A beautiful lake for a weekend trip, it's good elk-hunting country too. [T9N R22W S14]

SOUTH (or SOUTH FORK) LOST HORSE CREEK. See Lost Horse Creek, South.

SPUD LAKE. See Faith Lake.

South Kootenai Lake.
—Courtesy Michele Archie

STUART CREEK. This small stream flows through a heavily grazed area to Willow Creek, through the Calf Creek section of the Bitterroot Wildlife Management Area. There's no road or maintained trail, but it is fair fishing for 1½ miles above the mouth for pan-size rainbow and cutthroat trout. [T6N R19W S7]

SWEATHOUSE CREEK. A clear, fast stream flowing east for 6 miles down its steep, rocky canyon to the Bitterroot Valley, and then for another 5 miles through farmland to the Bitterroot River near Victor. The lower reaches can go completely dry in summer (due to irrigation diversions), but the upper canyon reaches are fun fishing for 6- to 9-inch cutthroat and a few rainbows. There are resident bull trout here as well. There's a trail following the stream west for several miles above the canyon mouth—and the falls, 2 miles in, are well worth the walk. [T8N R20W S29]

SWEENEY CREEK. About 8 miles long, from the junction of its north and south forks to its confluence with the Bitterroot River, 1½ miles south of Florence. The upper reaches flow down a heavily forested canyon, the lower reaches (within the Bitterroot Valley) are completely dewatered for irrigation. It's fair fishing above for small cutthroat and brook trout. There's no trail or road access to the reaches inside the National Forest. [T10N R20W S13]

SWEENEY CREEK, NORTH FORK. About 5 miles long, it's the outlet of Mills, Holloway, Duffy, and Peterson lakes; the lower couple of miles are good fishing for 7- to 9-inch cutthroat and rainbow trout. Have fun getting here—there's no road or trail. [T10N R21W S14]

TAG ALDER LAKE. This 9-acre lake is 32 feet deep, in a small, timbered cirque just below Mill Point, on the Mill Creek-Blodgett Creek divide. There is no trail—just gird your loins and head due west up the mountain front for a 2½-mile-long, 3,300-foot-high climb from the county road, 1 mile south of the mouth of Mill Creek Canyon. Or head south up the drainage from Mill Creek. This one is very seldom fished, but at last report it still contained a few 8- to 10-inch rainbow. [T6N R21W S7]

TAMARACK LAKE. This is the middle and largest (26 acres) of three glacial lakes beneath Sugarloaf Peak. It's reached by a good trail 8-plus miles west from the end of the Chaffin Creek road, west of US 93 between Darby and Conner. This lake is dammed at the outlet for irrigation, with a resultant 10 feet of water-level fluctuation. It is deep in the center, but with shallow drop-offs, and it used to be fished heavily for small and emaciated rainbows. Now it's stocked with cutts, last in 1990, but don't expect the fishing to be much more than marginal. [T2N R22W S10]

TAYLOR CREEK. A real small tributary of Hughes Creek, crossed by a gravel road at the mouth, 7 miles east of the Alta Ranger Station. There are roads and trails in the general vicinity, but none provide easy access. There is fair camp fishing here for small cutthroat and rainbow trout. [T3S R21W S3]

TENMILE LAKE. A deep, 20-acre lake at 6,700 feet in elevation, in barren muskeg-meadow country at the head of the Roaring Lion–Lost Horse divide. Reach it by foot (if you are ready, willing, and able) from the Lost Horse road, 4 miles north up Tenmile Creek. This lake is good fishing for 8- to 10-inch cutthroat—descendants of periodic plants dating from 1965. The most recent was in 1990. [T5N R22W S23]

TEPEE CREEK. A little bitty stream that flows into Howard Creek about 4 miles west of its confluence with Lolo Creek. Much of its length is accessible by logging roads, which are subject to seasonal closures. Maybe because it's so darn small, nobody seems to know much about the fishing here. Washed out in 1952, it offered up poor fishing for a while, but now you might expect to catch cutthroat—sized in proportion to the stream—in scattered pools for about 1 mile above the mouth. [T12N R23W S20]

THREEMILE CREEK. A small stream, crossed at the mouth by county roads about 4 miles north of Stevensville, then crossed often by county and rural roads along its 16-mile length. The lower 5 miles are mostly dewatered for irrigation, but still seem to produce some good catches of 6- to 14-inch brook and rainbow—the upper reaches are fair for small cutthroat and brookies. A kids' creek. [T10N R20W S25]

TIN CUP CREEK. The outlet of Tin Cup Lake, flowing north down a steep-walled glacial canyon for 16 miles to the Bitterroot River, near Darby. There's road access to the lower reaches, and 12 miles of trail that go all the way to the lake. The trail is well-suited to hikers and horses, and it sees a lot of use. The surrounding country is mostly heavily timbered, but the creek is easily fished for plentiful 6- to 12-inch cutthroat and some brook trout. [T3N R21W S21]

TIN CUP LAKE. A high-up lake at 6,296 feet, in a forested and talus-strewn cirque, reached by a good horse trail going 12 miles southwest along Tin Cup Creek from the end of the road, which is just southwest of Darby. Tin Cup is a fair-size (125-acre) lake, shallow at either end but fairly deep in the middle, with steep drop-offs along the sides. There is an irrigation dam that raises the water level as much as 15 feet. In spite of this, the lake is overpopulated with 8- to 16-inch, big-headed, snake-bodied cutthroat. [T2N R23W S1]

TOLAN CREEK. A good kids' stream for pan-size cutthroat, it's about 8 miles long and flows to the East Fork of the Bitterroot River, 3 miles east of Sula. Bull trout are abundant residents here, so make sure the kids can tell them apart from other trout. There's no trail. [T1N R19W S12]

TRAPPER CREEK. A small, steep stream that flows for 12 miles, down a rock-walled glacial canyon, to the West Fork of the Bitterroot River, about 4 miles south of Conner. It is good kids' fishing for 7- to 9-inch cutthroat, brook, and rainbow trout. There's a road following the creek west for about 3 miles, and then a trail goes another 6-plus miles upstream. [T2N R21W S27]

TRAPPER CREEK, North Fork. It flows for 7½ miles from its headwaters in the Selway-Bitterroot Wilderness to its confluence with Trapper Creek. There's no maintained trail, but if you're willing to bushwhack, you can have some fun fishing for small cutts. [T2N R21W S20]

Tin Cup Lake. —Courtesy U.S. Forest Service

TWELVEMILE LAKE. Take the Lost Horse road west from US 93 for 14 miles, then take a poor foot trail northwest for 4 miles or so to this lake. Or, you can bushwhack up from the drainage if you can't find the trail. The lake is fairly deep and about 10 acres in area, with some swampland about the margins, set in scattered-timbered, rocky country. The fishing is good for 8- to 11-inch cutthroat, but they seldom see a hook. Twelvemile was last planted in 1990. [T5N R23W S27]

TWIN LAKES. These two lakes (Lower and Upper), a few hundred yards apart, are reached by the Lost Horse Creek road, going 18 miles west from US 93. About 65 and 40 acres respectively, with a maximum depth of about 25 feet and gradual drop-offs, they're situated in a high cirque in predominantly barren, rocky country. There's a USFS campground at the lower lake, and motorboats are prohibited on both lakes. Both are slow to good fishing for small (8- to 10-inch) cutthroat and rainbow trout, and Upper Twin has some hybrids that run up to 18 inches or better. The lakes are planted annually with rainbow trout. [T5N R23W S29]

Twin Lakes. —Courtesy U.S. Forest Service

TWO BEAR CREEK. A small stream, about 6 miles long, flowing to Sleeping Child Creek near the end of the Sleeping Child road. There's road access only to the lower mile or so, which can be good early-season fishing for cutthroat up to 12 inches long. You might hook up with a small bull trout, as well. [T4N R19W S7]

UNNAMED LAKE AT THE HEAD OF HOPE CREEK. A high (elevation 7,500 feet) cirque lake just north of the Continental Divide in the Anaconda-Pintlar Wilderness Area, it sits just north and east of Hope Lake. It's only about 1½ acres in size, with some blue water and lots of lily pads around the margins. The immediate shore is mostly grassy meadow. We made these observations from a high promontory overlooking the lake in its beautiful setting—we wonder if there are any fish. [T1N R16W S4]

WARM SPRINGS CREEK. Twelve miles long and easily fished, this small tributary of the Bitterroot River is followed by gravel road, off US 93 northwest of Sula, going south to the Crazy Creek campground; from there, a USFS horse trail follows for 8 miles to headwaters. It produces good catches of 8- to 10-inch cutts and rainbows, and a few brook trout. A very few bulls live here, as well. [T1N R20W S1]

WATCHTOWER CREEK. The outlet of (barren) Watchtower Lake, this little stream flows down its deep, ice-scoured canyon for 9 miles to the Nez Perce Fork of the Bitterroot River, where it is crossed by the Nez Perce road 9 miles west of the West Fork Ranger Station. It's available pretty much to its source by a good trail, and it's excellent fishing for 7- to 9-inch cutthroat and some brookies. [T1S R23W S14]

WEST FORK BITTERROOT RESERVOIR. See Painted Rocks Lake.

WEST FORK BITTERROOT RIVER. See Bitterroot River, West Fork.

WEST FORK BUTTE CREEK. A small tributary of the South Fork of Lolo Creek that heads up near West Fork Butte. There is fair early-season fishing here for small cutthroat in the first 3 miles above its mouth, which is about 2 miles south of the mouth of the South Fork. The first 1½ miles are reached by a good gravel road; there is no trail to follow the rest. [T12N R22W S31]

WEST FORK CAMP CREEK. See Camp Creek, West Fork.

WEST FORK LOLO CREEK. See Lolo Creek, West Fork.

WILES CREEK. A small tributary of Warm Springs Creek, the lower reaches are followed somewhat by a footpath off the Warm Springs trail. There's fair fishing for small rainbow and cutthroat trout. [T1S R20W S9]

WILLOW CREEK. A fair-size, easily wadable fishing stream that used to flow from Willow Lake to the Bitterroot River near Corvallis, but it's now completely dewatered in the lower reaches. It's accessible for about 17 miles by a good gravel road that takes you east from US 93—mostly through private land—with a few "speed bumps," as one sign on the access through private land warns. The upper 3 miles are accessible by trail. This creek sees lots of fishing pressure and produces some fair-size cutthroats and small brook trout. [T7N R20W S19]

WILLOW (or FOOL HEN, or SAGE HEN) LAKE. From the end of the Willow Creek road, continue east on a good trail for a couple miles, then follow a poor, unmaintained, and in some spots nonexistent trail south for the next 2 miles to the lake, on the slopes of Skalkaho Mountain. At an elevation of 7,300 feet, in timber and parkland country, Willow is about 10 acres and 30 feet deep, with lots of aquatic vegetation around the shores. There's an old abandoned dam at the outlet. The lake was planted with rainbow many years ago, and westslope cuts in 1990. It contains a good population of 6- to 12-inchers, and old reports speak of a few lunkers. [T6N R18W S17]

WOODCHUCK RESERVOIR. Take the Eastside highway east from Florence, across the valley and over the river, to a point maybe ½ mile beyond where the main drag bends to the south. Take a little old gravel road to the north for ¾ of a mile, and then break off to the east again for 2¾ miles, and finally north once more on a farm road for 1¼ miles and you're there—at the Woodchuck Reservoir, which is no more than a couple of acres, if that, and gets pretty well drawn for irrigation in the summer. There are some trees and brush along the south side, a road across the lower end and up the north side, and a few stray trout you can pick up now and then, if you're the patient kind. Not a bad spot to while away a summer afternoon if you like a peaceful, bucolic atmosphere and don't wish to be bothered too much with fish. [T10N R19W S5]

WOODS CREEK. A small, eastward-flowing tributary of the West Fork of the Bitterroot River, crossed at the mouth by a gravel road 9 miles south of Painted Rocks Lake, then followed by a logging road west for 8 miles, almost to headwaters. It's good fishing for medium-size cutthroat and brookies. [T3S R22W S21]

WORNATH RESERVOIRS. The upper and lower reservoirs cover ⅓ and ½ acres respectively. They sit ¼ mile apart in a suburban development, 1 mile southeast across the railroad tracks from Lolo. The reservoirs have been planted with catchable (10- to 12-inch) rainbow. But they're strictly private, bordered by lawns, horse barns, etc. [T11N R20W S2]

Blackfoot River. —Courtesy Michele Archie

The Popular Blackfoot River

The Blackfoot River originates along the west slope of the Continental Divide near Rogers Pass and flows westerly 132 miles to Bonner, Montana. It varies in size from a small creek at its headwaters to places where it's over 150 feet wide with large, deep, turquoise pools in its lower reaches. The waters of the Blackfoot are turbulent, a result of the river's grade, which falls 10 to 25 feet per mile. Steep, stable, and confined channels, scoured to bedrock in many places, with a consistent presence of large boulders, provide a diversity of aquatic habitat. Bald eagles, bull trout, elk, and many other aquatic and terrestrial marvels share the Blackfoot River.

The Blackfoot is popular with floaters, bird watchers, picnickers, sunbathers, tubers, and fishers alike. Recreationists seeking solitude on the Blackfoot River will more than likely be frustrated by the high level of use this river has been getting in the last few years. Recreational access to the river improved during the 1970s, through the development of the Blackfoot River Recreational Corridor. The corridor is on mostly private lands, extending from the Missoula County line downstream to Johnsrud Park. It provides for camping, hiking, picnicking, fishing, hunting, and floater access, in specific areas only. Responsible public use of the Blackfoot River will assure continued landowner acceptance of recreational use of their land. Ongoing dialogues and planning efforts that include agencies, landowners, and recreationists are helping to address issues such as increasing use, limited resources, and conflicts among user groups.

Upstream of Lincoln, cutthroat and brook trout dominate the fish populations. Seasonal conditions in the headwaters vary greatly, with one section going underground and another heavily impacted by mine tailings and acid mine drainage. The Blackfoot River fishery downstream of Lincoln to the North Fork provides limited fishing opportunities for primarily brown trout—limited because of low densities of fish and poor access in the area. Downstream of the North Fork, rainbow trout dominate the fishery, with near equal numbers of browns in some areas. Fishery habitat restoration and restrictive angling regulations since 1990 have begun to rebuild this once-great fishery. The recovery of the native large river westslope cutthroat and bull trout populations is just beginning in the Blackfoot River. Anglers are reminded that these two native fish species must be released unharmed throughout the Blackfoot River and its tributaries.

The Blackfoot River receives an annual flush of spring snow melt, increasing significantly the volume of flow through the months of May and June. During this period, the river changes from a crystal-clear jewel to a raging torrent resembling Tom Sawyer's muddy Mississippi in clarity and the "River of No Return" (Salmon River in Idaho) in fury. The river above the North Fork weaves back and forth, frequently cutting off a meander in the process of developing a new one. This section of river is relatively slow but has abundant amounts of channel obstructions requiring portage, especially above the Helmville cut-off road, Highway 271. The section from the North Fork downstream to the mouth contains some rough whitewater with rapids, plunges, and standing waves, even in low flow. If you are experienced in whitewater, this is some fun water. If you are inexperienced, this river has real hazards that can be life threatening. Coast Guard-approved life jackets are not only required by law, but make good common sense on the Blackfoot River.

Don Peters
Fisheries Biologist
Montana Fish, Wildlife and Parks

Note: Special fishing regulations apply to the Blackfoot River and all of its tributaries (except the Clearwater River downstream from Lake Inez fish barrier). The limits are designed to increase the numbers of larger fish and to protect the native cutthroat trout. Check current regulations for details.

Meadows west of Seeley Lake. —Courtesy U.S. Forest Service

BLACKFOOT RIVER DRAINAGE

ALICE CREEK. It's crossed at the mouth by Montana 200, 12 miles east of Lincoln, and followed upstream by 11 miles of good gravel road and 2 miles of trail to the headwaters. The headwaters of Alice Creek are in elk winter and calving range, so watch for seasonal trail closures for motorized vehicles. A popular stream, in timber above and meadow below, it's good fishing for small brookies and cutts below, with the brookies thinning out above. It's catch-and-release only for the cutts. [T15N R7W S34]

ALVA LAKE. See Lake Alva.

ARCHIBALD CREEK. A real small creek, flowing to the Clearwater River at the outlet of Seeley Lake, crossed at the mouth by the West Lake road near Camp Paxson. There are only a few fingerling in this creek, but in early spring it is good largemouth bass fishing (up to 4 pounds) in the slough at its mouth. [T17N R15W S33]

ARRASTRA CREEK. It flows 11 miles south from Arrastra Mountain to the Blackfoot River, where it is crossed by Montana 200, about 2½ miles east of the Nevada Creek road. From its mouth, Arrastra is followed north for 4 miles by road across mostly posted land. From there, you might pick up an abandoned trail upstream. Or, drive to Reservoir Lake up the Beaver Creek road, and hoof it up the trail (no motorized vehicles) north to headwaters, east of Arrastra Mountain. Arrastra is a popular stream that is fair fishing for small cutthroat above, with some resident and spawning browns, an occasional brookie, and an even more occasional bull thrown in below. The lower 1½ miles sometimes go completely dry. [T14N R10W S30]

BAKING POWDER CREEK. A short, steep, inaccessible tributary of Falls Creek; the Landers Fork trail passes near the confluence as the trail enters the Scapegoat Wilderness. The lower reaches are fair to good fishing for pan-size cutthroat. It is fished only occasionally by horse packers or backpackers. [T16N R8W S26]

BEARTRAP CREEK RESERVOIR. Take Montana 200 east from Lincoln 16 miles, to the point where the main highway bears off to the left (north), up Pass Creek. Here you break off to the right and follow the Blackfoot River (secondary) road for 2 miles, right to this 10-acre private reservoir. Long and narrow, the water's followed by a service road along its west side, and, according to state records, it holds cutts to 16 inches—for the owners. [T15N R6W S27]

BEAVER CREEK. A very small tributary of Placid Creek, crossed at the mouth by the Jocko Lake-Placid Lake road, west off Montana 83 near Seeley Lake, then more or less followed by road for 3 miles to headwaters, in the Blackfoot-Clearwater Game Range. It's excellent fishing for small (6- to 8-inch) cutthroat and a few rainbow trout. [T16N R16W S14]

BEAVER CREEK. A rough, steep, narrow, and twisty stream, flowing south to the Blackfoot River, a couple of miles west of Lincoln. It is crossed at the mouth by Montana 200, and it's easily accessible by road north to the headwaters (about 10 miles in all). Beaver Creek is good early-season fishing near the mouth for cutthroat, brook trout, and a few browns—but it's mostly all posted down there. It's catch-and-release only for cutts. [T14N R9W S21]

BELMONT CREEK. Take the Blackfoot Recreational Corridor access road 7 miles west from Ninemile Prairie (12 miles east of Potomac) to the mouth of this creek, and then follow it north for 8 miles. A small creek in timbered country, it's fair fishing for small rainbow and cutthroat. [T14N R16W S24]

BERTHA CREEK. A small, swampy stream flowing from Summit Lake south for 3½ miles to Rainy Lake, paralleled by the Swan Lake-Seeley Lake highway. If you don't mind brush, it's easily accessible and good fishing (especially in the numerous beaver ponds) for 8- to 12-inch cutthroat trout. [T18N R16W S2]

BERTHA LAKE. See Colt Lake.

BIGHORN (or SHEEP) LAKE. A deep (54 feet), 14-acre cirque lake in the rough Lincoln backcountry just below the Continental Divide, it's just off the Continental Divide Scenic Trail. It's many miles back in, no matter which of the many trailheads you choose. It's a real hard-to-get-to lake that is very seldom fished, but it's reportedly excellent for large cutthroat and remnants of old plantings of rainbow trout. Surveys by fishery biologists show the lake to have an excellent self-sustaining population of Yellowstone cutthroat. [T17N R8W S34]

BIG SKY LAKE. See Fish Lake.

BLACK LAKE. See Elbow Lake.

BLACKFOOT RIVER, Dry Fork of the North Fork. You can reach the mouth by the North Fork trail just south of the guard station, then follow a good trail northwest through steep, timbered country for 15 miles to headwaters. A fair-size stream, the lower reaches (about 3 miles down) go almost dry except for a few holes. There is excellent fishing,

East Fork of the North Fork of the Blackfoot River. —Courtesy Michele Archie

especially in the upper reaches, for very nice 10- to 14-inch cutthroat trout. [T17N R10W S31]

BLACKFOOT RIVER, East Fork of the North Fork. An excellent fishing stream in mostly timbered country; good parts of this drainage burned in the 1988 Canyon Creek fire, so it's an ecologically interesting area. It is followed by a good USFS horse trail for 10 miles east from the mouth near the North Fork Guard Station, to headwaters, near Parker Lake. The East Fork flows through many open meadows and silted beaver ponds, and it supports large populations of 6- to 8-inch cutthroat trout. [T17N R10W S28]

BLACKFOOT RIVER, Landers Fork. Crossed at the mouth by Montana 200, 6 miles east of Lincoln, it's followed by road and trail for 30 miles through timbered mountains to headwaters in the Scapegoat Wilderness. The Landers Fork is tough water for fish to survive in—large floods have scoured parts of the streambed significantly in the last 20 years or so. As you move upstream, fishing improves for little cutts and brookies, and there are a few bulls hanging around. It's catch-and-release fishing for cutthroat and bull trout downstream from the wilderness boundary. [T14N R8W S13]

73

BLACKFOOT RIVER, North Fork. A beautiful clear stream that flows for 22 miles through steep, timbered mountains above, and for 14 miles through open meadowland below, to the Blackfoot River, 2 miles south of Ovando. The North Fork is crossed by Montana 200, 4 miles east of Ovando, and is followed north by road and well-maintained trail (nonmotorized vehicles only) to headwaters, deep in the Scapegoat Wilderness. After the 1988 Canyon Creek fire, the Forest Service closed a few of the trails in the area, so your trail maps may not be accurate. There's still plenty of access to this popular stream, which offers good fishing, mostly for cutthroat and a few rainbow—both residents and spawners up from the main river—along with whitefish and spawning browns and bulls. Above the falls, several miles back into the wilderness, cutthroat predominate. The North Fork is catch-and-release fishing for cutts and bull trout downstream from the wilderness boundary, and it's subject to the same limits for rainbow and brown trout as other Blackfoot tributaries. [T14N R12W S9]

North Fork Falls. —Courtesy U.S. Forest Service

BLANCHARD CREEK. A small tributary of the Clearwater River, crossed at the mouth by Montana 200, 1 mile west of the Seeley Lake turnoff, and followed by logging road, through steep, timbered mountains, west for 7 miles. After that, you're on your own. An easily fished stream with moderate brush cover, it is good for 9- to 10-inch brookies and rainbows, as well as a few cutthroat and an occasional spawning brown trout. [T14N R14W S4]

BLANCHARD CREEK, North Fork. The lower mile and a half of this small stream is followed by logging road off Montana 200, just west of Clearwater Junction. The upper reaches of this stream can be reached from nearby logging roads, if you don't mind a bit of a walk through timbered, brushy country. It's probably not worth the effort, since the lower reaches offer the best fishing, and that's only fair action for little brookies and cutts. [T15N R14W S31]

BLANCHARD LAKE. This "lake" is really a shallow, 10-acre, beaver-dammed wide spot on the Clearwater River, in logged-over land. Reach it from the Harpers Lake access road, 1 mile north of the Seeley Lake turnoff from Montana 200. It is moderately popular for an occasional large brown trout, nice yellow perch, cutthroat and rainbow to 10 inches, small brook trout, and lots of whitefish and rough fish. Fish, Wildlife and Parks says there are largemouth bass here, as well. [T15N R14W S33]

Blanchard Lake. —Courtesy Michele Archie

A Blackfoot brown. —Courtesy Tucker Lamberton

BLIND CANYON CREEK. A small stream, partly open and partly brushy, it ends up in some pretty swampy country as it approaches Trail Creek. It is available via an old logging road ½ mile north of Seeley Lake, and then 3 miles east on the Cottonwood Lake road. This road is closed sometimes, so ask at the Seeley Lake Ranger Station to check its status. The fishing here is fair for 6- to 8-inch cutthroat trout. [T17N R14W S31]

BOLES CREEK. This stream flows for 10 miles through timbered country to the west side of Placid Lake. There's logging-road access to a couple of miles of the lower reaches, and via the Finley Creek road to the upper reaches. The upper road is subject to a variety of closures, so know what you're doing before you go back there. It's pretty good fishing for 7- to 8-inch cutthroat, rainbow, and brook trout. [T16N R15W S30]

BOULDER LAKE. Don't believe anyone who tries to tell you that you have to bushwhack in to this one from the South Fork of the Jocko River! That route is off-limits to most folks, because it's in the South Fork Jocko primitive area on the Flathead Reservation—only tribal members are allowed. Anyway, it's easy enough to hike in to Boulder Lake, going west on 5 miles of good trail from the West Fork Gold Creek trailhead. Just watch for the cairns on your way through the clearcut, near the beginning of the trail. Boulder is a 20-acre lake in the Rattlesnake Wilderness, timbered on three sides but with talus on the south end; it's popular and real good fishing for good-size (10- to 13-inch) cutthroat. [T15N R18W S11]

BROWN'S LAKE. An open rangeland, 500-acre lake, with a maximum depth of about 25 feet and moderate drop-offs, mostly fished through the ice in winter. You can drive right to it on the county roads, 10 miles southwest out of Ovando. There's a public fishing access at the south end of the lake, with a boat ramp, outhouses, and places to camp. It has excellent fishing (especially through the ice) for large rainbow—it's stocked every year with Arlee and Kamloops strains. The lake receives less frequent plants of cutthroat, and you'll probably catch these in the 7- to 14-inch range. There are a few very nice brook trout and a rough-fish population that has increased in size in recent years. [T14N R11W S20]

BULL (or DEER PARK) CREEK. Bull Creek is a small stream that flows for no more than a couple of miles through Tupper Lakes to Ward Creek. Access is mostly on state land, from gravel roads. There's a minimal population of small cutts and rainbows. [T14N R11W S1]

CABIN CREEK. Take a USFS trail along the North Fork of the Blackfoot River to the mouth of this stream, near the guard station, then follow another trail north for 8 miles upstream, through timbered country, to headwaters, just below the Continental Divide. The lower reaches (about 3 miles down) are good fishing for 6- to 8-inch cutthroat trout. [T17N R11W S13]

CAMAS CREEK. A small, open meadowland stream that flows to Union Creek just west of Potomac, followed by a road southeast for 6 miles to headwaters. It's real good fishing for small to midsize brook trout. [T13N R16W S15]

CAMP CREEK. A small tributary of the East Fork of the North Fork of the Blackfoot River. It's reached by trail 1½ miles east of the confluence of the East and North Forks, 4 miles east of the North Fork Guard Station. Camp Creek flows through heavy timber with an open meadow here and there. There's no maintained trail, but it's good fishing for the first 3 miles above the mouth for 6- to 8-inch cutthroat trout. [T17N R10W S34]

CAMP LAKE. It's 15 feet deep, 19 acres, in heavily timbered country north of East Spread Mountain. Several trails provide access, and no matter which way you come at it, Camp Lake is several miles back. On

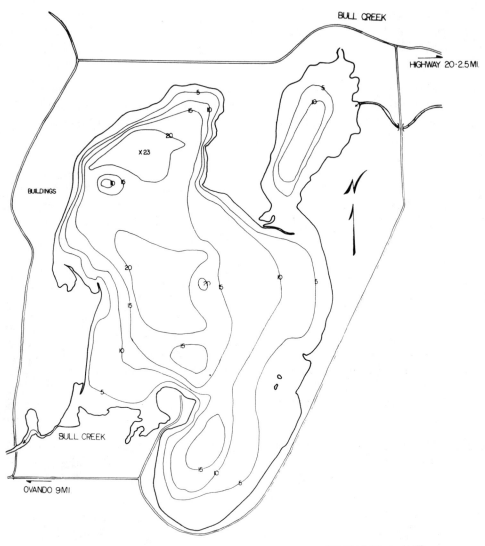

BULL CREEK

HIGHWAY 20 - 2.5 MI.

X 23

BUILDINGS

N

BULL CREEK

OVANDO 9 MI.

BROWNS LAKE

TI4N-RIIW-SI7,20,29

POWELL COUNTY

TOTAL SURFACE ACRES · 500

CONTOUR INTERVAL · 5 FT

SCALE

0   500   1000   2000

FEET

Montana Department of Fish, Wildlife and Parks

This map is not intended for navigational
purposes. Navigational hazards are not
shown. Access areas shown are public. Other
places may be open to public use through
the consent of individuals.

the Spread Creek trail, you'll reach Camp Lake about 8 miles northeast of the Monture Guard Station, or you might try the Lake Creek trail going north for about 10 miles from the North Fork of the Blackfoot trailhead. There is excellent fishing here, for nice fat rainbow up to 14 inches and long, snaky lunkers from 16 to 20 inches. [T17N R11W S32]

CANYON CREEK. A fair-size, wadable stream, mostly in the Scapegoat Wilderness. The big Canyon Creek fire of 1988, which burned about a quarter of a million acres, got its start and its name in this drainage. The country is mixed timber and burned areas—and the hike back in, northwest along the Dry Fork of the North Fork is a fascinating study in the effects of fire. Canyon Creek is followed by several miles of good trail going southwest to Canyon Lake. This one is good fishing for 8- to 10-inch cutthroat, with an occasional lunker. [T17N R11W S11]

CANYON LAKE. At the head of Canyon Creek, this lake pushes 20 acres and is 7 feet deep. It's reached by several trails, and no matter how you look at it, you're in for a hike of several miles. Reproduction is limited in Canyon Lake, and fishing is marginal for cutthroat. Some bull trout hang out here, too. [T17N R11W S28]

CHAMBERLAIN CREEK. A small stream in steep, timbered mountain country, reached near the mouth by a gravel road going south over Scotty Brown's Bridge across the Blackfoot River, 5 miles west of Ovando. There's some access from logging roads, and a trail follows the ridgeline between Chamberlain Creek and the East Fork drainages. There is fair fishing here for small cutthroats and rainbow-cutthroat hybrids. [T15N R13W S32]

CHIMNEY CREEK. A little stream flowing through steep, timbered country above and open benchland below to Douglas Creek, 5 miles west of Helmville. Chimney Creek is seldom fished but contains a few pan-size brook and cutthroat trout in the lower reaches. [T12N R12W S12]

CLEARWATER LAKE. Reach it by about ½ mile of trail from a good logging road northeast off Montana 83. The trail continues on around the lake, passing by a few good campsites along the way. This mountain lake in timbered country is about 125 acres and 40 feet deep, with steep drop-offs and a beaver dam at the outlet. Clearwater is popular with goldeneye, bufflehead, deer, and sometimes loons. The lake was poisoned in 1958 and since planted with cutthroat. The cutts can be big—up to 4 pounds—though they're predominantly in the 10- to 12-inch range. You've got to know what you're doing to catch them. [T19N R15W S19]

Clearwater Lake. —Courtesy Michele Archie

CLEARWATER RIVER. A heavily fished creek, in timber and mountain meadows, it flows for 35 miles from Clearwater Lake through Rainy, Alva, Inez, Seeley, Salmon, and Elbow lakes to the Blackfoot River. It's easily accessible where it flows through private land (make sure to get permission), and it's followed pretty closely for its entire length by Montana 83. In the upper reaches, it's a fun little creek with fair to good fishing, mostly for pan-size cutts. Down lower, there are more suckers and such, with some bull trout migrating through in season. With all the lakes along the way, you could hook into just about any kind of trout—and really, just about any kind of fish—somewhere along the length of this river. Northern pike are the latest discovery in the Clearwater system; they're likely to have significant impact on fishing, particularly for certain trout species, as they establish themselves. Look in the fishing regulations for special limits upstream from the Lake Inez fish barrier, and on all tributaries of the Clearwater. Downstream from the Lake Inez fish barrier, the Clearwater is open all year, with special salmon limits. [T14N R14W S16]

CLEARWATER RIVER, West Fork. An easily wadable stream that flows through steep timbered country north of Seeley Lake, it's followed by logging road for much of its length. There are about 10 miles of good fishing here for 7- to 8-inch cutthroat and brook trout. [T17N R15W S6]

COLT CREEK. A tiny stream, the outlet of Colt Lake, flowing 5 miles through timbered mountains to Rainy Lake. It's followed along most of its length to headwaters by a good logging road, northwest of Montana 83. There is fair fishing for pan-size cutthroat near the mouth and in the swampy middle reaches. [T18N R16W S12]

COLT CREEK RESERVOIR. This shallow reservoir is sort of a glorified swamp for most of the year, and, although it's pretty, it's not much to fish. But there are times when the water level comes up, and cutts from Colt Creek congregate here, making for some fast fishing. You can pitch off into the woods south of the Colt Creek logging road to get to this one. [T18N R16W S11]

COLT (or BERTHA) LAKE. Reach it within ½ mile by the Colt Creek logging road, 7 miles west of the Clearwater River, in logged-over country that's still being logged. It's been stocked with cutthroat. An outlet dam built by the Forest Service to create depth and spawning gravels, put in in 1977, has helped establish a spawning population here, with some success. [T19N R16W S32]

Colt Creek Reservoir. —Courtesy Michele Archie

CONGER CREEK. A real small stream flowing through steep, timbered mountains to Canyon Creek, ½ mile north of Canyon Lake, it is followed by a trail for 5 miles to headwaters. The lower 2 miles are fair to good fishing for 6- to 8-inch cutthroat trout. [T17N R11W S28]

COOPERS LAKE. A beautiful, clear mountain lake in heavily timbered country, reached by road 18 miles northeast from Ovando. Coopers is big—in the 180-acre range—and deep, with extremely steep drop-offs. Unfortunately, it's quite infertile and fished hard. That all translates into marginal fishing for the cutts that are planted there every year. They average 10 to 12 inches, but occasionally bigger ones are caught. Coopers was rehabilitated in 1967. [T15N R10W S7]

COPPER CREEK. A tributary of Landers Fork of the Blackfoot, followed by a sophisticated modern road—OK, so it's gravel—going northwest for 14 miles, through a narrow, timbered canyon below and then on up a timbered, flat-bottomed valley, to the end of the fishing water. The lower reaches (below the campground) are generally poor fishing, except for a few 3- to 4-pound bull trout that run up in the fall. The upper reaches are fair fishing in the numerous beaver dams, for 10- to 15-inch cutthroat and some resident and spawning bull trout. Copper Creek is great trout habitat, and it is catch-and-release for cutthroat and bull trout downstream from the wilderness boundary. The special limits on rainbow and brown trout that apply throughout the Blackfoot drainage also apply here. [T15N R8W S36]

COPPER (or LOWER COPPER) LAKE. A small (maybe 10 acres) but fairly deep lake, in high, timbered country, at 7,000 feet in elevation. It's reached by trail about two miles south from the end of the Copper Creek road, just west of Lincoln. Copper Lake was last stocked in 1979, and, at last report, contained lots of good-size cutthroat trout. They can be seen rising and feeding, but (reportedly) very few people can catch 'em. [T15N R9W S9]

COTTONWOOD CREEK. A small tributary of Douglas Creek that flows from timbered mountains above to meadowland below. The lower reaches are used mostly for irrigation, but they're fair fishing for 6- to 10-inch brook and brown trout; the upper reaches are decent for small cutthroat. The lower reaches are easily accessible by county roads, going south from Helmville. [T12N R11W S14]

COTTONWOOD CREEK. The outlet of Cottonwood Lake, it flows for 15 miles through hilly meadow and pothole country (ground moraine) to the Blackfoot River, about 3 miles northeast of Sperry Grade, west of Ovando. It's followed by a good gravel road for much of its length, and it's not hard to get permission to fish most of the private stretches. Cottonwood is a brushy creek that is difficult but good fishing for brown trout, and an occasional rainbow, brookie, and bull trout. Cutthroat are common in the upper reaches, but no matter where you catch them, it's catch-and-release only for cutts. [T15N R13W S29]

COTTONWOOD LAKES. These are two 15-acre lakes and one puddle, a few hundred yards apart, in steep timbered country. Reached by taking the Cottonwood Creek road 9 miles east from the Seeley Lake campground. The road is subject to variable closures, so it might be a good idea to check with the Seeley Lake Ranger Station, especially early and late in the year. Both lakes contain big cutthroat (reportedly up to 4 pounds) that are sometimes seen but seldom caught; fishing is quite difficult here. Arlee rainbows are planted here yearly, and they do well. The lower lake also has a good population of 6- to 9-inch brook trout. Both lakes are easily accessible. [T16N R14W S3]

DEADMAN LAKE. A 10-acre, shallow lake with floating logs all around, on the edge of farmland beneath heavily timbered Markham Mountain. Deadman is 10 miles east of Ovando, and it can be approached to within a few hundred yards by the Whitetail Ranch road. It was poisoned in 1957 and planted with rainbow in the late '50s and '60s. No plantings have been made since, and the status of the lake is unknown. Reports have it that the lake is seldom fished now, but it's fair for rainbow, plus a few brook and cutthroat trout from Bull Creek. It's on private land, so you'd best check with the owners before wetting a line. [T14N R11W S10]

DEER CREEK. A small stream flowing for 10 miles through steep, timbered mountains to the northwest end of Seeley Lake, it's easily accessible for most of its length by logging road. It's moderately popular, and good fishing for 6- to 8-inch cutthroat trout, along with a few brookies, browns, bulls, and whitefish. [T17N R15W S20]

DEER PARK CREEK. See Bull Creek.

DICK CREEK. A slow, meadowland stream flowing to Monture Creek, crossed at the mouth by a county road, 1¼ miles north of Ovando, easily accessible for its entire length (about 5 miles) by private road. Dick Creek is good fishing for 12- to 14-inch rainbow, quite a few 10- to 12-inch cutthroat, and an occasional large brown trout. [T15N R13W S24]

DINAH LAKE. A 34-acre lake, near timberline, at 6,700 feet in elevation, on the east side of the Mission Range. Take a 2-mile hike northwest from Elsina Lake to reach it. It can be fished either from shore or from a small island, but it's generally poor fishing (due to an overabundance of feed) for rainbow up to 5 pounds or better. In truth, it's said that most of the fish caught here are probably poached from the small inlet during spawning season—or through the ice in winter. [T17N R17W S1]

DOUGLAS CREEK. A slow, turbid stream, flowing to Nevada Creek 3 miles northwest of Helmville. It is followed along the lower reaches by the Helmville-Drummond road, then by poor (private) road to headwaters. It's possible to get permission to fish some of the lower reaches that run through private land. A marginal stream, Douglas Creek contains mostly small cutthroats with a few suckers and whitefish thrown in. [T13N R11W S8]

DRY FORK OF THE NORTH FORK OF THE BLACKFOOT RIVER. See Blackfoot River, Dry Fork of the North Fork.

DWIGHT CREEK. A small tributary of the Dry Fork of the North Fork of the Blackfoot River, crossed at the mouth by the Dry Fork trail, 8 miles northwest of the North Fork Guard Station. It's followed by a good USFS trail west for 5 miles, through steep, timbered mountains, to headwaters. The lower 3 miles are good fishing for small (6- to 8-inch) cutthroat trout. [T17N R11W S3]

Blackfoot River.
—Courtesy Michele Archie

EAST FORK OF THE NORTH FORK OF THE BLACKFOOT RIVER.
See Blackfoot River, East Fork of the North Fork.

EAST TWIN CREEK. A tiny stream in logged-off country, crossed at the mouth by Montana 200, 8 miles east of Bonner. It used to be excellent fishing for small cutthroat trout but has been ruined by logging. A 1986 sampling turned up no trout. [T13N R17W S2]

ELBOW (or BLACK) LAKE. This lake is a long, wide spot (about 40 acres) in the Clearwater River, 2½ miles north of Montana 200. You can drive close enough on a dirt road off Montana 83. It is considered to be fair fishing for largemouth bass and yellow perch, but it's poor for trout of all kinds. [T15N R14W S20]

ELK CREEK. A small, clear stream that is followed along the east side by a jeep road from its junction with the Blackfoot River, east of Ninemile Prairie, to headwaters, near "Top O' Deep." The upper reaches are in a timbered, brushy valley; the lower reaches are in open meadowland. It is mostly posted, but where you can get permission it's good fishing for 7- to 8-inch cutthroat, some brookies, a very few rainbow trout, and some rainbow-cutt hybrids. The North Fork Elk flows in about 7 miles south, and it's followed by a poor jeep road for 2 miles upstream. It is seldom fished, but it does contain a very few 6- to 8-inch cutthroat trout. [T14N R15W S26]

ELSINA LAKE. This lake is real shallow, about 15 acres, in timbered country right on top of the Clearwater-Jocko divide. It's quite popular and good fishing for 9- to 12-inch cutthroat and rainbow trout. Follow the signs west from Montana 83, near the northern end of Seeley Lake. The road is sometimes closed, so check at the Seeley Lake Ranger Station for current information. [T17N R17W S12]

FALLS CREEK. A short (6½ miles), steep stream in timbered country, it flows to Landers Fork of the Blackfoot, 4 miles east of the Indian Meadows Guard Station, north of Lincoln. It's about a 5-mile hike from the Indian Meadows trailhead to the mouth. Falls is reported to contain lots of small native cutthroat trout. [T16N R8W S35]

FALLS CREEK. It heads in Camp Pass, north of Ovando, and is followed by a good horse-and-hiker trail for 6 miles, down a narrow, heavily timbered mountain valley, to Monture Creek near the guard station. An open stream, it is fair fishing for 6- to 10-inch cutthroat and rainbow trout. [T16N R12W S17]

FAWN CREEK. A very small tributary of Deer Creek, crossed at headwaters by the Jocko road, 4 miles east of Upper Jocko Lake (in the

Flathead drainage). It's followed by road for its entire length—about 3 miles. In the past, the fishing in this small stream has been excellent for 10- to 12-inch cutthroat. [T17N R15W S24]

FINLEY CREEK. A small stream in timbered mountains above and swampy land below, it flows to Placid Creek 1½ miles west of Placid Lake, followed by logging road for much of its length. The road is open variably, so check with the ranger station for the latest. It is excellent fishing for 6- to 8-inch cutthroat, brook, and a few rainbow trout. [T16N R16W S24]

FISH CREEK. A tiny stream, about 3 miles long, flowing northwest from timbered country to the Blackfoot River, at the east side of Ninemile Prairie, north of Potomac. There's not much access, but it is very good fishing for such a small creek, with 7- to 10-inch brook, and a few rainbow and brown trout. [T14N R14W S28]

FISH CREEK. A little stream that drains Fish Lake and the old rearing ponds nearby, for 1½ miles southwest, through private timberland, to Salmon Lake, near the town of Seeley Lake. It is followed by Woodworth Road, and the lower end is fair fishing "the opening day of the season" for small brook trout. [T15N R14W S5]

FISH (or BIG SKY) LAKE. Drive 2½ miles north on Montana 83 from the south end of Salmon Lake to Woodworth Road, then head a mile or two east, then about a mile north, and you're there. The lake is 1 mile long by 1/8 mile wide, in dense timber right down to the water, good fishing for 14- to 16-inch rainbow trout—though, unfortunately, it's now privately owned and closed to the public. [T16N R14W S29]

FLESHER LAKE. This lake is about 10 miles east of Lincoln, right along Montana 200, near the mouth of Hardscrabble Creek. It was planted with rainbow in the 1960s, but since 1990 Flesher Lake has been planted with up to 4,000 small cutthroat each year. It's supposed to be pretty good fishing. [T15N R7W S33]

FRAZIER CREEK. A wee small tributary of the Blackfoot River, reached at the mouth by a poor road 8 miles south out of Ovando. A brushy stream in timbered country without a trail, it is seldom fished, but it contains quite a few small cutthroat. The lower reaches are on private land, so ask before you fish. [T14N R12W S28]

GOLD CREEK. A clear mountain stream, flowing for 17 miles through heavily timbered country to the Blackfoot River, 1 mile east of McNamara Bridge. Take Montana 200 east 10 miles from Bonner, to the Gold Creek logging road turnoff. Gold Creek is accessible along much of its length by logging road and trail. These logging roads have posed a problem for trout in this heavily logged drainage. A popular stream, Gold Creek is home to pan-size brook and cutthroat trout. Bull trout, once caught in the 15- to 21-inch range, are now rare in the drainage. [T13N R16W S6]

GREEN LAKES. See Tupper Lakes.

HARDSCRABBLE (or KROHN) CREEK. This stream drains Krohn Lake, flowing 3½ miles through mostly slough country to the Blackfoot River, where it is crossed by Montana 200, 8 miles east of Lincoln. It contains a few pan-size brook trout near the mouth. [T15N R7W S33]

HARPER'S LAKE. Take Montana 83 north for 1 mile from its junction with Montana 200. Head west on the clearly signed access road, about ¼ mile to the lake. A "landlocked" 18-acre lake surrounded by state land, about 28 feet maximum depth, with a gradual drop-off all around. There's a developed fishing access and a public campground nearby. It's stocked with rainbows every year, both young stock and "retired" brood stock from the hatchery. You're likely to catch rainbow to 13 inches, unless they're in the 6- to 10-pound category. And there are some nice cutts here, too. [T15N R14W S28]

Harper's Lake. —Courtesy Michele Archie

HEART LAKE. Take a good USFS trail from the public corrals on Copper Creek, near Indian Meadows, north 5 miles to Heart Lake. In steep, timbered mountains, Heart covers 33 acres, with a maximum depth of 50 feet in spots and steep drop-offs. It's very popular, so there are camping and stock restrictions along the lakeshore. You're likely to catch some nice grayling here, with an occasional cutthroat big enough to make it exciting. It's planted periodically. [T16N R8W S18]

HIDDEN LAKE. Covering about 20 acres, this lake sits a couple of miles west of Placid Lake. It's accessible by logging road, and is planted every year with 3- to 4-inch westslope cutts. [T16N R16W S13]

HOGUM CREEK. Take Montana 200 east 8 miles from Lincoln, to the Hogum Creek road. The creek is followed by road and trail for most of its length. There's good early season fishing for 9- to 10-inch cutthroat, and a few brook trout. [T14N R7W S8]

HORSEFLY CREEK. A real small stream in burned-over, brushy country, flowing for 3 miles to the Blackfoot River on the side opposite the highway, 9 miles east of Lincoln. It is followed by a jeep road, but it's very seldom fished. It's been rumored to produce good catches of 8- to 9-inch cutthroat, some brook, and a very few brown trout. [T14N R7W S4]

HOYT CREEK. A tiny meadowland stream that heads near Ovando and flows 3½ miles to McCabe Creek. It's crossed near the mouth, 2½ miles west of Ovando, by Montana 200, and it's fished occasionally by local residents for 8- to 9-inch brook trout. You might also hook into a few rainbow, browns, or cutts here, but don't expect monsters. [T15N R12W S18]

HUMBUG CREEK. A small meadowland stream flowing for about 6 miles to the Blackfoot River, a mile south of Lincoln. It is too small for a real fishing creek, but it does produce a few good early-season catches of 8- to 10-inch cutthroat and brook trout. Access is with permission only, as it's all on posted land. [T14N R9W S25]

INEZ LAKE. See Lake Inez.

JONES LAKE. A very shallow 40-acre lake on private sagebrush-and-meadow land, 1¼ miles northwest of Ovando. Jones Lake partly freezes out each year, fished mostly by local people for 6- to 10-inch yellow perch. [T15N R12W S20]

KEEP COOL CREEK. It drains the Keep Cool Lakes, flowing for about 8 miles to the Blackfoot River near Lincoln, accessible in a few spots by a poor road. It's an open meadowland stream that flows mostly through private land down low, and Forest Service land above. It is easily fished—and popular with local residents—for good catches of small brown trout, with some bigger ones running up from the river in the fall. There are a few cuts in this stream, too, and an occasional bull trout. Don't expect to catch anything above the lakes. The stream doesn't have enough water to support fish there. [T14N R9W S22]

KROHN CREEK. See Hardscrabble Creek.

LAKE ALVA. One mile north of Lake Inez on Montana 83, in timbered mountains, Lake Alva is about 300 acres and has a maximum depth of 90 feet, with lots of aquatic vegetation. There is a real nice public campground on the north end. This lake was rehabilitated in 1967 and has been stocked with cutthroat just about every year; it's good now for 8- to 12-inchers and lots of little yellow perch. You might also hook into a kokanee or an occasional bull trout. This is a real popular spot. There's a special limit on salmon here, ten per day and in possession. [T18N R16W S24]

LAKE CREEK. It drains Camp and Otatsy Lakes for 6½ miles through steep, timbered country, to the North Fork of the Blackfoot River, near the North Fork trailhead. It's reached near the mouth by a good USFS logging road, 11 miles north of the Whitetail Ranch turnoff (at the North Fork of the Blackfoot River road) from Montana 200. Lake Creek is followed by trail to its headwaters. The lower reaches go dry in summer, but the upper reaches are fair fishing for 6- to 8-inch cutthroat. [T16N R11W S27]

LAKE DINAH. See Dinah Lake.

LAKE INEZ. Take Montana 200 for 38 miles east from Missoula to Montana 83, and then north for 20 miles to Inez. The lake has a 4,100-foot elevation, covers 293 acres, and has a maximum depth of 70 feet. It's in timbered, mountainous country, with a good number of private cottages, and a public campground on the north end. It was rehabilitated at the same time as Lake Alva and, if anything, is a little better fishing for cutthroat, kokanee, and yellow perch, mostly, with a few bull trout. Until 1989, Inez was stocked with Yellowstone cutthroat, but now Montana Fish, Wildlife and Parks plants the lake with native westslope cutts. But illegally introduced pike are taking over, putting a dent in trout and kokanee populations. Your limit of salmon here is ten per day and in possession. [T18N R15W S31]

LANDERS FORK OF THE BLACKFOOT RIVER. See Blackfoot River, Landers Fork.

LINCOLN GULCH. A tiny stream that flows to the Blackfoot River a few miles west of Lincoln. It's fair fishing, through a couple of barnyards in the lower reaches, only for small brook trout. Incidentally, the lower reaches are further "enhanced" by dewatering for irrigation. [T14N R9W S28]

LIVERPOOL CREEK. A very small stream that almost dries up in the summertime, but it contains 8- to 10-inch brook and very few cutthroat trout in the lower reaches, for about ¼ mile between Montana 200 and Liverpool's junction with Keep Cool Creek, 2 miles west of Lincoln. This lower section is on private land, so ask permission before you get out your rod. [T14N R9W S14]

LODGEPOLE CREEK. A small tributary of Dunham Creek, reached at the mouth by a logging road going 6 miles north from the Monture campground, then it's followed by trail for 6 miles northwest, through real steep, timbered country, to headwaters at Youngs Pass. It's a good fishing stream for little (6- to 8-inch) cutthroat trout. There are also bulls in this stream, but how common they are is unknown. [T17N R13W S36]

LOWER COPPER LAKE. See Copper Lake.

MARSHALL CREEK. A small stream that flows for 4 miles, through steep, heavily timbered mountains, to Marshall Lake, then for 2½ miles to the West Fork of the Clearwater River. It is accessible at some points from the logging road that leads to Marshall Lake, going west off Montana 83. Above the lake, the road follows the creek, but the road's closed to motorized vehicles. Marshall is fair to good fishing for pan-size brookies and cutts. [T18N R16W S35]

MARSHALL LAKE. It's 150 acres, maximum depth 55 feet, with much aquatic vegetation around the margins, in what was once heavily timbered—but is now heavily logged—country. Marshall is 6 miles west of Montana 83; follow the signs off the West Fork Clearwater road. There are some informal campsites on the east end of the lake, and it's easy enough to walk down to the lake with a canoe or float tube. Cutts and brookies are common here and, depending on your luck, a bull trout or longnose sucker might spice up the action. Rumor has it that Marshall is full of little fish. [T18N R16W S28]

MCCABE CREEK. This stream flows southward for 7 miles from Spread Mountain, through a narrow, heavily timbered alley, past the Little Red Hills, to open meadow and pothole country, and then for a couple of miles into a boggy area, where it's anybody's guess where McCabe actually flows into Dick Creek, just northwest of Ovando. The lower reaches

Marshall Lake. —Courtesy U.S. Forest Service

are occasionally accessible by county road, the upper reaches by USFS trail. Especially in the upper reaches, it's excellent fishing for 9- to 10-inch cutthroat, rainbow-cutt hybrids, and brook trout, with a scattering of brown trout and an occasional rainbow. [T15N R13W S7]

MCDERMOTT CREEK. A very small stream, flowing for 3½ miles, through timbered country, to the north end of Coopers Lake. The upper reaches go dry, but the lower reaches, which are really a slough, contain some 10- to 12-inch cutthroat from the lake. There's a trail from Coopers Lake, or you can drop over, going southeast, from the North Fork of the Blackfoot trailhead. [T15N R11W S1]

MEADOW CREEK. A clear mountain stream flowing north, from timberland above and through meadowland below, to the East Fork of the North Fork of the Blackfoot River, 5½ miles southeast along the East Fork trail. It's followed by a good trail south for 8 miles to headwaters, and beyond to the Dry Creek trailhead. This is popular country with horse packers, and the stream's lower reaches receive lots of pressure. Fishing is excellent for 8- to 10-inch (and some bigger) rainbows, cutts, and hybrids. [T16N R10W S12]

MEADOW CREEK LAKE. It's really an oversize (17-acre) shallow beaver pond, with a boggy west shore, in timbered "way back" country. Take a good horse trail about 15 miles north from the end of the Beaver Creek road, where it crosses Arrastra Creek. The lake is lightly fished, but it has been good indeed for 12- to 13-inch cutthroat and a few lunkers that will go 3 to 4 pounds. The beaver dam, maintained in the past with help from an outfitter who fishes the lake, also boasts Yellowstone cutthroat-rainbow hybrids. [T16N R9W S18]

MIDDLE FORK CREEK. This little stream flows southwest through high, open park country to the Landers Fork of the Blackfoot. It's crossed at the mouth by the Landers Fork trail, then followed north and west to headwaters by a trail along its east bank. It contains small cutthroat. [T17N R9W S26]

MONTURE CREEK. A good fishing tributary of the Blackfoot River, crossed near the mouth by Montana 200, about 3 miles west of Ovando. It's accessible by gravel roads to 12 miles north of the mouth, through potholed and swampy meadowlands, to the Monture campground. From there, there's a good USFS horse trail following the stream north for another 18 miles, through steep, timbered mountains, to the headwaters. This is a popular stream in good hunting country, heavily fished for 8- to 10-inch cutthroat, along with some small brookies and rainbows (depending on where you fish), whitefish, and bull trout in the 10-inch range. It's catch-and-release only for cutthroat and bull trout downstream from the wilderness boundary. The special Blackfoot regulations on rainbow and brown trout also apply. [T15N R13W S27]

MOOSE CREEK. This small stream flows north, through timbered country, to the Blackfoot River, opposite the highway, about 8 miles west of Lincoln. It contains a few small brook, brown, and cutthroat trout. [T14N R10W S33]

MORRELL CREEK. Tributary to the Clearwater River, crossed near its mouth by Montana 83, about 2 miles south of Seeley Lake. There's logging-road access along the middle section to the Morrell Falls trailhead (check with the Seeley Lake Ranger Station to see whether the road is open, early and late in the season). The trail roughly follows the creek north to Morrell Lake, then to the falls, and beyond to headwaters, in the aptly named Grizzly Basin. Morrell is a popular stream that is fair fishing below the falls (10 miles upstream) for pan-size cutthroat and rainbow-cutthroat hybrids. Brookies and browns are common in the lower reaches, with a few brown trout spawners and some kokanee spawners in the fall. It's barren above the falls, which is just as well, because this is excellent grizzly country; so good, in fact, that lots of sportsmen do their hunting elsewhere! [T16N R15W S14]

MORRELL LAKE. This lake is reached by a good horse trail, going 3 miles north from the end of the Morrell Creek road. It's about 25 acres, fairly shallow, with lots of aquatic vegetation and a mud-and-gravel bottom. The fishing is poor to fair for cutthroat and rainbow-cutt hybrids— nothing here but 8- or 9-inchers, and it's a place that can't stand too much pressure. [T18N R15W S24]

MOUNTAIN CREEK. A very small stream, about 5 miles long, flowing southwest from Morrell Mountain to Trail Creek, just south of Seeley Lake. There's occasional access by logging road, and it's fair fishing for small cutthroat and brook trout. [T16N R15W S12]

MUD (or PENNY) LAKE. Mud Lake is about 5 acres, 20- to 25-feet deep, in heavy timber. It is hard to find, but it's reachable by a USFS trail ¼ mile north from Coopers Lake. It's not named on the map, and fishing reports are few and far between. Mud Lake was rehabilitated in 1967 and replanted with cutthroat. It was last stocked in 1984. A rubber boat or a float tube will come in handy here. [T16N R11W S36]

NEVADA CREEK. This 45-mile-long stream flows to the Blackfoot River, 4½ miles northwest of Helmville. In the lower reaches, it is mostly a slow, meandering stream in brushy swamp and meadowland, reached here and there by the Helmville-Avon road and county roads. The upper reaches are followed by logging road and trail for 15 miles, through timbered mountains, to headwaters, below Granite Butte on the Continental Divide. There aren't a lot of fish here, but down low you might hook into a nice brown or bull trout, and if you're lucky you'll avoid the squawfish and suckers. Above, there are small cutthroat and an occasional rainbow trout. Nevada Creek is catch-and-release only for cutthroat. [T13N R11W S7]

NEVADA (or NEVADA CREEK) LAKE. This is a narrow reservoir of a few hundred acres, right next to Montana 141 about 10 miles south out of Helmville. It's fairly popular, but it's almost completely dewatered in late summer, and it's only spotty fishing for 8- to 12-inch rainbow (which are planted yearly) and a very few whitefish, cutthroat, brook, and brown trout. The lake goes mostly dry occasionally, but a population of good fish still survives; the water in this lake is normally slightly turbid. [T12N R10W S13]

NORTH FORK OF THE BLACKFOOT RIVER. See Blackfoot River, North Fork.

NORTH FORK BLANCHARD CREEK. See Blanchard Creek, North Fork.

NORTH FORK ELK CREEK. See under Elk Creek.

NORTH FORK PLACID CREEK. See Placid Creek, North Fork.

OTATSY LAKE. You'll find this lake ¼ mile east, by a USFS trail, from Camp Lake, or 1½ miles south and west from Canyon Lake. You can come up the Lake Creek trail or up Spread Creek from the Monture Creek campground, but either way, it's several miles back. There is timber all around it (right down to the water's edge on the south and west sides), but it's swampy to the north and northeast. This is a very pretty 24-acre lake, 30 feet deep. It's full of 8- to 10-inch rainbow and it's fairly popular because of it. The Department of Fish, Wildlife and Parks reports that the lake's rainbow population is "overabundant," and they suggest that an increase in fisher harvest would be helpful in increasing the size of these fish. [T16N R11W S6]

OWL CREEK. This stream drains Placid Lake for 3 miles to the Clearwater River, ½ mile north of Salmon Lake. It's followed along the north side by the Placid Lake road, west off Montana 83. It's an easily fished stream that's pretty good for cutthroat and brookies, and some resident and spawning brown trout. [T16N R15W S25]

PARKER LAKE. On the East Fork of the North Fork of the Blackfoot River, in heavily timbered mountains, at about 6,000 feet in elevation, Parker Lake has an area of 22 acres and a maximum depth of 4 feet. A lot of the surrounding area was burned in the 1988 Canyon Creek fire, so watch and listen for woodpeckers on your way in. A mostly mud-bottomed lake, it has a few rocky bars, gravel beds, and some nice springs near the inlet. It can be good fishing for 8- to 16-inch cutthroat, plus a very few that run larger. They're hard to catch and so lightly colored they are often mistaken for goldens. If you strike out at Parker, you might try your luck behind the nearby beaver dams. Reach it by trail a few miles east of the Webb Lake Guard Station, in the Scapegoat Wilderness, Parker Lake is moderately popular with horse packers and hikers, and biologists fear that any increase in fishing pressure would be detrimental to the lake's self-sustaining cutthroat population. [T16N R9W S9]

PENNY LAKE. See Mud Lake.

PLACID CREEK. About 11 miles long, flowing from steep, timbered mountains above, through swampy flatland below, to Placid Lake. The middle and upper reaches are followed by logging road—check with the Seeley Lake Ranger Station to make sure it's open in early and late seasons. It was once a pretty good cutthroat creek, but now cutts are rare along the length of the stream. You're likely to catch brook trout in the middle reaches, and the lower 200 to 300 yards are good kokanee snagging in season (with permission only). The limit on kokanee is ten daily and in possession. It's open for salmon snagging from September 15 through December 31, and then the limit is thirty-five daily and seventy in possession. [T16N R15W S30]

PLACID CREEK, North Fork. The outlet of Elsina Lake, it flows for 3 miles, through timbered mountains, to Placid Creek, and it's accessible all along by road. There is some fair fishing here for 6- to 8-inch cutthroat. [T16N R16W S5]

PLACID LAKE. Take Montana 83 to ½ mile north of Salmon Lake, and then a good gravel road 3 miles west takes you to Placid Lake. This lake sits in timbered, mountainous country, with swampland to the west. Placid is a 1,143-acre lake, with a maximum depth of about 85 feet, marshy shores, dozens of cottages, and two public campgrounds. A good place to get run over by water-skiers. It's fair fishing for about anything you might want: 10- to 12-inch kokanee (a self-sustaining population), trout of all varieties (but not in great numbers), whitefish, perch, an occasional largemouth bass, and lots and lots of suckers. Fish, Wildlife and Parks is trying to up the trout populations with frequent plantings of cutthroat and rainbows. The limit on kokanee is ten daily and in possession. The salmon-snagging season runs from September 15 through December 31, and then the limit is thirty-five daily and seventy in possession. [T16N R15W S28]

POORMAN CREEK. A brushy, beaver-dammed stream, in timbered mountains above and brushy meadows below. It's followed by a gravel road for most of its 14-mile length, from headwaters below Stemple Pass to its junction with the Blackfoot River, 2 miles west of Lincoln. It's good fishing for 8- to 10-inch cutthroats and a few brook trout. The bull trout population is small and declining—there's been some hybridization with brook trout already. [T14N R9W S25]

RAINY LAKE. It's 70 acres, with a 30-foot maximum depth and steep drop-offs, and it's dammed. In steep, timbered country, it's reached by a dirt road ½ mile off Montana 83, just north of Lake Alva. Rainy Lake was poisoned in 1958 and planted with cutthroat, which now average between 10 and 11 inches and run up to 14 inches—good fishing! Grayling were planted here in 1970, but they didn't make it. There are also some good-size bull trout and lots of suckers. [T18N R16W S11]

RINGEYE CREEK. This is a small, steep, hard-to-fish stream in lodgepole and spruce country. It drains Webb Lake for 1½ miles to Landers

Fork of the Blackfoot, 6 miles north of the end of the Landers Fork road, at Indian Meadows. No one fishes above the lake, but it's fair fishing below for 8- to 10-inch cutthroat trout. [T16N R8W S18]

ROCK (or SALMON) CREEK. A meadowland stream that flows to the North Fork of the Blackfoot River, about 5 miles east of Ovando, crossed many times by various county roads. Ask permission to fish on private land, which is nearly the whole stream. There are resident rainbow and brown trout, along with a few brookies, and it's good early-season fishing for bigger cutthroat and rainbows up from the main river. [T14N R11W S6]

SALMON CREEK. See Rock Creek.

SALMON LAKE. About 45 miles east of Missoula, right along Montana 83, in heavily timbered mountains, at an elevation of 3,850 feet, Salmon Lake is a popular summer-home area, with a public campground on the east side. This 600-plus-acre lake has a maximum depth of 70 feet and contains fair numbers of 10- to 11-inch cutthroat, rainbow, and kokanee salmon; large populations of small yellow perch and sunfish; largemouth bass; and a few bull and brown trout. The bull trout are getting fewer— as are other trout species and kokanee—in part because of illegally planted northern pike that are taking over the lake. A fisheries biologist from the Department of Fish, Wildlife and Parks said that the only bull trout their 1995 gill-net surveys turned up were juveniles in the bellies of northern pike. Salmon Lake is at least as popular with picnickers, water-skiers, and swimmers as it is with anglers. In Salmon Lake and its tributaries, the limit for salmon is ten daily and in possession, except from September 15 through December 31, when snagging is allowed and the limits increase to thirty-five daily and seventy in possession. [T15N R14W S8]

SAUERKRAUT CREEK. A small, northward-flowing stream in timbered country, Sauerkraut joins the Blackfoot River about 4 miles west of Lincoln. It's accessible by gravel road and trail. The lower reaches contain cutthroat and a few small brook trout. [T14N R9W S29]

SEELEY LAKE. At a 4,000-foot elevation in heavily timbered mountains, Seeley Lake covers 1,025 acres and has a maximum depth of 125 feet. Drop-offs are mostly moderate, and there is much vegetation around the margins. It's about 55 miles northeast of Missoula on Montana 83. Seeley is a popular lake, with many cottages, resorts, public beaches, three public campgrounds, a great deal of waterskiing, swimming, picnicking, etc., and fair fishing in spite of it all. If you know where to go, you'll find some fun fishing for cutts, rainbows that can have some size to them, and kokanee salmon. Throw in some largemouth bass, yellow

SEELEY LAKE

Montana Department of Fish, Wildlife and Parks

perch, and a few bull trout, and it's hard to imagine getting bored at this lake. Seeley sees plantings of everything from rainbows and cutthroat to kokanee and bass. It has the standard Clearwater drainage limits on salmon—ten daily and in possession, except during snagging season, from September 15 through December 31, when the limits are thirty-five daily and seventy in possession. [T16N R15W S3]

SEVEN-UP PETE CREEK. A partly inaccessible "private" land creek that flows to the Blackfoot River about 5 miles east of Lincoln, it's followed by a logging road for 4 miles to headwaters. It's mostly reached from the 7-Up Dude Ranch, 5 miles east of Lincoln. The lower reaches sink, but it's good fishing for pan-size cutthroat and a few brook trout, in beaver ponds above and along the middle reaches. [T14N R8W S14]

SHEEP LAKE. See Bighorn Lake.

SHOUP CREEK. A small, short stream that drains Shoup Lake to Monture Creek across private timberland, crossed at the mouth by a logging road. It contains cutthroat, rainbow, and bull trout, but is seldom fished. It just ain't worth it. [T15N R12W S6]

SHOUP LAKE. In private, timbered country, Shoup is reached by gravel roads, going about 5 miles north from Ovando, then northwest another few miles to the lake. Shoup is about 15 acres and fairly shallow, with lots of grass and cattails around its margins and a tremendous population of freshwater shrimp. It contains good-size (14- to 16-inch) cutthroat and rainbow, plus a few 10- to 12-inch bull trout that are so well fed they're wonderfully hard to catch. Shoup Lake was last stocked in 1986, with rainbow trout. [T16N R13W S36]

SILVER KING LAKE. A private 16-acre lake, real deep (75 feet), with steep drop-offs all around, in heavily timbered mountains. It drains to the Landers Fork of the Blackfoot, and it's nearly reached by road, through the Silver King Ranch, north from Montana 200 up that drainage. It has some really nice (18- to 26-inch) rainbow trout from long- ago plantings. They are difficult to catch. [T15N R8W S1]

SNOWBANK LAKE. A 6½-acre, 35-foot maximum depth, glacial "kettle" lake in timbered country right at the junction of Snowbank Creek and Copper Creek. Reach it going north from Montana 200 on the Landers Fork road a couple of miles, then northwest on the Copper Creek road almost to the Copper Creek campground; from there, a good gravel road will take you to the lake. Snowbank has drop-offs steep enough to fish successfully from shore. Originally barren, it was stocked with rainbow until 1990, when fisheries managers began yearly plants of cutthroat. It's too cold here for swimming, and too cold for the trout to grow very fast. [T15N R8W S9]

SPOOK LAKE. About 3 miles southwest of Placid Lake as the crow flies, subcircular Spook Lake is at the head of Boles Creek, accessible by logging roads from a couple different directions. It's about 30 acres, timbered all around, with relatively shallow drop-offs, so it's best fished from a boat—which is OK, because you can make it in easily with a pickup. The fishing has been good, too, for cutthroat ranging from a few inches up to 6 pounds or better. The lake was last planted with cutthroat in 1993. You'll have company at this one, which hasn't been the best thing for the fishing. [T15N R16W S12]

SPRING CREEK. A small, spring-fed stream, flowing through open meadows for 3 miles to Nevada Creek, 1½ miles north of Helmville. It's on private land, easily accessible by county roads—fair fishing with permission for brown trout, plus a few cutts and brookies. [T13N R11W S11]

STONEWALL CREEK. A small tributary of Keep Cool Creek, crossed at the mouth by a county road, 1 mile west of Lincoln, and followed by road and trail to headwaters, near Stonewall Mountain. The upper reaches are mostly in timber; the lower reaches flow through numerous beaver dams in brushy meadows. It's good fishing for pan-size cutthroat. [T14N R9W S14]

SUMMIT LAKE. You'll find this lake 300 yards west of Montana 83, on the very top of the Clearwater-Swan divide, in steep, timbered country. Summit is a 25-acre lake, only about 10 feet deep, with overhanging bog all around the margins, and it's brushy as all get out. It's accessed by short trails from a couple of pullouts along the highway. It's been stocked and is fun fishing for midsize cutts, but you'll need a boat or a float tube if you want to catch more fish than brush. [T19N R16W S27]

SWAMP CREEK. Technically a tributary of Mountain Creek, this very small mountain stream basically ends in swampland, ½ mile east of Trail Creek. It's crossed by the Cottonwood Lake road, going east from Seeley Lake. It's fair fishing for pan-size cutthroat trout. [T16N R15W S1]

TOBACCO VALLEY CREEK. It's really the headwaters of the North Fork of the Blackfoot River, reached by the North Fork trail, ½ mile northeast of the guard station, and it's followed by trail for 4 miles to headwaters, on the Continental Divide. Almost an alpine stream, and it's reportedly fair to good fishing near the mouth for 8- to 10-inch cutthroat trout. [T18N R9W S31]

TUPPER (or GREEN) LAKES. One of two lakes, Big Tupper is about 14 acres and 20 feet deep, with a shallow drop-off all around. It's in the Marcum Mountain walk-in area, which is closed to motorized-vehicle travel from September 1 to April 30. Reach it from the Kleinschmidt Flat road, going 13 miles east from Ovando, off Montana 200. The lake was planted with rainbow in the late 1950s and through to 1966; however, there was no reproduction, and few if any are left. It is fair to good fishing, though, for some 10- to 14-inch brook trout that moved up from Bull Creek. The second lake, Little Tupper, is just a barren pothole. [T15N R10W S31]

TWIN CREEKS. See East and West Twin Creeks.

TWIN LAKES. Upper and Lower Twin Lakes are 1 mile apart, in timbered country, on the East Fork drainage (of the North Fork of the Blackfoot River, in the Scapegoat Wilderness). You can take a good USFS horse trail going several miles back from any of a number of trailheads, including the North Fork, Dry Creek, Reservoir Lake, and Indian Meadows. Upper Twin, 6 acres and 10 feet deep, is open around the east side, and it's slow fishing for 12- to 16-inch cutthroat (plus an occasional lunker to 5 or 6 pounds). It was last stocked in 1989. Lower Twin, at 16 acres, is 10 feet deep in the middle but has shallow drop-offs all around. It hasn't been stocked since the 1950s, but there's still fair action for smaller fish. [T16N R9W S6]

UHLER CREEK. A small stream in timbered country, Uhler flows southeastward to the Clearwater River, midway between Alva and Inez Lakes. It's reached for most of its length (7 miles) by logging road, off the West Fork Clearwater River road. It is good fishing for 8- to 10-inch cutthroat. [T18N R16W S24]

UNION CREEK. A small (jumpable) pastureland stream flowing westward for about 19 miles, down the Potomac Valley to the Blackfoot River, just above McNamara Bridge. It's fished some (by kids mostly) for lots of 6- to 7-inch fingerlings. [T13N R16W S6]

UNNAMED LAKES EAST OF HEART LAKE. Adjacent lakes, both small, just east of Heart Lake, in the Scapegoat Wilderness. The northern lake once contained a small population of large (13- to 15-inch) rainbow trout. The southern lake is suitable for fish, though none are in it, and it has no noticeable spawning facilities. Maybe you should hike on back there and see what's what. [T16N R8W S17]

UPSATA LAKE. Take Montana 200 west from Ovando for 2 miles, then follow the fishing-access signs north to the south end of this lake, in pothole, grass, and timber country. Upsata is about 85 acres, with shallow drop-offs and a maximum depth of 40 feet. The lake is surrounded by private land, but there's a public fishing access. Upsata is very popular, good ice fishing, and good fishing (especially near the center and deeper parts) for 5- to 17-inch rainbow trout. Hit the edges and weed beds for largemouth bass—but don't keep any, since Upsata is catch-and-release fishing only for bass. It's been stocked regularly with both species. This is a great spot for waterfowl watching if the fishing is slow. [T15N R13W S10]

WALES CREEK. A small stream flowing northeastward to the Blackfoot River, reached by a county road you can pick up near Ovando, following it south for 10 miles. From there, roads follow the stream for a few miles west, through open meadows. Wales contains lots of 4- to 6-inch cutthroat. [T13N R12W S34]

WARREN CREEK. A slow meadowland stream flowing southwestward for 13½ miles to the Blackfoot River, 3 miles southwest of Ovando. It's easily accessible all along by county roads. This stream flows mostly through private land, so get permission before you fish. It can be good fishing for small brookies and brown trout, with a few rainbows thrown in. [T14N R12W S6]

WASHINGTON CREEK. A little tributary of Nevada Creek, about 12 miles south of Lincoln, followed by road and trail to headwaters. Washington goes dry in the summer, but there is poor to fair fishing for 8- to 10-inch cutthroat in some dredge ponds, about a mile north of the Keily ranch. All in all, it's probably not worth bothering with. [T12N R9W S26]

WEBB LAKE. This is a shallow, 17-acre beaver pond (the site of the Webb Lake Guard Station) on the Ringeye Creek drainage, in steep, timbered mountains. Take a good trail 7 miles north of Indian Meadows on the Copper Creek road, or go 9 miles east along the East Fork (of the North Fork of the Blackfoot River) trail from the North Fork Guard Station. It is good early-season fishing for 10- to 11-inch cutthroat. Numerous spring areas in the lake bottom supply fresh water and keep the water temperatures low. However, biologists report that any substantial increase in the use of this lake could be detrimental to the existing fish population. [T16N R9W S14]

WEST FORK CLEARWATER RIVER. See Clearwater River, West Fork.

WEST TWIN CREEK. A very small stream crossed at the mouth by Montana 200, 8 miles east of Bonner, followed upstream to its headwaters

Webb Lake. —Courtesy Michele Archie

by logging roads. The roads are humped to discourage vehicle use, but some ORVs still go up during hunting season. It used to be good fishing for small cutthroat, but few are left now. [T13N R17W S2]

WILLOW CREEK. A brushy stream that heads below Dalton Lookout, flowing for 8 miles to the Blackfoot River, about 3 miles west of Lincoln. It is followed most of the way by a county road. Willow supports some small cutthroat and brook trout, but isn't much of a fishing stream. [T14N R9W S29]

The Clark Fork of the Columbia

To the anglers who know it best, the Clark Fork of the Columbia is a river with some pretty good fishing but unfulfilled potential. In spots, the river's fishing is as fine as can be found in western Montana. Its potential, however, is found in those stretches where trout are not plentiful, but where angling could rival that of the state's better-known blue-ribbon gems if only the river were allowed to heal from 125 years of heavy human impact.

With an annual discharge nearly twice what its more famous cousins, the Missouri and the Yellowstone, wring from the state, the Clark Fork travels some 300 miles, gathering water from fabled tributaries such as Rock Creek and the Bitterroot, Big Blackfoot, and Flathead rivers. The Clark Fork's northwest migration begins near Butte, where the mining-ravaged waters of Silver Bow Creek mix with Warm Springs, Mill, and Willow creeks in the upper Deer Lodge Valley, under the shadow of the 10,000-foot Flint Creek and Anaconda mountain ranges. There fishing begins almost immediately.

Anglers can track wily brown trout in the river just below the Warm Springs settling ponds that lie east of Anaconda. The Anaconda Copper Company constructed the ponds to settle out toxic metals that wash down from Butte and the contaminated floodplain of Silver Bow Creek. Steady summer flows from the ponds, robust streamside willow thickets, and stable stream banks combine to help maintain a nice brown trout fishery in the river for several miles below the ponds. This is one of the windows into what the whole river could be. The fish are tough to catch here, but fly anglers can coax them in with streamers such as wooly buggers or, in early to midsummer, on pale morning duns, blue-wing olives, and caddises.

Below this stretch, the angling gets substantially tougher. Metals pollution from streamside mine tailings, dewatering for irrigation, and riparian degradation combine to make living tough for trout above and well below Deer Lodge. Nonetheless, the resourceful angler can find the occasional large brown trout, a few rainbows, and more than a few mountain whitefish. Much of the better angling is downstream from major tributaries. Public access can be found at a number of bridges.

Bad Rock Canyon, where the Clark Fork River breaks through the mountain wall near Thompson Falls. —Courtesy U.S. Forest Service

After winding lazily through the wide, agricultural Deer Lodge and Flint Creek valleys, the river cuts through forested canyons, and by the time it gathers the clean waters of Rock Creek, 25 miles upstream of Missoula, fishing picks up again. Here, lucky anglers can fool browns and rainbows with well-placed streamers, beadhead nymphs, attractors, and spinners.

After the Big Blackfoot enters, above Missoula, the Clark Fork becomes a large river. And the sport fishery, still well under what it should be because of pollution, degraded habitat, and limited spawning tributaries, becomes dominated by rainbows and the occasional cutthroat. Whitefish and native rough fish, such as the northern squawfish and largescale sucker, also become abundant. From Missoula, through the whitewater of the Alberton Gorge and into the scenic canyon stretch between St. Regis and Paradise—nearly 200 miles from Butte—angling can be either terrific or spotty. River flows, temperature, and wind (or lack of it) can conspire to make angling either miserable or something to return for. When fishing is on, the angler gets a taste of what the river could regularly be, if nutrient pollution from municipal and rural sources, as well as chronic metals discharges from the Milltown reservoir above Missoula—a federal Superfund site—were controlled.

The best access between Missoula and Paradise is from state fishing-access sites, which are spaced at regular intervals, providing many float-trip options as well as ample elbow room for the wader or shoreline worm-dunker. Fly fishers usually fish streamers or nymphs in the spring or when the river is high. They switch to small mayfly patterns, attractors, and grasshopper imitations as summer arrives. Mepps and Cyclone lures are popular with spin fishers, and bait casters plunk that old standby, the night crawler, or the newer power baits. Bait anglers should note that, beginning in 1996, sculpins (or "bullhead") are no longer legal bait, because it's possible they carry whirling disease spores. In addition, if you happen to hook a bull trout, carefully release it. It is illegal to keep or even intentionally fish for these rare natives. The loss of even one spawning-age bull trout in the Clark Fork or one of its tributaries can be very harmful to the recovery chances of this fish.

Just above Paradise, the Flathead dumps into the Clark Fork. From here down to Thompson Falls, the river is big and slow, and angling slows down. Rainbows, a few brown trout, and slough-dwelling pike are occasionally caught on bait, lures, and flies. From Thompson Falls to the Idaho line, just a few miles upstream of where the river empties into Lake Pend Oreille, the Clark Fork is primarily a reservoir. Noxon Rapids and Cabinet Gorge dams tame a river that once featured mighty rapids and large runs of migratory bull trout. Today, Noxon Reservoir is gaining regional notoriety for its smallmouth and largemouth bass fishing, while Cabinet Gorge has a few brown trout and bass.

For 150 years, Montanans have asked much of the Clark Fork, using it as a repository for industrial and municipal wastes, and diverting its water to grow hay and to produce electricity. Now, after 20 years of improved pollution control and better land-use practices, the river is producing some pretty good fishing in certain reaches. With enough public concern, nurturing, and restoration, there's no reason the future of the whole river and its fishery—from top to bottom—shouldn't get a lot brighter.

Bruce Farling
Executive Director
Montana Council, Trout Unlimited

Clark Fork River near Plains. —Courtesy Ravalli County Museum, Ernst Peterson Collection

ACORN LAKE. This one covers only a couple of acres, but it's deep enough to keep from freezing out, maybe 15 feet deep in spots. Acorn Lake is a short 1-mile hike west from the Eddy Creek road, 5 miles south of the Clark Fork road west of Plains. Acorn is real good fishing for 9- to 12-inch cutthroat trout and not fished a heck of a lot, either. It's planted every few years or so. [T20N R28W S22]

ALBERT CREEK. A small stream, flowing for 12 miles through logged-off country from its headwaters, on the northern slopes of Petty Mountain, to the Clark Fork, 3 miles south of Frenchtown. Albert Creek is crossed at the mouth by the "Old River Road," about 18 miles west of Missoula, and it's followed for about 5 miles upstream by logging roads. A trail takes you from the end of the road to headwaters. It is decent fishing for 6- to 9-inch native cutthroat and imported brook trout, but it's been heavily impacted by logging. [T14N R21W S14]

ARROWHEAD LAKE. This 12-acre lake, in heavily timbered country at the head of Big Spruce Creek, has a maximum depth of about 40 feet. It's reached by a USFS trail 3 miles west of the West Fork Thompson River road. It's not fished a whole lot but does support a good population of 8- to 14-inch stocked cutthroat trout. You can watch 'em while you catch 'em in the gin-clear water. [T22N R29W S12]

ASHLEY CREEK. A tiny stream flowing for about 3 miles through a steep, timbered canyon above to flat ranchland below, where the lower reaches are entirely diverted for irrigation. Ashley is part of the Thompson Falls municipal water supply, and it's closed to fishing from the water supply intake to its source. It was seldom fished anyway, because all it contains are some small (6- to 7-inch) cutthroat trout. It's reached by road 3 miles northwest from town, then followed up from the reservoir by a hiking trail. [T49N R29W S3]

BALDY LAKE. In subalpine country, ½ mile southwest of Mount Baldy, 7 miles west as the eagle flies from Hot Springs. It is reached by a USFS trail going west 2 miles from the McGinnis Creek road, or east from USFS road 1025. Baldy is about 15 acres, deep in the upper end and shallow near the outlet, with steep cliffs along the southwest side. A lightly fished, spotty lake, it is only poor to fair fishing at best for 8- to 12-inch cutthroat trout, which are stocked every 4 years or so. [T22N R25W S32]

BEATRICE CREEK. A very brushy little stream that is paralleled by a logging road for 3 miles, through logged country, to its mouth on Fishtrap Creek. It is lightly fished and only poor to fair for 6- to 8-inch cutthroat. [T24N R27W S31]

BEAVER CREEK. A fair-size, easily fished stream, formed by the confluence of Big and Little Beaver creeks, it flows for 8 miles, across private ranchland on the Clark Fork floodplain, to empty into the Noxon Reservoir, a few miles southeast of Trout Creek. It is fairly popular and good fishing for mostly 8- to 12-inch rainbow, plus an occasional cutthroat, brook trout, or whitefish, and loads of trash fish. You might find a big brown trout or two here in the autumn. [T24N R31W S35]

BIG BEAVER CREEK. It flows eastward through a timbered, flat-bottomed canyon for about 11 miles, and then onto the Clark Fork floodplain for another 4 miles, to its junction with Little Beaver Creek. It is paralleled by a good gravel road from mouth to headwaters. An easily and heavily fished stream for mostly 8- to 10-inch cutthroat in the upper reaches, 6- to 14-inch brookies in beaver ponds along the middle reaches, and 10- to 12-inch rainbow below. [T23N R30W S30]

BIG BEAVER CREEK, South Branch. Four miles long in a steep canyon, this small stream is reached at the mouth by the Big Beaver road, then followed upstream by a good logging road. There is fair early-season fishing here for small cutthroat trout. [T22N R32W S11]

BIG CREEK. There are about 3 miles of fishing water here, from the junction of the East, West, and Middle forks to its mouth on the St. Regis River, a couple of miles west of DeBorgia, all accessible from the Big Creek road. Big Creek is very popular locally, and fair fishing for mostly 6- to 9-inch cutthroat, plus an occasional brook and rainbow trout. The East Fork is reached year-round by logging road, the Middle Fork road is closed from December 1 to May 15, and the West Fork is followed by a trail. All three are very small and offer fair fishing for small cuts and a few brookies. [T19N R30W S26]

BIG LAKE. Covering 38 acres in open subalpine country, this lake is reached by dropping into the Lake Creek basin to the north of Stuart Peak in the Rattlesnake Wilderness, a total of about 13 miles by trail. Or you could hike, bike, or ride horses to the end of the Rattlesnake Creek road (closed to motorized vehicles) and head west up the Lake Creek trail for a fairly strenuous (for the last mile or so) 4-mile hike up to the lake. It is fair fishing for skinny 8- to 12-inch rainbow trout. [T15N R18W S19]

BIG ROCK CREEK. It flows west from Bassoo Peak into the Thompson River, 3 miles south of the Bend Guard Station. Big Rock Creek flows over a falls 3 miles above its mouth, and then through a steep rocky and timbered gorge below. There's good fishing all along for 8- to 12-inch cutthroat and rainbow trout. It's paralleled by a logging road for the first mile upstream, and a USFS hiking trail for another 10 miles or so north up to headwaters. [T24N R27W S1]

BIG TERRACE LAKE. See Terrace Lake.

BLOSSOM LAKES. These two lakes are way up near the Idaho border, west of Thompson Falls, reached by a 2½-mile hike southwest from Prospect Creek road. The upper lake has a maximum depth of 17 feet, the lower one about 75 feet. Both are overpopulated with skinny (and ravenous) 6- to 8-inch brookies that provide fair to good fishing for not very many fishers. The lower one is now planted with rainbows, which are eating their way into the brook trout population and have potential to grow fairly large. [T21N R32W S30]

BLUE CREEK. A small stream that flows into Cabinet Gorge Reservoir, about 1 mile east of the Idaho border off Montana 200, Blue offers limited fishing opportunities for a shaky population of cutthroat trout. The East and West forks account for most of the stream's length. The West Fork is accessible by bushwhack and angler's trails as it crosses and recrosses the border, while the East Fork is followed by a logging road. Not worth the bother, though you may find a few cutthroat through the brush up either fork. [T27N R34W S19]

BOILING SPRINGS (or DUPONT) CREEK. A small, brushy, marshy stream in logging country, it's crossed at the mouth by a logging road around the south side of Lower Thompson Lake, and followed for its length by more logging roads. This creek is seldom fished, but it is loaded with brook trout and may have a cutthroat or two. [T26N R27W S11]

BONANZA LAKES. These two lakes are a few hundred yards apart in open alpine country (a sheepherder's paradise), about ⅓ mile east of the Idaho line, 15 miles southwest by crowflight from Superior. Take the Cedar Creek road southwest to USFS road 7763 north, then take the trail west up Bonanza Gulch 2 miles to the lakes. Or you can follow Cedar Creek road all the way to the State Line trailhead, then go north 2½ miles on the trail until the lakes appear below you. Right Bonanza is about 19 acres while Left Bonanza covers 10 acres. Both are deep, easily accessible all around, and good fishing for 6- to 9-inch brook trout. [T15N R28W S3]

BUCK LAKE. A beautiful alpine lake, fairly deep and covering 3 acres in a high, glaciated valley, ½ mile southeast of Wanless Lake, east of Noxon. Reach Buck Lake by a USFS trail 9½ miles northeast from the end of the McKay Creek road (around and beyond Goat Peak); or you can get in by trail going 7 miles north from the end of the Swamp Creek road. The lake is lightly fished (too far for most folks to hike) but it's good, for them that make it in, for 7- to 9-inch cutthroat. [T26N R31W S15]

BUFORD POND. See under Twomile Creek.

BULL RIVER. This is a fair-size, easily fished, moderately popular stream that flows 26 miles from the confluence of its North and Middle forks, through an open mountain valley, to the Clark Fork, 4 miles northwest of Noxon. It is followed by a good road all the way. The Bull is floatable for most of its length—easy floating above the East Fork, more difficult (due to faster water) below the East Fork, the last 3 miles of which is challenging whitewater (especially in high water). It's generally good fishing, for mostly 8- to 14-inch rainbow and cutthroat, plus a large variety of other species, including a few brown trout, brook trout, whitefish, and trash fish. The big browns make a spawning run in the fall, and some may hang out through the spring. Be aware that bull trout are present here, so don't catch 'em if you can help it. Much of the river bottom is private land, so ask first! [T26N R33W S3]

BULL RIVER, East Fork. This branch drains St. Paul Lake and flows for 9 miles, through a flat-bottomed, timbered valley, to the main river, at the historic ranger station. It is readily accessible by road for 7 miles to the Cabinet Mountains Wilderness boundary, and there's a trail on in to St. Paul Lake. The East Fork is lightly fished (it's pretty brushy), but it's good for small cutthroat. There is a decent population of resident and migratory bull trout—be kind to them. [T27N R33W S12]

BULL RIVER, Middle Fork. Crossed at the mouth by a road 2½ miles south of Bull Lake, it is then followed by a trail to headwaters, in the Cabinet Mountains Wilderness. There are about 4 miles of fishing water, in a timbered canyon with lots of downed cedar, logjams and the like. It's not bothered much (too tough), but it's good for 6- to 10-inch cutthroat trout. [T28N R33W S14]

BULL RIVER, North Fork. Offering about 5 miles of fishing water in a beautiful timbered canyon, it is accessible by a marginal USFS road for the first 2 miles, and then a horse trail 3 more miles into the wilderness. The North Fork is only lightly fished, but it's good for 6- to 10-inch cutthroat, with brown and bull trout spawners passing through as well. [T28N R33W S14]

BULL RIVER, North Fork of the East Fork. A real small stream in a steep, timbered canyon, it is crossed at the mouth by the East Fork road, and it's accessible by road and trail for about 2½ miles of fishing water. It's only lightly fished, but it's good for small cutthroat. Bull trout use this stream as well. [T27N R32W S4]

BULL RIVER, South Fork. This small stream is reached at the mouth by a road a few miles south of Bull Lake, and it's followed upstream for 3 miles through a logged canyon. It is terribly brushy, hard to fish, and seldom bothered, but it contains quite a few 6- to 10-inch cutthroat trout. [T28N R33W S14]

BURDETTE CREEK. Crossed at the mouth by the South Fork Fish Creek road, 8 miles north of Lolo Hot Springs, or 16 miles south of the Clark Fork, it is followed for 5 miles or so by a USFS trail. Burdette is a real swampy creek, with lots of beaver ponds and lots of fish—6- to 10-inch cutthroat. [T12N R24W S9]

BUTLER CREEK. From Ninemile House on US 10 (25 miles west of Missoula), take the Ninemile road northwest for 8 miles, to the mouth of Butler Creek; from there, you can take a county road for 4 miles northeast (or about halfway to headwaters), in timbered mountains. This is a

Falls on the North Fork of the Bull River. —Courtesy U.S. Forest Service

very small stream, but it's fair fishing for small cutthroat and brook trout. [T13N R20W S3]

CABIN LAKE. It's a 13½-acre, 40-foot deep lake with shallow drop-offs, in high (elevation 7,050) timbered mountain country. Take a USFS trail 1 mile north from the end of the West Fork Thompson River road. Cabin is planted with cutthroat every 4 years, and it's good fishing for trout that will average about 10 inches. Its popularity makes for very few large fish. [T23N R29W S35]

CABINET GORGE RESERVOIR. Extending from across the line in Idaho eastward to Noxon, Cabinet Gorge is about 12 miles long and has a maximum width of about 1 mile. It is easily accessible by good road on both sides, and it's a popular boating and fishing area. It contains a bit of everything, including rainbow, brown, and bull trout, largemouth and smallmouth bass, kokanee salmon, northern pike, yellow perch, whitefish, and plenty o' trash fish. Anglers, especially trollers, pull some big fish out of here. [T28N R32W S33]

Cabinet Gorge. —Courtesy U.S. Forest Service

CACHE CREEK. A moderately popular, good fishing stream in timbered mountains, reached at the mouth by the South Fork Fish Creek road (exit 66 off I-90), then followed by a good horse trail to headwaters. It produces good catches of 8- to 13- inch cutthroat and rainbow trout, as well as some brook trout, from all along its 9 miles of fishing water. [T12N R24W S8]

CANYON CREEK. A tiny creek in timbered country, crossed at the mouth by the Vermilion River road. It's followed upstream for about a mile by road, then for another 2 miles by trail. Only the lower mile is fair fishing, for 6- to 8-inch cutthroat trout. [T24N R30W S7]

CARTER (or CARTERS) LAKE. It lies ¼ mile east (down through the trees) from the old cabin near the middle of the Rattlesnake lake group— see directions to Worden Lake. It's in timber all around but has mostly open shores; it's 10 acres in size and about 20 feet deep at the most, with shallow drop-offs and water-level fluctuations of as much as 12 feet. It's not fished much, and usually with poor results, for skinny 8- to 12-inch rainbow trout. [T15N R18W S30]

CATARACT CREEK. Take the Vermilion River road 5 miles east from the east side of the Noxon Reservoir to the mouth of Cataract; from there, a USFS trail crosses Vermilion and follows Cataract for 5 miles, around a gorge below and up a narrow, flat-bottomed canyon above, to its headwaters on Seven Point Mountain. This moderately popular stream is good fishing for 6- to 9-inch cutthroat trout. [T24N R30W S8]

CEDAR CREEK. A nice little stream about 15 miles long (in country that was heavily mined in the early 1900s), it is followed by a good gravel road for its entire length, down a steep, timbered canyon to the Clark Fork, 1½ miles southeast of Superior. Cedar Creek is mostly open, easily and heavily fished for fair catches of a mix of rainbow, brown, cutthroat, and brook trout. It's mostly on private land and fished by locals. [T16N R26W S3]

CEDAR LOG CREEK. This one flows north from Cedar Log Lakes for 7 miles, through real rough, timbered country, to the West Fork of Fish Creek. It's reached at the mouth by the West Fork trail, and paralleled for a few miles upstream by a trail along the ridge. There is some pretty steep water below, but it flattens above with quite a few nice holes. Cedar Log is seldom fished, but fair for 6- to 8-inch cutthroat trout. [T13N R25W S19]

CEDAR LOG LAKES. These two lakes, a mile apart, are in alpine timber just east of the Idaho line, 22 miles southwest (as the crow flies) from

Cataract Creek at Saturday Night Falls.
—Courtesy U.S. Forest Service

Alberton. There are two or three ways in, and each involves at least an 8-mile hike, so you can pick your poison. Either head in west from Montana Creek (off the South Fork Fish Creek road), or south from the West Fork Fish Creek trail. Your last ½ mile is cross-country to the lakes. They are both good fishing for 8- to 14-inch cutthroat, with the bigger lake (East Cedar) perhaps a bit better. [T21N R13W S24]

CEMENT GULCH. A real small tributary of Trout Creek, it is reached at the mouth by the Trout Creek road, southeast of Superior, then followed upstream by a closed logging road for 2 miles; from there, it's a walk up the stream to headwaters. It is lightly fished, but it's good in the lower reaches for pan-size cutthroat trout. [T15N R27W S26]

CHERRY CREEK. This one flows for about 10 miles, through steep mountains, to the Clark Fork, 4 miles east of Thompson Falls. It is easily accessible by road for 5 miles and trail for 2 more, and it's fairly popular for nice catches of 6- to 8-inch cutthroat and brook trout. [T21N R29W S23]

CHIPPEWA CREEK. A small, brushy stream in a timbered canyon, it flows from the north side of Dad Peak in the Cabinet Mountains Wilderness to the South Fork Bull River. Chippewa is crossed near the mouth by the South Fork road, and it's a bushwhack east from there upstream. The lower mile is spotty but sometimes good fishing for 6- to 10-inch cutthroat trout. [T28N R33W S24]

CHIPPY CREEK. It's crossed at the mouth by the Thompson River road, 10 miles south of the Bend Guard Station, and followed upstream for 1 ½ miles by a logging road, then by trail for 7 miles to headwaters. It is a small, brushy, hard-to-fish stream that is seldom bothered, but there's fair fishing in the lower reaches for small brook trout, and cutthroat above. [T23N R27W S1]

CIRQUE LAKES. See Upper Wanless Lakes.

CLEAR CREEK. It flows east through steep mountains for 14 miles, from Clear Peak to Prospect Creek near Thompson Falls. It is followed by a logging road and is heavily fished along the lower reaches for fair catches of 6- to 8-inch brook and cutthroat trout. [T21N R30W S13]

CLEAR LAKE. At the head of Deer Creek, a couple of miles west of Ward Peak, in a little timbered glacial cirque with some open camping spots, lies Clear Lake. It is about 9 acres and 40 feet deep, and there's good fishing for 6- to 10-inch brookies. It is reached (by a few) by taking the Little Joe Creek road to the Montana state line, then turning north on the State Line road for about 8 miles, and finally going by shank's mare for a final ½ mile to the shore. [T17N R30W S3]

CLIFF LAKE. Fifty acres and real deep, with aquatic vegetation around the lower end and rock cliffs above the upper end, Cliff lies in subalpine country, 1 mile above Diamond Lake. Take the Dry Creek road, off I-90 north of Superior, to the end, about 20 miles south; continue on a good trail 1½ miles to the lake. This is a beautiful lake that is lightly fished, because it supports only a small population of 7- to 16-inch cutthroat, though there are a few bigger fish here. [T16N R28W S18]

COMBPEST (or COMBEST) CREEK. This is a small stream, mostly on river-bottom ranchland across the Clark Fork from Plains. The lower 3 miles are readily accessible by road and are poor fishing for 6- to 8-inch rainbow trout. [T20N R26W S33]

COOPER GULCH. A small, clear mountain stream, reached at the mouth by the Prospect Creek road (near Thompson Falls), then followed by a logging road to headwaters. The lower 2 miles are heavily fished for small cutthroat trout, though it can go dry as it nears Prospect Creek. [T21N R31W S29]

Cliff Lake. —Courtesy U.S. Forest Service

COPPER (or SILVEX) LAKE. An old mine reservoir 3 miles south of Lookout Pass, it is reached by a trail 1½ miles from I-90. Copper Lake covers 6 acres and is fairly shallow, with some aquatic vegetation, logs, etc., and a real muddy bottom. It is planted every 4 years or so with cutts, and it's fair to good fishing now for 7- to 13- inchers. [T19N R32W S8]

CORONA LAKE. Taking the county road north from Plains to USFS road 1025 for 14 miles or so, then an old logging road just before Corona Creek, will get you to this small lake. It has been planted for the last few years with rainbow trout and grayling, and it should offer good fishing. Let us know! [T22N R25W S30]

CRATER LAKE. It covers 16 acres in steep timbered mountains, and it's (seldom) reached by taking the North Fork Fish Creek trail 5 miles north to the Crater Creek (too small for fish) drainage, and then cross-country 2 miles southwest to the shore. It is planted with cutthroat every 10 years or so, and it isn't fished a heck of a lot, but it's good at times for cutts ranging up to 16 inches. [T14N R26W S34]

CRYSTAL LAKE. A 118-foot-deep lake in timbered mountains south of De Borgia, it is reached by a steep trail 1½ miles southwest from the Deer Creek road. A healthy population of naturally reproducing brook

116

trout are found here. One Crystal Lake brookie measured 21.3 inches long and weighed 4.5 pounds—though most are between 4 and 9 inches. [T18N R30W S28]

DALTON LAKE. A 6-acre cirque lake, ⅓ mile east of the Idaho line, in the old 1910 burn, it is reached by a 3-plus-mile hike from the trailhead at the end of the South Fork Trout Creek road (which you take 15 miles southeast of Superior). Once you get to Pearl Lake, head south over the saddle to Dalton. It is planted every four years with westslope cutthroat trout, which are eager to please the angler who has taken the time to get there. They seldom see anyone. [T14N R27W S5]

DEEP CREEK. Not much of a fishing stream, it is small and in a narrow timbered canyon. Deep Creek is crossed at the mouth by a county road 15 miles north of Thompson Falls, and followed to headwaters by a USFS trail. There are a few small cutthroat here and there along the lower 3 miles, but they seldom see a hook. [T23N R30W S21]

DEER CREEK. A small stream, flowing north through a narrow, timbered canyon to the St. Regis River opposite De Borgia, it is followed by a logging road for 6 miles upstream. The lower reaches are sometimes fished by local residents for 8- to 12-inch brookies and a few cutthroat. [T19N R30W S25]

DEER LAKE. This Deer Lake (there is at least one in most every major drainage) is only about 3½ acres in area, in rocky bluff country that is open around the shores. It is maybe 15 feet deep beneath cliffs at the west end, and shallower towards the outlet. It is planted every three or four years with cutthroat, and it's good fishing for 10- to 12-inchers. To get there, take a USFS trail 3 miles west up the Honeymoon Creek drainage toward Roundtop Mountain. [T22N R29W S24]

DENNA MORA CREEK. It's reached at the mouth by I-90, right by the rest stop 4 miles east of Lookout Pass—now how's that for service? A real small stream with only about a mile of fishable water in the lower, flat reaches, it is seldom fished but fair for a few messes each spring of 7- to 9-inch brook trout. [T19N R32W S10]

DEVIL GAP CREEK. A very small, seldom-if-ever-fished stream, its lower stretches can go dry in the summer. The upper reaches reportedly harbor a few small cutts, but it's a bushwhack to get there. It is crossed at the mouth by the Marten Creek road, 4 miles west of Noxon Reservoir. [T25N R33W S26]

DIAMOND LAKE. With an area of 17 acres in heavily timbered country, it is reached by the Dry Creek road (4 miles northwest of Superior) right to the Diamond Lake campground. Diamond Lake is deep in the upper end, generally logged-up around the margins, and mostly fished from raft or boat. It is quite popular and has good fishing for 6- to 11-inch brook trout. [T16N R28W S17]

DOMINION CREEK. A short (about 2 miles of fishable water), brushy little stream, it is a tributary to the St. Regis River, 3 miles west of Saltese. To get there, leave I-90 at exit 5 and follow the river for a mile by an access road to the mouths of Dominion and Randolph creeks. It's not fished much except by local people, but it does produce fair catches of small brook and cutthroat trout. [T19N R31W S8]

DRY CREEK. There are about 8 miles of fair to good fishing here for small brookies and cutthroat along the Dry Creek road, and another 4 miles of paralleling trail, in open country above and timbered country below. Located 4 miles west of Superior (and south of the Clark Fork River), it's a fairly popular stream with local anglers. [T17N R26W S19]

DRY CREEK, East and West Forks. A very small stream is reached by a logging road going 5 miles south from Thompson Falls. The lower sections of each fork provide fair fishing for small cutthroat. The main stream goes dry below the confluence of the forks. [T21N R29W S31]

DUCKHEAD LAKE. Good and deep, about 500 yards long by 150 yards wide, it's surrounded by steep grassy slopes and scattered timber, with some talus along the east side. It is reached by a trail up Big Spruce Creek, 3½ miles west from the West Fork Thompson River road. There's some fair fishing here for cutthroat, planted every four years, that run up to 18 inches but average around 12. [T22N R29W S13]

DUPONT CREEK. See Boiling Spring Creek.

EAGLE PEAK LAKE. This Mineral County lake, in the eastern shadow of Eagle Peak at a 6,200-foot elevation, is slightly over 3 acres with a maximum depth of 30 feet. It is reached 2½ miles west up a trailless creek from a loop on the Ward Creek road, ½ mile past Ward Creek and its trailhead. Eagle Peak Lake is unnamed on most maps. It was planted in 1977 and 1982 with westslope cutthroat, and, to tell you the truth, I haven't heard how they're doing. [T18N R30W S35]

EAST FORK BIG CREEK. See under Big Creek.

EAST FORK BLUE CREEK. See under Blue Creek.

EAST CEDAR LAKE. See under Cedar Log Lakes.

EAST FORK ELK CREEK. See under Elk Creek.

EAST FORK PETTY CREEK. See under Petty Creek.

EAST FORK ROCK CREEK. See under Rock Creek.

EAST FORK TWELVEMILE CREEK. See under Twelvemile Creek.

EDDY CREEK. A small stream in a narrow valley, it is crossed at the mouth by the frontage road 7½ miles southeast of Superior and followed by a logging road for 3 miles. The lower reaches go almost dry in late summer, and most people don't realize that there is enough water above to float the few trout that are in it. Some of the locals fish it for pan-size cutthroat. [T16N R25W S28]

EDDY CREEK. A small stream flowing down a real steep, rocky gorge to the Clark Fork, about 6 miles west of Weeksville, it is followed by a logging road that is gated after 3 miles. No matter, the lower 2 miles are the only place worth fishing, for 6- to 8-inch cutthroat trout. [T21N R27W S32]

ELK CREEK. A moderately popular stream, it flows from the junction of its east and west forks for 6 miles, through private meadowland, to the Clark Fork, 1 mile east of Heron. Elk Creek is easily accessible by road (with permission), and is fair to good fishing throughout its length for 6- to 10-inch brook and some cutthroat. The East Fork supports a declining population of cutthroat in its first few miles, all accessible by road in logged country. [T27N R34W S35]

ELK (or SIMS) LAKE. You can drive to within ½ mile of this one, up the Sims Creek road. Take off from the Vermilion River road, about 2½ miles east above the West Fork, then 2½ miles up the creek, and finally a pack trail into the shore, at 4,100 feet above sea level. It's 7 acres in a steep timbered pocket, with brush around the shore. There's lots of fish food here, and some good fishing for 1- to 2-pound cutthroat—summer and winter. The fish can be a bit choosy here, due to the abundance of natural food. [T25N R30W S25]

ENGLE (or ENGLE PEAK) LAKE. This is a small alpine lake in the western shadow of Engle Peak, just inside the Cabinet Mountains Wilderness, northeast of Noxon. It is reached by a 2-mile hike on USFS trail 932, off the end of the Orr Creek logging road, or by USFS trail 926, a couple of drainages to the south. It has been planted every three or four years, and is due again, with westslope cutts that will range from 6 to 13 inches. [T26N R31W S18]

FARMER'S LAKES 5 and 6. Lake 5 is about 25 acres, and Lake 6 is 18 acres. They're ⅓ mile apart, in a couple of small glacial cirques east of, and 1,300 feet or so straight down from, Stuart Peak. (Lake 5 is 120 feet higher and to the south.) Both are drained by the headwaters of High Falls Creek, which is too small and much too steep to support fish. The best way to get there is to head back to Stuart Peak, 10 miles north and east of the Sawmill Gulch trailhead in the Rattlesnake Wilderness. Skirt Stuart Peak by trail, heading north and then east for another 1½ miles to the lakes. Farmer's Lakes haven't been planted for quite some time, but both offer fair fishing for a small population of cutthroat of all sizes. [T14N R18W S5]

FIRST CREEK. A small, brushy stream that occupies a narrow, 4-mile-long valley in steep, logged mountains. It is crossed at the mouth by a county road 7 miles southeast of Superior, and upstream by a logging road. The lower reaches can go dry, but the upper reaches contain a few small cutthroat trout. [T16N R25W S20]

FISH CREEK. A good-size stream with lots of nice big holes, it flows to the Clark Fork across the river from, and 2 miles east of, Tarkio. The entire stream (to the junction of the North and West forks, east of Clearwater Crossing) is followed by good logging road. This is a heavily fished, open stream that offers good fishing for numerous 9- to 13-inch rainbow, a bunch of brookies, even more whitefish, and enough cutts to let you know they are there. Rainbow, brown, bull, and cutthroat all make spawning runs up this stream. [T14N R25W S1]

FISH CREEK, North Fork. A decent fishing stream in a narrow, timbered, and brushed-up canyon, it is followed to headwaters (9 miles) by a good trail from Clearwater Crossing. This creek is lightly fished for small rainbow and cutthroat trout. It is also excellent bull trout habitat, so be kind to these endangered fish. [T13N R25W S6]

FISH CREEK, South Fork. This branch offers 15 miles of fair fishing for 6- to 10-inch rainbow, cutthroat, and brook trout. A declining population of bull trout also uses the stream. The South Fork is accessed for its entire length by good logging road. Be aware of the private land in the upper reaches of the creek. [T14N R25W S36]

FISH CREEK, West Fork. Accessible by a good USFS trail for all of its 9 miles, the first 5 miles or so of this branch are the only ones worth the bother. It doesn't get much pressure but it's good fishing for a mix of cutts, 'bows, and brookies. The farther up you get, the more bull trout you'll find, as this is prime habitat for them. [T13N R25W S6]

FISHTRAP CREEK. A fair-size but wadable stream, about 17 miles long in logged mountains, it is crossed at the mouth by the Thompson River road, then followed upstream (north) by a logging road. Fishtrap is heavily

Clark Fork River above Thompson Falls. —Courtesy U.S. Forest Service

fished and a consistent producer of 7- to 8-inch cutthroat, plus a few brook and rainbow trout. Don't look for trophy fish here. [T23N R27W S33]

FISHTRAP CREEK, West Fork. A very small stream that drains Stony, Terrace, and three unnamed alpine lakes through a steep, narrow canyon, for about 6 miles of fishing. It is not very popular, but it's readily accessible by a logging road, and there's fair fishing for 6- to 8-inch cutthroat trout. The last 2 or 3 miles of the road are closed to vehicles in the spring until June 15. [T24N R28W S26]

FISHTRAP LAKE. A long, narrow, boomerang-shaped lake, about 50 acres, shallow at the upper end but 60 feet deep or better at the outlet. Fishtrap is accessible by the Lazier Creek road, 11 miles southwest of Lazier's mouth on the Thompson River. The lake is excellent fishing (although lots of folks skip it) for 6- to 12-inch cutthroat trout, a very few brook trout, and too many suckers. There is a USFS campground here. [T24N R28W S4]

FLAT CREEK. A "kids only" creek, too small for them to get into trouble but still fair fishing for 6- to 10-inch cutthroat, brook, and rainbow trout.

There's a logging road that follows it up, through some old mining claims, from its mouth at Superior. [T17N R26W S34]

FLAT ROCK CREEK. A small stream with about 3 miles of fishing, in timbered country, it is crossed at the mouth by the Twelvemile Creek road, then followed by a good trail east to headwaters. It's fair to good for 6- to 10-inch rainbow and brook trout, plus a few cutthroat in some nice beaver dams scattered along the upper reaches. Go around to the Tamarack Creek trailhead to more easily access the upper section of Flat Rock. [T19N R29W S3]

FOUR LAKES CREEK. A very small stream (less than 2 miles of fishing) in high mountains, it is reached by the West Fork of the Thompson River road, followed to headwaters (i.e., Frog, Grass, Porcupine, and Knowles Lakes—all barren) by logging road and trail. It's moderately popular (with disappointed lake anglers perhaps?) for small cutthroat and rainbow trout. [T23N R28W S32]

FRENCH LAKE. A deep cirque lake covering 14 acres in timbered mountains, French Lake is reached by a USFS trail up the North Fork of Fish Creek, 8 miles northwest of Clearwater Crossing. It is seldom fished, but it contains large numbers of hard-to-catch cutthroat and rainbow-cutthroat hybrids, which average 8 inches and range from 6 to 17 inches. [T14N R26W S18]

FRENCHTOWN POND. This popular little number lies adjacent to I-90, a mile west of Frenchtown. It is a nice recreation pond for locals and passersby, covering about 5 acres, with a maximum depth of perhaps 10 feet and some springs that keep it from freezing out. It's a good place to swim in the summer, iceboat in winter, and fish for pike, bass, and perch year-round. It is heavily fished. [T15N R21W S28]

GLACIER LAKE. A deep, 25-acre cirque lake in barren rocky country in the Rattlesnake Wilderness north of Missoula, reached by better than 14 miles of trail from the Sawmill Gulch trailhead. Another route takes you on a 4-mile hike west up Wrangle Creek from the end of Rattlesnake Creek road (which is closed to motorized vehicles through the recreation area). Glacier was gill-netted in 1970 and confirmed to be barren but suitable for fish. Yellowstone cutts were planted the next year, and their progeny are still around. [T15N R19W S24]

GOLD LAKE. Take the Ward Creek road 3 miles west from the mouth, to the Up-Up Lookout road, then follow that road for about 8 miles to USFS trail 250. Hike about a mile on the trail, then head west and downhill ½ mile cross-country to the lake, nestled on the north side of Gold

Peak. A good topo map might help find this one. Rainbow trout live here, of 7 to 14 inches or so. [T18N R30W S23]

GRANT CREEK. A pretty little stream in heavily timbered mountains above, it is mostly dewatered for irrigation below. Grant Creek is crossed by I-90 a couple of miles west of Missoula, and it's followed by a county road and trail for 12 miles to headwaters, in the Rattlesnake Wilderness. Grant Creek is moderately popular fishing for small cutthroat and brook trout. [T13N R19W S5]

GRAVES CREEK. A small stream, it is followed by road from its head-waters for 10 miles, through a timbered canyon, down to the Clark Fork, 7 miles west of Thompson Falls. It is readily accessible, heavily fished, and fair for 7- to 12-inch cutthroat, rainbow, brookies, and a very few brown trout. Bull trout use the stream as well. [T22N R30W S11]

HAZEL (or WARD) LAKE. Seven acres and deep, but with considerable aquatic vegetation around the margins, Hazel lies between Eagle and Ward Peaks in alpine timber. Approach it via a good USFS trail (262), a couple of miles southwest of the end of the Ward Creek road. It was last planted with westslope cutthroat in 1989, and it's reported to be good fishing for your average cutts. [T18N R30W S36]

HEART LAKE. This one's a deep, 60-acre alpine lake, whose upper end lies below a big cliff (right next to Idaho) and the lower portions in the open country of the old 1910 burn, southwest of Tarkio. Take the Trout Creek road south from I-90 to a good trail on the South Fork, then follow the trail about 2 miles to the lake. Heart is lightly fished for good-size (7 to 16 inches) brook trout, and cutthroat as well. [T14N R27W S23]

HEART LAKE. It kind of looks like a heart from the air. Heart Lake lies south of Haugan at the base of a steep cliff, in a little timbered cirque, maybe ⅛ mile northeast of Idaho. Mostly open around the shore, it's drained by the East Fork of Big Creek. Reach it to within ¾ mile by the East Fork Big Creek logging road, and then it's a tough steep climb to the south. From October 15 through May 15, you'll have to tack on a little extra distance to your hike, since the East Fork road is gated about a mile from the trailhead. The lake has an area of 6½ acres, with a maximum depth of 60 feet. It's no better than fair fishing for 6- to 15-inch rainbow trout, but it is moderately popular for all of that. [T18N R30W S29]

HENDERSON (or LITTLE NINEMILE) CREEK. This is a real small stream, flowing for 4 miles in a narrow, timbered canyon across (south of) the river from I-90, 12 miles west of St. Regis. It's seldom fished, but the lower mile contains 6- to 8-inch rainbow, cutthroat, and brook trout that migrate up from the main river. There's an unmaintained trail, of sorts. [T18N R29W S4]

HOODOO CREEK. A tiny, open meadow creek, it offers about 2 miles of poor, kids' fishing before it disappears underground. Don't bother fishing this one, at the head of Trout Creek, ½ mile north of Hoodoo Pass, but the country is nice. [T14N R27W S3]

HOODOO LAKE. Covering 10½ acres with a 35-foot maximum depth, Hoodoo sits in high alpine meadows at the upper end, and timber below. It's a short hike to the lake—a bit better than a mile—along USFS trail 111T, which takes off to the south from the Trout Creek-Hoodoo Pass road, about 3 miles north of Hoodoo Pass. It is only lightly fished, but it's excellent for small (6- to 9-inch) brookies. [T14N R27W S15]

HUB LAKE. Five acres with a maximum depth of 18 feet, it lies in sub-alpine timber, ½ mile west of Hazel Lake. You get there by driving up the Ward Creek road to trailhead 262, then hiking south on 262 and west on trail 280, for a total of 2½ miles to the lake. There are a couple of good campsites here, and some westslope cutthroat as well, ranging up to 13 inches or so. [T18N R30W S35]

ILLINOIS CREEK (or GULCH). Real short (about 2 miles) and real small (goes dry in spots), it has numerous beaver dams from ½ mile above its mouth on up. It is followed by an informal trail from its mouth on Cedar Creek (ask permission to cross the private land here), and it is fair fishing for 6- to 10-inch rainbow trout in the dammed areas. [T15N R27W S17]

IMAGE (or IMAGINE) LAKE. At the headwaters between the Vermilion River and Graves Creek, Image is reached within ¼ mile by a logging road. No fish here due to winterkill (it's not planted anymore), but a nice place to visit. [T23W R29W S10]

INDIAN CREEK. At the headwaters of the West Fork Fish Creek, it is accessible by trail for 4 miles from end to end. The Middle Fork has a 2-acre beaver pond, located about 1½ miles above its mouth, that is good fishing for small cutthroat trout. Otherwise, this stream is a flop, including its forks. [T13N R26W S25]

IRISH CREEK. This little stream in timbered country is reached at its mouth by the Cache Creek trail, then followed by trail for 3 miles to its headwaters. It is good fishing for 6- to 8-inch native cutthroat trout. [T12N R25W S28]

JOHNSON CREEK. It's about 5 miles long, very small; it's followed much of the way by a good logging road, down its narrow canyon, to the Clark

Fork, 2 miles east of Superior. The lower reaches can go dry, but the upper reaches are fair fishing for small (6 to 8 inches) cutthroat trout. [T16N R26W S3]

JUNGLE CREEK. Flows through logged country to Fishtrap Creek, 1 mile above the mouth, and it's followed upstream by a logging road. Jungle Creek is only occasionally fished, but it contains fair numbers of small cutthroat trout. [T23N R27W S28]

KREIS (or KREISES) POND (or LAKE). A 9½-acre, fairly deep, timbered pocket that was dammed up years ago and water-ditched in. Take the Remount road, in the Ninemile drainage, to the USFS remount depot, then go a couple of miles east on the Ninemile road. Kreis used to be stocked with cutthroat, but bass were planted last time (in 1987), with mediocre results. No matter now, they drained it a year or so back for repairs and haven't planted it since. It's a nice place for a picnic and even comes equipped with a real picnic area. [T16N R22W S31]

LAKE CREEK. A small tributary (2½ miles) of Rattlesnake Creek, it drains Carter and Sheridan lakes, among others. It is fair fishing for small cutts and brookies. [T15N R18W S21]

LANG CREEK. A very small stream that flows through open grazing land to the Thompson River, 1½ miles east of Lower Thompson Lake. The lower reaches are readily accessible by the Thompson River road (on private land), but they're seldom fished, though they contain a few trout and yellow perch that have migrated up from the main stream. [T26N R26W S18]

LAWN LAKE. Get your topo maps out to find your way to this one, way up near the headwaters of Graves Creek. There are at least three ways (trail, gated road, old road) to get to within ½ mile or so, then it's cross-country the rest of the way. If you find it, you'll also find fair fishing for cutthroat planters, ranging up to 12 inches and replenished every three or four years. [T23N R29W S27]

LENORE LAKE. In a small cirque in logged-over country up near Idaho, it's reached within ½ mile by USFS road 1180, off the Twomile Creek road. You are on your own from there. It is 2.5 acres, 20 feet deep, and contains westslope cutthroat trout from a 1993 plant (and 1982 before that). [T17N R29W S9]

LITTLE BEAVER CREEK. A small stream, it is easily accessible by road, flowing through a timbered canyon above and hay and pastureland below to Big Beaver Creek, 2 miles south of Whitepine. It is posted, but the lower 7 miles are good fishing for 10- to 14-inch brook, and some rainbow, trout. [T23N R30W S30]

125

LITTLE JOE CREEK. The whole stream, including both the north and south forks, offers good fishing for 6- to 10-inch cutthroat, and maybe some rainbow in the lower reaches. The first mile, just west of St. Regis, flows through private land, but the rest of it is followed by good logging road and is fished quite a bit. Be kind to the bull trout that use this (or any) stream, please. [T18N R28W S26]

LITTLE LAKE. This lake is in the Rattlesnake Wilderness, and is not a short hike in, no matter how you approach it. You could hoof it or take a mountain bike to the end of the Rattlesnake Creek road, which runs through the heart of the Rattlesnake National Recreation Area and is closed year-round to motorized vehicles. From the end of the road, it's a 3-mile hike into the lake along USFS trail 502. Or you could drop into the basin from Stuart Peak (itself a 10-mile hike from the trailhead at Sawmill Gulch), heading north and then east on USFS trails around Mosquito Peak and Glacier Lake. Open to the southwest, in timber to the northeast, Little Lake covers 16 acres and provides pretty good fishing for lean 6- to 10-inch cutthroat trout. [T15N R18W S19]

LITTLE (or UPPER) MCGREGOR LAKE. Located just across US 2, north of McGregor Lake, it covers 30 acres, is 30 feet deep with a muddy bottom, and has a marshy shoreline. It is most effectively fished by boat for brook and rainbow trout, yellow perch, and largemouth bass. The trout are planted regularly and have been known to reach 20 inches or so, especially the brookies. [T26N R25W S4]

LITTLE NINEMILE CREEK. See Henderson Creek.

LITTLE ROCK CREEK. Flowing through logged-over country for 7 miles to the Little Thompson River, it is intermittently accessible for the lower 4 miles by logging roads. It's moderately popular and fair fishing (in the lower reaches) for 6- to 8-inch rainbow trout. [T23N R27W S25]

LITTLE THOMPSON RIVER. A good-size stream, it is crossed at the mouth by the Thompson River road and followed by a logging road (except for 3 miles in the middle) upstream for about 10 miles. The lower mile flows through a rocky gorge, the middle reaches in open rangeland and willows, and the upper reaches in timbered mountains. Heavily fished in the lower 11 miles it's good for 7- to 10-inch rainbow, brook, and cutthroat trout, as well as whitefish. Bull trout can be found here, too. [T23N R27W S26]

LITTLE THOMPSON RIVER, North Fork. There are about 3 miles of fair fishing here, for 6- to 8-inch rainbow and brook trout. It is crossed near the mouth by a logging road and followed upstream by trail. This is a moderately popular stream. [T23N R27W S26]

LITTLE TROUT CREEK. A small steam flowing for 4 miles through steep, timbered mountains to Trout Creek. It is followed by a logging road through private land for about 2½ miles upstream. It goes dry in the upper reaches, but below it's fair for 6- to 8-inch brook trout and a few cutthroat. [T24N R31W S19]

LOST CREEK. Small, in a moderately brushy, timbered canyon, it's about 6 miles long, with 4 miles of fairly popular fishing water. Reached by taking the Cedar Creek-Oregon Gulch road, 1 mile south of Superior, Lost Creek is followed for most of its length by a logging road, and the last 2½ miles by USFS trail 112T, to Lost Lake. The stream is good fishing for 6- to 10-inch rainbow and cutthroat trout. There is a nice meadow with lots of meanders at the headwaters. [T16N R27W S21]

LOST LAKE. A high lake in the old 1910 burn, it's about 25 acres and fairly deep, with cliffs at the upper end. Drained by Lost Creek, it's reached by taking the Lost Creek road to the end, then a 2½-mile hike southwest to the lake. Lost Lake is not fished much but it's good for 6- to 10-inch brook trout. [T16N R28W S34]

LOWELL (or SNOWSHOE) LAKE. A beautiful 28-acre, 70-foot-deep lake with steep drop-offs along the southwest side. It is in a northeast-facing Cabinet Mountain cirque, below talus slopes to the south and west and some stunted alpine fir on the east. To get there, hike 1½ miles cross-country, up the right-hand drainage from the end of the North Fork Bull River trail, in steep, grizzly bear country. This is truly a superb trip for the scenery as well as the fishing, which is excellent when (and if) you get there, for 8- to 12-inch cutthroat. [T29N R32W S32]

LOWER THOMPSON LAKE. Just east of Middle Thompson Lake, 240 acres and 140 feet deep in places, it is easily accessible by US 2 along the north side. It's planted regularly with rainbow and brown trout, as well as kokanee salmon. Neither the kokanee nor the browns have established viable populations in the last five years of planting, but the rainbows are doing fairly well. Trout have been known to grow to 5 or 10 pounds here. Largemouth bass have established an extremely viable population (they probably feast on the salmon and trout plants), and they are the reason most people fish here, for sometimes-large bass. You can also find the occasional pike, and more small perch and pumpkinseeds than you can shake a stick at. You'll need a boat to fish this one effectively. Check current regulations for special limits on trout and bass. [T26N R27W S11]

LOWER TRIO LAKE. See under Trio Lakes.

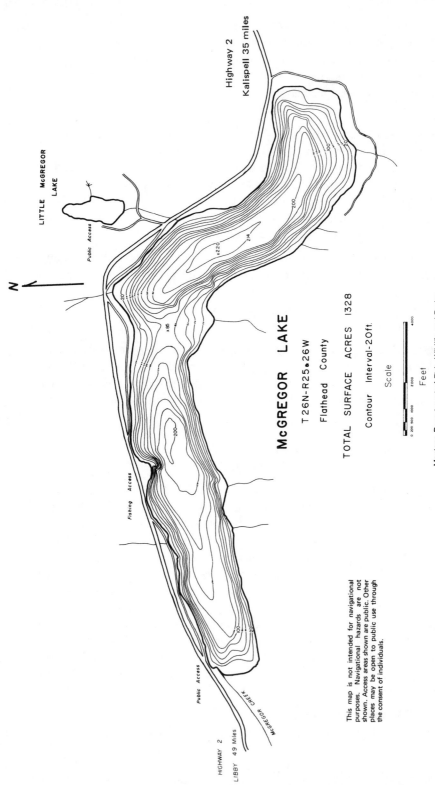

LITTLE McGREGOR LAKE

N

Public Access

Highway 2
Kalispell 35 miles

Public Access

Fishing Access

McGREGOR CREEK

Public Access

HIGHWAY 2
LIBBY 49 Miles

McGREGOR LAKE

T26N-R25•26W
Flathead County

TOTAL SURFACE ACRES 1328

Contour Interval-20 ft.

Scale

0 200 500 1000   2000   4000

Feet

This map is not intended for navigational purposes. Navigational hazards are not shown. Access areas shown are public. Other places may be open to public use through the consent of individuals.

Montana Department of Fish, Wildlife and Parks

LYNCH CREEK. An easily fished, pastureland "kids' creek," with about 3 miles of fair fishing water, it is available by county roads north of Plains. Lynch contains 6- to 8- inch cutthroat and brook trout, and it flows mostly through private land. [T20N R26W S16]

MARTEN CREEK. Flowing through a timbered canyon for 10 miles to the Noxon Reservoir at Marten Creek Bay, it is accessible at the mouth by the South Fork road, 5 miles south of the dam site. There is a campground here, where a logging road takes off and follows on up to headwaters. It is generally good fishing for 6- to 10- inch brook and rainbow trout below, and cutthroat and rainbow trout above. The South Fork is followed by a closed road, for 3 miles of fair fishing for small cutts. [T25N R32W S32]

MCCORMICK CREEK. Small, about 7 miles long, in timbered country, it is crossed at the mouth by the Ninemile Creek road, 1 mile north of Stark, and followed upstream by a logging road for 2 miles beyond the gold dredgings. It's fair fishing above the dredgings for 6- to 8-inch cutthroat and rainbow trout. [T16N R23W S21]

MCGREGOR CREEK. The outlet of McGregor Lake, it flows for 5 miles right next to US 2, down to Lang Creek. It is lightly fished, but it's fairly good in early season for small cutthroat and brook trout, plus a few rainbow. Larger fish have been known to use the stream as well. [T26N R26W S18]

MCGREGOR LAKE. This is a large (1,328 acres) lake in timbered country, 30 miles west of Kalispell on US 2. It is a fairly popular recreational area, with summer homes and resorts. The fishing is good (mostly from boats) for 16- to 18-inch (and a few to 16 pounds) lake trout, plus loads of rainbow (planted in large batches every year) and a few cutthroat. There are yellow perch and whitefish here as well. Check current regulations for special limits on trout. [T26N R25W S9]

MCKINLEY LAKE. In timber all around but with mostly open shores, it covers 20 acres of a nice little glacial cirque in the Rattlesnake Wilderness. It is reached by a good USFS trail about 1 mile north of Stuart Peak, 11 miles from the Sawmill Gulch trailhead. It can also be accessed by trail up Lake Creek (from the end of the Rattlesnake Creek road, which is closed to motorized vehicles) to Carter Lake and continuing ½ mile to the southeast. McKinley is moderately popular but pretty slow fishing for 8- to 12-inch heavy-bodied rainbow trout. [T15N R18W S31]

MIDDLE FORK BIG CREEK. See under Big Creek.

MIDDLE FORK BULL RIVER. See Bull River, Middle Fork.

McGregor Lake. —Courtesy Ravalli County Museum, Ernst Peterson Collection

MIDDLE FORK INDIAN CREEK. See under Indian Creek.

MIDDLE THOMPSON LAKE. A big (602 acres), deep lake in timbered country, 8 miles west of McGregor Lake on US 2. It is a fairly popular recreational area, with lots of summer homes and plenty of boating action. The fishing is excellent (mostly from boats) for 10- to 18-inch kokanee, and largemouth bass from 10 inches to 5 pounds. Rainbow and brown trout are planted regularly and provide steady fishing, with some trout reaching 10 pounds or so. Smallish yellow perch and sunfish, some lake trout, and a few brookies can be found here as well. Check current regulations for special limits on trout and bass. [T26N R27W S4]

MIDDLE TRIO LAKE. See under Trio Lakes.

MILL CREEK. This stream offers 10 miles of fishing water, in open meadow above and in a steep, rocky gorge below. Its lower reaches are almost completely dewatered for irrigation, and what's left is crossed by the highway at Frenchtown. The upper reaches are followed by a logging road for about 8 miles to headwaters. It is good fishing in the gorge for 4- to 10-inch cutthroat, while up in the meadows it's mostly brook trout. This is an excellent kids' creek, but it's declining due to development and logging. [T14N R21W S4]

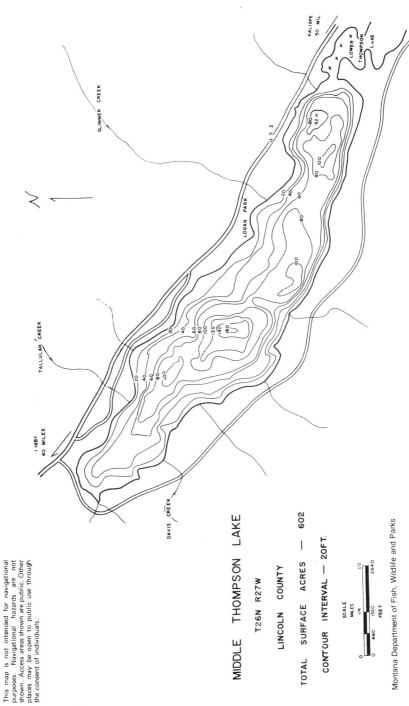

This map is not intended for navigational purposes. Navigational hazards are not shown. Access areas shown are public. Other places may be open to public use through the consent of individuals.

MIDDLE THOMPSON LAKE

T26N R27W

LINCOLN COUNTY

TOTAL SURFACE ACRES — 602

CONTOUR INTERVAL — 20 FT.

SCALE

MILES
0   1/4   1/2

FEET
0   660   1320   2640

Montana Department of Fish, Wildlife and Parks

SLIMMER CREEK

TALLULAH CREEK

LIBBY 40 MILES

DAVIS CREEK

LOGAN PARK

U S 2

KALISPE 50 MIL

LOWER THOMPSON LAKE

MISSOULA GULCH. Small and brushy, it drains Missoula Lake for 2 miles to Bonanza Gulch, and from there to Oregon Gulch. It is crossed by a logging road ½ mile above the mouth. The lower ¼ mile (below Bonanza Gulch) is in a big flat and is fair fishing for 8- to 12-inch cutthroat trout. [T15N R28W S2]

MISSOULA LAKE. Reached by the Cedar Creek road, and then a short hike on USFS trail 108, it's about 25 miles southwest of Superior, in the old 1910 burn. It covers 12 acres and is over 50 feet deep, with mostly steep drop-offs; it's partly brushy and partly open around the shore. It is planted off and on with rainbow and cutthroat, and it's fair fishing for these, in the 8- to 13-inch range. [T15N R28W S15]

MONTANA CREEK. A small tributary of Cache Creek, it is followed by a seasonally gated road (October 15 through June 15). There are about 3 ½ miles of meandering fishing water, where you'll find enough 6- to 8-inch cutts to keep you busy. [T12N R24W S18]

MOORE LAKE. A deep, 13-acre subalpine lake in timbered country, it is accessible by the South Fork Little Joe Creek road, going 14 miles south from St. Regis. Moore Lake lies below talus slopes at the upper end and a small cliff on the east side. It has quite a few aquatic plants around the margins, and it's heavily fished for good catches of 6- to 13-inch brook trout. There is a USFS campground here. [T16N R29W S3]

MORAN BASIN LAKES. There are two lakes, but the lower one is a barren pothole. Upper Moran is a deep, 14-acre lake that sits at about 5,700 feet in elevation in a cirque in the Cabinet Mountains Wilderness. It's reached by about 6 miles of USFS trail that take off from the end of a short spur road that heads east from the Bull River Guard Station. It isn't fished much but it has been excellent for skinny, 10- to 11-inch cutthroat and it surely does support a burgeoning population of ravenous mosquitoes. [T27N R32W S14]

MOSQUITO CREEK. A small kids' creek flowing from the mountains, down across the open floodplain, to the Clark Fork River at Belknap. It is followed by a road for about 3 miles of fair fishing, for 6- to 8-inch brook trout, most all of it on private land. [T22N R30W S11]

MURR CREEK. This little stream flows through rocky, sparsely timbered country. It is crossed at the mouth by the Thompson River road, then followed upstream by a trail, for about 2 miles of good fishing for 6- to 8-inch cutthroat and brook trout. It's only lightly fished. [T25N R26W S8]

NEMOTE CREEK. A brushy little stream with about 2 miles of fishing, in hay and pastureland, it's crossed by I-90, 2 miles northwest of the Tarkio turnoff. This seldom-fished creek has some good holes, which are fair in early season for 6- to 10-inch brook trout and some rainbow trout. Most of the fishable water, down low, is on private land. The upper reaches, including the South Fork, are generally too small to be bothered with, except for the occasional hole. [T15N R25W S16]

NINEMILE CREEK. A fair-size, easily wadable stream in open hay and pastureland, followed by county roads from its mouth, near US 10 (25 miles west of Missoula), upstream for about 25 miles of fishing water. Ninemile used to be an excellent cutthroat stream, but logging, dredging, and irrigation operations have hurt it badly. Much of the land is private, and access is very limited. It is now mostly an early-season stream that is good for nice-size rainbow, cutthroat trout, and whitefish that migrate up from the Clark Fork. [T15N R22W S28]

NORTH CACHE LAKE. In Mineral County, at a 6,500-foot elevation, this lake is 13.1 acres and 74 feet deep, ½ mile west of the Cache Creek trail. Last planted in 1993, it should offer good fishing for hungry cutts to 13 inches or so. [T11N R25W S8]

NORTH FORK FISH CREEK. See Fish Creek, North Fork.

NORTH FORK LITTLE JOE CREEK. See under Little Joe Creek.

NORTH FORK LITTLE THOMPSON RIVER. See Little Thompson River, North Fork.

NORTH FORK TROUT CREEK. See under Trout Creek.

NOXON RAPIDS RESERVOIR. A large reservoir on the Clark Fork, about ½ mile wide at its maximum by 38 miles long, it is accessible along both sides by good roads, and there are several recreation, picnic, and camping areas. Noxon is fished mostly by boat, though other boating activities would be more consistently enjoyable and productive. You can catch most any species of fish known to Montanans here, the most likely being perch, pumpkinseeds, and brown trout—as well as the large- and smallmouth bass for which the reservoir becomes better known each year. There are smaller populations of rainbow, cutthroat, pike, whitefish, and bull trout, plus a full complement of trash fish. The only stretch much worth fishing is the tailwater section, below Thompson Falls Dam. It helps to know the water here. Check current regulations for special limits on bass in the early season. [T26N R32W S4]

Gorge on Oregon Creek. —Courtesy U.S. Forest Service

OREGON GULCH. This stream flows for 11 miles from Oregon Lakes to Cedar Creek. The upper and lower sections are reached by the Cedar Creek and Lost Creek roads, the middle stretches by foot trail only. It is moderately popular, and fair fishing for 7- to 8-inch cutthroat, plus a very few rainbow trout. The lower 5 miles are on private property, so ask permission. [T16N R27W S14]

OREGON LAKES. Three moderately popular, deep cirque lakes in high (but heavily timbered) country, at the head of Oregon Gulch. Lower Oregon Lake is 3 acres in size and accessible by ½ mile of steep trail going south from the Cedar Creek road. Middle Oregon, 27 acres, is accessible by trail ½ mile beyond the lower lake. Upper Oregon Lake is 11 acres in area and about 40 feet deep, lying ½ mile up the drainage from Middle Oregon. However, it is most easily reached by a 300-yard hike from the Idaho state line trail. All three lakes are spotty, but offer some good fishing for 6- to 10-inch brook trout. [T15N R28W S13]

OUTLAW LAKE. It's reached by a cross-country hike a mile or so north from the end of the Eddy Mountain road, or you could choose to bush-whack up Outlaw Creek from the Clark Fork, about 10 miles east of

Thompson Falls. Planted with cutthroat every three or four years, it is good fishing for those with desire and a good topo map. [T21N R28W S28]

PACKER CREEK. It flows right through Saltese and is followed by logging roads for 2½ miles of fair fishing, in brushy alder-choked country, for pan-size cutthroat. Not much worth the bother, and neither are its forks. [T19N R31W S14]

PEAR LAKE. This one is snug up against the Idaho border in the Prospect Creek drainage, 17 miles west of Thompson Falls. Take USFS trail 404, from the end of the Prospect Creek road, past the first of the Blossom Lakes, then another ¾ mile to Pear Lake. They have recently begun stocking cutthroat here every four years, so it should provide some good fishing now. It certainly doesn't get much pressure. [T21N R32W S31]

PEARL LAKE. A 14-acre alpine lake in the old 1910 burn, it is reached by a 3-mile hike south from the trailhead on Trout Creek road, past Heart Lake and on to Pearl Lake. Pearl was last planted in 1979 with cutthroat, which seem to have developed a self-sustaining population. It is good fishing for 8- to 12-inchers and the occasional old-timer. [T14N R27W S25]

PETTY CREEK. An open ranchland stream, it is reached near headwaters via the Graves Creek road from Lolo Creek, then followed by a county road for 12 miles from its headwaters to its mouth on the Clark Fork, 1 mile east and across the river from Alberton. The upper reaches have lots of nice water; the lower end sinks in summer. It is heavily fished in the early season, good for 6- to 9-inch cutthroat, brook, and whitefish, plus a few rainbow trout. Petty Creek is experiencing major subdivision activity right now, and access has been severely restricted in recent years. [T14N R23W S12]

PETTY CREEK, East Fork. This fork is crossed at the mouth by the Petty Creek road (either from Alberton or the Lolo drainage) and followed by a logging road for about 2 miles. The East Fork is easy to miss and not many people hit it—so it's pretty fair fishing for pan-size cutthroat trout. [T13N R22W S30]

PILCHER CREEK. This small (3 miles), steep tributary of Rattlesnake Creek has been closed to fishing for many years, as it is utilized for the Missoula municipal water supply. [T14N R18W S20]

PILGRIM CREEK. It's followed upstream from its mouth, near Noxon, by a good gravel road for 6 miles, through hay and pastureland, to the junction of its South and West forks. A moderately popular creek, it's good fishing for 8- to 10-inch rainbow, cutthroat, brook, and brown trout. Some brown trout spawners can be found in the fall. Pilgrim flows mostly through private land. [T26N R32W S19]

POACHER LAKE. You don't have to be one to fish it, but you do have to hike cross-country a ways to get there. Unnamed on most maps, it sits at the head of Poacher Gulch, 2½ miles west of the Eddy Creek road, a couple of miles south of Montana 200. Or you could head up to Eddy Mountain from the Cherry Creek side, hit USFS trail 1130, and drop in from the west. It's 8½ acres in size by 34 feet maximum in depth; planted periodically with cutthroat, it's good fishing indeed for 10- to 12-inchers. Planting records indicate that Tuffys Lake, ½ mile to the north, may have been accidentally planted with cutts intended for Poacher, but nobody at Fish, Wildlife and Parks seems to know. It might be worth an investigation. [T20N R28W S10]

PROSPECT CREEK. A fair-size stream, it is 21 miles long, mostly in timbered country, and it's followed by a good gravel road from headwaters to the Clark Fork, opposite Thompson Falls. The entire stream is fair fishing for 8- to 13-inch rainbow, cutthroat, and brook trout. Cutthroat become more numerous in the upper reaches, and brown trout are found in the lower reaches. Whitefish and bull trout also live here. It is a popular stream for Thompson Falls folk, especially the first few miles. Angling is closed within a 100-yard radius of the stream mouth, unless otherwise posted, from June 1 through August 30. [T21N R29W S7]

QUARTZ CREEK. A small stream, crossed at the mouth by a county road along the south side of the Clark Fork, 1 mile west of Tarkio, it's followed upstream by a logging road through about 5 miles of steep mining country. Quartz Creek has been polluted by mining, but it's fair fishing along the lower 3½ miles for small resident rainbow and a few large springtime spawners from the main river. [T15N R25W S27]

RAINY CREEK. Quite a small stream (about 2 miles of fishing) in fairly open country, south of Lookout Pass, it is reached at the mouth by I-90, 4½ miles west of Saltese, then followed past headwaters by a logging road. It is lightly fished and only poor to fair in early season for small rainbow, brook trout, and an occasional whitefish. [T19N R31W S7]

RANDOLPH CREEK. A small, brushy stream, it's crossed at the mouth by I-90, 4 miles west of Saltese (see Dominion Creek). It is seldom fished, but it's fair for a few miles above the road for pan-size cutthroat and brook trout, and a few whitefish. [T19W R31W S7]

RATTLESNAKE CREEK. Part of the city of Missoula's municipal water supply, Rattlesnake Creek is a clear mountain stream that flows to the Clark Fork at Missoula. It's followed by road and trail for 20 miles up a narrow, steep canyon to headwaters. It heads in as many as thirteen sub-alpine cirque lakes, some of which contain fish. The creek itself is closed for 7 miles or so, from the dam up to the mouth of Beeskove Creek. From there up, it is open year-round for catch-and-release fishing, with artificial lures only. This stretch offers good fishing, especially for the fly fisher, for 12- to 17-inch cutthroat and rainbow-cutthroat hybrids, and many smaller brook trout. The lower 3½ miles, up to the dam, are good for slightly smaller rainbow, brook, and cutthroat, with larger trout up from the river on spawning and feeding runs. Bull trout are present throughout. [T13N R19W S22]

RATTLESNAKE LAKES. See Big, Carters, Farmer's, Little, McKinley, Sheridan, and Worden lakes.

Rattlesnake Creek above Missoula.
—Courtesy U.S. Forest Service

Greenough Park in Missoula, showing Rattlesnake Creek.
—Courtesy U.S. Forest Service

RATTLESNAKE LAKE Number 3. This lake in the Rattlesnake Wilderness is unnamed on most maps and not easy to get to. It was last planted in 1978 with westslope cutts, which, if they are reproducing, should still be around in good numbers. Grab your map: See the lake about ½ mile southeast of Carter Lake? That's the one, and the best way to get there (unless you enjoy scaling nearly vertical walls) is a tiring bushwhack up the outlet stream from Rattlesnake Creek. Good luck, and let us know if there are still fish there! [T15N R18W S32]

ROCK CREEK. This little stream is crossed at the mouth by a road 2 miles east of, and across the Clark Fork from, Tarkio, and it's followed upstream by a logging road through steep mountains. It's seldom fished, but it's fair for 6- to 8-inch cutthroat trout for about 1½ miles, in early season, before the lower reaches go dry in summer. [T14N R25W S2]

ROCK CREEK. Crossed at the mouth by Montana 200, 1 mile north of the Noxon Dam, it's followed upstream by a logging road to the junction

138

of its East and West forks. Heavily fished for about 6 miles, it's good for 6- to 12-inch cutthroat and brook trout. Bull trout live here in good numbers as well. [T26N R32W S29]

ROCK CREEK, East Fork. This branch flows from Rock Lake for 1 mile down a barren valley, then 1½ miles through Rock Creek Meadows, and from there another 2½ miles through a narrow, timbered valley to the main stream. The East Fork is followed by a logging road up to the meadows, where it widens and meanders to form many nice pools, which are heavily fished for some of the best 6- to 10-inch cutthroat fishing in this part of the state. There is a gate shown on the map, about 1 mile south of the meadows, so it might pay to check with the Forest Service before heading up. [T26N R32W S1]

ROCK (or ROCK CREEK) LAKE. This lake, 42 acres and deep, in a barren, glaciated valley below Rock Peak, is reached by trail, 3 miles north of the gate on the East Fork of Rock Creek road. Rock Lake sustains

Fisherman on Rock Creek. —Courtesy U.S. Forest Service

a moderate amount of fishing pressure, for 12- to 14-inch cutthroat (some pushing 20 inches) that can be seen but are seldom caught. This lake is just inside the Cabinet Mountains Wilderness. [T27N R32W S31]

ROCK MEADOWS PONDS. These are considered to be part of Rock Meadows, on the East Fork of Rock Creek, though they sit nearly 2 miles off. There is no maintained trail. From the lower meadows (about 2 miles below Rock Lake), take the small tributary due south for 1½ miles to the first of a string of five ponds, each about ⅛ mile apart. They're all reported to be very good fishing for 6- to 10-inch cutthroat trout, but you will pay dearly for them (with your blood—once the hordes of ravenous mosquitoes find you). [T26N R31W S7]

RUDIE LAKE. Found ¾ mile south of Crystal Lake (on the contour, through timbered country), Rudie is reached cross-country, going east off USFS trail 269, a mile or so past Crystal. Rudie is about 12 feet at its deepest, 7 acres in area, and seldom fished, but it's excellent indeed for 6- to 9-inch brook trout. [T18N R30W S28]

ST. LOUIS CREEK. A tiny tributary of Ninemile creek, it is crossed at the mouth by the Ninemile road at Old Town, then followed upstream for about 1½ miles by old logging and mining roads. This is a moderately popular, early-season stream that is good fishing for 6- to 8-inch rainbow and cutthroat trout. [T17N R24W S18]

ST. PAUL LAKE. A deep, 14-acre lake in barren glaciated country (elevation 7,200 feet), it is reached by a USFS horse trail, 3 miles southeast from near the end of the East Fork Bull River road. St. Paul is in the Cabinet Mountains Wilderness. It has been planted periodically with cutthroat, and is good fishing for 12- to 14-inchers. [T27N R32W S24]

ST. REGIS LAKES. Two lakes (East and West) in high alpine country, they are accessible by trail at the end of a mining road, about a mile south of Lookout Pass and ½ mile west of I-90. West St. Regis is only 2 acres and is barren. East St. Regis is 7 acres and 44 feet deep in at least one spot, with some scattered timber around it. It offers fair to good fishing, though seldom does anyone bother, for 6- to 9-inch brook trout. [T19N R32W S12]

ST. REGIS RIVER. A fair-size but wadable, heavily fished stream, it's followed by I-90 for nearly 40 miles, through timbered mountains, from its headwaters below Lookout Pass to the Clark Fork at St. Regis. It is fair fishing for 6- to 12-inch cutthroat, rainbow, brown, and brook trout. You'll find a few bigger trout, but not many, due mainly to fishing pressure and habitat degradation. There are enough whitefish here to keep you busy as well. [T18N R27W S30]

SAVENAC CREEK. A brushy little stream that flows from timbered mountains to the St. Regis River, 2½ miles west of De Borgia. It is crossed at the mouth by I-90, then followed upstream by a (private) logging road for about 2 miles of good fishing. The upper reaches are followed by trail. Savenac contains mostly 4- to 10-inch cutthroat and brook trout, and it's a good kids' creek. [T19N R30W S26]

SAVENAC NURSERY POND. A 1-acre kids' pond on the north side of I-90 at Haugan. It has been periodically stocked with rainbow trout that never grow too large, but it can offer fun fishing for the youngsters. [T19N R30W S22]

SCHLEY LAKE. Unnamed on most maps, this deep, 2-acre lake lies just southeast of Schley Mountain, at the head of Montana Creek. It is best reached (if you can find it) by the Schley Mountain trail, way up at the end of Surveyors Creek road. Hike about a mile south, past the mountain, and dive down to the east with your topo map in hand. There are no official records of cutthroat plantings since 1941, though rumors fly that it is planted fairly regularly and can be very good fishing. When you get back let us know, or maybe we'll see you up there. [T12N R25W S8]

SEMEM CREEK. Not much of a creek, it is very brushy and seldom fished, although it contains a fair population of 6- to 8-inch cutthroat and rainbow trout. It is crossed at the mouth by the Thompson River road, 9 miles south of the Bend Guard Station, then followed by logging roads up through Plum Creek land. [T23N R27W S1]

SHERIDAN LAKE. A shallow, 20-acre, dammed Rattlesnake Wilderness lake, with about 10 feet of water-level fluctuation, it's in timber all around but with mostly open shoreline. Sheridan lies ¼ mile east of, and 250 feet down the outlet from, Big Lake. At last report, it had lots of little 8- to 10-inch rainbow trout in it, just right for the skillet. [T15N R18W S20]

SHRODER CREEK. A little tributary of the Thompson River, 3 miles north of the Bend Guard Station, Shroder is accessible by road for about 2 miles of fair fishing in a narrow, rocky gorge, and it's lightly fished for 6- to 8-inch cutthroat and rainbow trout. [T25N R26W S18]

SIAMESE LAKES. Lower Siamese is real deep, 35 acres in area, with cliffs along its upper side in timbered alpine country. It is a steep ½-mile hike west to Upper Siamese, which is 28 acres and deep. To reach them, take a 10-mile trek west up Straight Creek (USFS trail 99), from the Clearwater Crossing at the end of the West Fork of Fish Creek road. Both lakes are popular with the dudes, and they're fair to excellent at times for 9- to 15-inch rainbow and 7- to 14-inch cutthroat trout. [T13N R26W S29]

SILVER CREEK. This small stream drains Silver Lake down into the St. Regis River at Saltese. It is followed its entire length by a road of sorts, and it's fair fishing for 6- to 10-inch cutthroat and brook trout. [T19N R31W S14]

SILVER LAKE. A high alpine lake in the old 1910 burn, just east of the Idaho line, it is reached by a very steep jeep road, going 7 miles south from Saltese. The lake is 17½ acres in area, and it's deep but with mostly shallow drop-offs, bordered by rocks at the upper end, timber and willow elsewhere. There is an unofficial campground at the lower end. It is moderately popular and good fishing for mostly 5- to 10-inch brook trout. There may be a brown trout or two lurking in the depths as well. [T19N R31W S32]

SILVEX LAKE. See Copper Lake.

SIMS LAKE. See Elk Lake.

SIXMILE CREEK. A small, open ranchland creek, crossed at the mouth by I-90, 6 miles west of Frenchtown, then followed upstream by county roads. It's fair kids' fishing for mostly small brook trout, plus a few cutthroat and rainbow trout up from the Clark Fork. It flows through mostly private land. [T15N R22W S27]

SLIMMER CREEK. Four miles long, with two lakes and some beaver ponds in the upper reaches, it is crossed at the mouth by US 2 at Logan Park, then followed to headwaters by logging roads. It is fair fishing for small brook and cutthroat trout. [T26N R27W S10]

SNOWSHOE LAKE. See Lowell Lake.

SOUTH BRANCH WEST FORK TROUT CREEK. See under Trout Creek.

SOUTH FORK FISH CREEK. See Fish Creek, South Fork.

SOUTH FORK LITTLE JOE CREEK. See under Little Joe Creek.

SOUTH FORK MARTEN CREEK. See under Marten Creek.

SOUTH FORK NEMOTE CREEK. See under Nemote Creek.

SOUTH FORK TROUT CREEK. See under Trout Creek.

SQUARE LAKE. This is a 12-acre alpine lake in timber a mile southeast of Hazel Lake, beneath Ward Peak. To reach this one take Little Joe Creek road southwest from St. Regis to the State Line road, then north about 4 miles to the trailhead (just past USFS trail 262) and downhill to the north ¼ mile or so to the lake. There's a parking spot at the takeoff point and you won't have much company once you've arrived. Fishing is pretty good for brook trout and a few cutthroat hanging on from old plantings. [T17N R30W S1]

STONY LAKE. This 8½-acre lake is no more than 7 feet deep (but it doesn't freeze out, thanks to some springs), in timbered, windfall country. It is reached by road, about 7 miles north along the West Fork of Fishtrap Creek from the main stem. The last 4 miles of the road are closed to motorized vehicles from April 1 through June 15. Stony is mostly open around the shore, moderately popular, and good fishing for 8- to 12-inch cutthroat trout. [T23N R29W S1]

STRAIGHT CREEK. A really nice stream to fish, with about 5 miles of good water in the old 1910 burn. It is followed by a trail all the way, from its mouth on the North Fork of Fish Creek, just above the Clearwater Crossing, to some big falls at the head of the fishing water. Not many people come here, but the fishing is good for 7- to 9-inch rainbow, cutthroat, and maybe a few brook trout. There are no lunkers 'tis true, but this one you ought to hit. [T13N R25W S6]

STRAIGHT (or STRAIGHT PEAK) LAKE. In the Bitterroot Range, it's 7½ acres in area and 50 feet deep. You can get there hiking ½ mile east off the state line trail near Straight Creek, or go 9 miles west on the USFS trail along Straight Creek from the Clearwater Crossing—the last 2½ miles to the lake have no trail. Straight Lake was last planted with cutts in 1993, and it provides good fishing for 8- to 14-inchers. [T13N R26W S30]

SURVEYOR CREEK. It drains Surveyor Lake, for 4 miles through timbered country, to the South Fork of Fish Creek. The entire creek is accessible by a logging road, traveling west from the Fish Creek road, and it's fair fishing for 6- to 10-inch cutthroat, brook, and rainbow trout. [T13N R24W S31]

SURVEYOR LAKE. It is reached to within ½ mile by the Surveyor Creek road, and then it's an easy trail on in. It covers 18 acres and is about 50 feet at the deepest, offering fair fishing for 6- to 11-inch rainbow trout. [T12N R25W S4]

SWAMP CREEK. This creek drains Wanless Lake in the Cabinet Mountains Wilderness, flowing for 13 miles south and west into Noxon Reservoir, midway between the towns of Trout Creek and Noxon. The lower 4½ miles of stream flow through private land, offering limited access for fishing. On the other hand, the upper reaches are plenty easy to access

Surveyor Lake.
—Courtesy U.S.
Forest Service

from the Forest Service trail that follows the creek from the National Forest boundary, into the wilderness, and on up to Buck Lake, just downstream from Wanless Lake. Brookies are likely to be the catch of the day here, and you might hook into some little cutts as well. [T25N R32W S14]

SWAMP CREEK. About 7 miles of fishing water, in pasture and scattered timberland. It is easily accessible all the way, by a road about 10 miles northwest of, and across the river from, Plains. It's a heavily fished, early-season creek for most anything that swims in the Clark Fork, mostly 6- to 10-inch cutthroat, rainbow, and a few 12- and 16-inch brown trout in the fall. The West Fork is basically too small to worry about. [T20N R27W S3]

SYLVAN LAKE. Take the Vermilion River road east from Montana 200 for 20 miles to USFS road 154 at Happy Gulch, then follow the road north up the gulch to within ¾ mile east of this very shallow 6-acre lake, which occupies a cirque high on the southern slopes of Sliderock Mountain. You might want your topo map to be sure where you're going. It is reported to be fair fishing for brook and cutthroat trout. [T25N R29W S24]

TADPOLE LAKE. It's unnamed on most maps, tucked up next to the Idaho border, 5 miles south of Saltese. The easiest way in is off the state line road on USFS trail 255. The lake will be ¼ mile to the east, about ½ mile from the trailhead. It was last planted in 1993, with westslope cutthroat. [T18N R31W S4]

TAMARACK CREEK. It is about 3 miles north of St. Regis (at the mouth) by paved road (Montana 135), and then you can drive on up it for 7 miles through some open but mostly timbered land. It pretty well dries up in the lower (open) reaches, but is fair fishing above for pan-size cutthroat, brook, and rainbow trout. [T18N R27W S9]

TERRACE (or BIG TERRACE) LAKE. This lake is only 16 acres but has a 160-foot maximum depth with mostly shallow drop-offs and lots of drowned logs, and cliffs at the upper end. The West Fork Fishtrap Creek road will get you within ¾ mile of the lake (except between April 1 and June 15, when the last 3 miles of the road are closed to motorized vehicles). Then it's cross-country west up the drainage to the lake. Terrace Lake is planted with cutthroat every four years and is good fishing for 10- to 14-inchers. [T23N R29W S12]

THOMPSON CREEK. A small stream, it is reached at the mouth, 1½ miles west of Superior, and for 3 miles upstream by road. A trail takes you up toward headwaters, though it wanders from the stream a bit. No matter, since there are only about 4 miles of fishing, which is fairly good for the first mile above the end of the road (brushy here), but poor below, for small cutthroat. A kids' creek. [T17N R26W S28]

THOMPSON LAKES. See Upper, Middle, and Lower Thompson Lakes.

THOMPSON RIVER. A good-size stream flowing south from Lower Thompson Lake for 50 miles, through a wide range of open meadow and timber, private and National Forest land, to the Clark Fork, 7 miles east of Thompson Falls. It is easily accessible all the way by public and private roads, and it can be floated for almost its entire length. This is a moderately popular river that is generally good fishing for mostly 8- to 12-inch brook, rainbow, and cutthroat trout in the upper reaches. Down lower, you'll find mostly rainbow, up to 20 inches, and whitefish. Just above the Clark Fork, you could run into some browns up from the river, as well as rainbow and whitefish. Bull trout are present throughout the river. Some of the trout here may surprise you with their size. Thompson has an extended season for whitefish—check current regulations. [T21N R28W S18]

THOMPSON RIVER, West Fork. A nice-size, open stream that is easily accessible by road, for about 6 miles of fishing. It is heavily fished, fair to

Looking northwest up the Thompson River. —Courtesy U.S. Forest Service

good for small cutthroat, rainbow, and brook trout. Bull trout use this stream as well. [T22N R28W S22]

TORINO CREEK. A small headwater tributary of Dry Creek, it drains Diamond and Cliff Lakes; it is accessible by road for 1 mile of poor to fair fishing (from the mouth to the big falls). Torino contains mostly 6- to 8-inch brook, and a few cutthroat and rainbow, trout. [T16N R28W S3]

TRAIL LAKE. Nineteen feet deep at the most, 11½ acres, Trail Lake sits in a timbered pocket reached by USFS trail 156, 2 miles from the end of the Trail Creek road on the headwaters of Trout Creek. The lake was planted years ago and is now fair fishing, but spotty, for 6- to 13-inch brook trout. [T14N R27W S5]

TRIANGLE POND. Drive 3 miles northwest from Noxon, along the south side of Noxon Rapids Reservoir, to this 7½-acre, maximum 32-foot deep, triangular flooded borrow pit along the road. It is planted annually with rainbow trout of all sizes, and it provides some good fishing for these, up to 22 inches or so. There is a picnic area here, so you might as well take the kids and hook them up with some nice trout. See current regulations for special limits on trout. [T26N R33W S9]

TRIO LAKES. Three seldom visited alpine lakes, about ¼ mile apart, in the old 1910 burn. The easiest way in is by the Trout Creek road (from the Clark Fork, 5 miles east of Superior) to the South Fork, then take a trail for 3 miles to the state line, then south for 3 miles, and finally a short, steep cross-country hike east to the lakes. Upper Trio is about 5 acres in size and fair fishing for 6- to 10-inch brook trout. Middle Trio is only 3 acres, but fairly deep, and it's fair to good fishing for 7- to 10-inch brook trout and 6- to 14-inch rainbow. Lower Trio, about 14 acres, offers fair fishing for 9- to 18- inch rainbow and 12- to 14-inch cutthroat trout. [T14N R26W S31]

TROUT CREEK. A heavily fished stream flowing through a brushy canyon to the Noxon Reservoir, a mile west of the town of Trout Creek. It's accessible by a logging road for 6 miles, to the junction of the East and West forks. Trout Creek is easily fished for fair catches of 8- to 12-inch rainbow and cutthroat trout, and brook trout in some beaver ponds about 3 miles above the mouth. The first 4 miles or so flow through private land. Each of the forks, East and West (including the South Branch of the West Fork), are followed by trails, offering fair to good fishing for small cutthroat and brook trout. [T24N R31W S18]

TROUT CREEK. A fair-size stream, with 15 miles of heavily fished water in a timbered canyon. It is followed by a good road from its mouth on the Clark Fork River, 5 miles southeast of Superior, to some nice falls 9 miles upstream, and for another 6 miles to the confluence of the North and South forks. There's a steep canyon directly below the falls that is always good fishing, though difficult to work, for 9- to 12-inch cutthroat, rainbow, and whitefish. Above the falls, it is mostly good fishing too, for 8- to 10-inch cutthroat. Bull trout will come upstream from the river to the falls. [T16N R26W S13]

TROUT CREEK, North Fork. Here is a small, seldom fished stream, in heavily timbered country, at the headwaters of Trout Creek. It is crossed by a logging road, but access is basically on foot, for 2 miles of fair fishing for pan-size cutthroat trout. [T14N R27W S3]

TROUT CREEK, South Fork. This fork is followed by the Trout Creek road for 2 miles, then for another 2 miles by USFS trail 171, up to Heart Lake. A nice open stream in high, timbered country, it's moderately popular for fair catches of small native cutthroat trout. [T14N R27W S3]

Upper Trout Creek below Hoodoo Meadows. —Courtesy U.S. Forest Service

TWELVEMILE CREEK. About 12 miles long, with 11 miles of fishing water, in a narrow canyon that is easily accessible all the way by a logging road, it is crossed at the mouth by I-90, a dozen miles west of St. Regis. Twelvemile is moderately popular and fair to good fishing for 8- to 10-inch brook trout and cutthroat, plus an occasional rainbow, brown trout, or whitefish. The lower reaches are perhaps overfished; the upper reaches are better. [T18N R27W S4]

TWELVEMILE CREEK, East Fork. This is a tiny stream, crossed at the mouth by the Twelvemile road, then followed by Old Mullan Road, for about 3 miles of slow fishing for small cutthroat. [T19N R29W S35]

TWENTYFOUR MILE CREEK. A tiny, headwater tributary of Prospect Creek, in steep, timbered country, it is crossed at the mouth by the Prospect road and followed upstream by a USFS trail, for 2 miles of fair fishing. It contains 6- to 8-inch cutthroat trout that don't often see a hook. [T21N R32W S13]

TWIN LAKES. Two 4-acre potholes (the upper one deep, the lower fairly shallow) about 200 yards apart, in timbered country 6 miles north of the Bend Historic Ranger Station, near Happy's Inn. Reached by the Twin

Lakes Creek logging road, both lakes are decent fishing for 10- to 16-inch rainbow trout, which are planted every two years or so. [T26N R27W S27]

TWIN LAKES. These two lakes are found in the northern shadow of Stuart Peak, on the southern edge of the Rattlesnake Wilderness near Missoula. They look really good for fishing, but they are barren. We thought you might like to know. [T15N R18W S31]

TWOMILE CREEK. A small, fair to good fishing stream in mostly timbered country, it is accessible by road from the mouth (across the river from I-90, 4 miles west of St. Regis) and upstream, for 6 miles of fishing water. There are some open-meadow beaver ponds (including Buford Pond) a couple of miles above the mouth. Twomile contains mostly 8- to 10- inch cutthroat and brook trout. [T18N R28W S28]

UNNAMED LAKE AT HEAD OF CATARACT GULCH. A tiny (maybe an acre) pothole in timber at the head of (barren) Cataract Gulch, which drains for 1 mile to Missoula Gulch, ½ mile above the mouth of Bonanza Gulch. We've never been there, but a fellow we know said he saw baby submarines erupting from the surface. They couldn't have been too big or the lake wouldn't have floated 'em. [T15N R28W S10]

UNNAMED LAKE NEAR OREGON PEAK. A 1-acre pothole in timber 1½ miles north and a little east of Oregon Peak. To get there, take the Cedar Creek road, as though you were going to Missoula Lake, until you hit Oregon Gulch. Now follow along the gulch (still on the road) north for about ¼ mile, until you cross a little tributary coming in from the southwest. This is it. Follow it up for maybe 500 yards and you are there. Someone wrote several years ago and said he saw fish rising from the surface while he was flying over in a Cessna 180. Why don't you try it—and let us know? [T15N R28W S11]

UPPER MCGREGOR LAKE. See Little McGregor Lake.

UPPER THOMPSON LAKE. Almost a continuation of the Middle and Lower Thompson lakes, it lies in flat, timbered country on the divide between the Thompson and Fisher river drainages. Upper Thompson is followed along the north shore by US 2, about 35 miles west of Kalispell. It covers about 232 acres and has a maximum depth of about 100 feet (though most of it is about 10 feet). Pike, pumpkinseeds, and yellow perch dominate this lake. There is a good largemouth bass fishery here, which is declining as the pike population rises. Trout don't do so well here, especially small ones, so lately a few hundred brood-stock rainbow and more in the 8-inch range have been planted, offering limited opportunities for trophy trout. There are loads of trash fish here as well. Check current regulations for special limits on bass and trout. [T27N R27W S30]

UPPER WANLESS (or CIRQUE) LAKES. Take the McKay Creek road from its mouth on Montana 200, near the northern end of Noxon Reservoir, north for 5 miles to the end, then take the Wanless Lake trail 6 miles on to Upper Wanless (or Cirque) Lake number 1. Number 2 is about 1 mile below, and numbers 3 and 4 are about ½ mile apart, another mile or so down the trail, in a steep, partly timbered glacial canyon. Number 1 covers about 3 acres. All are deep enough to support fish. Numbers 1, 2, and 3 are good fishing, indeed, for 8- to 14-inch cutthroat and number 4 is fair fishing for 6- to 14-inch cutthroat. Quite a few folks stop at number 3 on their way in to Wanless. [T26N R31W S16]

VERMILION RIVER. This is a fair-size stream that heads below Vermilion Peak and forms a 25-mile half circle on its way to Noxon Reservoir, near Trout Creek. The uppermost stretches are in high open country, while most of the river flows through a narrow timbered valley. About 11 miles up, you'll find Vermilion Falls, which divides the river into two distinct sections. Below, it is slow fishing for a mix of small trout and whitefish. Occasionally some bigger fish will come up from the reservoir, but more often than not these are trash fish. Above, fishing picks up quite a bit, for cutthroat and brook trout, in some pretty appealing water. [T24N R31W S14]

WANLESS LAKE. This lake, 120 acres in area and 165 feet deep, lies in a big cirque, at the head of a barren glaciated valley, that is drained by Swamp Creek. You get there by good trail 1 mile east of Upper Wanless, or take the Swamp Creek trail (which goes north from Noxon reservoir) pretty much all the way to the lake. This lake is heavily fished for 6- to 16-inch Yellowstone and westslope cutthroat, and it's also being turned into a garbage dump by careless sportsmen, making it seem not so much a wilderness lake. [T26N R31W S15]

WARD CREEK. A small tributary of the St. Regis River, 6 miles west of town. It is followed upstream for 7 miles, through a narrow canyon, by a logging road, and then for 2 miles by a beautiful trail, through towering white pine and huge cedar trees (if they haven't been chopped down by now), to some falls at the head of the fishing water. Ward Creek is moderately popular, and it's good fishing for 8- to 11-inch cutthroat and brook trout. Bull trout are found throughout this stream. [T18N R29W S24]

WARD LAKE. See Hazel Lake.

Wanless Lake.
—Courtesy U.S.
Forest Service

WEEKSVILLE CREEK. A small stream that flows south down its timbered canyon to the Clark Fork at Weeksville. It is crossed at the mouth by Montana 200, 8 miles west of Plains. There are about 1½ miles of fishing water, which are accessible by road, seldom fished, and average at best 6- to 10-inch brook trout. [T20N R27W S2]

WEST CEDAR LAKE. See under Cedar Log Lakes.

WEST FORK BIG CREEK. See under Big Creek.

WEST FORK BLUE CREEK. See under Blue Creek.

WEST FORK FISH CREEK. See Fish Creek, West Fork.

WEST FORK FISHTRAP CREEK. See Fishtrap Creek, West Fork.

WEST FORK SWAMP CREEK. See under Swamp Creek.

WEST FORK THOMPSON RIVER. See Thompson River, West Fork.

WEST FORK TROUT CREEK. See under Trout Creek.

WHITE PINE CREEK. A small tributary of Beaver Creek, it is reached at the mouth by a county road a couple of miles west of White Pine. It's followed by a logging road (past some beaver ponds about 4 miles upstream) for a total of 12 miles, to headwaters, in logged-over country.

This one is fairly good fishing, hit hard for 7- to 8-inch cutthroat above the ponds and 8- to 10-inch brook trout below. The best fishing is on private land. [T23N R31W S13]

WILLOW CREEK. Another small stream with only about 2½ miles of fishing water, in a big beaver-dammed flat on the upper reaches of the Vermilion River. Easily accessible by road, it's heavily fished for plentiful small cutthroat and brook trout. [T24N R29W S4]

WORDEN LAKE. Tucked back in the Rattlesnake Wilderness, Worden has a good 750-foot high, bare rocky cliff at the upper end, a dam at the lower end, and trees all around. It covers 10½ acres with mostly shallow drop-offs and a maximum depth of 19 feet. To get there, either head 3 miles or so southwest up the Lake Creek trail from the end of the Rattle-snake Creek road (closed year-round to motorized vehicles), or drop into the Lake Creek Basin on the trail that heads north from Stuart Peak—all told, a 12-mile hike from the Sawmill Gulch trailhead. Worden has been a fair producer of pan-size cutthroat trout, but it was last planted in 1978, so it's a bit questionable. [T15N R18W S30]

WRANGLE CREEK. This is a headwaters tributary of Rattlesnake Creek, draining Sanders Lake (among others) and flowing for about 4 miles. It is an excellent stream, with westslope and Yellowstone cutts, brookies, rainbow, and rainbow-cutthroat hybrids all common. It is also an impor-tant bull trout stream. It's catch-and-release fishing, with artificial lures only, on Wrangle (and all the upper Rattlesnake streams). [T15N R18W S21]

ALBICAULIS LAKE. A high (elevation about 7,950 feet) cirque lake, 17 acres in area, 57 feet deep, and dammed at the outlet, it has as much as 14 feet of seasonal water-level fluctuation and lots of submerged timber around the shores. Pick up USFS road 169, heading west from I-90 at the Racetrack exit, taking it to the Racetrack Creek campground. Continue up the Racetrack Creek drainage 6 miles past the campground, on a progressively poorer jeep road, and then go 2 miles further in timbered country up the North Fork of Racetrack Creek to the lake. This is real good water for 8- to 12-inch rainbow trout that are stocked here regularly, as well as some rainbow-cutthroat hybrids. [T7N R12W S26]

ALDER CREEK. About 8 miles long, with 500 feet of drop per mile, in steep, heavily timbered mountains, Alder Creek debouches to Rock Creek on the side opposite the Rock Creek road. It is reached by a private bridge across Rock Creek, then followed upstream to the headwaters by a good USFS trail. This stream is really "liquid ice"; it has innumerable good holes overflowing with zillions of 4- to 7-inch cutthroat, and it's easily but, because of the size of the fish and inaccessibility of the stream, seldom fished—except a little right around the mouth, for rainbow spawners up from Rock Creek. Bull trout spawners use this stream, too. [T8N R17W S6]

ALPINE LAKE. It's 22 acres, dammed at the outlet, with 29 feet of water-level fluctuation and lots of water-killed timber around the margins. Alpine is a clear subalpine lake, at 7,850 feet in elevation, just north of Racetrack Creek. The shoreline is about a third talus and boulders. It is reached via a poor jeep road ½ mile northeast of Albicaulis Lake. It is planted regularly with rainbow, last in 1996. It's good fishing for rainbows in the 12- to 16-inch range. [T7N R12W S25]

ALTOONA LAKES. Big (or North) and Little (or South) Altoona cover about 3 acres and 1 acre respectively, both 15 feet at the deepest. These lakes lie about ⅛ mile apart, in mining country at the head of the Royal Creek drainage. To reach them, continue south on a pickup road off the Boulder Creek road. Big Altoona is mostly steep offshore, except for a shallow shelf on the northeast side, and it's good fishing at best (not so hot at times) for 8- to 13-inch cutthroat up to 1 pound. Little Altoona is reached by a trail directly south from Big Altoona, and it also contains cutthroat trout. [T8N R12W S34]

AMC SETTLING PONDS. See Anaconda Settling Ponds.

AMERICAN GULCH. A small gulch, through which flows an equally small stream, which is paralleled by a good gravel road for about 3 miles from its junction with Brown's Gulch. It is poor fishing in occasional beaver dams for small resident cutthroat trout. [T5N R8W S35]

ANACONDA (or AMC) SETTLING PONDS. A series of several ponds constructed along Silver Bow Creek to keep toxic sediments from washing downstream to the Clark Fork River. Take the Warm Springs exit off I-90 and head a short distance east. The ponds lie in a wildlife-management area upstream from Warm Springs Bridge. They are catch-and-release fishing only, and other regulations apply, so check into the legalities before you fish here. The place is low on aesthetics, but high on the big-trout scale—one of the ponds is named Hog Hole, and not because of any pig farms in the neighborhood. Pond number 3 is stocked yearly with rainbow. [T5N R9W S31]

ANTELOPE CREEK. This stream is followed by rough gravel road and trail along most of its length, all on private land. It flows into Rock Creek 45 river miles south of I-90. The lower 1½ miles flow through open, but private, land, and there's fair fishing for 6- to 8-inch cutthroat. [T6N R15W S17]

B&B FISHPOND (or BISON CREEK RESERVOIR). Take I-15 north from Butte about 10 miles to exit 134. Head north for a couple of miles along the frontage road, and then east across the interstate another couple of miles to the reservoir, in the Elk Park meadowland. This is really two ponds that total about 10 acres and which are private, stocked with rainbow and brook trout, and reportedly excellent fishing. [T4N R7W S25]

BARKER LAKES. Two lakes—Big and Little, Upper and Lower, East and West, take your pick—high up near Mount Haggin. From a point about 8 miles west of Anaconda on Montana 1, head south up Barker Creek on 5 miles of rough jeep road, and then about a mile of trail to Little Barker, in a small, timbered cirque at 7,850 feet above sea level. It is about 10 acres, mostly less than 5 feet deep, but it has two small, deep holes about a fourth of the way out from the inlet, which are probably what keeps it from freezing out. Big Barker is a ½-mile hike and a 400-foot climb around and over the ridge southeast of Little Barker. It's a kidney-shaped lake, 11 acres in area and deep along the west shore, with steep drop-offs beneath steep, rocky cliffs, but shallow along the timbered west side. Both lakes are planted every couple of years with rainbow, last in 1996. They are good fishing for rainbow in the 10- to 16-inch range. [T4N R12W S17]

BASIN CREEK. It flows for 12 miles from the Basin Creek Reservoir to Blacktail Creek, within the city limits of Butte, and it's followed all the way by a county road. It is poor fishing for 5- to 7-inch brook trout. Basin Creek—including all reservoirs and tributaries—is closed to fishing from the lower Butte water-supply reservoir dam to headwaters. [T3N R7W S29]

BASIN CREEK RESERVOIRS. Two reservoirs, Upper and Lower, reached by an oiled road up Basin Creek, going 12 miles south from Butte. They provide the city water supply and are closed to fishing. [T1N R8W S12]

BEAR CREEK. It's crossed at the mouth by I-90 at Bearmouth, then followed upstream for 8 miles by a good gravel road. Back in the good old days, it was excellent fishing for native cutthroat, but it has since been extensively placer mined and is now virtually barren. [T11N R14W S14]

BEARMOUTH ACCESS POND. A small (1-plus-acre) borrow pit on the Clark Fork floodplain, just off I-90 northeast of Bearmouth, designed as a recreational pond after completion of the highway. You can get to it by hiking 100 feet or so from the rest stop. It was planted regularly with rainbow until 1985. The water is full of shrimp, so the fish that have survived the heavy fishing pressure can be on the large side. The pond is closed to motorized watercraft. [T11N R14W S15]

BEAVER CREEK. A small stream, flowing through swampy, beaver-dammed country to the West Fork of Rock Creek, about ¾ mile west of the West Fork Guard Station. There's some access to Beaver Creek by a logging road that is closed seasonally for elk calving. The stream is fair fishing in the ponds for 8- to 9-inch cutthroat and brook trout. [T6N R16W S35]

BEAVERTAIL (or BEAVERTAIL HILL) POND. This borrow pit from construction of I-90 lies right along the interstate, about 30 miles east of Missoula. It's accessed from the Bearmouth exit, and there's a public fishing access. It's stocked every year with rainbow, which get stiff competition from a growing population of stunted sunfish. There's some good bass fishing here, too. [T11N R16W S11]

BEEFSTRAIGHT CREEK. A very small tributary of German Gulch, crossed at the mouth by a gravel road 6 miles south of Fairmont Hot Springs. The road is open seasonally. Beefstraight is excellent fishing for small, 5- to 7-inch brook and cutthroat trout that thrive in its numerous falls and pools. [T3N R10W S26]

BIG ALTOONA LAKE. See under Altoona Lakes.

BIG BARKER LAKE. See under Barker Lakes.

BIG HOGBACK CREEK. See Hogback Creek.

BIG POZEGA (or DEEP) LAKE. A high (elevation 7,600 feet), 52-acre cirque lake in sparsely timbered, mountain goat country. Reach it by a good trail, 3 miles south from the Racetrack Creek road, or (if you are brave or foolish) you can drive on the rough road up Modesty Creek past the Thornton Creek drainage and continue west on to the lake. Pozega is over 100 feet deep in places and dammed, with water-level fluctuations of as much as 18 feet and lots of dead timber around the shores. The fishing pressure is heavy for fair catches of 5- to 22-inch rainbow and cutthroat trout, and rainbow-cutthroat hybrids. The hybrids especially run towards the big end of the scale. [T6N R12W S11]

BIG SPRING CREEK. A small stream flowing southward to Rock Creek, across from the road and just upstream from the Siria campground. There is about ½ mile of trail up this brushy creek, but it is seldom fished for the few small cutthroat it contains. [T8N R17W S27]

BIG THORNTON LAKE. See Thornton Lake.

BISON CREEK RESERVOIR. See B&B Fishpond.

BLACKTAIL CREEK. A small stream that flows for about 13 miles from Pipestone Pass to Butte, where it joins Silver Bow Creek at the headwaters of the Clark Fork. There's not much access, since the stream runs mostly through private land, and it is poor fishing anyway for a few small rainbow and brook trout. [T3N R8W S24]

BLUM CREEK. Take the Gold Creek road 5½ miles south from I-90 to the mouth of Blum Creek, near Lingenpelter. It is a very small stream that's crossed by gravel road in a couple of spots. Blum's not much to fish, but there is fair action for 8- to 12-inch trout in a few beaver ponds along the lower ½ mile. [T9N R11W S15]

BOHN LAKE. At about 7,100 feet in elevation, this 25-acre lake sits in a cirque in timbered country at the head of Dempsey Creek. It's dammed at the outlet, runs 15 feet deep at most, with steep drop-offs all around. Bohn Lake is reached by a jeep road heading west from the Montana State Prison Ranch near Deer Lodge, up Dempsey Creek 8½ miles above the Perkins ranch. It's good fishing for good-size cutthroat trout, if you know what you're doing. Bohn was last planted in 1990. [T7N R11W S34]

BOULDER CREEK. A small tributary of Flint Creek, crossed at the mouth by Montana 1 (the Pintlar Scenic Route), a mile south of Maxville, and followed by gravel road and trail 14 miles to headwaters. It is good fishing for 8- to 10-inch cutthroat trout, with browns and brookies in various stretches to add variety. [T8N R13W S4]

BOULDER CREEK, South. This stream flows north through steep, timbered country (the northern slopes of the Flint Creek Range) to Boulder Creek, 2 miles south of Maxville. It is reached at the mouth by the Boulder Creek road, followed upstream for 5 miles by a road, and then 2½ miles by a trail to Stewart Lake. This stream is easily accessible and good fishing for 9- to 12-inch cutthroat, rainbow, and brook trout. There are a few bull trout here as well. [T8N R13W S15]

BOULDER LAKES. Two lakes at the head of the Boulder Creek drainage, in an area closed to motorized vehicle use. You'll hike in on 3 miles of USFS trail from the Boulder Creek road, about 9 miles southeast from its junction with Montana 1 at Maxville. The trail heads southeast for about 1½ mile before branching off to the southwest for the last half of the hike. The lakes, in alpine country, are about 9 acres each and real deep. Small plants of westslope cutthroat trout were made in 1990 and 1994. Fishing is decent for cutts in the 8- to 10-inch range. [T7N R12W S20]

BOWLES CREEK. A small stream that rises in timber and flows eastward through meadowland for about 4 miles to the West Fork of Rock Creek. Bowles is followed by trail—closed to motorized vehicles—to headwaters near the crest of the Sapphire Mountains. The trail takes off to the east from the Forest Service road that heads south from Montana 38 to follow the West Fork of Rock Creek. Bowles Creek is good fishing in the lower reaches for 8- to 10-inch cutthroat trout. [T5N R17W S17]

BOWMAN LAKES. Three lakes in the Racetrack Creek drainage, each dammed at the outlet, at the end of the Bielenberg Canyon road (USFS road 5147), west of I-90 between Deer Lodge and Warm Springs. Taken together, the lakes cover an area of about 20 acres in high, sparsely timbered, rocky country. They are generally good, although sometimes temperamental, fishing for 8- to 13-inch cutthroat and rainbow-cutt hybrids. [T7N R11W S31]

BREWSTER CREEK. Take the Rock Creek road 9 miles south from I-90 to the mouth of this stream. It's followed upstream by gravel road for 6½ miles south, and 3,000 feet up, to headwaters near Sliderock Mountain. It is a small stream in timbered country, fairly good fishing for cutthroat, rainbow, cutt-rainbow hybrids, and brook trout to 9 inches—and it is very badly overfished. [T10N R16W S19]

BREWSTER CREEK, East Fork. A very small stream reached by a gravel road 5 miles up Brewster Creek, then followed by a jeep road and trail for about a mile above the mouth. This is a brushy stream in timbered country. It is seldom fished but contains a few pan-size cutthroat. [T10N R16W S23]

BROWN'S GULCH. It's reached at the mouth by I-90 near Silver Bow, a few miles west of Butte, and it's followed upstream for about 10 miles by good county roads. This stream flows mostly through private pastureland in its lower reaches (but you can usually get permission to fish if you ask), and it's the site of numerous beaver dams above. It is generally good fishing for pan-size cutthroat and brook trout. [T3N R9W S22]

BRYAN CREEK. It flows to Telegraph Creek about 10 miles south of Elliston, and it's followed for 1½ miles upstream by a county road. It is a small creek, about 3 miles long, mostly in timber but with a few meadows and some beaver ponds below. The fishing is excellent in the ponds for small cutthroat trout, but there is not enough water to stand much fishing pressure. [T9N R6W S10]

BURNS SLOUGH. A group of small sloughs totaling about 25 acres, they used to extend for 1½ miles along both sides of the railroad tracks east of Bearmouth. Years ago, they were partly filled in and reoriented by road construction, but they still offer excellent warm-water fishing for largemouth bass and rainbows, which are planted there every year. It is also real good duck-hunting country. [T11N R14W S12]

BUTTE CABIN CREEK. A small stream, flowing through a densely forested canyon for 6 miles to Rock Creek, upstream from the Harry's Flat campground, about 20 miles south of I-90. It's followed by a road for about a mile, and then by trail to headwaters, near Quigg Peak. There is much willow, alder, and brush along the banks, and it's tough fishing for little rainbows, cutts, and their hybrids. [T9N R17W S20]

CABLE CREEK. A small tributary of Warm Springs Creek, crossed at the mouth by US 1, a couple of miles east of Silver Lake. It's followed by a county road for 3 miles, through mining country, to headwaters. It is fair early-season fishing for pan-size rainbow, brook, and cutthroat. You might bump into a few bull trout, too. [T5N R13W S24]

CARPENTER CREEK. It is reached near the mouth by a county road 2 miles east of Avon. This is a very small stream that was dredged for gold in the 1930s, and it's poor to fair fishing in a small, 2-acre pond at its mouth for 8- to 10-inch brook and brown trout. The pond is on private land, with fishing by permission only. [T10N R8W S23]

CARPP CREEK. A beautiful little stream in the Anaconda-Pintlar Wilderness, flowing west for 7 miles, through timbered mountains, to the Middle Fork of Rock Creek. Carpp Creek is reached at the mouth by the Middle Fork road, about a mile south of Moose Lake, and it's followed by a trail to the headwaters. You can also hit the middle reaches via the

Carpp Creek.
—Courtesy U.S. Forest
Service

good East Fork of Rock Creek road to the Meadow Creek road. A trailhead there provides quick access. A few big bull trout spawn up this stream in the fall, and a few fingerling live in the upper reaches. Otherwise it is, oddly enough, barren for all practical purposes. [T3N R16W S1]

CARPP LAKES. There are three lakes—two in a high cirque (elevation 7,750 feet), and one up higher, near 8,300 feet. The lower lakes are reached by a fair trail, 3 miles south from the trailhead at the end of the Meadow Creek road, or 6 miles southeast from the Moose Lake trailhead. Lower Carpp Lake is a shallow alpine-meadow lake that covers about 15 acres. Carpp Lake—the middle one—is 25 acres and shallow. Upper Carpp is about 1½ miles past the middle lake, and it's smaller than the other two. These lakes are fast fishing for little cutts that never seem to get much bigger than 7 or 8 inches. Middle Carpp was planted with cutts in 1988. [T3N R15W S15]

CARUTHERS LAKE. A fairly deep, 22-acre lake, dammed at the outlet like all lakes in the Dempsey Basin. It's reached by a jeep road 3 miles west of Bohn Lake. It is reportedly good fishing for 6- to 9-inch cutthroat trout. [T7N R11W S29]

CINNABAR CREEK. Access the stream mouth from the Welcome Creek trail, about 3 miles west of the trailhead along Rock Creek. The upper reaches are accessible by driving north along the Bitterroot-Rock Creek divide from Ambrose Saddle, then heading east from Cinnabar Saddle for a couple of miles of rough road. Cinnabar is a very small, and obviously almost inaccessible, stream that flows through mountain meadows and timbered gulches to Welcome Creek. It is fair fishing for 6- to 8-inch cutthroat trout. [T9N R17W S4]

CLEAR CREEK. A tiny stream flowing through timbered country to Beefstraight Creek. There is no trail, and it is seldom fished because of its lack of accessibility, but it contains a fair number of 7- to 10-inch cutthroat trout. [T3N R10W S34]

CONLEY'S LAKE. Head west out of Deer Lodge past the Montana State Prison. Conley's Lake sits about 3 miles west of the prison, near the end of the road. It's about 3 acres and fairly shallow, bordered by brush and willow. It has been rehabilitated and stocked with rainbow trout, last in 1990. [T7N R10W S4]

COPPER CREEK. A small stream flowing northward for 4 miles from the Copper Creek Lakes to Boulder Creek, about 2 miles south of Princeton. It's followed by gravel road and a USFS trail to the headwaters. Brook trout are abundant in the upper reaches, and you'll catch some cutts. The lower reaches contain some small cutthroat, were once stocked with rainbow, and are good spawning and rearing habitat for bull trout. [T8N R12W S31]

COPPER CREEK. Originating in the Anaconda-Pintlar Wilderness west of Anaconda, Copper Creek flows northeastward to the Middle Fork of Rock Creek, about a mile north of Moose Lake. It's followed by good gravel road, and then by trail to the headwaters, near Bitterroot Pass. This is a mostly open stream, except for willow and brush along the middle reaches. It is heavily fished and reportedly good for 8- to 11-inch cutthroat. You might hook into a very occasional resident bull trout in the lower reaches, along with a brook trout or two. [T4N R16W S25]

COPPER CREEK LAKES. Three high lakes at elevations of about 7,250 feet. The upper lake (also called Crystal Lake) is the largest, measuring 14 acres. This lake was planted with rainbow in the 1940s, and with westslope cutthroat trout in 1977. It's reached by a good hikers' trail, ½ mile north of a jeep road that runs 4 miles east from Granite (which is west of Philipsburg). Or you can hike in about 3 miles from the Copper Creek road. The lower two lakes string out, ⅛ mile apart, down the drainage. The middle lake covers 4 acres, the lower lake 12 acres. All three of the Copper Creek lakes are real deep, but with gradual drop-offs all around, and have good gravel bottoms. All are excellent fishing for 6-

to 10-inch brook trout; number 3 also has lots of rainbow-cutthroat hybrids and a few of their progenitors. [T7N R13W S24]

COTTONWOOD CREEK. A pretty little stream, flowing to the Clark Fork River at Deer Lodge, then followed by county road and trail 12 miles to headwaters, near Electric Peak. It is mostly dewatered for irrigation in the summer, but the lower reaches—even right in town—are poor to fair fishing in the early season for brook, brown, and cutthroat trout. There are some small cutts upstream, as well. [T8N R9W S33]

COUGAR CREEK. It's about 25 miles south along Rock Creek to the mouth of Cougar Creek, on the east side. It's good fishing for pan-size (exceptionally to 10 inches) rainbow, rainbow-cutt hybrids, and brookies for a couple of miles up this little creek, in heavily timbered mountain country. It gets fished a fair amount in early spring, and not much thereafter. It's good spawning and rearing habitat for bull trout, but bull trout numbers are not high here. [T8N R17W S7]

CRAMER CREEK. A small tributary of the Clark Fork River, crossed at the mouth by I-90 between Beavertail Hill and Bonita. It's followed for 10 miles by good gravel road to the headwaters. The lower reaches are heavily fished for small cutthroat and brook trout. [T11N R16W S10]

CRAMER CREEK, West Fork. Take the Cramer Creek road 1½ miles north from I-90 to the mouth of the West Fork, then follow a dirt road for a short stretch, then a footpath, and finally cow trails for 3 miles to the headwaters. It's easily and heavily fished for good early-season catches of 8- to 10-inch cutthroat trout. [T12N R16W S35]

CREVICE CREEK. This stream flows eastward for 5 miles from Lone Tree Hill to Gold Creek near Lingenpelter. The lower reaches are followed by gravel road, and there's no road or trail access to the upper reaches. This is a small stream that is mostly overlooked by all save local fishermen, for whom it produces good catches of 6- to 8-inch trout. The lower reaches are on private land, so ask first if you decide to give small-stream fishing a try here. [T9N R11W S15]

CRYSTAL LAKE. See under Copper Creek Lakes.

DAVIS RESERVOIR. See Dog Lake.

DEAD (or DEAD MAN'S) LAKE. An alpine lake in a small cirque, about ¼ mile south of, and 100 feet lower than, Albicaulis Lake. At a 7,850-foot elevation, Dead Lake measures 8 acres, with a 27-foot maximum depth. Go ¼ mile across the spillway and down the unmaintained trail from Albicaulis Lake. Dead Lake is fair fishing for cutthroat trout that average around a foot or better and sometimes grow to a foot and a half in length. [T7N R12W S26]

DEEP CREEK. A little bitty stream, about 5 miles long, that flows to Bear Creek at "Old Bear Town," 7 miles upstream from Bearmouth, to I-90. In BIWP (Before It Was Placered) days, Bear Creek was an excellent trout stream, and Deep Creek still supports a few small cutthroat trout, but they're seldom fished for. [T12N R14W S9]

DEEP LAKE. See Big Pozega Lake.

DEMPSEY CREEK. It's about 17 miles long, from its headwaters in several high lakes to its mouth on the Clark Fork, 6 miles south of Deer Lodge. Dempsey Creek is followed by county and USFS roads (that grow rougher as you get farther upstream) along most of its length. The lower reaches are mostly dewatered for irrigation, only poor fishing for brook and brown trout, but the upper reaches, just below the lakes, are generally excellent for 7- to 8-inch cutts. [T7N R9W S33]

DOG (or SPOTTED DOG) CREEK. A small stream flowing northward for 14 miles to the Little Blackfoot River, just east of Elliston. The lower stretches flow through a narrow, rocky gorge and are followed by cattle trails. The upper 13 miles flow through open pasture and timberland, and they're followed and crossed by county and private roads, and (incidentally) by the old abandoned Fort Benton highway. This is a fair to poor fishing stream in the early season for small brook and cutthroat trout. In late season, it produces some fair-size browns and an occasional whitefish from its lower reaches—plus lots of suckers. [T9N R6W S6]

DOG LAKE (or DAVIS RESERVOIR). It's 11 acres and deep, with real black water and a 10-foot dam, but little or no drawdown, in open rangeland at the head of a deep gorge on Spotted Dog Creek. Dog Lake is reached by county and private roads, going 4 miles south from Avon. Dog Lake is lightly fished by local residents for 7- to 14-inch cutthroat, brook, and a few brown trout. Other denizens of this lake may include beaver and mink. [T9N R8W S15]

DOLUS LAKES. Four alpine cirque lakes, ranging in area from 3 to 14 acres. They lie about ¾ mile apart, and are between 7,800 and 8,000 feet in elevation, in an area closed to motorized vehicles (except snowmobiles). The lower and middle lakes on the main drainage are along a good trail, 3 miles west of Rock Creek Lake; they offer slow to fair fishing for 7- to 10-inch cutthroat and 9- to 16-inch brown trout, descended from a long-ago plant. The upper lake is fair fishing for 6- to 11-inch cutthroat trout. The remaining lake (a little to the north of Middle Dolus) is barren. [T8N R11W S28]

DORA THORN LAKE. This alpine lake sits at 7,350 feet, covers 6 acres, and runs fairly deep, with gradual drop-offs and much aquatic vegetation around the margins. Dora is reached by a good trail about a mile north of a jeep road from Granite (which is east of Philipsburg). Or you can hike up along the trail to the Copper Creek Lakes from the end of the Copper Creek road, southeast of Maxville. Dora is a spotty lake where you get skunked more often than not, as there is too much feed, but you can occasionally hit it right for cutthroat trout, and maybe some rainbow-cutt hybrids, that will range from 6 to 17 inches. [T7N R12W S19]

DUTCHMAN CREEK. A 5-mile "pickup" stream between the Lost Creek and Warm Springs Creek fans. Never more than a mile from a good county road in marshy farmland, Dutchman is good fishing for 8- to 14-inch rainbow, brook, brown trout, and grayling. It is usually subjected to moderately heavy fishing pressure by local residents, and occasionally to extreme pressure by way of a D-8 Caterpillar in the act of blocking off a section or two while effecting ditch repairs. [T5N R10W S14]

EAST BARKER LAKE. See under Barker Lakes.

EAST FORK BREWSTER CREEK. See Brewster Creek, East Fork.

EAST FORK RESERVOIR. Near the middle of the East Fork Rock Creek drainage, the reservoir is reached by a good gravel road off Montana 38, southwest of Phillipsburg, or a short drive around Georgetown Lake. There are two USFS campgrounds near the lake. The East Fork Reservoir covers 500 acres and is 75 feet deep, with shallow drop-offs near the dam and inlet, and straight down elsewhere. It has about 50 feet of water-level fluctuation, but in spite of that there's good fishing in the summer, before dewatering, for 10- to 14-inch rainbow and brook trout. It's moderately popular. There are also bull trout here. [T4N R14W S5]

EAST FORK ROCK CREEK. See Rock Creek, East Fork.

ECHO LAKE. Take Montana 1 to a point ¾ mile northwest of Georgetown Lake, then turn north on a county road for 1½ miles to the Echo Lake campground. This is a summer resort lake at 6,650 feet above sea level, about 75 acres in area and around 20 feet deep, with a mud bottom. It gets real warm in the summer, and there is a lot of swimming and waterskiing, quite a few summer homes, and a lodge (or rather the remains of a lodge). It is planted annually with 4- to 6-inch rainbow trout. It's fair fishing, and heavily fished, for rainbow and brook trout that range from 9 inches up to 1½ pounds. Check your regulations for seasonal and other special limits for Echo Lake. [T6N R13W S32]

EDITH LAKE. From the Middle Fork of Rock Creek trailhead, take a good USFS horse trail 5 miles southeast to this lake. Edith is a deep, 40-acre cirque lake in alpine country. It's been stocked with rainbow in the past, and it was planted with Yellowstone cutts in 1989. Whether it's rainbows or cutts or some combination, Edith is good fishing for 9- to 15-inch fish, but you'll have to work for them. [T3N R15W S28]

EIGHTMILE CREEK. Head west on good county roads from Hall, along Montana 1 (the Pintlar Scenic Route). Follow logging roads into the Harvey Creek drainage, and then to the mouth of Eightmile Creek. Eightmile is followed upstream by trail to headwaters, east of Sliderock Mountain. It is a scenic stream in timbered country, easily fished for good early-season catches of 6- to 8-inch cutthroat, rainbow, and brook trout, but it is seldom fished because you have to walk. [T10N R15W S24]

ELBOW LAKE. A high-elevation (7,500 feet) alpine lake, about 12 acres in size and no more than 10 feet deep anywhere. There's a short trail over to Elbow Lake from the Trask Lakes basin, at the head of the South Fork of Rock Creek, west of Deer Lodge. This lake is poor to fair fishing for rainbow that will average 10 inches. [T7N R11W S18]

ELK CREEK. A small, swampy stream, flowing to the Ross Fork of Rock Creek about 7 miles south of the East Fork road. It's accessible along the lower reaches by a rough logging road that heads up toward Medicine Lake. It is only occasionally fished, but produces excellent catches of small cutthroat trout. [T5N R16W S34]

ELK'S TIN CUP CREEK POND. This is found on the Montana State Prison Ranch, about 6 miles west of Deer Lodge, at the end of the prison road and immediately west of the brick "residential" building. It is a shallow, 5-acre lake, dammed, with about 5 feet of drawdown, and it's good fishing for 8- to 10-inch brook trout. It is not stocked. [T7N R10W S4]

ELLIOT LAKES. Two cirque lakes at 8,500 feet in elevation, in alpine country in the Dempsey Basin. Reach them by several miles of trail up the Tin Cup Joe drainage, west from the road from Deer Lodge, going past Martin Lake over into the Dempsey Basin. Or you can take a jeep road up the Dempsey Creek drainage (you can make it if you're a wild one), which will get you to within ½ mile of the lower lake. Lower Elliot has an area of perhaps 63 acres, and it's more than 80 feet deep with steep drop-offs, dammed but with only 3 feet of drawdown—just enough to drown the lower fringe of trees around the edges. It is seldom visited, but it's a good producer of 6- to 9-inch cutthroat trout. Upper Elliot (or Mount Powell) Lake is 73 acres in area and 55 feet deep with steep drop-offs, and there's about 5 feet of water-level fluctuation due to an irrigation dam at the outlet. It is seldom fished but good for camp-fare cutthroat trout. [T7N R11W S21]

EMERINE LAKE. It is easily reached by logging road at the very end of the West Fork of Rock Creek, near the top of Emerine Ridge. This small Granite County lake is planted with westslope cutthroat occasionally, last in 1984. Fishing is reported to be fair. [T5N R16W S8]

FALLS FORK CREEK. Flowing out of the Anaconda-Pintlar Wilderness to the Middle Fork of Rock Creek, the Falls Fork is accessible by trail for most of its 5-mile length (although the trail is rarely close to the stream). Use the Middle Fork trailhead, several miles south of Moose Lake, and follow the trail signs for Johnson Lake. In open timber country, Falls Fork is lightly fished for good catches of 8- to 10-inch cutthroat. A few bull trout come through in the fall. [T3N R16W S18]

FINLEN CREEK. See Gilbert Creek.

FISHER (or JONES) LAKE. A high-elevation (7,350 feet) cirque lake in partly timbered alpine country, Fisher is dammed, with 20 feet of drawdown. It covers about 30 acres and runs 36 feet deep in the center, with shallow margins. Fisher is barely reachable by jeep road from the end of the North Fork Flint Creek road, or you can hike in a couple of miles north and west from Green Lake. It is poor to sometimes fair fishing for 7- to 11-inch Yellowstone cutthroat trout that average about 10 inches. Not many folks bother it. [T6N R12W S4]

FIVEMILE BARROW PIT (or WARM SPRINGS GRAVEL PIT). Here are about 5 acres of long, narrow ponds in open meadow, just south of Montana 48 and about a mile west of I-90. Anacondites fish it quite a bit for excellent catches of rainbow trout, planted by the Department of Fish, Wildlife and Parks on a put-and-take basis. [T5N R10W S24]

FLINT CREEK. A large tributary of the Clark Fork River, Flint Creek flows northward from Georgetown Lake, through mostly farm- and meadowland, for 43 miles to its mouth at Drummond. It's followed all the way by Montana 1, the Pintlar Scenic Route. It is heavily and, for the most part, easily fished for good catches of cutthroat, rainbow, brook, and brown trout, and some whitefish. Flint Creek flows through mostly private land, so ask permission before you fish. Rainbow, brown trout, and whitefish are the predominant species in the lower reaches. They're joined by cutthroat and brook trout in the upper reaches (south of Philipsburg). The cutthroat, rainbow, and brook trout average around 9 to 10 inches, the whitefish and browns 14 to 16 inches. Oh, and you'll find lots of suckers below, with their numbers decreasing some upstream. Flint Creek has an extended season for whitefish and is catch-and-release for trout. Check your regulations. [T10N R12W S6]

165

FLINT CREEK, North Fork. This fork flows from the southern slopes of the Flint Creek Range to Georgetown Lake, and it's followed by a good gravel road for 7 miles, from its mouth to headwaters. The North Fork is a small, heavily fished stream for limited catches of 7- to 8-inch brook, and a few rainbow and cutthroat, trout. There's a restricted open season here, and special limits for trout. Check current regulations. [T5N R13W S7]

FOSTER CREEK. A small tributary of Warm Springs Creek in steep timbered country, crossed at the mouth by Montana 1, about 8 miles west of Anaconda, then followed by road and trail for 10 miles to head-waters, in the Flint Creek Range. Foster Creek is heavily fished, without too much success, for small cutthroat and brook trout. [T5N R12W S29]

FOURMILE BASIN LAKES. Two deep, 5-acre lakes, a few hundred yards apart, plus three shallow ponds, in alpine cirques. Take a good trail 3 miles from the end of the Twin Lakes Creek jeep road (off Montana 1 near the Spring Hill campground). Lower Fourmile is usually good fishing for 8- to 10-inch brookies, and it was planted with golden trout in 1976. Upper Fourmile supports a good population of 7- to 11-inch golden trout from plants in 1976 and 1983. [T4N R13W S16]

FRED BURR CREEK. A small, open stream flowing west from the Flint Creek Range to Warm Springs Creek, about 2½ miles south of Philipsburg. There is limited road access to the lower reaches, which are mostly on private land. Down here, Philipsburgians and local ranchers hook into fair catches of 7- to 9-inch cutthroat. You will need permission here. [T6N R14W S3]

FRED BURR LAKE. A high-elevation (7,600 feet) alpine lake, 161 acres in area and as much as 88 feet deep. It is nip and tuck getting there, by a poor jeep road, 7 miles east from Philipsburg. Fred Burr is dammed and used for the municipal water supply. Although closed to all fishing, it reportedly contains some real nice 13- to 14-inch rainbow trout and rainbow-cutthroat hybrids. [T6N R13W S1]

FUSE LAKE. Take Montana 38 for 2½ miles east of Skalkaho Pass, then follow a good USFS trail about 1½ miles north to this lake, which lies in a high-elevation (7,950 feet) cirque. Fuse is 13 acres and at most 37 feet deep, with gradual drop-offs all around. It is a real pretty, easily acces-sible (after you stumble across the clear-cuts), and moderately popular "green algae" lake that is fast fishing for mostly 5- to 10-inch arctic gray-ling. [T6N R17W S27]

GALEN HOSPITAL POND. This pond, on the grounds of the state sani-tarium at Galen, is stocked regularly with rainbows, last in 1993. It also

Fred Burr Lake Reservoir. —Courtesy U.S. Forest Service

receives periodic plantings of cutts, the last one being in 1990. [T6N R9W S31]

GEORGETOWN LAKE. A large (4½ square miles) lake at a 6,350-foot elevation, Georgetown Lake is really a drowned meadow converted into a reservoir. It's easily accessible by Montana 1, about 20 miles west of Anaconda. This is one of Montana's most popular fishing lakes, and justly so. There are eleven Forest Service campgrounds, a boat landing, and many summer residences. It is a popular recreation lake for boating, waterskiing, and fishing, frequented mostly by vacationers from Butte, Anaconda, Deer Lodge, and Missoula. It's heavily fished both summer and winter. During the winter, small kokanee salmon are the mainstays, along with big rainbows that hang out near the bottom. Early and late season, brook trout fishing is a draw, and some of the many rainbows stocked here each year turn out to be lunkers. The rainbows are helping to keep the kokanee population in check, and kokanee size is increasing.

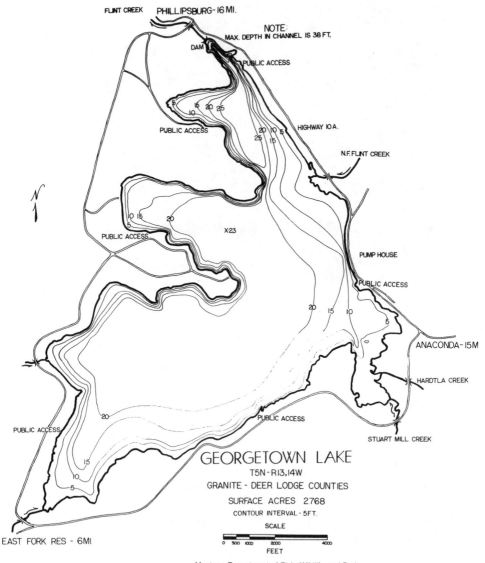

This map is not intended for navigational purposes. Navigational hazards are not shown. Access areas shown are public. Other places may be open to public use through the consent of individuals.

FLINT CREEK   PHILLIPSBURG- 16 MI.

NOTE:
MAX. DEPTH IN CHANNEL IS 38 FT.

DAM

PUBLIC ACCESS

10 15 20 25

PUBLIC ACCESS

HIGHWAY 10 A.

20 10 5
25 15

N.F. FLINT CREEK

N

10 15 20
5

X23

PUBLIC ACCESS

PUMP HOUSE

PUBLIC ACCESS

20 15 10
5

ANACONDA - 15 M

HARDTLA CREEK

20

PUBLIC ACCESS

STUART MILL CREEK

PUBLIC ACCESS

15

10
5

GEORGETOWN LAKE

T5N - R13,14W

GRANITE - DEER LODGE COUNTIES

SURFACE ACRES 2768

CONTOUR INTERVAL - 5 FT.

SCALE

0   500 1000   2000   4000
FEET

EAST FORK RES - 6 MI.

Montana Department of Fish, Wildlife and Parks

This is a real productive lake. Lots of special regulations apply here—special seasons, lakeshore closures, and special limits. Check them out before you fish. [T5N R13W S6]

GERMAN GULCH. A small stream flowing to Silver Bow Creek at the headwaters of the Clark Fork River. There's access by gravel road and trail to the upper reaches, south of Beefstraight Creek. The upper reaches were extensively placered in the late 1800s, and the stream can't seem to do much better than 6- to 8-inch cutts and brookies. [T3N R10W S12]

GILBERT CREEK. Also known locally as "Finlen Creek," after the owner of the property just above the mouth. Access is a little tricky, since you have to drive through the Finlen ranch from the Rock Creek road, about 4 miles south of I-90. But ask and ye may receive permission to fish and to access the mile or so of trail above the ranch. You can also get to the upper reaches by logging road from the Schwartz Creek drainage. It's been pretty well logged up there. Gilbert Creek is easily and heavily fished near the mouth for a smorgasbord of small brook, rainbow, and brown trout, with some whitefish and a few cutts thrown in for good measure. There are four little artificial ponds, progressively 2.6, 2.8, 2.9, and 3 miles above the mouth; the upper three cover about ½ acre each, the lower one about 6 acres. All have been planted in the past and are used as private fishing ponds. The upper 4 miles of this stream contain cutthroat and brook trout of unknown size and number. [T11N R17W S25]

Georgetown Lake. —Courtesy U.S. Forest Service

169

GILBERT CREEK, South Fork. Here is a small stream that flows through brushy, timbered country to Gilbert Creek at the old Finlen ranch. There's no road or trail access, and the mouth is on private land. That may help to explain why the South Fork is seldom fished for the fair catches of cutthroat and brook trout it could provide. [T11N R17W S27]

GLOVER LAKE. See Tamarack Lake.

GOAT LAKE. An 18-foot deep, 12-acre cirque lake in alpine country (elevation 8,075 feet), Goat is reached by ¼ mile of trail west of Caruthers Lake in the Dempsey Basin. With open talus slopes to the south and timber to the north, the lake has an open shore and is easily fished for good catches of 7- to 13-inch cutthroat and rainbow-cutthroat hybrids. [T11N R17W S27]

GOAT MOUNTAIN (or THOMPSON) LAKES. Six little alpine lakes in cirques on the upper flanks of Goat Mountain. Five are about 5 acres each and are reached by trail from the sixth and largest (about 15 acres), called Thompson Lake. If you've got an ATV or a motorcycle and don't mind winding around on worn-out roads, you can drive to the shore of Thompson Lake. Head north up the Little Gold Creek road from the Boulder Creek road, about 6 miles southeast of its junction with Montana 83 at Maxville. From there, a Forest Service map or instinct will lead you up and over the Flint Creek divide and from there 5 or 6 rough miles to Thompson Lake. With the exception of this old road, the area

Thompson Lake. —Courtesy U.S. Forest Service

east of the divide is closed to motorized vehicles. By staying on the road, you'll help protect the wet meadows in this slow-to-recover area. Better yet, lace up your boots and hike west up the Rock Creek drainage from Rock Creek Lake about 5 miles, until the trail meets up with the old road (mentioned above) that heads southwest for a couple of miles to the lakes. These lakes are excellent fishing for 8- to 9-inch cutthroat. [T7N R12W S1]

GOLD BAR LAKES. From Anaconda, take Montana 1 for 10 miles west, and then turn north up the Warm Springs Creek road for 7 miles, and continue north about 1 mile cross-country, to four small (1 to 3 acres), shallow lakes in heavily timbered mountain country. They are hard to find, and poor fishing when you do, for small cutthroat trout. [T6N R12W S18]

GOLD CREEK. Site of the first major gold strike in Montana, Gold Creek flows to the Clark Fork across from I-90, some 11 miles south of Drummond. It is followed by gravel road, past the old ghost town of Pioneer (now completely vandalized), for 20 miles to the headwaters at the Gold Creek Lakes. It is an easily fished stream that flows through meadows below and heavy timber (where it hasn't been logged) above. It produces good catches of 7- to 10-inch rainbow and cutthroat trout below, with lots of brown trout, especially in the fall. Upstream, the fishing mostly consists of a few 6-inch cutthroat. [T10N R10W S31]

GOLD CREEK LAKES. Two high-elevation (about 7,250 feet) cirque lakes on the western slopes of Rose Mountain, they cover 30 acres and 5 acres, respectively. They're reached by the Gold Creek Forest Service road, driving 20 miles southwest from I-90. Both are fair fishing for foot-long rainbow trout and hordes upon hordes of suckers. [T9N R11W S31]

GOLD CREEK, North. A small tributary of Gold Creek, crossed at the mouth by the Gold Creek road ½ mile south of Jones Mountain, accessed here and there by logging roads. It isn't much for fishing, but it's good spawning habitat and supports lots of 5- to 7-inch trout. [T9N R11W S31]

GREEN CANYON LAKE. A deep cirque lake of about 8 acres and a depth of 50 feet, just east of and beneath Whetstone Ridge. You can get within 1½ miles by a logging road up the Copper Creek drainage, south of Moose Lake. This lake is stocked every couple of years with cutthroat, and it can be good fishing for cutts in the 12-inch (and a little better) range. There may be some rainbow-cutthroat hybrids from the old days, when rainbows were planted in the lake. [T4N R16W S31]

GREEN (or POZEGA NUMBER 3) LAKE. A high cirque lake at 7,850 feet, southwest of Deer Lodge in the Flint Creek Range, Green Lake runs 34 feet deep and covers 13 acres. It is known locally as Pozega Number 3 Lake. It's reached by about a mile of jeep road (but you might want to leave your jeep somewhere down this rough road and walk up) to the west of Pozega Lake or by about 3 miles of trail south and a bit east from Fisher Lake, in the Racetrack Creek drainage. Green is partly dammed, with water-level fluctuations of as much as 6 feet, and it's fair to good fishing for rainbow, cutthroat, and rainbow-cutthroat hybrids, which range from 6 to 18 inches. [T6N R12W S10]

GRIZZLY CREEK. A very small, brushy stream flowing to Ranch Creek at the Grizzly campground in the Rock Creek drainage. It is a hard, exasperating stream to fish, mostly ignored by would-be anglers on the trail that follows the creek from mouth to headwaters. It does contain fair numbers of 6- to 8-inch cutthroat-rainbow hybrids and brook trout. [T10N R16W S31]

HAGGIN LAKE. A real deep little lake, covering about 8 acres, in a cirque just north of Mountain Haggin in the Anaconda Range, at 8,250 feet above sea level. There's no road or trail access up Big Gulch, which

Rock Creek at Grizzly Creek. —Courtesy U.S. Forest Service

heads up at Haggin Lake—there may be an old footpath from the trail that runs southwest from Stump Town (along Montana 1 west of Anaconda). Otherwise your best bet may be to bushwhack over from the Barker Lakes to the west. Not much word gets out about Haggin Lake, but there have been reports of good fishing for 10- to 15-inch rainbow trout, last planted there in 1976. In 1984, westslope cutts were stocked there. [T4N R12W S16]

HAIL COLUMBIA CREEK. A kids' creek, tributary to Brown's Gulch, it's followed through open country for about 5 miles by county roads. It contains a few 6-inch and smaller brook and rainbow trout. [T4N R8W S29]

HARVEY CREEK. A real pretty little stream that flows through low, open hill country to the Clark Fork, about a mile north of Bearmouth and across the river from I-90. It is followed by trail along nearly its entire length to headwaters, south of Sliderock Mountain in the John Long Mountains east of Rock Creek. This one is mostly skipped by all but local anglers, but it's easily fished and excellent for 6- to 8-inch cutthroat, plus an occasional rainbow or brown trout. Bull trout are common in the upper reaches, with fewer below. [T11N R14W S16]

HEARST LAKE. This 18-acre lake occupies a barren, rocky cirque at 8,200 feet in elevation just north of Mount Haggin, about 5 air miles southwest of Anaconda. It is reached by a 3½ mile hike over a rough trail, from the old city reservoir at the head of Ice House Gulch. It is real deep and excellent fishing for cutthroat and rainbow-cutt hybrids that range from 10 to 16 inches. Lower Hearst is a tiny pond about ⅛ mile below Hearst Lake, and it reportedly contains a very few 12- to 14-inch cutthroat trout, but not enough to make it worthwhile fishing. Hearst Lake proper has been planted with both westslope cutthroat trout (last in 1984) and rainbow (last in 1976). [T4N R12W S15]

HIDDEN LAKES. See Trask Lakes.

HOGBACK (or BIG HOGBACK) CREEK. Take the Rock Creek road south from I-90 for 31 miles to the Siria campground, then about another mile to the mouth of Hogback Creek. This is a very small stream, whose lower reaches flow through meadowland and are easily fished for 6-inch cutthroat and a few brook trout. You might see an occasional bull trout here, especially in the fall. [T8N R17W S35]

HOOVER CREEK. A small tributary of the Clark Fork River, crossed at the mouth by I-90 at Jens, then paralleled by a gravel road for 11 miles to the headwaters. Miller's Lake, at the mouth of Elk Swamp Creek about 6 miles upstream, has been heavily fished for 6- to 9-inch rainbow and brook trout, but Hoover Creek itself is generally neglected. It has a bad siltation problem and is very turbid, with warm water. There are cutts and rainbow-cutt hybrids here, but the fishing isn't much. [T10N R11W S20]

HOPE CREEK. It flows from Faith and Charity gulches for 4 miles, through alpine meadows, to Dog Creek. It's followed by good gravel roads to headwaters. Hope is quite a small stream that is fair fishing, although almost never bothered, for 8- to 9-inch cutthroat, brown, and brook trout. Cutthroat populations are declining, at least in part because of competition from the brookies and browns. [T11N R6W S29]

HUNTERS LAKE. This high alpine lake lies at a 7,850-foot elevation in a broad timbered cirque. It measures 9 acres and is dammed with 5 feet of drawdown. It's reached by about a mile of trail west from the Thornton Creek road, which is accessible from the Modesty Creek drainage. It has been fair fishing for 7- to 12-inch rainbow trout in the past, but it is a shallow, marginal lake, and no recent report on it is available. [T6N R12W S13]

IVANHOE LAKE. This alpine cirque lake covers 7 acres and is 45 feet deep, on the headwaters of the Middle Fork of Rock Creek, just inside the Anaconda-Pintlar Wilderness. It's reached by a jeep road 4½ miles south of Moose Lake, then continuing on a steep switchbacked USFS horse trail ½ mile to the shore. The wilderness is closed to stock use April 1 through July 1. Ivanhoe is only fair fishing for 8- to 12-inch rainbow trout. [T3N R16W S26]

JACOBUS PONDS. Two little ½-acre private ponds, 2 miles west of Elliston, just south of US 12, in open meadows. They are fair fishing for 6- to 8-inch cutthroat and brook trout. [T9N R7W S3]

JOB CORPS PONDS. These four ponds are part of the Anaconda settling pond system, at the headwaters of the Clark Fork River. They're right next to I-90 near Warm Springs. They're shallow ponds constructed by, you guessed it, the Job Corps! They're planted yearly with rainbow, and every so often there's a planting of cutts. It's good fishing for good-size trout. [T5N R9W S7]

JOHNSON LAKE. This 70-acre, 68-foot-deep lake in the Anaconda-Pintlar Wilderness is a couple of miles south of Edith Lake. Johnson is 5 miles by trail southeast of the Middle Fork Rock Creek trailhead. It's surrounded by exceptionally scenic country, and it's a good base camp for day hikes to other lakes. Put it all together and you get a lake that sees plenty of use. Watch for camping and stock restrictions along the shoreline. Johnson's fair fishing for skinny cutthroat. [T3N R15W S32]

JONES LAKE. See Fisher Lake.

JONES POND. A private, 2-acre, earth-dammed, spring-fed reservoir right by the owner's house, 2 miles north of Warm Springs and a mile west of I-90. It is very good fishing indeed for 12- to 24-inch brown trout, with the owner's permission only. [T5N R9W S1]

KAISER LAKE. A 12-acre lake, 22 feet deep, in conifer-covered mountains. Reach it via 1 mile of pickup road from the Middle Fork of Rock Creek road, 7 miles south of the creek's mouth. Kaiser is poor fishing at best for small cutthroat, bull trout, rainbow, and hordes of suckers. [T4N R15W S18]

LAKE ABUNDANCE. A high alpine lake in heavily timbered country, 4 miles south of Congdon Peak in the Sapphire Mountains. Lake Abundance is only 4 acres, long, narrow, and shallow (but it does not freeze out), with swampy margins and much aquatic vegetation—really sort of a dammed-up mountain meadow. Abundance is reached by 14 miles of horse trail southwest of Moose Meadows along the Ross Fork of Rock

Creek fishing. —Courtesy Michele Archie

Creek, or you can hike in on a number of trails from the Bitterroot side of the divide. It is excellent fishing for 6- to 10-inch cutthroat trout, but it's hit only occasionally. It's real good elk hunting country too, but rough! [T3N R18W S1]

LAKE ELLEN (at YMCA Camp). A shallow beaver pond in a ground moraine outwash plain, reached by the Little Blackfoot road 3 miles south of Elliston. It's good 6- to 14-inch brook trout fishing for the kids at summer camp. [T9N R6W S19]

LAKE OF THE ISLES. A high-elevation (8,150 feet) lake just north of the Continental Divide in the Anaconda Range, 11 miles west of Anaconda. It's reached by trail a mile or so east of Twin Lakes, in an area closed to motorized vehicles. Lake of the Isles lies in a timbered basin, covers about 3 acres, is fairly deep in the upper end, and offers only poor to fair fishing for cutthroat that range up to 2 pounds. It was planted with cutthroat trout in the early '60s and again in 1984. [T4N R13W S26]

LITTLE ALTOONA LAKE. See under Altoona Lakes.

LITTLE BARKER LAKE. See under Barker Lakes.

LITTLE BLACKFOOT RIVER. Good-size for a mountain stream but small for a river, the Little Blackfoot flows for 50 miles from Electric Peak, elevation 8,100 feet, through a mostly broad, flat-bottomed agricultural valley to it's eventual junction with the Clark Fork at Garrison, elevation 4,650 feet. It is paralleled all the way by US 12 and good county roads. This is a heavily fished stream, whose flow is sometimes entirely diverted for irrigation, but it is somehow consistently good fishing for 9- to 12-inch browns and whitefish below Elliston, and fair for cutthroat and brook trout above. This stream has suffered from senselessly brutal stream channelization and straightening in its lower stretches. The Little Blackfoot has an extended whitefish season and is catch-and-release for trout. Check current regulations for details. [T9N R12W S24]

LITTLE BLACKFOOT SPRING CREEK. This spring creek flows for 5 miles to join the Little Blackfoot River west of Elliston. It's tough to get permission to fish this small stream, and the fishing would be better if the cattle had been kept away from it, but you still might hook into some cutts, browns, or brookies. [T10N R7W S33]

LITTLE FISH LAKE. A mostly shallow, 9-acre mountain lake with much vegetation around the shores. You might be able to find the old, unmarked trail that heads up from the South Fork of the Ross Fork of the Rock Creek trail. This trail is closed to motorized vehicles for much of the year, to give elk a place to calve in peace. Little Fish Lake is good to excellent fishing, although seldom bothered, for small (6- to 10-inch) cutthroat trout. [T4N R17W S23]

LITTLE HOGBACK CREEK. A tiny, brushy stream flowing north for 3 miles to Rock Creek, between the Bitterroot Flat and Siria campgrounds. It's too small to be of much note, and the few small bull trout that live near the mouth should be left alone. [T8N R17W S17]

LITTLE POZEGA LAKE. A high-elevation (7,650 feet) alpine lake about ⅛ mile above Big Pozega by jeep, in real good mountain-goat country. Little Pozega has a maximum area of about 13 acres, is as much as 35 feet deep in places, and is dammed, with 8 feet of water-level fluctuation and lots of drowned timber around the margins. It is fished a fair amount for this neck of the woods, and it's good, too, for 5- to 15-inch rainbow trout. [T6N R12W S14]

LITTLE RACETRACK LAKE. Reached by a ¾-mile hike southeast from Racetrack Lake, in a high (7,450-foot elevation) alpine cirque, Little Race-track covers 6 acres, with a 27-foot maximum depth. It's dammed, with 5 feet of drawdown and lots of boulders and drowned timber around the edges. It is lightly fished, and no better than poor to fair for 10- to 11-inch rainbow and a few rainbow-cutthroat hybrids. Fishing would probably be better but for the excessive drawdown. [T6N R12W S5]

LITTLE THORNTON LAKE. About 500 yards east of Big Thornton, Little Thornton is 4 acres in area and 42 feet deep. It's real slow fishing for 14- to 18-inch rainbows and cutts that were planted there in 1984. [T6N R11W S19]

LOST CREEK. A small, easily wadable stream flowing to the Clark Fork River through about 15 miles of open meadow and cropland (just over the hump north of Anaconda) and 5 miles of heavily timbered mountain canyon. Lost Creek is easily accessible for its entire length by good county roads and a short stretch of trail to headwaters, past the Lost Creek campground. It is heavily fished for good catches of small brook, cutthroat, and brown trout, with an occasional 3- to 4-pound brown from the lower reaches in the fall. [T6N R9W S32]

LOWER BARKER LAKE. See under Barker Lakes.

LOWER ELLIOT LAKE. See under Elliot Lakes.

LOWER WILLOW CREEK. A small, jumpable stream, flowing for about 9 miles through farmland in the Flint Creek Valley west of Hall, is easily accessible by county roads. It is heavily fished by local ranchers for good catches of 7- to 9-inch cutthroat, brook, and brown trout. Permission to fish the lower reaches can be hard to come by. [T10N R12W S19]

LOWER WILLOW CREEK, North Fork. It is easily accessible by 11 miles of county road from Hall, or by 14 miles of private and county roads from Bearmouth. There are about 7 miles of open, easily fished water, good early-season kids' fishing for 6- to 8-inch cutthroat and a few brook trout. [T9N R14W S2]

LOWER WILLOW CREEK, West Fork. Take a county road 10 miles west from Hall to the mouth of this creek, and then go 3 miles on up-stream. A timber and meadowland creek, it's only fair fishing for small cutthroat and brook trout. [T9N R14W S3]

LOWER WILLOW CREEK RESERVOIR. A 170-acre, 85-foot-maxi-mum-depth reservoir behind a 940-foot-long, earth-filled dam in open grassland, at the junction of the North and South forks of Lower Willow Creek. It's reached by good county roads about 9 miles southwest from Hall. The water rights to this reservoir are all taken for irrigation—the thing can be drained completely dry, and therefore it's not stocked. How-ever, it does provide an excellent habitat for native cutthroat trout from the creek, and it's sometimes excellent fishing for 14- to 16-inchers. It's also used for a moderate amount of waterskiing. [T9N R14W S2]

MALLARD CREEK. A very small stream flowing for 3 miles north to Rock Creek, about 4 miles north of the West Fork Guard Station. The lower mile is on private land, with fishing by permission only; it is easily fished and contains goodly numbers of 6- to 7-inch cutthroat trout. [T6N R15W S29]

MARSHALL CREEK. An open, easily accessible stream, flowing for about 6 miles through mostly farmland to Flint Creek, 3 miles north of Philipsburg. It is only fair fishing for 6- to 7-inch cutthroat trout. [T7N R14W S11]

MARTIN LAKE. Martin Lake is a real high-elevation (8,700 feet) cirque lake in barren "way back" country at the headwaters of Tin Cup Joe Creek. It can be reached by horse trail a little more than a mile north from Elliot Lakes, or even farther back by trail heading west and south from Conleys Lake. It is as much as 50 feet deep in spots, covers 45 surface acres when full, and is so far back and high up that it is seldom visited, much less fished. Martin Lake does support a small population 7- to 13-inch cutthroat trout, and it's planted every so often, last in 1990. [T7N R11W S17]

MEADOW CREEK. A small, easily wadable tributary of the East Fork of Rock Creek, west of Georgetown, followed along most of its length by trail and good road. Here is an open, muchly beaver-dammed stream that is fair fishing for 7- to 10-inch cutthroat trout. [T5N R15W S26]

Martin Lake from Rainbow Pass. —Courtesy U.S. Forest Service

MEADOW CREEK. This little stream flows from some springs just below the Continental Divide, west of Helena and north of Mullan Pass, for 2 miles through alpine meadows to Dog Creek. It is fair to good fishing for small brookies and cutthroat trout in some beaver ponds about ½ mile above the mouth. [T11N R6W S28]

MEADOW LAKES. Six alpine lakes (elevation between 7,650 and 8,650 feet) at the headwaters of Racetrack Creek, in sparsely timbered, rock and mountain-meadow country east of Phillipsburg. They're reached most easily by a 1½-mile pack trip east and then south around the hill from Fisher Lake. The lakes are strung out within a mile of one another. They range in size from 5 to 13 acres. While all the lakes were once stocked with rainbow, now just four of them—the four largest—receive periodic plants of cutthroat. The Meadow Lakes offer fishing that varies from fantastic (one lake—we won't say which one—is known to grow big fish) to mediocre to nonexistent. [T6N R12W S3]

MEADOW LAKES. Five little alpine lakes, around 7,500 feet above sea level, at the headwaters of Rock Creek, between Phillipsburg and Deer Lodge. They're reached by 5 miles of trail west from the upper end of

Rock Creek Lake. Or head south for ½ mile from the ATV trail that heads up to the Goat Mountain Lakes from Little Gold Creek, east of Maxville. Off-road vehicles have caused a fair amount of damage to meadows near the lakes, so help the area recover by sticking to designated trails. Only West Meadow Lake contains fish. It lies east of and below a 350-foot high, mostly open rocky ridge but it is in timber to the north and east. West Meadow covers 16 acres, runs fairly deep, and is pretty good fishing for 6- to 14-inch rainbow-cutthroat hybrids. It was last planted with rainbow in 1977. [T8N R12W S36]

MEDICINE LAKE. A 72-acre lake at 7,000 feet in elevation in heavily timbered mountains. Take a jeep road 4½ miles west from the junction of Elk Creek and the Ross Fork of Rock Creek. You can also get in by hiking a couple of miles south from the end of the Sand Basin road. It is about 35 feet deep, with gradual drop-offs, a muddy bottom, lots of lilies, and a beaver dam at the outlet. The fishing is no less than excellent for 6- to 14-inch cutthroat trout. There's a special season on this lake and its tributaries, and the lake is closed to all gasoline motors. Consult your fishing regulations and the Philipsburg Ranger Station on the Deerlodge National Forest for details. [T4N R17W S2]

MIDDLE FORK ROCK CREEK. See Rock Creek, Middle Fork.

MIKE RENIG GULCH. A small stream paralleled from its headwaters on Jericho Mountain for 6 miles to its mouth on the Little Blackfoot at Elliston by good gravel and jeep roads. Mike Renig is generally poor fishing, except for a string of beaver ponds in meadowland about 3 miles above its mouth—there you might catch a good mess of 6- to 8-inch brook and cutthroat trout. [T9N R6W S7]

MILL CREEK. A clear mountain stream that rises in the Anaconda Range and flows eastward, behind the barren slopes of Mount Haggin, for about 14 miles to the Deer Lodge Valley and from there for 5 miles through meadowland to Silver Bow Creek, in the headwaters of the Clark Fork River. The lower and middle reaches are followed by road, and they're easily and heavily fished for fair catches (if you could call them that) of 5- to 6-inch cutthroat, brook, and rainbow trout. Also look for brown trout and whitefish. The upper reaches are followed by trail to headwaters at Miller Lake. [T5N R9W S31]

MILL CREEK, South Fork. A tiny stream flowing for 4 miles to Mill Creek, through a brushy, beaver-dammed flat, a few hundred feet west of the Anaconda-Big Hole highway (Route 274). It contains quite a few 5- to 7-inch cutthroat trout. [T4N R11W S28]

MILLER (or MILL CREEK) LAKE. It's really just a small (2½ acres), shallow, swampy pond, in subalpine scattered-timber and meadow country near the head of Mill Creek, just north of the Continental Divide. Miller Lake is reached by 8 miles of foot trail from the end of the Mill Creek road. It's very seldom visited, but it's excellent fishing for 6- to 10-inch native cutthroat trout. [T4N R12W S30]

MILLER'S LAKE. See under Hoover Creek.

MINNESOTA GULCH. A very small (2½ miles) tributary of Beefstraight Creek. It's crossed about halfway upstream by a trail, but, other than that, there's no access. It's fair small-stream fishing for pan-size cutthroat and brook trout. [T3N R10W S29]

MODESTY CREEK. This 12-mile creek heads just east of Thornton Ridge and flows into the Clark Fork River just north of Galen. It goes dry in its lower stretches. No report on its fishery is available, but it's a likely stream for small cutthroat, brook, and brown trout. [T6N R9W S20]

MONARCH CREEK. A tiny (4-mile) tributary of Ontario Creek, in the Little Blackfoot drainage south of Elliston. Followed by a road for 2½ miles above the mouth, it's fair fishing for a small population of little trout—6- to 7-inch cutthroat. [T8N R6W S20]

MOOSE MEADOW (or MOOSE) CREEK. This small stream flows for 6 miles through boggy, floating turf in the Moose Meadows country to the Ross Fork of Rock Creek. It is crossed at the mouth by the Ross Fork road and followed upstream for a couple of miles by a jeep road (that you should stay on if you don't want to get stuck). If you stray far from the creek, you could easily break through and provide food for the fish, which are mostly 6- to 8-inch cutthroat and hungry. [T5N R16W S34]

MOOSE LAKE. A beautiful little 21-acre-area, 26-foot-deep lake, reached by a good road a mile south of the Copper Creek campground. There is only limited public access, and the fishing is poor anyway for a very few small brook trout, cutthroat, and hordes of suckers. The lake is planted annually with westslope cutthroat trout. In the fall, there might be a few big bull trout up from Rock Creek hanging around. [T4N R16W S36]

MOSQUITO LAKE. This lake lies ½ mile north of the Copper Creek Lakes, at the head of Swamp Gulch. It is in heavily timbered mountains, about 5 acres in area, with a muddy bottom but clear water, in which live numerous salamanders. The lake was last planted with westslope cutthroat trout in 1958, but it's no longer on the planting program. Old reports say that Mosquito Lake has a fair population of 6- to 8-inch rainbow trout plus a few *BIG* cutthroat, remnants of way-back plantings.

Bull moose. —Courtesy U.S. Forest Service

New reports are hard to come by, and there's a good chance that the trout have left the lake to the mosquitoes and salamanders. [T7N R13W S24]

MOUNTAIN BEN LAKE. Reach this lake by a good trail ½ mile from Caruthers Lake, about a mile south of Racetrack Peak (there's a nice view from here at 9,524 feet, and it's a pleasant hike after the morning's fishing). Mountain Ben is 33 acres and over 50 feet deep, in timbered country with rocky talus sloped to the west. It's slow fishing for 7- to 15-inch rainbow-cutthroat hybrids. [T7N R11W S30]

MOUNT POWELL (or UPPER ELLIOT) LAKE. See under Elliot Lakes.

MUD LAKE. A muddy little 2-acre pothole at the top of Tin Cup Joe's moraine, reached by a good gravel road 2 miles west of the Deer Lodge prison farm. It's poor fishing for 7- to 10-inch brook trout and a few sunfish. [T7N R10W S3]

MUD LAKE. Take a poor jeep road 2 miles north from Racetrack Lake, east of Phillipsburg. The only thing is, you can't take your Jeep: it's closed to road vehicles, but open to trail bikes, ATVs, and feet. The lake is about 12 acres, mostly shallow but up to 17 feet deep in places. It's slow fishing for 16- to 17-inch rainbow trout, as well as westslope cutthroat, which were last planted in 1976. [T7N R12W S28]

MUD LAKE. Proceed west on Montana 38 from Montana 1, to about a mile east of the Skalkaho Pass. Mud Lake sits just south of the road along the North Fork of Rock Creek, east of Hamilton. There's a Forest Service campground here. Mud Lake is 4½ acres in area, swampy, and mostly shallow but up to 34 feet deep in the middle, so it doesn't freeze out. It's slow fishing for the blackest pan-size cutthroat you've ever seen. [T6N R17W S32]

NORTH FORK FLINT CREEK. See Flint Creek, North Fork.

NORTH (or NORTH FORK) GOLD CREEK. See Gold Creek, North.

NORTH FORK LOWER WILLOW CREEK. See Lower Willow Creek, North Fork.

NORTH FORK ROCK CREEK. See Rock Creek, North Fork.

ONTARIO CREEK. It's followed by a good gravel road, through heavy timber, for 8 miles northwestward between Treasure and Bison mountains, to the Little Blackfoot River, about 8 miles south of Elliston. Ontario gets real low in late summer, and its trout "take to the holes," which are fair fishing then for 6- to 8-inch cutthroat and brookies. [T8N R7W S12]

OPHIR CREEK. A wee-small stream flowing for about 8 miles to Carpenter Creek, 4½ miles northeast of Avon, crossed at the mouth by the Carpenter Creek road. Ophir "picks up" irrigation water during the summer months and supports a few 6- to 10-inch cutthroat and brook trout, but on the whole it's poor fishing and very seldom bothered. [T10N R8W S12]

PERKINS POND (or RESERVOIR). A dammed-up 4-acre pothole on the toe of the Dempsey Creek moraine. Perkins has a maximum depth of about 20 feet, goes almost dry in late summer, and somehow supports a fair crop of 8- to 12-inch, muddy-tasting brook trout. It hasn't been fished much since some enterprising individuals tried to seine it out years ago. It's on private land, so ask permission before you try your luck. [T7N R10W S32]

PETERSON CREEK. A small stream flowing for 11 miles westward to the Clark Fork at Deer Lodge. The lower reaches are mostly dewatered for irrigation, but there is fair fishing for small trout—mostly cutthroat and brookies—in an occasional pothole here and there upstream. This is a kids' creek that is followed by county roads to headwaters. It's just about all on private land, with limited access, so be sure to ask before you fish. [T7N R9W S4]

PFISTER POND. A private ½-acre pond, a mile east of Elliston on the south side of US 12. Pfister was planted years ago, and it has been fair fishing for 8- to 10-inch brook trout in the past. It's seldom visited, but you might want to give it a shot if you get permission. [T9N R6W S6]

PHYLLIS LAKES. Take a good USFS trail 5 miles south and then 1 mile east from the Middle Fork Rock Creek trailhead to this pair of high alpine lakes in the Anaconda-Pintlar Wilderness. The lakes are about 10 acres each and very deep, with steep drop-offs and rocky bluffs to the south, and timber on around. The upper lake is spotty for 8- to 14-inch cutthroat. The lower lake is planted occasionally and is a bit better fishing. Upper Phyllis was last planted in 1981 and Lower Phyllis in 1988. [T2N R16W S1]

PORCUPINE LAKE. A very small lake, about ½ mile off the jeep road that leads up the Thornton Creek drainage and over to Pozega Lake. It's not much, but it was stocked with westslope cutthroat in 1990, so it may be worth a peek if for some reason you're in that neck of the woods. [T6N R12W S14]

POWELL LAKE. It measures 9 acres and is 40 feet deep in at least two places, sitting in timbered country on the eastern flanks of the Flint Creek Range. Powell is reached to within ½ mile by a jeep road from the Montana State Prison, west of Deer Lodge. It is seldom fished and only poor fishing anyway, for 11- to 15-inch brown trout and hordes of suckers. [T7N R10W S18]

POZEGA LAKES. See Big and Little Pozega Lakes.

POZEGA NUMBER 3 LAKE. See Green Lake.

RACETRACK CREEK. This easily wadable fishing stream flows from Racetrack Lake for 15 miles, down a deeply glaciated, heavily timbered canyon; then for 2½ miles, through the great hummocky Racetrack terminal moraine; and finally for 6 miles, across the wide open meadows of the Racetrack-Dempsey Creek alluvial flat, to the Clark Fork River, 2 miles north of Galen. It is easily accessible for its entire length by good county roads, jeep roads, and USFS trails. The middle and upper reaches are heavily fished for good catches of 6- to 9-inch cutthroat and brook trout, plus a few browns. Bull trout are common in the drainage. [T6N R9W S9]

RACETRACK LAKE. A high-elevation (around 7,700 feet above sea level) alpine lake in deeply glaciated country, just north of Twin Peaks. Racetrack is reached by a rough jeep road continuing north from the end of the North Fork of Flint Creek road. Little Racetrack lies about ¾ of a mile beyond. Racetrack is about 80 feet deep and 35 acres in area; it's dammed, with perhaps 14 feet of drawdown. It's good fishing for cutthroat, rainbows, and hybrids in the foot-long range. It's planted every few years with cutthroat, last in 1994. [T6N R12W S5]

RAINBOW LAKE. This lake sits at a 7,200-foot elevation in heavy timber at the headwaters of Gold Creek, about ⅛ mile north of Gold Creek Lakes. It covers 20 acres and is up to 35 feet deep in spots. Rainbow is reached by the same Gold Creek road that leads to the Gold Creek Lakes, then a short stretch of trail heading west from just about the end of that road. It is moderately popular, and it used to be excellent fishing for 10- to 30-inch rainbow—but poachers made sure to leave danged few of those fish in their wake. The Rainbow Lake fishery is recovering, in part due to recent plantings of cutthroat and rainbow. Now the fishing is demanding, but rewarding, for cutts in the foot-and-a-half range and some big rainbows. [T8N R12W S14]

RANCH CREEK. Take the Rock Creek road south for 10 miles from I-90, to the mouth of Ranch Creek, then go southeast up that creek for a mile to the Grizzly campground. From there, you're on foot or horseback for 10 miles of trail, to the headwaters of Ranch Creek. Here is a beautiful mountain stream, flowing through steep, timbered country above and open meadows below, that provides decent fishing for mostly small cutthroat and brook trout, plus a few rainbow, brown trout, and whitefish near the mouth. A few bull trout hang out in Ranch Creek, especially in the fall. It is heavily fished near the campground, but pressure peters out as you move upstream. [T10N R17W S36]

ROCK CREEK. This stream drains as many as nineteen alpine lakes, running eastward for 7 miles through heavily timbered, glaciated canyons to Rock Creek Lake; from there, it flows for another 10 miles down the great Rock Creek boulder moraine, through a narrow, rocky gorge, and finally out across the Clark Fork floodplain to the river, near Garrison. It is readily accessible by road to the lake, and by trail above, and it's lightly fished in the lower and middle reaches for good catches of 7- to 12-inch whitefish, plus a few brook and rainbow trout, and lots of suckers. Cutthroat dominate the fishery above the lake. [T9N R10W S23]

ROCK CREEK. Certainly one of the most beautiful and probably the most famous and heavily fished stream in Montana west of the Continental

Rock Creek near Phillipsburg. —Courtesy Ravalli County Museum, Ernst Peterson Collection

Divide, Rock Creek flows for 50 miles from the junction of its west and Middle forks to the Clark Fork River, 24 miles east of Missoula, south of Clinton. It is readily accessible all along by oiled and graveled roads that natives want kept that way. Rock Creek is a comparatively small, easily waded stream in open rangeland above, but it quickly becomes a large, swift, and often unfordable stream for most of its length, through heavily timbered hills between the Long John and Sapphire Mountains. It is good to excellent summertime fishing for all levels of fishers in its upper reaches, for 8- to 10-inch rainbow and cutthroat trout. It's excellent fishing below for the experienced angler, and fair for most everybody else, for mostly 10- to 16-inch rainbow trout and lesser numbers of brook, cutthroat, and brown trout, plus plenty of whitefish. Bull trout are not unusual in the upper and middle reaches—remember to release the bull trout you hook. There's good winter whitefishing here, for 10-inch to 4-pound whitefish that could stand a lot more pressure than they get. Rock Creek was the site of a highly successful controlled catch-and-keep restriction in recent years; these new regulations have brought the stream back from severe fishery declines, brought on by too much fishing impact. Check current regulations for restrictions on bait usage, fishing from boats, and special limits. [T11N R17W S12]

ROCK CREEK, East Fork. Eighteen miles long, it's crossed at the mouth by Montana 38, followed by a county road for 12 miles past the East Fork Reservoir, and from there by a good USFS trail for 6 miles to headwaters, in the Anaconda-Pintlar Wilderness. The East Fork flows through partly timbered and partly open country; it's fairly popular, producing good catches of 8- to 12-inch cutthroat, with a few whitefish, brookies, and rainbows thrown in. [T4N R14W S6]

ROCK CREEK, Middle Fork. A clear mountain stream flowing northward, from its headwaters in the Anaconda-Pintlar Wilderness for about 24 miles to its mouth. It's followed for the first 19 miles upstream by a good gravel road, and the remaining 5 miles by a good USFS trail. The Middle Fork is an easily wadable steam that is heavily fished for good catches of 6- to 10-inch rainbow, whitefish, and a few cutthroat trout. There are also some small bull trout here. [T6N R15W S31]

ROCK CREEK, North Fork. The North Fork is an easily wadable, very popular stream that flows through heavily timbered mountains. It's followed for 4 miles from its headwaters near the Skalkaho Pass to its confluence with the West Fork. It is a consistent producer of small cutthroat trout. [T5N R17W S2]

ROCK CREEK, Ross Fork. This stream flows for about 20 miles from its headwaters at Lake Abundance to the West Fork of Rock Creek, a couple of miles east of the West Fork Guard Station. Its middle and upper reaches are accessible by jeep road, and then by trail on up to the lake. Ross Fork flows mostly through timber and swampland. Easily wadable, it's considered to be fair fishing for 9- to 10-inch cutthroat trout, and a few brookies, rainbow, brown trout, and whitefish in season. Watch for small bull trout here as well, especially in the fall. The lower end is mostly on private (posted) land. [T6N R15W S31]

ROCK CREEK, South Fork Ross Fork. This small, open stream is followed by a good USFS trail for 6 miles from its mouth past headwaters. The trail is open to motorized vehicles from June 16 through the end of August only, to give calving elk some peace and quiet, and to provide walk-in opportunities for hunters in the fall. The South Fork is not all that popular, but it's good fishing for 7- to 9-inch cutthroat trout. [T4N R17W S12]

ROCK CREEK, West Fork. A small, open stream in mountain-peak and timber country, the West Fork flows for 22 miles to its confluence with

West Fork of Rock Creek.
—Courtesy U.S. Forest Service

the Middle Fork—the headwaters of Rock Creek. It is followed by good road to headwaters near Signal Rock. This is a popular, easily fished stream that produces good catches of small cutthroat trout and whitefish. Some small bull trout hang out in the West Fork, as well. [T6N R15W S31]

ROCK CREEK LAKE. Covering 180 acres, deep, with a concrete dam and 30 feet of drawdown, Rock Creek Lake is easily accessible by 12 miles of good gravel road northwest from Deer Lodge, and it has been a popular boating, swimming, and waterskiing area. It was poisoned in 1959, but there was only a partial kill, and it has since been planted repeatedly with rainbow, and later cutthroat, trout (last in 1988). As of last report it is only fair fishing, with rough fish taking over again. The lake is surrounded by private land with no public fishing access. [T8N R11W S23]

RYAN LAKE. A little old reservoir lake, 6 acres in area and 10 feet deep (almost), reached (almost) by jeep road off the Bielenberg Canyon road. At last report, it was slow fishing for big brooks in the 15- to 18-inch class. [T7N R11W S33]

SAND BASIN CREEK. A small, open-meadow stream, flowing for 5 miles to the West Fork of Rock Creek and followed by good gravel road to headwaters. It is easily fished for fair catches of pan-size cutthroat trout, but the stream's water carries a heavy sediment load. [T5N R17W S11]

SAUER LAKE. Six miles by trail from the East Fork Rock Creek trailhead, Sauer Lake sits in high (elevation 8,050 feet), timbered country in the Anaconda-Pintlar Wilderness. It's about 8 acres, and it used to be good to excellent for 6- to 9-inch cutthroat trout, but it's now reportedly barren and seldom if ever fished. [T3N R14W S6]

SAWMILL CREEK. You've got to ford Rock Creek to get to this one, almost 8 miles south of I-90, but once you're across, a trail follows the creek west almost to headwaters. It's a darned good little stream for 6- to 10-inch brookies and cutts for a couple of miles up its timbered canyon. [T10N R16W S19]

SCHWARTZ CREEK. This stream flows east from the Bitterroot-Clark Fork drainage divide for 7 miles to the Clark Fork River, 1 mile south of Clinton. It's followed by good logging roads almost all the way. It is fished near the mouth for brookies and westslope cutts in good numbers, of the 6- to 10-inch size, and a few brown and rainbow trout during spawning season. [T12N R17W S34]

SENATE CREEK. A small open stream that drains Kaiser Lake for 1 mile to the Middle Fork of Rock Creek. The lower ½ mile is fair fishing for 6- to 9-inch cutthroat trout. [T4N R15W S7]

SENECAL PONDS. Two artificial ponds, of about 1 and 2 acres, at the mouth of the North Trout Creek canyon. Take US 12 for 3 miles east of Avon, then the Snowshoe Creek and county roads for 7½ miles to these private ponds, below the old Senecal residence. Fishing, with the owner's permission only, is reportedly good for 8- to 14- inch cutthroat and rainbow trout. [T10N R7W S10]

SIDNEY (or SYDNEY) LAKE. This is a very deep, 15-acre alpine lake, reached by trail ½ mile northeast from Dora Thorn Lake. In the past it was good fishing for rainbow and cutts in the 12-inch range, but now it's reported to be almost barren. [T7N R12W S19]

SILVER LAKE. An ACM (the old Anaconda mining company) reservoir, about a mile long and ½ mile wide, in timbered country 1 mile east of Georgetown Lake. Take Montana 1, going 13 miles west from Anaconda. Silver Lake is lightly fished (in favor of Georgetown), and it's usually poor at best for 8- to 10-inch rainbow trout and kokanee salmon, plus a few lake trout and cutthroat. There are small numbers of big bull trout in this lake, too. [T5N R13W S21]

SMART CREEK. A small, open stream, flowing north to Flint Creek 6 miles south of Hall, it's followed by road for much of its 11-mile length. It is not much for fishing, but it looks good, is easily accessible, and is subjected to moderate fishing pressure for 6- to 7-inch cutthroat trout. [T9N R13W S21]

SNOWSHOE CREEK. This tributary to the Little Blackfoot River flows for 11 miles from headwaters, west of Esmeralda Hill. It's followed along its entire length by good gravel road. It can be good fishing for cutthroat, and for spawning brown trout in the fall. [T10N R8W S26]

SNOWSHOE PONDS (or LAKES). Two scenic used-to-be-fish-rearing ponds of about 3 and 4 acres, 100 feet apart, in scattered timber and open meadowland hills at the mouth of Snowshoe Canyon. You get there by taking US 12 about 4 miles east from Avon, then the Snowshoe Creek road north for 6 miles, and a private road ¼ mile west to the ponds. Permission only here. [T10N R7W S4]

SOUTH (or SOUTH FORK) BOULDER CREEK. See Boulder Creek, South.

SOUTH FORK OF GILBERT CREEK. See Gilbert Creek, South Fork.

SOUTH FORK OF MILL CREEK. See Mill Creek, South Fork.

SOUTH FORK ROSS FORK ROCK CREEK. See Rock Creek, South Fork Ross Fork.

SPOTTED DOG CREEK. See Dog Creek.

SPRING CREEK. Take the Rock Creek road for 6 miles south from I-90 to the lower pastureland reaches of Spring Creek, on the Randley Ranch (fish with permission only there). From the trailhead, you can head on upstream for a short distance on a USFS trail that quickly climbs away from the creek. You may be able to pick up the traces of an old footpath that follows the stream up through a timbered gorge to the headwaters. The lower reaches offer the best fishing, but they are on private land with very limited access. The fishing can be good for mostly 8- to 10-inch (and a few up to 14-inch) rainbow, cutthroat, and brook trout. You might find an occasional bull trout, especially in the upper reaches. [T10N R16W S6]

STEWART LAKE. A 20-acre mountain lake in heavy timber, reached by logging road 4 miles northeast of Philipsburg. Stewart was rehabilitated in the 1950s and is planted yearly with rainbow trout. It's quite popular, with only fair to good fishing for 9- to 11- inch rainbows. There's a Forest Service campground at the lake. [T7N R13W S16]

STONY CREEK. This is the outlet of Stony Lake, flowing for 10 miles, through steep, heavily timbered country, northeastward to Rock Creek at the Squaw Rock campground. It's followed upstream by a road for 5 miles, then a USFS trail for 6 miles to headwaters. Stony is an open, easily fished stream that is quite popular for good catches of 7- to 9-inch cutthroat trout. [T7N R16W S21]

STONY LAKE. With a 24-foot maximum depth, this 12-acre alpine cirque lake is reached by a real steep USFS trail, 6 miles southwest up Stony Creek from the end of the road. Or you can hike in 6 miles north from the Crystal Creek campground, a couple of miles east of Skalkaho Pass. The fishing is slow here, for 6- to 12-inch cutthroat trout—you have to work for 'em. [T6N R17W S17]

STORM LAKE. This 55-acre lake is about 8,700 feet above sea level, in a cirque on the northern slopes of Mount Tiny, in the Anaconda Range. It is reached by road going 7 miles south from Montana 1, just east of Silver Lake. Storm Lake is over 100 feet deep, with steep drop-offs all around. It was originally barren, but it's been planted a number of times and is now fairly good fishing for cutthroat and rainbow that will range from 9 to 18 inches. It was last planted with cutthroat in 1994; this is a good weekend lake. [T4N R13W S30]

STORM LAKE CREEK. The small, fast, and clear outlet of Storm Lake, it flows northward down a steep timbered canyon. It's followed by the Storm Lake road for about 11 miles to Warm Springs Creek, ½ mile east of Silver Lake. It's not fished much, but it does contain (here and there along its course) a few 6- to 10-inch cutthroat and brook trout. [T5N R13W S27]

STUART MILL CREEK. A 200-yard-long inlet to the northwest end of Georgetown Lake, it's heavily used by spawning rainbow trout in the spring, and kokanee salmon in the fall. It is open July 1 through November 30, with special creel limits for all trout. [T5N R13W S19]

SYDNEY LAKE. See Sidney Lake.

TAMARACK (or GLOVER) LAKE. It's reached by 4 miles of good trail and 1 mile of lousy, rough, and unmaintained footpath into the Anaconda-Pintlar Wilderness from the Meadow Creek trailhead, at the end of USFS road 5141, which heads southwest from the East Fork Rock Creek Reservoir. Tamarack is a high lake in a timbered cirque, about a mile west of Warren Peak. It covers about 15 acres and is of only moderate depth; it's swampy, with shallow drop-offs all around and quite a few aquatic plants around the shores. It is seldom fished, but it's good for small to midsize cutthroat—last planted in 1988. [T3N R15W S21]

Tamarack Lake.
—Courtesy U.S. Forest
Service

TELEGRAPH CREEK. A small tributary of the Little Blackfoot River, Telegraph is followed by good gravel roads for 8 miles from its headwaters to its mouth, near Elliston. The lower 3 miles flow through meadow and willow land, and are fair fishing for 6- to 8- inch cutthroat and a few brook trout. [T9N R6W S18]

THOMPSON LAKES. See Goat Mountain Lakes.

THORNTON (or BIG THORNTON) LAKE. A 30-acre cirque lake, perhaps 25 feet deep, in timbered country on the headwaters of Racetrack Creek. It's most easily reached by taking a 4x4 vehicle up Modesty Creek (west from Galen) and over into the Thornton Creek drainage. Then you hit the trail for a 1½-mile walk south to the lake. Thornton is moderately popular and good fishing for 8- to 10-inch rainbow trout. [T6N R11W S19]

THREEMILE CREEK. A small stream that is mostly a series of meadowland springs above. It flows for 1 mile through a flat-bottomed canyon below to its junction with the Little Blackfoot River, 2 miles west of Avon. The lower reaches—on private land—are good fishing for 8- to 12-inch cutthroat and browns. [T10N R8W S20]

TIN CUP JOE CREEK. A small stream flowing eastward from the Flint Creek Range for 8 miles, across the state (Deer Lodge) prison farm meadowland and the Deer Lodge Country Club, to the Clark Fork at Deer Lodge. The lower reaches are easily fished (mostly by kids) for poor catches of 5- to 6-inch rainbow and cutthroat trout, and trash fish. [T7N R9W S4]

TRASK LAKES (or HIDDEN LAKES). There are four lakes and several potholes here, all in alpine country above 8,000 feet in elevation. The largest of the group is Trask Lake, at 10 acres. The lakes are reached by a trail 7 miles southwest from the end of Rock Creek Lake. Or come in from the south by about 2 miles of good trail from Alpine Lake. The trail are both in a special management area, closed to motorized vehicles. Trask Lake is overpopulated with 8- to 9-inch brook trout and some cutthroat. Some of the other lakes have brook trout and a few cutts in them, too. [T7N R11W S18]

TROUT CREEK. It's about 12 miles long, in open ranchland, occasionally accessible by private and county roads from its junction with Flint Creek, 5 miles south of Philipsburg, to headwaters. The fishing here is real good for pan-size brook and cutthroat trout, but the stream is too small to stand much more than local pressure. [T6N R14W S15]

TROUT CREEK. A small stream flowing for 10 miles, through private ranchland, northward to the Little Blackfoot River, 2½ miles east of Avon. The lower reaches are used for irrigation, but they're good in early season for 8- to 10-inch brookies, cutthroat, and brown trout. [T10N R8W S27]

TWIN LAKES. These two lakes are reached by a good trail, a mile from the end of the Twin Lakes Creek jeep road, in subalpine country. Lower Twin is small, shallow, and contains few if any fish. Upper Twin, about ⅛ mile above Lower Twin, is 18 acres, fairly shallow, and bordered by scattered timber, alpine meadow, and talus slopes. It was planted in 1963 and 1971 with westslope cutthroat, and it's usually good fishing for 8- to 12-inch fish. [T4N R13W S22]

TWIN LAKES CREEK. A real fast, steep stream, flowing down a steep timbered canyon for 8 miles from Twin Lakes to Warm Springs Creek, ½ mile east of the Spring Hill campground (3½ miles east of Silver Lake). It's followed all the way by a logging road and USFS trail. The first 4 miles are fair for small cutthroat and brook trout, but are seldom fished. Fish, Wildlife and Parks surveys have also found rainbow and golden trout in the stream, from earlier plantings in Twin Lakes. [T5N R12W S19]

Lower Twin Lake. —Courtesy U.S. Forest Service

Upper Twin Lake. —Courtesy U.S. Forest Service

TYLER CREEK. Take I-90, 12 miles south from the Rock Creek junction to Byrne, then cross the Clark Fork River to the mouth of Tyler Creek, on private property. It is followed by a logging road that's closed to motorized vehicles, and the creek is brushy and hard to fish for the small cutthroat it contains. [T11N R15W S23]

UPPER BARKER LAKE. See under Barker Lakes.

UPPER ELLIOT LAKE. See under Elliot Lakes.

UPPER WILLOW CREEK. A pretty little stream flowing from heavily timbered hill country in the Long John Mountains for 17 miles to Rock Creek, 4 miles above the Squaw Rock campground. It's followed by a road all the way, except for maybe the last 2 or 3 miles. The lower reaches, flowing through meadowland, are wadable and easily and heavily fished (with owner's permission) for excellent catches of 8- to 12-inch cutthroat, rainbow, and some brook trout. Most of the creek is on private land. [T7N R16W S25]

WAHLQUIST CREEK. A real small, brushy stream in a timbered draw, flowing to Rock Creek on the side opposite the road, 3 miles above the Harry's Flat Guard Station. It's accessible by logging road from the Bitterroot drainage over Ambrose Saddle. Not so long ago, small cutthroat and brook trout were plentiful here. Now Fish, Wildlife and Parks surveys find them rare. [T9N R17W S30]

WALLACE CREEK. A small (4-mile) stream flowing through heavily timbered hills east of Clinton, followed by a logging road to its headwaters. The lower reaches have been known to contain a few 8- to 10-inch brook and cutthroat trout, but a mine, mill, and cyanide leach plant operated in the drainage for a while during the 1980s, and there are no reports on whether the fishery suffered. [T12N R17W S26]

WALLACE RESERVOIR. It's about 9 acres, with a 10-foot maximum depth, behind a 300-foot-long earthfill dam in a partly open draw, a couple of miles east (by good gravel road) of I-90 at Clinton. It is sometimes drawn clear down to nothing for summertime irrigation, but it has been known to somehow harbor a fair population of nice fat 6- to 15-inch cutthroat that are not often fished for. [T12N R17W S24]

WARM SPRINGS CREEK. It heads in heavily timbered mountains at the southern end of the Flint Creek Range, flowing southward for 9 miles (past the Upper and Lower Warm Springs campgrounds) to the Warm Springs Valley, and from there for 20 miles eastward through open meadow and farmland, past Anaconda, to the Clark Fork at the town of Warm Springs. Here is an easily accessible (by state highway and county roads) and easily fished stream, which is good fishing in its upper reaches for cutthroat, and in its middle section for rainbow, cutthroat, brook, and brown trout. It is strictly "kids' fishing" in and near Anaconda. [T5N R9W S18]

WARM SPRINGS CREEK. A small, tepid stream, flowing through limestone terrain for 10 miles to the Clark Fork River. It's crossed near the mouth by I-90, 3½ miles south of Garrison, then followed upstream all the way to its headwaters by a good gravel road. The upper reaches are overpopulated with 3- to 5-inch fingerling and trash fish; the lower reaches flow through private land (no fishing allowed) but would be excellent fishing for 8- to 10-inch brown trout, some bigger, and an abundant supply of suckers in its very turbid water. [T10N R10W S15]

WARM SPRINGS GRAVEL PIT. See Five Mile Barrow Pit.

WARM SPRINGS HOSPITAL POND. A shallow 2-acre pond on the hospital grounds, 100 yards west of I-90. It is planted yearly with rainbows, for children 13 years old and younger. [T5N R10W S24]

WELCOME CREEK. This small stream is followed by a good USFS trail for 11 miles up a heavily timbered canyon from its mouth on Rock Creek, opposite the Dallas Creek campground, to headwaters. (The middle 3 miles or so are hazardous foot trail only.) It is only occasionally fished (probably because it is on the opposite side of Rock Creek from the road), but it's fairly good for pan-size cutthroat, plus a few rainbow trout, brown trout, and whitefish. Bull trout are common, especially late in the season. [T9N R17W S2]

WEST BARKER LAKE. See under Barker Lakes.

WEST FORK CRAMER CREEK. See Cramer Creek, West Fork.

WEST FORK LOWER WILLOW CREEK. See Lower Willow Creek, West Fork.

WEST FORK OF ROCK CREEK. See Rock Creek, West Fork.

WEST FORK WILLOW CREEK. See Willow Creek, West Fork.

WILLOW CREEK. A small, jumpable stream, flowing to the Clark Fork River a mile north of and opposite Garrison; it's crossed by the old Pioneer highway, 10 miles north of Deer Lodge. This one is real easy to fish, a popular kids' creek that consistently produces excellent catches of eatin'-size brook and cutthroat trout. [T9N R10W S14]

WILLOW CREEK. This open meadow stream flows through 11 miles of grassy bank to Mill Creek, a mile northeast of Opportunity. It is fair to good fishing, through the meadowlands of the Willow Glen Ranch (about 2½ miles), for 6- to 7-inch brook and cutthroat trout. Ask for permission to fish, and chances are good that you'll get it. [T4N R10W S11]

WILLOW CREEK, West Fork. There's about 2½ miles of creek here, mostly in swampy meadowland in the Mount Haggin Wildlife Management Area, 6 miles east of Anaconda. The West Fork provides fair meadow fishing for 6- to 8-inch brook trout, if you want to hoof it all the way out there. [T3N R11W S1]

WYMAN GULCH (or WYMAN CREEK). A small stream west of Phillipsburg. Take the Rock Creek road from I-90, 2½ miles south of the guard station, then take a federal cable car across Rock Creek to the mouth of Wyman Creek, and from there a good trail 3 miles upstream. This ice-cold mountain stream flows through a heavily timbered canyon, producing fair catches of 4- to 7-inch scarlet red cutthroat and brook trout, which because of their small size are popular for eating. This stream is quite accessible, and there is lots of fishing in its lower reaches. An occasional bull trout comes up from Rock Creek. [T7N R17W S2]

WYMAN GULCH. A tiny stream, flowing for 5 miles to South Boulder Creek, south of Maxville, paralleled by a road from mouth to headwaters. The lower couple of miles, mostly in meadow, are easily fished for fair catches of pan-size cutthroat trout. [T8N R13W S22]

Brown trout. —Courtesy Tucker Lamberton

Flathead River. —Courtesy U.S. Forest Service

The Scenic Flathead River

While fishing the Flathead usually means fishing Flathead Lake, the main stem of the Flathead River, below the lake to its junction with the Clark Fork and above the lake to its three forks (North, Middle, and South), can provide some excellent fishing. There are several access sites along the river both above and below the lake, providing some walk-wading opportunities, but the most productive fishing is done by floating the river. Above the lake, from the confluence of the South Fork down to Kalispell, the primary catches will be westslope cutthroat trout, with rainbow trout, whitefish, lake trout, and a few bull trout. Below Kalispell, the catch will be rainbow trout, westslope cutthroat trout, whitefish, lake trout, a few bass, and northern pike in the slower moving water. From the lake (below Kerr Dam) downstream to the Clark Fork, rainbow trout, brown trout, largemouth bass, and northern pike will be the fare.

With the spectacular Mission Mountains and Glacier Park as backdrops, Flathead Lake is one of the most scenic fishing holes in the West. Twenty-eight miles long and sprawling over 126,080 acres, Flathead is the largest natural body of fresh water west of the Mississippi River. Clear, cold water, countless bays and islands, and twenty-six species of fish would seem to make this an angler's paradise. But there's trouble in paradise.

Gouged out by glaciers, Flathead filled with glacial meltwater and seven native fish species. Explorers in the mid-1800s found westslope cutthroat and bull trout as common gamefish. Not content to leave well enough alone, early settlers started adding new species to the pot, and by the 1930s, abundant tasty kokanee and trophy lake trout combined to make Flathead the most popular fishery in Montana. Yellow perch and lake whitefish filled out the catch.

By the 1960s, kokanee started to show the impact of heavy harvest, dam operations, and lake trout predation. *Mysis* shrimp were added to the system in the 1980s, in hopes of rejuvenating the kokanee, but it proved to be the last straw. The food chain was thrown into total chaos, and the kokanee fishery collapsed, while yellow perch, westslope cutthroat, and bull trout declined. Lake trout and lake whitefish boomed. There's a major kokanee recovery effort under way, but the system's still in flux, and where it will settle out is unknown. There's no doubt that Flathead Lake will be used in the future to illustrate both the good and bad points of new species introductions.

The good news is, there's still lots of great fishing available! The *Mysis*-based food chain is producing lots of tasty 1- to 4-pound lake trout (mackinaw). The "macs" can be taken by shoreline casting, or flat-line trolling lures and plugs in 10 to 30 feet of water, in May, June, October, and November. They can also be taken year-round by vertically jigging spoons or jigs in 30 to 110 feet of water from a boat, or through the ice when the bays freeze. The river mouth, Painted Rocks, Blue Bay, and the Narrows are consistent producers. Be aware that the south half of the lake and the lower stretch of the river are in the Flathead Indian Reservation, and fishing requires tribal licenses.

Big macs are still around too, and a number of lakers over 30 pounds are taken each year. The big fish are commonly found in 100 to 200 feet of water. Vertical jigging and trolling with down-riggers are the most popular methods of tempting the big guys. Woods Bay Point, Painted Rocks, the Mid- lake Bar, Mac Alley, and Skidoo Bay are all big fish haunts. Finding a concentration of bait fish is the key, but the bait (and the big macs) rove a lot.

Polson Bay, at the south end of the lake, still provides good catches of yellow perch. Mid- to late April finds concentrations of spawners, but anglers can still locate schools of perch during both the summer and winter. Anglers typically rove until they find a school of fish to work on. Don't be surprised to catch lake trout and lake whitefish along with the perch.

Lake whitefish have grown greatly in popularity in recent years. Hard-fighting and tasty, these fish hit light but hang on when you hook them! Lake whitefish are commonly found in 30 to 50 feet of water over gravel. Look for schools off points in mid- to late summer, and along points and flats in the winter. Gravel shelves in November can be great places for both spawning lake whitefish and spawning lake trout.

The native fish have fallen on hard times. Bull trout fishing is closed at this time, and while the cutthroat limit is already greatly reduced, catch-and-release fishing is encouraged.

Flathead offers both the trophy of a lifetime and some great fish fries. The sheer size of the lake makes it a challenge, and the beauty of the surroundings makes it hard to concentrate on the business at hand. It's no wonder it's the place I end up fishing the most. Come give it a try.

Jim Vashro
Regional Fisheries Manager
Montana Fish, Wildlife and Parks

NOTE: Since the above information was written, there have been substantial changes in fishing regulations. Please check current regulations for limits and other important information.

ABBOT CREEK. A small stream, Abbot flows through timber and pastureland to the Flathead River at Martin City. It's paralleled by a good road and provides about 2¹/₂ miles of good kids' fishing for 6- to 8-inch brookies and rainbow. As always, ask permission to fish on private lands. [T30N R19W S5]

ALDER CREEK. A very small stream, crossed at the mouth by the Good Creek road, 15 miles west of Lower Stillwater Lake. It's followed all along by a road (you'll need permission to access the first mile) and is fair fishing for 3- to 9-inch cutthroat trout. [T31N R25W S11]

ASHLEY CREEK. The outlet of Ashley Lake, this stream flows for 35 miles through Lone Lake, Lake Monroe, Smith Lake, and eventually past (just south of) Kalispell to the Flathead River, 5 miles southeast of town. It is all easily accessible by US 2 and county and farm roads, though it flows through a lot of private property. Permission reportedly comes easier in the upper reaches, above Smith Lake. Below Smith Lake, Ashley Creek is open to fishing year-round. You'll find a mix of rainbow and brook trout, yellow perch, whitefish, squawfish, and suckers throughout Ashley Creek. [T28N R21W S25]

ASHLEY (or BIG ASHLEY) LAKE. Four and a half miles long by almost 2 miles wide at the west end, this lake is over 200 feet deep with mostly steep drop-offs, and 40 or 50 acres of lilies and rushes. It's reached and followed all around by good county roads, 12 miles west of Kalispell. There are fifty or sixty summer homes and two public campgrounds on this popular, dammed lake, which has a water-level fluctuation of about 2 or 3 feet. It is excellent fishing for 10- to 12-inch kokanee (check regulations for special limits), good for 10- to 12-inch cutthroat, an occasional rainbow-cutthroat hybrid weighing 30 pounds or more (the world record was caught here), and some of the nicest yellow perch in the state. All of Ashley Lake's inlet tributaries are closed to fishing the entire year. [T28N R23W S1]

BANEY (or BARNEY) LAKE. Located on state lands southwest of Whitefish, you get to this one by heading west off Farm to Market Road, at the south end of the Kuhns Wildlife Management Area. We don't know what you'll find when you get there, but you can try to find out. [T30N R22W S30]

BEAVER (or BIG BEAVER) LAKE. A deep, 106-acre lake with lilies and aquatic plants along the north side, Beaver is on state land and can be

ASHLEY LAKE

T28N - R23 - 24W

Flathead County

TOTAL SURFACE ACRES – 3,244

Contour Interval – 20 ft.

Scale

Feet

Montana Department of Fish, Wildlife and Parks

Highway 2 - 10.4

Highway 2 - 8.5

Rand Creek

Wade Creek

Green Mountain Creek

Public Access

This map is not intended for navigational purposes. Navigational hazards are not shown. Access areas shown are public. Other places may be open to public use through the consent of individuals.

reached easily on seasonally good roads, 5 miles west of Whitefish. There are summer homes and a developed public access here, as well as pretty good fishing for rainbow that run from 10 inches up to 5-plus pounds. Beaver Lake was last stocked with rainbow in 1996, and brook trout have been planted here in the past. [T31N R22W S17]

BIG ASHLEY LAKE. See Ashley Lake.

BIG BEAVER LAKE. See Beaver Lake.

BIG LOST CREEK. This stream is 12 miles long from its headwaters in the hills, a few miles north of Ashley Lake, to its lower end in the Flathead Valley, where it sinks about 5 miles northwest of Kalispell. It is reached and followed all the way by good county roads. Big Lost Creek is mostly fished by local people, for average catches of 8- to 10-inch brook trout and a few rainbow and cutthroat. [T29N R22W S28]

BLANCHARD LAKE. A 147-acre body of water, it's accessible by road a couple of miles south of Whitefish. There is a public sportsman's access on the east side. Blanchard is up to 32 feet deep in places, with plenty of aquatic vegetation and a mossy bottom. It gets pretty warm in the summer, and it's good fishing from boats, for mostly 10- to 12-inch largemouth bass (and some recorded to 4 pounds deep down in the weeds), 8- to 10-inch yellow perch, and lots of "keeper-size" sunfish. You'll probably find a pike or two as well. In a rather odd regulatory turn, designed to give other species a chance, Blanchard Lake is open to spearing and gigging for northern pike and nongame fish through the ice and by persons submerged in the water. [T30N R22W S2]

BLAST (or CRATER) LAKE. Three acres, 20 feet deep, in an old rocky burn, it's reached to within 200 yards by road, 3 miles south of Whitefish. Crater was poisoned out in 1961 and is now planted every other year with rainbow, so it's fair to good fishing at times. [T30N R22W S13]

BLUE (or GREEN) LAKE. Misnamed Green Lake on some maps, it is located just west of the Sunday Creek road, 1 mile south of Stryker. The entire south side of this 12-acre lake lies along the edge of a big rock slide, and is real deep straight off from shore. It is spotty but sometimes good fishing for small brookies and some rainbow trout, which are planted every two years or so. [T33N R25W S1]

BLUE LAKE. An 8-acre pothole, 40 feet deep, it straddles private and Plum Creek land just west of the road, on the northwest corner of Echo Lake, north of Big Fork. Access is as questionable as the fishing, which was once reported to be good for sunfish and planted bass. We don't think it gets stocked anymore, but there could be some cranky old bass still hanging around. [T27N R19W S6]

BOCK LAKE. This is a private lake, unnamed on most maps, next to Kohler Lake between Bigfork and Creston. It was last planted in 1957 with rainbow. By now it is not worth your time, or the farmer's, to try to fish it. [T28N R19W S25]

BOOTJACK LAKE. Covering 65 acres with fairly steep drop-offs but a swampy area on the south end, Bootjack lies in timbered hills, 7 miles west of Whitefish. It's reached by a rough road on its west side. There is a new parking area and a good carry-on access trail (for float tubes, canoes, etc.) to the lake. Managed as a trophy trout lake, it was poisoned in fall 1996 due to the illegal introduction of perch and sunfish. In spring 1997 it was planted with 2,500 Eagle Lake rainbows and a few brood stock. Plans are to plant the rainbows in alternating years with westslope cutthroat. [T31N R23W S26]

BOWSER LAKE. This one is on state land southwest of Kuhns Wildlife Management Area, off Farm to Market Road. It is shallow, subject to freezing out during cold winters and drying up during hot summers, hard to get to, and has few fish. [T29N R22W S6]

BOYLE LAKE. It's about 46 acres and 50 feet deep, set in conifers, near the railroad a mile west of the northwest end of Whitefish Lake. Boyle contains only sunfish now. [T31N R22W S7]

BULL LAKE. Take a right off US 93 in Stryker, following the Stillwater River to the Loon's Echo road. Go to the south end of Fish Lake, and hang a right on a little 4WD track for ¼ mile or so (on foot or on wheels) to the inlet of Bull Lake. It's a long lake, set in timbered mountains, 106 acres, over 70 feet deep, and with mostly steep drop-offs all around. There are summer cottages here and there, and good fishing for 10- to 12-inch cutthroat trout, and sunfish. Kamloops rainbow have also been planted there recently. [T34N R24W S29]

BURNT LAKE. With an area of 4½ acres and a 40-foot maximum depth, Burnt Lake gets planted with cutthroat every other year and is reportedly pretty fair fishing for cutts, and brookies as well. To get there, take the Sunday Creek road south from Stryker, past Sunday Lakes ½ mile, then take a left and drive up USFS road 3738. You may have to walk about a mile on this road if it's not passable. Good luck! [T33N R24W S17]

CABIN LAKE. A pretty little 16.8-acre pothole, 20 feet deep, in timber a couple of miles north of Echo Lake. This one is private, with unknown (to us) fishing potential. [T28N R20W S25]

CANYON LAKE(S). See Hidden Lake(s).

CEDAR CREEK. A small, brushy stream in an old burn, Cedar Creek flows south for 10 miles towards the Flathead River, and eventually sinks just north of Columbia Falls. It's impounded north of town for the municipal water supply and is closed in that area. However, it is open above the impoundment, and fair fishing for 6- to 7-inch brook trout. The North Fork road follows Cedar Creek along its upper reaches. [T30N R20W S8]

CEDAR LAKE. Really a shallow, 15-acre peat bog in brushy burned-over country, accessible by a logging road to within a couple of hundred feet from the shore, 3½ miles north of Columbia Falls. It is seldom fished (a boat is a must), but it's fair for 8- to 10-inch cutthroat. It's on private land, so get permission if you really have your heart set on fishing there. [T31N R20W S29]

CHINOOK LAKE. This is a small, shallow, private lake just over a mile northeast of Tally Lake. It was last planted in the late '70s with grayling. It's doubtful that anything is left now, but you could ask the owners if you're interested. [T31N R23W S21]

CHURCH SLOUGH. This is a classic oxbow slough, typical of the lower Flathead Valley area, reached easily by county road 6 miles southeast of Kalispell. It provides good fishing for largemouth bass, northern pike, and yellow perch, with the occasional whitefish thrown in. Boats come in handy here. Church Slough is open year-round—check current regulations for special limits on bass. [T28N R30W S31]

CIRCLE LAKE. This is a 2-acre pothole on private land, a mile or so northwest of Echo Lake. Not only is it private, it probably doesn't have any fish in it. [T28N R20W S36]

CLIFF LAKE. A 5-acre pothole lake on state land. You get there by taking Farm to Market Road and hanging a left ¼ mile north of Kuhns Road, then a left at the Y, and finally the next main right. Or, you could just follow the empty beer cans and bottles to the lake, as this is a popular party spot. The fishing isn't too bad through the weeds for fat pan-size rainbow, a few cutts, and some grayling they're trying out here. [T30N R22W S30]

CORDUROY CREEK. A tiny, brushy tributary of Good Creek, it is crossed near the mouth by the Good Creek road, 10 miles west of the Stillwater Ranger Station, and followed upstream by a trail. It's not fished much, but it's fair for 6- to 10-inch brookies in some beaver ponds about ½ mile above the mouth, and small cutthroat through most of its length. [T31N R25W S1]

CRATER LAKE. See Blast Lake.

CRESTON LAKE. See Jessup Mill Pond.

CRYSTAL CREEK. A small "kids' creek," it's a tributary to Cedar Creek and accessible by road 5 miles north from Columbia Falls. There are about 3 miles of fair fishing here, for 6- to 7-inch cutthroat trout. [T31N R20W S16]

DOG CREEK. It flows into and out of Dog Lake, for about 4 miles above and 3 miles below, and eventually into the Stillwater River, about a mile above Lower Stillwater Lake. The lower mile contains a few small brookies—it's marginal at best. [T32N R23W S18]

DOG LAKE. A 99-acre lake that is only about 25 feet deep at most, it sits in rolling timber just west of US 93, about 3 miles north of Olney. Whether you come in from the south end of Upper Stillwater Lake or from the highway side of the lake, be prepared for a fairly rough road. Dog Lake has a shallow, narrow neck in the middle, and it's fairly deep at the north end and marshy at the south end. There are a few brook trout, maybe some rainbow, and enough good-size pike to keep you busy. [T33N R23W S31]

DOLLAR LAKE. A deep, 8-acre pothole in rolling timberland, ¹/₂ mile west of Whitefish Lake and a mile north of Beaver Lake, it's accessible by a logging road 5 miles from US 93. Here is a moderately popular pond that's been planted every other year with rainbow and has offered fair to good fishing for midsize cutthroat and rainbow. Illegal introductions of Fathead minnows, however, have put Dollar Lake on the short list of lakes to be rehabilitated. [T31N R22W S16]

DUCK LAKE. It's really just a wide, brushy spot in the Stillwater River (about 60 acres), 1¹/₂ miles above Upper Stillwater Lake and right beside US 93, 29 miles north of Whitefish. It's fair fishing for 8- to 10-inch brook and cutthroat, plus a few northern pike. [T33N R24W S15]

DUNSIRE CREEK. Go from Whitefish to Tally Lake, then take the Logan Creek road and next the Sheppard Creek road, for 5 miles above the Star Meadow Guard Station to Dunsire Creek. It is mostly too small to fish, but it's fair in some beaver ponds near the mouth for 6- to 10-inch brook and native cutthroat trout. [T30N R25W S8]

EAST BASS (or SKYLINE, or RAINBOW) LAKE. A private, 4-acre pothole, ¹/₄ mile east of Sawdust Lake in the "Many Lakes" housing development east of Creston. It has been good fishing for largemouth bass and rainbow trout in the past, but it's no longer stocked and probably isn't much worth the effort. [T28N R20W S24]

It doesn't get any better. —Courtesy Michele Archie

ECHO LAKE. A 725-acre, mud-bottomed lake of a most uneven outline, it reaches 75 feet deep in spots. Reached by good county roads 5 miles north of Bigfork, Echo Lake has one small inlet (Echo Creek) but no surface drainage, and is mostly spring fed. It is a popular summer recreation lake, meaning waterskiing, jet boats, etc. Northern pike had taken over the lake for a while, but recent efforts at rehabilitating the largemouth bass and rainbow trout fisheries have been fairly successful. Kokanee salmon have also been stocked here in recent years. There are some large fish in this lake. Check current regulations for special limits on bass and restrictions on spearing. [T27N R19W S5]

EGAN SLOUGH. This is a classic oxbow slough, off the Flathead River 2 miles west of Creston. Access is pretty informal—you may have to ask permission and might end up carrying your boat a short distance. The fishing is well worth the minimal trouble, excellent for yellow perch and northern pike. State-record pike have come out of the Flathead River in these parts—they're in there! [T28N R20W S20]

EMMET (or SUN FISH) SLOUGH, or HORSESHOE BEND. This one makes almost a complete circle ³/₄ mile in diameter, in open farmland with cottonwood along the banks. Located ¹/₂ mile southwest of Church Slough, it is reached by good county road north of Somers. Emmet is good fishing for largemouth bass that are reported up to better than 5 pounds, and also contains a large population of yellow perch and sunfish. [T27N R21W S1]

ESTES LAKE. Take Montana 35 for 5 miles south from Bigfork, and then a washed-out, rocky mountain road for 1½ miles east from Woods Bay, to Estes. It is about 3 acres, not too deep, and it's fair to good brook and rainbow trout fishing for mostly 10-inchers, plus a few recorded to 1½ pounds. [T26N R19W S20]

EVERS CREEK. A small, swampy stream, about 8 miles long, with lots of beaver ponds that are known locally as "Short's Meadows." Evers flows to Logan Creek, 3 miles north of Tally Lake, and is accessible in turns by the Star Meadow road and various smaller logging roads. It is hard to fish but contains a fair number of small brookies and cutts. [T31N R23W S8]

FENNON (or FENAN, or RUSSELL, or MOON) SLOUGH. Take the Somers road 4 miles west from Bigfork to the south end of this slough, which is about 150 yards across, and forms almost a complete circle about ½ mile in diameter. Despite the fact that nobody can agree on what to call it, Fennon is moderately popular with local people and tourists from Bigfork, and it provides some of the best largemouth bass fishing in this area, for fish weighing from 1 to 5 pounds. There's decent northern pike fishing as well. It's open the whole year—check current regulations for special bass limits. [T27N R20W S15]

FINGER (or WALL) LAKE. Set in timbered rocky-ridge country, it's about ¾ mile long, narrow, and deep in places with steep, rocky shores. It is reached by trail 200 yards from the end of a logging road, up the west side of Duck Lake (not so easy to find), or by a 1-mile hike on USFS trail 802, just south of the Upper Stillwater Lake campground. This neck of the woods is being discovered, by more and more people, as a nice day-hiking area, and the lakes are getting more pressure than ever (still not very much). Look to catch some nice brook trout out of this one, ranging up to 18 inches. [T33N R24W S22]

FIRE LAKES. Three lakes, two of them about 7 acres and the other about 13 acres, in an old burn, accessible to within 200 yards or so by USFS road 3738, off the Sunday Creek road, just south of Sunday Lakes. The road may or may not be passable, and walking is always an option. They are lightly fished in winter, almost never in the summer, but they're good for brooks that average a pound and grow bigger. [T33N R24W S17]

FISH (or STRYKER) LAKE. A deep lake, covering 32 acres, right next to Bull Lake in the Stillwater State Forest, it's reached by a 2-mile drive right out of Stryker. Fish Lake is moderately popular, good fishing for 9- to 10-inch brookies, and quite a few nice ones—up to 3 pounds.[T34N R24W S29]

FITZSIMMONS CREEK. This small tributary of the Stillwater River is followed by road the length of its main and west forks, and by trail up its north fork. The main stem is the only one worth fishing, and that's for small cutts and brookies. A severely declining run of bull trout uses the stream as well. [T34W R24N S5]

FOY LAKES. Three lakes, Lower Foy (20 acres), Middle Foy (35 acres), and Foy (273 acres and over 130 feet deep), about ⅛ mile apart in open country. They're reached by paved road, 2 miles southwest from Kalispell. The lower and middle lakes are as good as barren. The upper lake is heavily fished for good catches of 10-inch to 2- pound rainbow trout, as well as some kokanee salmon that were planted in '92 and '93. This is a very busy lake in the summer, packed with ski boats and jet skis and the like. Not the place to go if you're looking to get away from it all. Check current regulations for special limits on trout. [T28N R22W S26]

FROG LAKE. See Summit Lake.

GOOD CREEK. A fair-size stream, emptying into Logan Creek 3 miles below Lower Stillwater Lake, and fishable from shore in most areas. There are about 20 miles of fishing water, clear to the mouth of Plume Creek, and it is followed most of the way by a good logging road west from the Stillwater Ranger Station. There are many beaver ponds along the middle reaches, and ½ mile of box canyon near the mouth. The entire stream is good fishing for 3- to 11-inch brook and cutthroat trout. [T31N R23W S3]

GREEN LAKE. See Blue Lake.

GRIFFIN CREEK. This stream heads just north of Pleasant Valley Mountain, and flows over 20 miles to its junction with Logan Creek, in the north end of Star Meadows. It's followed by USFS road 538 for most of its length, through some heavily logged country. Catches of cutthroat and brook trout have declined in the past several years, but the fishing is still pretty good for the small ones. [T30N R24W S8]

HALF MOON LAKE. A fairly deep, 54-acre lake in relatively flat, timbered country, just across the road from Lake Five, near West Glacier. Half Moon was rehabilitated and planted with bass in 1969. It was subsequently planted again and is a bass lake now, with fairly good fishing. Brook trout were just recently planted, with unknown results. [T31N R19W S11]

HAND CREEK. A small tributary of Griffin Creek, in formerly timbered mountains, it used to be home to a solid population of native cutthroat. These days, it's hard to find anything but real small brookies. There are about 3 miles of fishing, most of it easily accessed from logging road. [T29N R25W S2]

HANSON (or PIKE) LAKE. A private lake located 4 miles southeast of Tally Lake, this is a shallow, 5-acre pond in rocky, mostly logged-over country. It had some brookies swimming around at last report, and had at least one pike in it a long time ago. [T30N R23W S24]

HASKILL CREEK. About 10 miles long, in timber above and ranchland below, it's part of the Whitefish municipal water supply—meaning that a portion of this stream is regularly closed. Check the current regulations to make sure. Haskill flows to the Whitefish River, a few miles below town, and is crossed here and there by county roads, for 6 miles of fair fishing for 6- to 7-inch cutthroat and brook trout. Good kids' fishing. [T31N R21W S8]

HERRIG CREEK. It drains from Herrig Lake, on the southern slopes of Pleasant Valley Mountain, for 5 miles to the north end of Little Bitterroot Lake, and it's followed along the lower reaches by a good gravel road. Herrig is presently closed to fishing the entire year, to protect spawning cutthroat and rainbow. [T28N R25W S36]

HERRIG LAKE. Located in the Stillwater State Forest, between Stryker Peak and Herrig Mountain, you can get within $1/4$ mile on a primitive road off the Stryker Ridge road (if the road isn't gated). Since 1982, it has been planted every few years (most recently in 1996), with cutthroat, and should offer good fishing if you can get there. [T34N R24W S14]

HIDDEN (or CANYON) LAKE(S). About $3/8$ mile long by 200 yards or so wide, and pinched to a narrow, shallow channel in the middle so that it's almost two lakes, Hidden is basically a trench on the Little Bitterroot River. It's reached by a $1/2$-mile hike (a steep drop) from the road, about 3 miles north of Hubbart Reservoir. It's in heavily timbered country, is fairly deep in spots, and is fair fishing for rainbow and brook trout. [T26N R24W S20]

HOLE-IN-THE-WALL LAKE. From just south of the Upper Stillwater Lake campground, take USFS trail 803 directly to Hole-in-the-Wall, which is more or less round, deep, and used to be relatively unknown when it was a cross-country hike in. Still, it has been only slightly discovered since the trail went in, and it can be good fishing for 10- to 13-inch brookies and the occasional lunker. [T33N R24W S22]

HORSESHOE BEND. See Emmet Slough.

HUBBART RESERVOIR. It's 430 acres, but drawn down very low at times, in logged country. A poor road (high clearance recommended)

Hidden Lake.
—Courtesy Michele Archie

leads to the east side of the reservoir. Hubbart has been poisoned and replanted at least twice in the past, but "bucket biologists" insist on planting undesirable species. This time around it's yellow perch, which threaten to choke out a potentially healthy kokanee and rainbow fishery. You can still catch a fat rainbow or two, if you can work your way through the perch. [T25N R24W S7]

JESSUP MILL POND (or CRESTON LAKE). It's just east of, and it supplies the water for, the Creston Hatchery. It's reached by paved highway, either 10 miles east from Kalispell, or an equal distance north from Bigfork. Lying in an east-west direction, it's about ⅝ mile long by a couple of hundred yards wide, mostly in cut-over timber but open on the west end. Spring fed and very fertile, it has been planted now and again with this and that, was poisoned out, and is no longer stocked, but it's presently fair fishing for nice fat brook trout. [T28N R20W S11]

JOHNSON LAKES. Three private, pretty little potholes—North, South, and East—in cut-over timber and farmland. Go 1 mile east on the Swan highway (Montana 83) from the junction with Montana 35, and you'll see the lakes in the field to the north. You need to get permission, and they might give you an idea of where to fish for a mix of perch, sunfish, and bass. [T27N R19W S18]

KILA LAKE. See Smith Lake.

LAGONI LAKE. It's reached by rough road 1 mile south from the Upper Stillwater Lake campground, but it's not quite as easy to find as it looks on the map—there is a maze of old roads that isn't shown. Lagoni is 20 acres, deep on the northeast side, with steep rocky cliffs on the south side and timber to the north. It should be fished from a boat (if you're going to fish). There are some nice northern pike here, as well as a few brookies, some rainbow and cutthroat planters, and a good share of trash fish. [T33N R24W S26]

LAGONI LAKE, Upper. This one is unnamed on many maps, but can be found by hiking, trailless, upstream from Lagoni Lake. That's a long bushwhack, but it may be preferable to the shorter but more up-and-down trek from Hole-in-the-Wall Lake. However you get there, you'll probably find yourself alone with a lake full of 10- to 12- inch cutthroat. [T33N R24W S21]

LAKE BLAINE. A popular summer-home, waterskiing, and picnicking lake, with one resort and a private campground. It covers 372 acres of timber and farmland right at the foot of the Swan Range. From Kalispell, take good county roads 10 miles east. Blaine used to be stocked annually with all kinds of fish, but hasn't been since 1984. It's got a mix of bass, pike, perch, rainbow, and kokanee, with the cold-water species in decline. There are some sizable largemouth and pike holed up in this lake. It's closed to spearing. [T29N R20W S26]

LAKE FIVE. Covering 235 acres, it's up to 62 feet deep in spots, with a gradual drop-off and a gravel bottom. It's located 3 miles south of West Glacier, 4 miles north of Coram, off a good county road. Lake Five is fairly popular in the summer with water-sports enthusiasts. It was formerly a good trout fishery, but it was taken over by trash fish, then rehabilitated in 1969. It is now a decent largemouth bass fishery, and Montana Fish, Wildlife and Parks is trying to get kokanee started as well. [T31N R19W S9]

LAKE MARY RONAN. A 1,500-acre lake that features resorts, summer homes, and the attendant water-sports enthusiasts, Mary Ronan is still a high-quality fishery with several species of fish. Good catches of 10- to

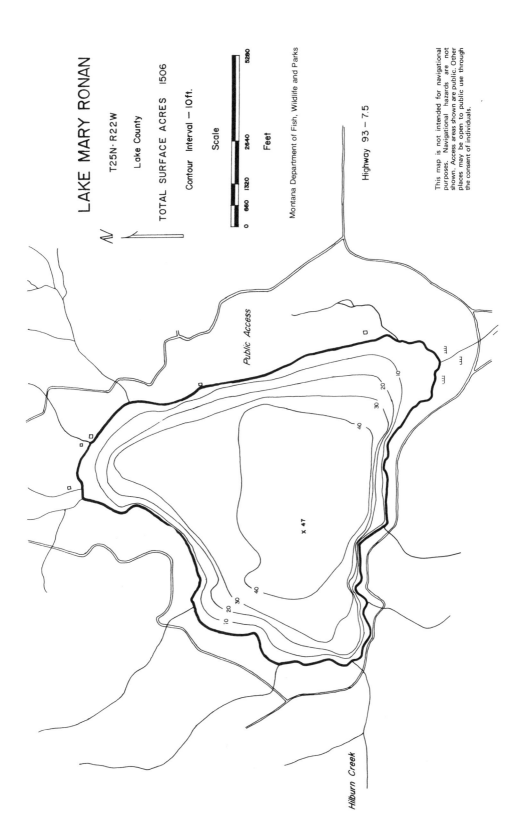

LAKE MARY RONAN

T25N- R22W

Lake County

TOTAL SURFACE ACRES 1506

Contour Interval — 10 ft.

Scale

| 0 | 660 | 1320 | 2640 | 5280 |

Feet

Montana Department of Fish, Wildlife and Parks

Highway 93 — 7.5

This map is not intended for navigational purposes. Navigational hazards are not shown. Access areas shown are public. Other places may be open to public use through the consent of individuals.

Public Access

Hilburn Creek

X 47

20-inch rainbow, 10- to 16-inch kokanee salmon, 10- to 14-inch cut-throat, and 2- to 5-pound largemouth bass can be had here. Unfortunately there is now a growing population of perch, which were illegally introduced in 1993, and although the lake is stocked heavily (particularly with kokanee) the prognosis for the fishery is uncertain. Lake Mary Ronan is subject to special seasons and limits, so check the regulations carefully. From Dayton, along the west side of Flathead Lake, take a good county road 8 miles northwest to the lake. There is a state campground on the east side of the lake, which, as the Plum Creek timber company goes forward with the planned sale of its lands around the lake, may become the only free public access. [T25N R22W S11]

LAKE MONROE (or LOWER ASHLEY LAKE). Monroe is a private lake connected with Lone (or Middle Ashley) Lake by a swampy but passable-by-boat area, so that the two lakes are almost one. From Ashley (Big Ashley) Lake, follow a good road 4 miles south, to where the road crosses Ashley Creek. Monroe contains a little bit of everything, from rainbow and cutthroat to bass, perch, and squawfish, due to the ease of travel up and down Ashley Creek. [T27N R23W S4]

LAKE OF THE WOODS. A pothole lake, 62 acres and fairly deep, it is located on private land ½ mile north of Echo Lake, north of Bigfork. It used to be planted with trout and may still harbor a remnant population. If you're really interested in fishing here, the only way to do it is to ask first. [T28N R19W S31]

LAZY CREEK. A small, swampy stream with lots of beaver ponds, it flows through exceptionally brushy country into the northwest corner of Whitefish Lake. It is accessible at the mouth (but surrounded by private land) via East Lakeshore Drive, then a few miles up through a maze of logging roads on Plum Creek land. In short, access is difficult. The dedicated angler will find fair to good fishing for 6- to 12-inch brookies. [T31N R22W S5]

LEBEAU CREEK. A small, brushy stream in a rocky, beaver-dammed canyon, LeBeau sinks about ½ mile above its mouth and rises into Upper Stillwater Lake. Get to the middle reaches by going 8 miles west of the Stillwater Ranger Station on the Martin Creek logging road. There are reported to be about 4 miles of good fishing here, for 10- to 12-inch brookies. [T33N R24W S36]

LITTLE BEAVER LAKE. About 23 acres in area, it's almost an extension of the north end of Big Beaver Lake, separated by a narrow swampy area. Little Beaver is reached by road, through rolling timberland, 5 miles west of Whitefish. It is planted regularly with rainbow and is pretty good fishing for 10- to 14-inchers, with the occasional old-timer showing up as well. [T31N R22W S17]

LITTLE BITTERROOT LAKE. This lake is about 3 miles long by $1/2$ mile wide, fairly deep, and dammed, with 4 feet of water-level fluctuation. Located $1^1/2$ miles west of Marion, this lake can be reached via any of several good roads. This is a moderately popular recreational lake. There is a state park at the north end, a couple of resorts, and sixty or seventy summer homes, with all the attendant activities. It is planted regularly with kokanee salmon and two strains of rainbow, and supports a healthy population of yellow perch as well. Fishing is fairly good for these species, in the 8- to 14-inch range, but watch out: you could hook into a rainbow much bigger than you had bargained for! [T28N R25W S36]

LOGAN CREEK. It flows for about 25 miles, through a mix of public and private lands, into and out of Tally Lake, and dumps into the Stillwater River. You'll find brookies, whitefish, and squawfish in the lower reaches, from the mouth to Tally Lake. The first couple of miles above Tally Lake offer fair to good fishing for cutthroat, brookies, and whitefish. Farther up, you'll find only very small brook trout and the occasional whitefish, except maybe in the private beaver ponds in Star Meadows. Logan Creek is followed for most of its length by good logging roads. Be especially aware of the private land in the area. [T31N R23W S3]

LONE (or MIDDLE ASHLEY) LAKE. Four miles south of Ashley Lake, in timberland, reached by the Ashley Creek road, it covers 200 acres, all under 50 feet deep, with shallow drop-offs, lots of vegetation, and a muddy bottom. Lone Lake is connected with Lake Monroe (or Lower Ashley) by a swampy but passable-by-boat area. Access is very poor to Lone Lake, as it sits mostly in private land, but there is some state land on its shores, so you can get to it. This lake holds a wide variety of fish, mostly warm-water species, but anything might be found there, due to the ease of travel up and down Ashley Creek. [T28N R24W S36]

LORE LAKE. From Kalispell, take the Farm to Market road north for 12 miles, then a private lane west for $1/2$ mile, where you'll find Lore right behind a ranch house. It's $1/2$ mile long but only 100 feet or so across, below timber on the west and open ranchland to the east, and so shallow as to freeze out during hard winters. It's also drawn down every year for irrigation purposes, but it's fair fishing for brook trout in spite of a heavy amount of aquatic vegetation. Once again, ask first to fish here. [T30N R22W S32]

LITTLE BITTERROOT LAKE

T27N-B24W

FLATHEAD COUNTY

TOTAL SURFACE ACRES 2,925
CONTOUR INTERVAL 20 ft.

Scale

500   1000'   1/2 MILE   1 MILE

FEET

Montana Department of Fish, Wildlife and Parks

This map is not intended for navigational purposes. Navigational hazards are not shown. Access areas shown are public. Other places may be open to public use through the consent of individuals.

LOST CREEK. It flows north for about 3 miles to some 90-foot falls, and then for another mile almost to the south end of Tally Lake, where it makes a 135-degree turn and flows to the southeast for another 10 miles, through Lore Lake to the Stillwater River. The lower reaches are not much worth fishing, and they're mostly on private land. The upper reaches, both below and above the falls, are good fishing for small brook and cutthroat trout. [T30N R22W S33]

LOST LAKE. It's ⅛ mile by easy hike, through private land, off the Stoner Creek road, 5½ miles west of Lakeside, near the headwaters of the Stoner Creek drainage. It's good fishing for a large number of small brook trout. [T26N R21W S21]

LOWER ASHLEY LAKE. See Lake Monroe.

LOWER STILLWATER LAKE. In a timbered flat alongside US 93, 17 miles north of Whitefish, Lower Stillwater is about 248 acres, with mostly shallow drop-offs. It is best fished by boat or through the ice for abundant yellow perch, pike in the 5- to 12- pound range, and some brook and cutthroat trout. Decent rainbow fishing can be found around the outlet area, especially in springtime. Check current regulations for special limits on trout, and restrictions on spearing. [T32N R23W S20]

LUPINE LAKE. It's 13 acres, steep off-shore and deep in the middle, located about a mile west of Ashley Mountain. Reach it by a 2-mile trail from either the Ashley Mountain road or from the Griffin Creek road. Lupine is moderately popular, and it's good fishing for 10- to 16-inch westslope cutthroat (stocked regularly) and possibly some remnants of a Yellowstone cutthroat population. [T29N R25W S12]

MARTHA LAKE. It's only 2 acres in size, but it's deep, sitting in alpine country (there's not even any brush around it) on Birch Creek. It's reached by a mountain climber's nightmare of a trip, ½ mile below Birch Lake in the Jewel Basin hiking area. This lake is almost never fished, but it contains a fair population of rainbow and rainbow-cutthroat hybrids. It's unnamed on most maps. [T28N R18W S31]

MARTIN LAKES. To reach these two lakes in timbered hills, take the Martin Creek logging road from Lower Stillwater Lake about 3 miles west, then USFS road 9629 north for 1 mile. Upper Martin, in a steep rocky canyon, is about 13 acres and very deep, but marshy around the shore. It is fair fishing for 8- to 10-inch brookies, a very few rainbow, and plenty of trash fish. Lower Martin lies at the head of a meadow, fed with seepage from Upper Martin. It is about 6 acres and shallow, with a muddy bottom; it's fair ice fishing, for about the same kinds of fish as in the upper lake. [T32N R24W S11]

MCGILRAY (or MCGILBRAY, or MCGILVRAY) LAKE. A most irregularly shaped 34-acre pothole in rolling timberland, McGilray sits on a section of state land near the Boy Scout camp between Creston and Bigfork. You'll probably have to walk a short way down a gated road to the lake itself. The water level is variable, depending on the year and the season, so it may seem more like two or three lakes rather than one, if the water is low. There are probably still some largemouth bass hanging out here, and it has been planted for the last few years with rainbow (including a plant of brood stock for a kids' fishing derby). [T28N R20W S36]

MCWENNEGER (or MCWINEGAR) SLOUGH. Located just north of Montana 35, 2 miles west of its junction with Montana 206, this slough covers about 50 acres. Loaded with weed beds and lily pads, McWenneger offers prime habitat for northern pike, largemouth bass, and yellow perch. It is popular with water-skiers in the summer and ice fishers in the winter. Boaters may need to be a bit creative when putting in, since the boat ramp is marginal at best. [T28N R20W S6]

McGilray Lake. —Courtesy John Fraley

MCWHORTER'S POND. Unnamed on most maps, this small pond is located near the Danielson ranch, about 7 miles west of Kalispell and not far from Batavia. It has been stocked with rainbow and cutthroat trout in the last few years. [T28N R23W S25]

MEADOW LAKE. This is a pretty little lake, actually a drowned meadow complete with partially submerged outbuildings at its fringe. It sits north of the Upper Whitefish Lake road (road 487) about 3 miles east of Olney. Meadow Lake is best fished from a boat, and it's stocked with rainbow trout every few years, most recently in 1996. [T32N R23W S4]

MIDDLE ASHLEY LAKE. See Lone Lake.

MOON SLOUGH. See Russell Slough.

MUD LAKE. This is a small lake, located on private land just west of Lake Five, bordering Blankenship Road. It's probably not worth the bother of getting permission to fish here, for small sunfish. [T31N R19W S9]

MURRAY LAKE. Follow the signs in the Beaver Lake complex, west of Whitefish, to find this deep 45-acre lake. It is stocked every year and has been fairly popular—especially among people fishing from boats—for good catches of 10- to 17-inch rainbow. But thanks to illegal introductions of Fathead minnows, Murray is due for rehabilitation in the near future. [T31N R22W S18]

MYSTERY LAKE. From a take-off point on the Stryker Ridge road, take a fair State Forest trail for 1¼ miles, across a drainage and over to the lake. It's a small, shallow lake three-quarters of the way up a steep, exceptionally brushy flank. Occasionally impacted by winter kill, it contains 8- to 10-inch cutthroat. [T33N R23W S8]

NO TELLUM LAKE. No Tellum is a small reservoir, unnamed on most maps, located just south of the southeast end of McGregor Lake. Take the Murr Creek road south from US 2 and hang the first right. Unfortunately, you're likely to find not much of a lake left. Plans are to remove the dam, which has been judged to be unsafe, and pretty well drain the lake. If you make it to No Tellum before all of that happens, you'll find a trophy rainbow lake (artificial lure only, special creel limits) with dark brown water that the rainbow seem to like just fine. After No Tellum is drained, look for the management of one of the other small lakes in the Thompson Chain of Lakes—perhaps Cad or Cibid—to change, in order to create a replacement trophy fishery. [T26N R25W S16]

OLIVE LAKE. This little pothole is on private land between Kohler and Angel Lakes, north of Echo Lake. With permission you can hike the ¼ mile or so to fish for largemouth bass. If you find the owners, they'll have more information on the present conditions there. It is unnamed on some maps. [T28N R19W S30]

PETERSON LAKE. This one covers 80 acres with a very irregular shoreline; it's timbered on the east side, with farmland on the west. Peterson can be reached by boat from Echo Lake during periods of high water. Otherwise, access is all private, as the Plum Creek land shown on some maps has been sold to other private interests. The lake is good fishing for largemouth bass, yellow perch, and sunfish, as well as some northern pike. [T27N R19W S7]

PIKE LAKE. See Hanson Lake.

RAINBOW LAKE (east of Creston). See East Bass Lake.

RAINBOW LAKE. In timbered hills (second growth) west of Whitefish. North of the road to Little Beaver Lake, this lake is about midway between Murray and Beaver Lakes, about ½ mile from each. Rainbow has been fairly popular in past years, but stocking efforts have been stopped because of its frequent winterkill. It's doubtful that there are any fish there now. [T31N R22W S19]

REDMOND CREEK. A road just south of Hubbart Reservoir takes you to the mouth of this very small tributary of Briggs Creek. Redmond flows through a wide, timbered canyon and provides about 3 miles of fair 6- to 8-inch cutthroat fishing, but it is really too small to bother. [T25N R24W S18]

ROGERS LAKE. This lake is 237 acres in area and 20 feet at its deepest. To get there from Kalispell, take US 2 south about 20 miles, then the Rogers Lake road south to the lake. Rogers was one of the original grayling lakes in this part of the country, but some "bucket biologist" introduced perch a few years back. The lake was poisoned in the early '90s and has been planted with grayling, cutthroat, and rainbow since. The grayling fishing is out of this world. By all reports, Rogers Lake is a great success story of rehabilitation and recovery. Let's hope it keeps going that way. The spawning inlet is closed to fishing the entire year. [T27N R23W S30]

RUSSELL SLOUGH. See Fennon Slough.

SHEPPARD CREEK. This is a small, willowed, brushy, beaver-dammed stream. You can reach it at the mouth by the Logan Creek road, 7½ miles west of Tally Lake. It's followed upstream by a logging road for 7 miles of fishing. Sheppard is a tough one to fish due to the brush, but it's a fair pro-ducer of 6- to 12-inch brook trout and some cutthroat. [T30N R24W S8]

SKAGGS (or SKAGS) LAKE. Forty-two acres and 17 feet deep, it's lo-cated a couple of miles northeast of Proctor, west of Flathead Lake. Word is that public access has been denied and that fishing is poor anyway. Go on ahead to Lake Mary Ronan if you're already in the area. [T25N R21W S22]

SKYLES LAKE. To reach this shallow, 37-acre lake, go 3 miles west of Whitefish on US 93. There's a state fish and game access area here, and it's close enough to town to be moderately popular. It used to be consis-tently stocked with trout until 1984, when the state realized the lake wasn't particularly suited to trout. Now you'll find some largemouth bass there, and maybe some leftover trout. Perch and sunfish are likely as well. [T31N R22W S33]

SKYLINE LAKE. See East Bass Lake.

SMITH (or KILA) LAKE. This lake covers about 300 shallow acres in a flat-bottomed mountain valley beside the town of Kila. From Kalispell, take US 2 southwest for 9 miles. Smith Lake is followed all the way around by a road, but it's so marshy and boggy that about the only place you can get to the water is along the south side, where there is a Depart-ment of Fish, Wildlife and Parks access site. Most people fish from boats, or they wait until winter. It is excellent fishing, though, for 6- to 12-inch yellow perch, a few largemouth bass, brooks, some small sunfish, and a very few 8- to 12-inch rainbow trout. It's also a great place to view water-fowl and birds of all sorts. [T27N R22W S9]

SMOKEY LAKE. About 10 acres with a 20-foot maximum depth, Smokey's located along the road to Burnt Lake, a mile or so south of Sunday Lakes. It was planted about 5 years ago with brook and Kamloops rainbow trout, and again in 1996 with westslope cutts. Kind of a crapshoot, but worth a try. [T33N R24W S17]

SPENCER LAKE. Spencer is 28.5 acres and no more than 15 feet deep anywhere, with a mud bottom. It sits just south of US 93, 4 miles west of Whitefish, just before the Twin Bridges Road-Tally Lake turnoff. It was managed for a while as a trophy rainbow lake, until pumpkinseeds and perch were introduced (by some bright soul) and took over. You might still be able to catch a rainbow or two here, but you'll get real tired of taking sunfish off your hook in the meantime. [T30N R22W S4]

SPILL LAKE. It's just over the bank from Blackie's Bay on Echo Lake. At 9.7 acres, it used to be good fishing for rainbow, but it's now gone private and no longer stocked. [T27N R19W S6]

SPRING CREEK. A tiny stream that rises about 3 miles northwest of Kalispell and flows to the southwest through private farmland to town (and the Stillwater River); Trumbull Creek flows into it. It is fished mostly by kids, year-round for fair to good catches of small brook, and now and then a rainbow or cutthroat, trout. [T28N R21W S9]

SPRING CREEK. This small stream drains Morning Slough and runs south for 4 miles through farmland to Lake Blaine, south of Columbia Falls. It's accessible by county road at the mouth and at intervals here and there upstream. The inlet area harbors some largemouth bass, while small brookies can be found on up to the slough. [T29N R20W S23]

SPRING LAKES. Take US 93 north about 3 miles past Radnor, then right on the Spring Creek road to the end, then hike northeast ¼ mile cross-country to find the upper lake. It is stocked every two or three years with cutthroat and is rarely fished. There may be some nice trout in this one. The lower lake can go dry, so don't bother with it. [T33N R24W S4]

STILLWATER RIVER. This stream flows for nearly 60 miles, beginning as a small mountain stream in the Whitefish Range and ending up a sluggish tributary of the Flathead River, a couple of miles south of Kalispell. The upper 10 miles are followed by a logging road out of Stryker, and offer good fishing for cutthroat, brookies, and mountain whitefish. The next 25 miles or so are followed fairly closely by US 93. There are few formal access sites but many bridges on logging roads. The river is floatable, except for the sections just below both Upper and Lower Stillwater Lakes, where logjams, fences, and heavy brush can make for some interesting portages. You'll find cutthroat, rainbow, brookies, and whitefish scattered throughout this section, as well as the occasional northern pike cruising in from one of the lakes. The next stretch is through farmland in the Flathead Valley, and with the farmer's permission you might catch some rainbow, cutthroat, or suckers. The 5-mile section from the mouth to the confluence with the Whitefish River offers good pike fishing, and even some lake trout wandering up from Flathead Lake. Check current regulations for special seasons and limits. [T28N R21W S16]

STONER CREEK. A very small stream, it flows for 5 miles eastward to Flathead Lake at Lakeside, where it is crossed by US 93. It is mostly too small to fish, but there is about ½ mile of meadow in the upper reaches (available by road) where the creek has been impounded by beaver dams, and where a fair number of brook trout live. [T26N R20W S18]

STRAWBERRY LAKE. This beautiful lake is located near the crest of the Swan Range, just north of the Jewel Basin hiking area. From Foothills Road, north of Echo Lake, take a logging road to a well-used trail. From there, it's a 2-mile hike to the lake. Just look for the signs. Strawberry doesn't get planted these days, so the fishing is slow at best, but the scenery is spectacular. [T28N R19W S11]

STRYKER LAKE. See Fish Lake.

SUN FISH SLOUGH. See Emmet Slough.

SUNDAY CREEK. A small stream, flowing for several miles northeastward from Skillet Mountain, through heavily logged mountains, to Duck Lake, it is followed for most of its length by the Sunday Creek road out of Stryker. There are a lot of beaver ponds up and down this creek, and they are fair fishing for pan-size brookies, though the fishery has declined due to logging activity that resulted in siltation and lack of cover. [T33N R24W S9]

SUNDAY LAKES. Lower and Upper, they are 3 miles south of Stryker on the Sunday Creek road. Upper Sunday is right by the road, and is now planted with cutthroat trout. You might also find brookies and maybe a bass or two here. Lower Sunday is cross-country ¼ mile northeast of Upper, now stocked with rainbow trout. It used to have way too many pumpkinseeds, so the success of the plantings is questionable. [T33N R24W S7]

SWIFT CREEK. It flows for nearly 25 miles (including forks), from high in the Whitefish Range, through Upper Whitefish Lake, and down to its mouth at the north end of Whitefish Lake. It is fair fishing for a mix of cutthroat, brookies, and rainbow, with whitefish becoming more and more prevalent. The upper reaches hold primarily small cutthroat. There used to be a good run of bull trout, but they're in serious decline now. Logging in the drainage has severely degraded this fishery in the past several years. [T31N R22W S5]

SYLVIA LAKE. This lake covers 22 acres, is fairly deep, with gradual drop-offs, and is best fished by boat. Reach it via the Sheppard Creek road out of Star Meadow. There's a USFS campground on the east shore. Sylvia is stocked regularly with grayling and is good fishing for 6- to 16-inchers. There are some state-record-class grayling swimming around in here as well. [T30N R25W S20]

TALLY LAKE. It's the deepest lake in the state, at 492 feet, and covers 1,326 acres. This is a popular recreation lake (big boats, waterskiing,

Tally Lake. —Courtesy U.S. Forest Service

cliff jumping, etc.) with a fairly large USFS campground at the north-west end. The best way to get there is from Whitefish, taking the Star Meadow road 10 miles northwest, since the road from the south can be in poor condition at times. Tally offers only poor fishing for cutthroat, rainbow, bull trout, whitefish, kokanee, and northern pike. Check regulations for special limits on salmon. [T31N R23W S30]

TAMARACK CREEK. A small, beaver-dammed stream in logged Plum Creek land, flowing east to the Little Bitterroot River 2 miles above Hubbart Reservoir, it's accessible by a poor jeep road for about 1 mile upstream. All told, there are about 2½ miles of poor to fair fishing here, for small cutthroat, rainbow, and brook trout. It's a marginal stream. [T26N R24W S31]

UPPER LAGONI LAKE. See Lagoni Lake, Upper.

UPPER STILLWATER LAKE. From Whitefish, take US 93 north 25 miles, then southwest ½ mile to a campground on the north shore. A poor logging road follows the lake around the east side and goes on down to Olney. Mostly shallow, but reaching 70 feet at its deepest, this lake covers 630 acres, with marshy areas along the west side and south end. It is fair fishing for cutthroat (in decline) and brook trout, and good fishing for northern pike. The best fishing is for yellow perch and sunfish, and you can find your share of trash fish here as well. Check current regulations for special limits and restrictions on spearing. [T33N R23W S25]

UPPER WHITEFISH LAKE. It covers 88 acres in logged-over land, with a maximum depth of 34 feet. There is a popular state campground on the east shore of this lake, which is reached by logging roads 20 miles above Whitefish Lake. Although the Upper Whitefish road will take you there all the way from the north end of Whitefish Lake, it's easier on your vehicle if you cut some of the back-road miles off by heading east off US 93 at Olney. This lake offers only fair fishing for 6- to 12-inch cutthroat, though it is planted frequently. Best fished by boat. [T34N R23W S28]

WALL LAKE. See Finger Lake.

WEST FORK SWIFT CREEK. See under Swift Creek.

WHITEFISH LAKE. A popular resort lake with many summer homes and public recreational facilities, it provides excellent fishing for lake trout that run up to 30 pounds or so. You can catch just about anything in Whitefish Lake, from northern pike (in the shallow bays) and largemouth bass (a few) to kokanee, cutthroat, rainbow, and lake whitefish. The lake is stocked yearly with westslope cutts. Whitefish is over 220

Upper Whitefish Lake. —Courtesy U.S. Forest Service

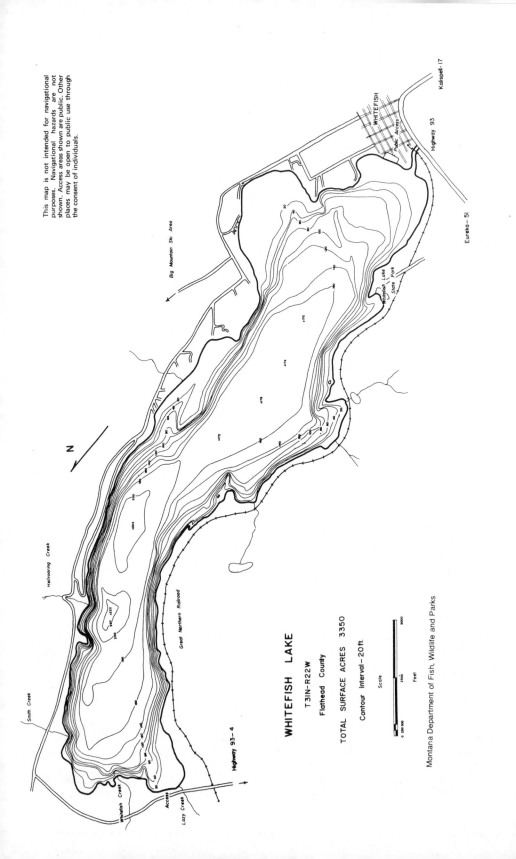

This map is not intended for navigational purposes. Navigational hazards are not shown. Access areas shown are public. Other places may be open to public use through the consent of individuals.

N

Big Mountain Ski Area

Hellroaring Creek

Smith Creek

Whitefish Creek

Lazy Creek

Access

Highway 93 – 4

Great Northern Railroad

Whitefish Lake State Park

WHITEFISH

Public Access

Highway 93

Kalispell – 17

Eureka – 51

WHITEFISH LAKE

T3IN–R22W

Flathead County

TOTAL SURFACE ACRES 3350

Contour Interval – 20 ft.

Scale

0 250 500   2500   5000

Feet

Montana Department of Fish, Wildlife and Parks

feet deep, 6 miles long by a mile wide, in the upper Flathead Valley, with its south shore within the city limits of Whitefish. It's easily accessible around each end and along the east side by good county roads. There is a state park on the south end. Check current regulations for special limits. [T31N R22W S26]

WHITEFISH RIVER. Twenty-four miles long from its head at Whitefish Lake to its juncture with the Stillwater River, a mile east of Kalispell, it is easily accessible by good county roads all the way. It is an easy floating stream, but it's fished mostly from shore for good early-season catches of rainbow trout, and sometimes large pike if you know where to find them. Suckers and whitefish abound throughout. This river is really nicer to float than to fish. Check current regulations for special seasons on part of the river. [T28N R21W S5]

WOODS LAKE (or LAKE of the WOODS). Located west of Whitefish Lake in the Beaver Lake complex, Woods has been managed as a trophy rainbow lake, with special regulations and big fish. Big fish, that is, until a combination of heavy illegal fishing (including ice fishing) and a freeze-out a couple of years back decimated the population. Montana Fish, Wildlife and Parks began replanting the lake in hope of reestablishing the excellent fishery of the past, but the current plan is to abandon Woods as a trophy lake. [T31N R22W S17]

Crazy Fish Lake and Mount McLeod. —Courtesy U.S. Forest Service

The Flathead Indian Reservation

The Flathead Indian Reservation contains a wide variety of waters supporting fish for food and sport. More than seventy high mountain lakes provide clear, cold water and support trout populations. Mid-mountain irrigation reservoirs, which in some cases are dammed natural lakes, support hatchery-stocked trout and remnant populations of bull trout. Valley irrigation reservoirs hold populations of largemouth bass, northern pike, and yellow perch. Flathead Lake provides a fishery for lake and cutthroat trout, kokanee salmon, lake whitefish, and yellow perch, as well as supporting one of the last viable (or nearly viable) populations of bull trout.

The lower Flathead River runs for 68 miles through the reservation. The Jocko and Little Bitterroot rivers and Post, Mission, and Crow creeks are the major tributaries to the Lower Flathead. These rivers and streams support important fisheries for five species of trout, mountain whitefish, and northern pike. These tributaries also provide important spawning habitat for main river trout stocks.

Due to the activities of man, much of the tribal fishery resources have been degraded. The construction of water diversions for irrigation blocked native bull and westslope cutthroat as they attempted to reach their spawning grounds. As a result, these two species are now almost nonexistent over much of their original range. In addition, sediment-laden irrigation water reentering the streams compacts and covers spawning gravel, reducing the potential for successful reproduction. Kerr Dam has been identified as contributing to significant degradation of aquatic habitat and fisheries in the lower Flathead River and in Flathead Lake. Managed for money rather than for healthy waters, the dam's variable emissions wreak havoc in the surrounding waters.

Over the past 100 years, the fisheries resources of the tribes have been managed by the Bureau of Indian Affairs, the United States Fish and Wildlife Service, and the state of Montana. The results of non-tribal management have been documented above. Management for the protection, enhancement, and wise use of tribal fish stocks and aquatic habitat is now directed by the Tribal Fisheries Program, and the outlook is bright for the future of reservation waters.

A separate reservation fishing permit is required to fish any tribal waters. Please read the regulations carefully, as there are many site- and species-specific rules designed to ensure the health of the fishery. Enjoy your visit, while respecting our land and its resources.

Joe DosSantos
Tribal Fisheries Manager

Adapted with permission from:
Fisheries Management Plan for the Flathead Indian Reservation
Amended February 1993

NOTE: Since the above information was written, there have been substantial changes in fishing regulations. Please check current regulations for limits and other important information.

Lake trout, Flathead Lake. —Courtesy John Fraley

AGENCY CREEK. A little stream flowing from McLeod Peak for 8 miles northwest towards the Jocko River. The lower, farmland reaches, near Old Agency, are accessible by county roads and are occasionally fished by kids for 5- to 8-inch westslope cutthroat. [T16N R20W S13]

ASHLEY (or HIDDEN) LAKES. About 4 miles north of St. Ignatius, take Ashley Lake Road east for 3½ miles to the trailhead. The lakes are 3 more miles up the drainage, at about 5,200 feet above sea level. The lower lake covers 14 acres and is 73 feet deep. It was last stocked in 1968, but the cutthroat are reproducing naturally now, providing good fishing for 8- to 14-inchers. The upper lake is barren. [T19N R19W S25]

BURGESS LAKE. This 10-acre lake, with a maximum depth of 52 feet, is a very productive trout lake, giving up rainbow and cutthroat to 18 inches. It is planted regularly. To get there, park at the river turnout on the north side of Montana 200, about 4 miles west of Perma. The trailhead is on the south side of the road, about ½ mile from the lake. [T18N R24W S9]

CLIFF LAKE. See under First Lake.

COURVILLE (or PABLO) LAKE. From Pablo, drive 3 miles east on gravel and logging roads, and then hike another 3 miles (and 3,000 feet up) on an old trail on the west face of the Mission Range, along the ridge between Goat and Crow Creeks, to this lake. It's 6,550 feet above sea level in a beautiful rocky cirque, 30 acres and 45 feet deep. It used to be barren, but it was stocked with cutthroat in 1994 and should provide good fishing now. [T21N R19W S11]

CROW CREEK. From the junction of its north and south forks, at the base of the Mission Range, Crow Creek is readily accessible by county roads. It flows for 15 miles, through mostly open farmland, to the Lower Crow Reservoir and eventually to the Flathead River. A pretty stream, its lower reaches have been impacted by agricultural activities, though restoration efforts are under way. This creek supports 8- to 10-inch rainbow and brown trout, with larger fish showing up occasionally. The upper reaches support brook and cutthroat trout as well. [T20N R21W S28]

CROW CREEK, Middle. See Middle Crow Creek.

CROW CREEK, North Fork. See North Fork Crow Creek.

CROW CREEK, South. See South Crow Creek.

CROW CREEK (or TERRACE) LAKES. These are five beautiful alpine lakes in three timber-bottomed, rock-walled glacial cirques at the head of South Crow Creek, near the crest of the Mission Range. Take the South Crow trail a little over 3 steep miles to Crow Creek Lake Number 2, at 6,590 feet above sea level, then ½ mile beyond to Number 1, if you need the exercise and enjoy the scenery (it's barren). You can follow the outlet about a mile downstream from Crow Number 2 to the first main tributary, and then up that stream for ½ mile to Crow Number 4, at 6,270 feet in elevation, and a mile beyond to Number 3, at 6,725 feet. Number 5 is at 6,720 feet above sea level, reached by going ¼ mile downstream from Number 4, then ½ mile up the south tributary. Crow Number 2, 59 acres in area and 110 feet deep, has a few very nice 13- to 20-inch Yellowstone cutthroat. Crow Number 3 is 11 acres and 35 feet deep; it used to be barren, but it was planted with cutthroat the summer of '68 and provides fair fishing. Crow Number 4 is 35 acres, 115 feet deep, and full of 8- to 14-inch cutthroat. Crow Number 5 is 30 acres in size and 73 feet deep, and it's routinely planted with cutthroat that provide some real fine fishing. [T20N R18W S7]

DISAPPOINTMENT LAKE. See under First Lake.

DOG LAKE. See Rainbow Lake.

DRY FORK (or LONE PINE) RESERVOIRS. These two reservoirs (Upper and Lower) are located 2 miles west of the town of Lonepine. Both are irrigation reservoirs that generally fill in the spring and are drawn down during the summer. Boats with motors of 15 horsepower or less are permitted, but shallow slopes and extreme drawdown can make boat launching difficult. Shore angling is productive and wading is effective. Both reservoirs are pike and perch fisheries. Lower Dry Fork generally produces more, but smaller, fish, while Upper Dry Fork gets less pressure and gives up fewer (though larger) fish. Both reservoirs have produced pike in the 20-pound range. Good ice fishing here, too! [T23N R24W S34]

DUCHARME CREEK. A tiny kids' creek that flows through open pastureland and into Moss Creek, just south of Flathead Lake, 5 miles east of Polson. It's crossed by Montana 35 and houses a few small brookies. If you get to the mouth of the stream, you may find some good largemouth bass fishing as well. [T22N R19W S5]

DUNCAN LAKE. A barren lake in open scrub timber below McDonald Peak, 7 air miles east of St. Ignatius on the Flathead Indian Reservation. Cutthroat were planted here, but unsuccessfully. Beautiful surroundings! [T19N R18W S30]

FINLEY CREEK. A small stream emptying to the Jocko River near the US 93 crossing, 1 mile north of Arlee, it is accessible by US 93 and county roads for 13 miles to headwaters. Mostly a pastureland creek, anglers can expect to find 8- to 10-inch brook and rainbow trout in its waters. At the right times of the year, you may find larger cutthroat and brown trout here as well. [T16N R20W S2]

FINLEY LAKES. Two small mountain lakes, southwest of and just beneath Murphy Peak. Take US 93 north from Evaro about 4 miles, then McClure Road east for ½ mile, and a jeep road southeast to the trailhead. Take the lightly maintained trail up the East Fork for 3 miles to Lower Finley, and another ¾ mile to Upper Finley. The lower lake contains quite a few 10-inch cutthroat. The upper lake is overpopulated with 6- to 10-inch, half-starved, bug-eyed cutthroat that bite like mad. Seldom fished, these lakes provide a good day hike and plenty of action. [T15N R19W S11]

FIRST LAKE. It's the lowest (at 6,400 feet above sea level) of a group of five glacial lakes just east of McDonald Glacier and west of the crest of the Mission Range on the Flathead Indian Reservation. There is no trail, and any way in is nothing but rugged. Perhaps the two easiest routes, if you can call them that, are either cross-country a couple of miles up over the top of the range from Island Lake in the Swan drainage, or from the McDonald Reservoir-Summit Lake trail. From this trail, at the top of the switchbacks about 3 miles up from the reservoir, you take off to the south up the creek, over talus and through brush, to First Lake. It's 53 acres in area, a good 75 feet deep and it will taste like champagne by the time you get there. Another ¼ mile and 400 feet up the drainage, through more brush and scrub timber, brings you to the 14-acre, 77-foot-deep Disappointment Lake, which offers excellent cutthroat fishing (up to 16 inches). Now if you're still in the mood and the body is willing, Cliff Lake is another 500 feet up and ¼ mile beyond (surrounded by cliffs, naturally); it's 7 acres and 180 feet deep. Cliff is barren, as are the lakes above. These lakes are in the Special Grizzly Bear Management Zone, closed to human travel July 15 through October 1. [T19N R18W S21]

FLATHEAD LAKE. It's about as big as lakes naturally get in these parts—nearly 30 miles long, covering over 125,000 acres, with 185 miles of shoreline. You should have no problem finding your way to Flathead Lake once you're in Polson. It's surrounded by private property, except for the thirteen public access sites scattered around the lake, and is a very popular recreational lake in the summer. Lake trout is the prime sport fish in Flathead Lake. Trophy fish, up to 40 pounds, are best pursued by boat or with the help of one of the many commercial outfitters

Flathead Lake. —Courtesy Montana Fish, Wildlife and Parks

operating on the lake. Shore fishing for lake trout is excellent in the spring and fall, when water temperatures are cool enough for the trout to move into the shallows. Lake whitefish are abundant in the lake but are seldom caught by anglers, except when the fish move up into the Flathead River. Yellow perch are available in East Bay during their spawning period in the spring, but they've been greatly reduced in recent years due to heavy predation by lake trout. A major effort to recover a fishable population of kokanee is under way, with plantings of hatchery fish. This effort is scheduled to continue until 1998, longer if anglers are able to catch enough of the released fish before the lake trout do. [T22N R20W S4]

FROG LAKE. See under Summit Lake.

HEWOLF CREEK. Very small, it flows for 5 miles through mostly private (posted) land to Valley Creek. The lower 2 miles are followed by a road of sorts. Hewolf is extensively beaver dammed, fair fishing for 6- to 7-inch brook, plus a few cutthroat and rainbow, trout. [T17N R21W S25]

HIDDEN LAKES. See Ashley Lakes.

Kicking Horse Reservoir.
—Courtesy Ravalli County Museum,
Ernst Peterson Collection

JOCKO RIVER. This is a medium-size trout stream that has good access and is easy to wade. From its confluence with the Flathead River upstream to the town of Arlee are healthy populations of rainbow and brown trout, with catches common in the 12- to 16-inch range and opportunities for larger trout. This section of river also offers good mountain whitefish angling, which is open year-round. Upstream of the town of Arlee, the stream gradient steepens and flows through more mountainous terrain. The primary trout species are cutthroat and brook trout, in the 8- to 14-inch range. [T18N R21W S17]

JOCKO SPRING CREEK. See Spring Creek.

KICKING HORSE RESERVOIR. It's about 800 acres, in open farmland, ¹/₂ mile east of US 93 and a mile from Nine Pipe Reservoir. This reservoir provides the best opportunity in the area to fish for bass from a boat (15 horsepower restriction), due to closures on other reservoirs. It contains an abundance of largemouth bass, some up to 20 inches, and good rainbow trout fishing, especially in the summer. [T19N R20W S25]

LITTLE BITTERROOT RIVER. A small stream that was once fair-size but is now impacted by irrigation. It heads in Little Bitterroot Lake and is followed southward by good county roads for 11 miles to Hubbart Reservoir, and then another 45 or so to the Flathead River, 15 miles north of Dixon. The lower reaches, below the reservoir, are fairly flat and fair early-spring fishing, while the upper reaches are steep and

Lower falls of the Little Bitterroot River. —Courtesy U.S. Forest Service

generally fair to good for 8- to 10-inch rainbow and cutthroat, plus occasional concentrations of brookies. There are also quite a few northern pike from Lone Pine down. [T20N R22W S13]

LONE PINE RESERVOIRS. See Dry Fork Reservoirs.

LONG LAKE. See under Summit Lake.

LOST (or MORIGEAU) LAKES. Upper and Lower, or East and West, these lakes lie 450 yards apart, at 6,200 and 5,800 feet in elevation respectively, in timber and rocky cliff country on the steep west face of the Mission Range, one mile northwest of Terrace Lake. Unnamed on most maps, the 20-acre, 7-foot-deep Upper and the 7-acre, 78-foot-deep Lower Lake feed Lost Creek. They're reached by a cross-country mile north through timber and downfalls from the South Crow trail. Both were barren originally, but they now produce good catches of 10- to 14-inch Yellowstone cutthroat. This is most definitely a bushwhack, so you'd better use a good topographical map. [T21N R18W S31]

LOST SHEEP LAKE. Drive to the end of the Middle Fork Jocko road, at the mouth of Deep Creek. Now take the well-used trail up toward Grey Wolf Lake (not on the reservation). Walk 3-plus miles until you make two major stream crossings, within ½ mile of each other. Lost Sheep Lake is just out of sight, about 200 yards up the second creek. It's 9 acres in area, rarely visited, and even more rarely fished, but it's good fishing for fair-size cutthroat. It is regularly stocked with westslope cutts. [T18N R17W S32]

LOWER CROW RESERVOIR. A very productive irrigation reservoir, it covers about 700 acres in the semi-arid prairie portion of the Mission Valley. From Ronan, take a county road 6 miles west. This reservoir provides a diversity of angling opportunities for both warm- and cold-water species, mostly the result of illegal introductions. Large brown trout can be found here, along with numerous smaller rainbow trout. Pike and smallmouth and largemouth bass were recently introduced and have flourished. Yellow perch are also common and primarily support the ice fishery. [T20N R21W S11]

LUCIFER LAKE. As you drive north on US 93 over the hill by the National Bison Range from Ravalli, look ahead and to your right and you will see Elizabeth Falls, at the top of a great rock-walled glacial cirque on the southwest end of the Mission Range. Drive on to St. Ignatius, then turn right on the Mission Dam road for 3 miles, to the Mission Reservoir and the wilderness trailhead. This good trail follows along the creek and up the cliff to the north side of the falls, then on up to the lake, making about 5 miles all told. With an area of 41.4 acres and a depth of 110 feet, the lake harbors a healthy population of Yellowstone cutthroat, ranging up to 15 inches. [T18N R18W S5]

MAGPIE CREEK. This is a small, steep stream that flows into the Flathead River about 6 miles east of Perma. The lower reach often goes dry in the summer, but upstream the canyon area offers fair fishing for cutts and brookies up to 10 inches. A jeep road takes you up from the mouth a couple of miles. [T18N R23W S12]

MCDONALD LAKE (or RESERVOIR). Covering 250 acres, behind a glacial moraine that was raised higher with earth fill, it is located in a rock-walled canyon on the precipitous western slopes of the Mission Range. From US 93, take good county roads 5½ miles west to McDonald, which is a mile south of the Nine Pipe Reservoir. Moderately popular, McDonald is good fishing for 7- to 10-inch cutthroat. Ice fishermen report catches of much larger fish. There is a tribal campground at the lower end. [T18N R19W S16]

MIDDLE CROW CREEK. A small, snow-fed stream above, the lower reaches flow through mostly timberland along the base of the Mission Range, for about 4 miles of excellent 8- to 10-inch brook, rainbow, and cutthroat trout fishing. From Ronan, take county roads a couple of miles southwest to the mouth. Middle Crow is followed by an unimproved jeep road. [T19N R20W S6]

MINESINGER CREEK. It heads just north of Haystack Mountain and flows rapidly down the steep western slopes of the Mission Range, until it sinks just above the Pablo Feeder canal. From US 93, 6 miles south of Polson, take logging roads 4 miles east. The stream is small and cold, and fair kids' fishing for pan-size brookies. [T22N R19W S16]

MISSION CREEK. A small, brushy, pastureland stream, it is the outlet of Mission Reservoir and a tributary of Post Creek. Mission Creek is followed and crossed by county roads along its entire 15-mile course across the Flathead Valley, from St. Ignatius through Moiese. It is moderately popular with local residents and decent fishing for 8- to 12-inch rainbow and brown trout, with occasional brookies or cutts. [T18N R21W S4]

MISSION RESERVOIR. It covers 289 acres in a steep, rock-walled canyon behind a 30-foot earth-fill dam on the lower slopes of the Mission Range. From St. Ignatius take a good county road 3½ miles west. There is a poor road clear around the reservoir. Mission Reservoir is very good fishing at times for pan-size rainbow and cutthroat, and also contains a few large ones. The inflow stream is closed to fishing. [T18N R19W S16]

MOON LAKE. See under Summit Lake.

MORIGEAU LAKES. See Lost Lakes.

MUD CREEK. A narrow, brushy, 25-mile creek in pastureland, it is crossed by US 93, 1½ miles south of Pablo, and flows to the Lower Crow Reservoir. Mud Creek is easily accessible by county roads and is fair fishing in spots for mostly 6- to 10-inch brook trout, plus a few cutthroat and rainbow as well as some larger brown trout near the reservoir. [T20N R21W S12]

MUD LAKES. There are fourteen lakes in all, but only the lower four have fish. They lie between 5,790 and 6,820 feet above sea level, in an east-west string. From 50 to 400 yards apart, they're at the head of a rocky, glaciated canyon on the precipitous western front of the Mission Range. Reach the Mud Lakes by taking Mud Lake Road, 2 miles north of Pablo off US 93, all the way to the end. Then you just hike on up the drainage to the lakes. The lower lake is 20 acres in area, a good 155 feet deep, and swarming with 6- to 10-inch brook and some 7- to 15-inch rainbow trout. The next lake is 10 acres, 75 feet deep, and has a good population of nice fat 8- to 10-inch rainbow, plus some 7- to 12-inch cutthroat trout. The next one is 20 acres, 60 feet deep, and provides good catches of nice fat 6- to 11-inch rainbow trout. The uppermost of the fishable lakes is 9 acres in area and only 30 feet at maximum depth; it used to be barren but is now stocked with cutthroat and is good fishing. [T22N R19W S35]

NINEPIPE RESERVOIR. This 1,800-acre irrigation reservoir, on a National Migratory Waterfowl Refuge, sits out in open, rolling farmland in the middle of the Flathead Valley, right beside US 93, 19 miles south of Polson. As a waterfowl refuge, it greatly enhances migratory-bird hunting throughout the entire region. It is also an outstanding bass fishery, with some fish reaching 20 inches or more. Both black and yellow perch have found niches here and can be caught in good numbers. There is a picnic area south of the dam, as well as a visitor interpretive center, and there's handicapped fishing access off US 93 on the north side of the reservoir. [T20N R20W S34]

NORTH FORK CROW CREEK. It is 10 miles long, with the upper reaches on the steep western slopes of the Mission Range and the lower in brushy pastureland west of Ronan. Easily available by county roads, it's excellent fishing for 4- to 10-inch brook and cutthroat trout. [T20N R19W S6]

Ninepipe Reservoir. —Courtesy Ravalli County Museum, Ernst Peterson Collection

PABLO LAKE. See Courville Lake.

PICTURE LAKE. This lake is 450 yards up the drainage from Lucifer Lake, in a stupendous glacial cirque the likes of which you've never seen before. It's at 6,450 feet above sea level, in lodgepole timber, below great 2,000- to 3,000-foot vertical rock walls all around. With an area of 20.4 acres and a depth of 50 feet, it used to be barren. However, it was planted with a good supply of cutthroat (left over from Lucifer) and has since been fair to good fishing for up to 12-inchers—for the few fishermen who make it in. [T18N R18W S4]

POST CREEK. This is a small, farmland stream, the outlet of McDonald Lake and a tributary of Mission Creek. The stream is readily accessible by county roads and is fair fishing for 6- to 12-inch rainbow, cutthroat, and brook trout. The lower reaches may harbor a few larger fish. [T19N R20W S33]

Lakes at the head of Post Creek. —Courtesy U.S. Forest Service

RAINBOW (or DOG) LAKE. Located just off Montana 28, about 10 miles southwest of Hot Springs, it is a 207-acre lake, full of beaver dams at the inlet, and has been used for a mill pond. Once a popular rainbow fishery, it is now home to illegally planted northern pike and so is a popular northern fishery, for pike up to 7 pounds or so. [T20N R25W S2]

REVAIS CREEK. It's a small stream whose lower reaches can dry up, crossed by Montana 200, 2½ miles west of Dixon. The upper reaches are in foothill rangeland and are followed by a road, for about 3 miles of fair fishing for pan-size brookies and cutthroat. [T18N R22W S10]

RONAN SPRING CREEK. See Spring Creek.

ST. MARY LAKE (or TABOR RESERVOIR). A 274-acre irrigation reservoir, in heavy timber at the base of the Mission Range. From St.Ignatius, take the Dry Creek road 10 miles east. St. Mary is a popular camping spot, but there is a very large drawdown, and the fishing is no better than fair for 8- to 10-inch cutthroat trout. [T17N R18W S6]

SONIELEM LAKE. Drive to the trailhead at Mission Reservoir, hike upstream about 2 miles past the reservoir, then gird your loins and take off up the south tributary for 1½ miles of rugged steepness and that's it— Sonielem Lake. In a rocky glacial canyon at 6,700 feet above sea level, it's 20 acres and 40 feet deep. It used to be barren, but it was stocked with fingerling cutthroat in the summer of '68, and their progeny is still going, providing fair fishing for 6- to 12-inchers. [T18N R18W S18]

SOUTH CROW CREEK. This little stream flows down a steep timbered canyon above but is fairly flat below. From Ronan, take county roads 4 miles south. It's fair fishing for 8- to 10-inch brook, rainbow, and cutthroat trout. [T20N R19W S18]

SPRING (or RONAN SPRING) CREEK. This spring-fed creek originates 1½ miles northeast of Ronan, flows through downtown, and continues 5 miles to its confluence with Crow Creek. It flows through agricultural lands and has had water quality problems in the past. As are most spring creeks, this is a highly productive system with the potential to produce large trout. An extensive restoration effort in 1995 and '96 has given the stream new hopes of living up to its full potential. The stream produces good catches of brook and rainbow trout. The entire length of the stream is on private land, though access is fair. [T20N R20W S15]

SPRING (or JOCKO SPRING) CREEK. This spring-fed creek rises 2 miles north of Arlee and flows northwest about 4 miles to its confluence with the Jocko River. It is a productive stream, with rainbow and brown trout being the most abundant species. In addition brook trout and mountain whitefish are present. [T17N R20W S17]

SUMMIT LAKE. From the end of the McDonald Lake road (at the lower, dam end of the reservoir), take the wilderness trail up the north side of the lake for a moderately flat 1½ miles, and then a steep switchbacked 2½ miles to Moon Lake. In a brushy, steep-walled canyon, it's 15.3 acres, mostly between 10 and 20 feet deep, and it receives cutthroat by natural migration downstream from Long Lake, about ⅛ mile to the north. Long Lake is ½ mile long in a north-south direction, covers 29 acres, and is slow fishing (as a rule) for 14- to 16-inch cutthroat. The trail follows along the brushy west side of Long Lake, and beyond for another ½ mile to Frog Lake (which is only about 6 acres and quite shallow, but it does support a healthy population of cutthroat). Another ½ mile northwestward up the trail brings you to Summit Lake (68 acres and 55 feet deep), beneath steep slopes to the northwest but a fairly flat swale to the southeast, where there is lots of room for your camp. Summit provides fair

Camp fare at Summit Lake.
—Courtesy James Pelland

fishing for 12- to 16-inch cutthroat trout. If you don't want to retrace your steps on the way out, you can proceed westward through Eagle Pass and on down the western slopes of the Mission Range, along a steep, switchback trail for 4½ miles to the Cheff ranch, 4 miles due east of the Allentown Motel on US 93. [T20N R18W S32]

SWARTZ LAKE. This is a 5-acre, shallow swamphole with muddy margins, surrounded by timber, at the western base of the Mission Range. From Ronan, take the South Crow Creek road 5 miles east. It's good fishing for 6- to 8-inch brookies. Keep your eye on this one: it will soon become a westslope cutthroat fishery. [T20N R19W S10]

TABOR RESERVOIR. See St. Mary Lake.

TERRACE LAKE. See Crow Creek Lakes.

TURTLE LAKE (or RESERVOIR). This irrigation reservoir is stocked annually with trout but also has a self-sustaining largemouth bass population. The reservoir grows large fish of both species. It is generally filled with spring runoff and drawdown during the summer months. From Polson, take Montana 35 east 2½ miles and turn south on a county road. The reservoir is just to the west of the road and surrounded by a housing complex. Access is not a problem. [T22N R19W S18]

TWIN LAKES. These lakes are located on the southwestern flank of the Mission Range at a 4,500-foot elevation. From St. Ignatius, head southeast toward St. Mary Lake and continue past the reservoir 2 miles. There is a campground between the two lakes. Both lakes are fairly deep, with moderate drop-offs, and are stocked annually with trout, producing good catches of average size. [T17N R18W S8]

VALLEY CREEK. This is a small, brushy creek that enters the Jocko River a couple of miles south of Ravalli. The stream flows through tribal and private lands; access is good but please respect private property. It is populated primarily with brook trout, and fewer cutthroat trout, in the 10- to 12-inch range. [T17N R20W S8]

WHITE EARTH CREEK. This is a small, spring-fed farmland creek flowing for 2½ miles to the Flathead River southwest of Polson. It's fished (mostly by kids) in the upper reaches only for fair catches of 6- to 10-inch brookies. [T22N R22W S36]

Lower Tranquil Lake. —Courtesy John Fraley

The Middle Fork of the Flathead— Montana's Wildest River

The Middle Fork of the Flathead River originates 1 mile above Gooseberry Park, at the confluence of Strawberry and Bowl creeks, below the spectacular western slopes of the Continental Divide. For 90 miles, the river rushes untamed from the remote heart of the Bob Marshall Wilderness complex to meet the North Fork of the Flathead River near West Glacier.

For the first 14 miles of its length, the Middle Fork winds through a remote, timbered valley to Schafer Meadows. This portion of the river features good fishing from July, when runoff diminishes, through October for westslope cutthroat trout, a state-designated "Species of Special Concern." Dark or dull dry fly patterns seem to be most effective, although almost any pattern will tempt these backcountry cutthroat. Anglers using spinning gear find success with small spinners and spoons, and natural baits such as grasshoppers. Anglers can expect to catch cutthroat ranging from 6 to 15 inches, with 10 inches about average.

Anglers should not overlook the excellent fishing for mountain whitefish available on this river reach. Mountain whitefish, many times more numerous than trout, will strike wet or dry flies. And contrary to the opinion of some anglers, whitefish fillets dipped in flour and pan-fried make an excellent complement to a backcountry meal.

Anglers can access this upper stretch of the Middle Fork by main trails from the east side of the Continental Divide over Sun River, Teton, Gateway, and Badger passes. The Big River trail, which follows the entire length of the river, can be reached from the west side of the divide at Morrison Creek and Granite Creek trailheads.

At Schafer Meadows, an active airstrip and a Forest Service administrative guard station provide access for float and bank anglers. From 2 miles below Schafer Meadows to US 2 near Bear Creek, the Middle Fork flows for 32 miles through a steep, rocky canyon. This portion of the river offers spectacular and challenging whitewater floating in a wilderness setting. Floating is best during June and the first half of July; the wise rafter will check with the Forest Service on river levels before planning a trip.

The fishing on this portion of the river provides the same thrills as the upper stretch. Fishing is best from mid-July through August, when low water levels restrict floating. Anglers access this river reach by main trails through the Great Bear Wilderness down Granite and Morrison creeks, and by the Big River trail, which begins east of Essex.

The river from Bear Creek to below West Glacier follows US 2 for 44 miles, forming the southern boundary of Glacier National Park. Challenging whitewater amid boulder and canyon, with the awesome peaks of Glacier National Park in the background, draws rafters to this section of the Middle Fork. Westslope cutthroat trout are not numerous in this section, and fishing is not considered as good as in the upper reaches of the river. In recent years, anglers have caught non-native lake trout from Flathead Lake in this river reach.

Bull trout, the inland cousin of the Dolly Varden, are present in all sections of the river and its larger tributaries from June to October. These fall spawners, migrating upstream from Flathead Lake, range from 19 to 36 inches and can weigh up to 15 pounds or more. Fishing for this declining "Species of Special Concern" is off-limits. For further protection, the Fish, Wildlife and Parks Commission maintains complete fishing closures on the following tributaries: Morrison, Lodgepole, Granite, Long (all draining U.S. Forest Service lands); and Ole, Park, Muir, and Nyack (which drain Glacier National Park). In addition, the river is closed to fishing 100 feet above and 100 feet below the mouth of Bear Creek.

The Middle Fork remains one of the finest free-flowing rivers in the United States, and it is biologically closely tied to the Flathead Lake and River system. This system is not highly productive and exists in a delicate ecological balance. By recognizing its fragile nature, you can help maintain the beauty and integrity of Montana's wildest river.

John Fraley
Information/Education Officer
Montana Fish, Wildlife and Parks

NOTE: Since the above introduction was written there have been substantial changes in fishing regulations. Also, all streams in the Middle Fork drainage that lie within wilderness boundaries have special restrictions. Please check current regulations for limits and other important informtion.

ALMEDA LAKE. The headwater of Essex Creek, it's a 4-mile hike by trail, just west of the town of Essex. This lake at the edge of the Great Bear Wilderness is planted every four to five years with cutthroat. [T29N R17W S24]

BASIN CREEK. It rises on the slopes of the Continental Divide, at an elevation of more than 7,000 feet, and flows eastward for 8½ miles to Bowl Creek (elevation 5,800 feet), just west of the Sun River Pass. There's no maintained trail, and it's off the beaten path, so it's seldom fished for the good number of small cutthroat it contains. The middle reaches are heavily beaver dammed. You might see a few spawning bull trout come through here in the fall, but their numbers are declining in this creek, and there weren't a whole heck of a lot of them to start out with. [T26N R11W S35]

BEAR CREEK. A fair-size tributary of the Middle Fork of the Flathead River, Bear Creek is followed along its whole 16-mile length by US 2, down a brushy, timbered valley with some pastureland (Steven's Canyon). It was practically scoured out by the 1964 spring flood, and even at this late date contains less-than-optimal numbers of 8- to 10- inch cutthroat, but it's making a comeback. You're as likely to hook into a brook trout or a whitefish as you are a cutt. And bull trout come up from the river on their way to their spawning grounds—but remember, it's illegal to intentionally fish for bull trout, and if you hook one accidentally, you should release it right away. Angling is closed within a 100-yard radius of the stream mouth, or as posted, from June 1 through August 30. [T29N R15W S31]

BERGSICKER CREEK. Bergsicker is followed by trail for 5 miles from its mouth at Long Creek nearly to its headwaters on Mt. Baptiste. It flows down a narrow, timbered canyon and is marginal fishing in the lower reaches for small cutthroat, since the stream has a habit of drying up occasionally. [T27N R15W S5]

BERGSICKER LAKE. A small lake reached by trail about 5 miles up the Bergsicker Creek drainage. It's been stocked unsuccessfully in the past, but Fish, Wildlife and Parks is giving it another chance. It was stocked three times in the past several years, and if you go fish there, you should come out with a report on how the cutts are faring this time around. [T27N R16W S14]

BOWL CREEK. A high, snow-fed stream that heads on the Continental Divide at Teton Pass. It's followed by a trail for 11 miles, through timbered mountains, past the Sun River Pass to its junction with Strawberry Creek, the headwaters of the Middle Fork of the Flathead River. The mouth is 20 miles above the Schafer Ranger Station, or 12 miles over Teton Pass from the West Fork Teton trailhead. It is fished a moderate amount by parties in transit over the passes, and it's fair to good fishing in the middle reaches for 8- to 10-inch cutthroat. Bull trout are uncommon in the drainage, and their population is declining. [T26N R11W S20]

BRADLEY LAKE. There's no maintained trail to this lake; it's a tough, 2½-mile, uphill hike from the Big River trail west up Bradley Creek—after fording the Middle Fork of the Flathead. This high lake attracts a few hardy souls each year, but, alas, there are no fish. It has been planted but fruitlessly, since the lake loses its water by the end of summer. [T27N R14W S23]

CALBICK CREEK. A small stream, about 4 miles long, in a narrow, timbered canyon. It's followed by a trail from headwaters to its mouth on the Middle Fork of the Flathead River, 4 miles above the Schafer Ranger Station. It is mostly passed up for larger streams, but the lower 2 miles are fair fishing for 6- to 8-inch cutthroat. [T27N R12W S29]

CASTLE LAKE. Getting here is a rugged, steep, 3-mile, killer hike—sometimes straight up—from the Big River trail south, across the Middle Fork of the Flathead River at a point about 5 miles downstream from the mouth of Granite Creek. It's good fishing for nice cutthroat. [T27N R14W S9]

CHALLENGE CREEK. A very small headwaters tributary of Granite Creek that joins the creek near the Challenge Guard Station. It's reached at the mouth by the road to the Granite Creek trailhead. There's a good population of cutthroat trout here, but Challenge, like all streams in the Granite Creek drainage, is closed year-round to give the bull trout a place to spawn and grow up undisturbed. [T29N R13W S32]

CHARLIE CREEK. The outlet of Cup Lake, Charlie Creek is followed by a USFS trail for 4 miles through timbered, brushy country to the Middle Fork of the Flathead River, 6 miles above Nimrod. It is lightly fished for 8- to 10-inch cutthroat. An occasional bull trout makes its way upstream in the fall. [T28N R15W S30]

CLACK CREEK. The outlet of (barren) Dean Lake in the Trilobite Range, Clack also drains the Trilobite Lakes. It is followed by a trail for 7 miles down its narrow, steep-walled canyon to the Middle Fork of the Flathead

Westslope cutthroat, Tranquil Lake. —Courtesy John Fraley

River at Gooseberry Park. The lower 2 miles are good fishing for resident 8- to 10-inch cutthroat, but it is an out-of-the-way stream and not bothered much. At the upper part of the stream there is about a mile of good beaver-pond water, but no fish. [T26N R12W S13]

COX CREEK. The outlet of Beaver Lake, Cox Creek is followed for 8 miles through steep, timbered mountains to the Middle Fork of the Flathead River, 5 miles above the Schafer Ranger Station. It is not heavily or even moderately fished, but the lower 5 miles are good for 8- to 10-inch cutthroat. [T27N R12W S28]

CRIMSON LAKE. This lake sits at the head of a tight drainage between Leota and Crimson peaks at the south end of the Bob Marshall Wilderness. There's no maintained trail to it, so the best way in may be a short but steep walk from the Crimson Peak trail. The lake was stocked in 1988 with cutthroat, and your guess is as good as ours about the fishing. [T18N R14W S23]

CUP LAKE. Hike along Charlie Creek from its confluence with the Middle Fork of the Flathead, near Spruce Park, for 6 miles, mostly on maintained

USFS trail. This lake, on the western edge of the Great Bear Wilderness, was stocked with cutthroat in the past, but heavy winterkill discouraged fisheries managers. They're giving it another shot, though—Cup Lake has been stocked with cutts every four years since 1988. [T27N R16W S4]

DEERLICK CREEK. A small stream flowing down a steep, timbered canyon, through fairly flat pastureland, below the Middle Fork of the Flathead River near the Nyack Ranger Station. It is crossed at the mouth by US 2 and is followed by a trail for 2 miles of fair, 6- to 7-inch brookie and cutthroat fishing. [T32N R18W S36]

DICKEY LAKE. Drive to the end of the Dickey Lake road near Essex; then hike a little over 2 miles by rough trail to the lake on the edge of the Great Bear Wilderness. It's had winterkills in the past, but it's been stocked with cutts in recent years to rebuild the fishery. [T29N R17W S13]

DIRTYFACE CREEK. This short stream flows in a steep, V-shaped, heavily timbered canyon below; the terrain levels out somewhat above. Dirtyface is reached at the mouth by the Elk Creek trail and is followed by trail to headwaters and beyond—over the South Fork-Middle Fork

Westslope cutthroat, Dickey Lake. —Courtesy John Fraley

divide to Logan Creek. The lower 3 miles are poor to fair cutthroat fishing. Elk Creek, which flows into Dirtyface, is too small to fish. [T28N R16W S12]

DOLLY VARDEN CREEK. Dolly Varden flows northward for 11 miles to Schafer Creek near Schafer Meadows, but only the lower 2 miles are decent fishing. There are some real good holes here where the cutthroat hide out. And you might find a bull trout or two, especially in the fall. A moderately popular stream, it is easily accessible by a good USFS trail. [T27N R13W S26]

ELK LAKE. Reach it from Moose Lake, 4 miles by a fair trail, or from US 2, 7 miles by rough trail up Devil's Creek and around Devil's Hump. It's good fishing for cutthroat that can get pretty big. [T28N R15W S15]

ESSEX CREEK. A small stream, the outlet of Almeda Lake, it's followed by 4 miles of good USFS horse trail along its narrow, steep-walled, timbered canyon, and then a couple of miles of road to the Middle Fork of the Flathead River, opposite the Walton Ranger Station. Crossed at the mouth by US 2, Essex Creek is moderately popular with the younger set, with 2½ miles of fishing for lots of 6- to 8-inch cutthroat. [T29N R16W S15]

FLOTILLA LAKE. A heavily fished but excellent lake for 8- to 15-inch cutthroat, Flotilla is about 146 acres in size and deep, with rocky shores in subalpine scrub-timber country. It's reached by a very steep trail 2 miles (and maybe a shade more) above Scott Lake, in the Great Bear Wilderness. [T27N R14W S25]

GATEWAY CREEK. A most spectacular stream, Gateway heads in the Big River Meadows near the Continental Divide, and flows through the Gateway Gorge, where it is dwarfed below vertical limestone walls that rise over 1,100 feet above it. Six miles from headwaters, it joins Strawberry Creek. The 3 miles below the gorge, in a timbered valley, are good fishing for 8- to 10-inch cutthroat. The Big River Meadows stretch is full of small cutthroat. [T26N R11W S9]

GRANITE CREEK. A nice stream that heads at the confluence of Challenge and Dodge creeks, near the Challenge Guard Station. It's followed by a couple of miles of logging road and 7 miles of good USFS trail down a narrow, steep-walled, heavily timbered canyon to the Middle Fork of the Flathead River, 9 miles below the Schafer Ranger Station. Granite Creek and its tributaries are closed the entire year to give the bull trout some privacy. There's a good population of cutts here, too. [T28N R14W S35]

Westslope cutthroat, Middle Fork of the Flathead River. —Courtesy John Fraley

LAKE CREEK. It's about 4 miles long, in timber and burned-over country between Scott Lake and the Middle Fork of the Flathead River, near Three Forks. It's followed by a good horse trail pretty much all the way. This is a pretty little stream with some 25-foot falls near the mouth. It is lightly fished, but good for 8- to 10-inch cutthroat. Watch for an occasional bull trout. [T27N R14W S12]

LODGEPOLE CREEK. About 8 miles long, Lodgepole flows southwest down a fairly low gradient canyon to Morrison Creek, a few miles upstream of the Middle Fork of the Flathead River. It is followed from the mouth nearly to headwaters by a good horse trail. Lodgepole Creek and all its tributaries are closed to fishing the entire year—they're great spawning habitat for both bull trout and cutthroat. [T27N R13W S10]

LONG CREEK. Actually a short stream, about 5 miles long, in a timbered canyon, it's followed by a USFS trail from its headwaters to the mouth on the Middle Fork of the Flathead River, 6 miles above the Nimrod campground. Long Creek and its tributaries are closed the entire year. [T28N R15W S27]

MARION LAKE. A fairly deep (145-foot maximum), 80-acre lake in a high, brushy pocket on the north side of Essex Mountain. The trailhead is about 1½ miles west of US 2 at Essex; from there, an easy 3 miles of trail up Marion Creek. Marion Lake is moderately popular and excellent fishing for 7- to 14-inch cutthroat. In the 1920s, the lake was stocked with rainbow trout, so there might be some rainbow-cutt hybrids hanging out. There are no big ones. [T29N R16W S20]

MINER CREEK. A small inlet of Scott Lake, followed by a trail for 4 miles down its steep, timbered canyon. The lower mile is fair fishing for small cutthroat. [T27N R13W S30]

MOOSE LAKE. This lake is in the Twentyfive Mile Creek drainage— from there it's about a 3-mile hike from the end of the logging road. It's poor fishing, too shallow to maintain a population of fish, although it was stocked with cutts in 1969. It grows moose, not trout. [T28N R14W S16]

MORRISON CREEK. A small, southward-flowing tributary of the Middle Fork of the Flathead River, it empties in at Three Forks. It is followed from its mouth by a trail for 11 miles up its narrow, timbered canyon. Gated logging roads provide access to the upper reaches, north and west of Slippery Bill Mountain. It's just as well that they're gated, since Morrison Creek and all its tributaries are closed to fishing year-round. They're great habitat for bulls and cutthroat—two native species that are in trouble. [T27N R13W S8]

PYRAMID LAKE. This small lake sits on the southwestern edge of the Bob Marshall Wilderness, just up from Pyramid Pass. It's accessed by about 5 miles of trail up the Morrell Creek drainage, east of the town of Seeley Lake. It's been stocked yearly since 1988 and is reported to be good fishing for cutts in the 12- to 15-inch range. [T18N R14W S33]

SCHAFER CREEK. About 8 miles long, in a narrow, timbered canyon, Schafer Creek flows to the Middle Fork of the Flathead River, 5 miles below the Schafer Ranger Station. It's followed by a trail to its West Fork— 6 miles of fair fishing for cutthroat. Bull trout are common visitors to the lower section. [T27N R13W S26]

SCOTT LAKE. Here is a really shallow (no more than 4 feet deep anywhere, not counting the mud), 30-acre lake in good moose country: the beasts walk right across and feed in the middle of it. From Three Forks, on the Middle Fork of the Flathead River, 5 miles below the Schafer Ranger Station, the lake is reached by 3 miles of trail. There are some nice springs here that keep the lake from freezing out, and it's excellent fishing for 12- to 14-inch cutthroat. [T27N R13W S30]

SHEEP LAKES. These two lakes drain into Sheep Creek, south of Snowshed Mountain, in the Great Bear Wilderness. There's no trail to the lakes, but the Sheep Creek trail gets you to within a mile or so of the lower lake. The upper lake was planted with cutthroat in 1993, and it might be worth a trip back there to satisfy your curiosity about how they're doing. [T28N R16W S5]

STANTON CREEK. A small stream that heads in Stanton Glacier and flows 5 miles eastward through an old, brushy burn to Stanton Lake, then for 1½ miles past the lake to the Middle Fork of the Flathead River, 7 miles east of Nyack. It's followed by good trail to about a mile above the lake. It is fair fishing below the lake, and it used to be good for about 1 mile above, in some old beaver ponds, for 8- to 10-inch cutthroat trout. [T31N R17W S36]

STANTON LAKE. This lake is 1,300 yards long by 300 yards wide, no more than 29 feet deep anywhere, in a timbered valley, 1½ miles by good trail from Stanton Creek. There is some open ground at the lower end and along the west side, and there are some big, swampy beaver ponds above, with lots of logs and brush, so it is difficult to get around during high water. Quite a few folks hike in, although the fishing is poor for

Upper Tranquil Lake. —Courtesy John Fraley

rainbow, cutthroat, and rainbow-cutthroat hybrids, mostly in the 6- to 9-inch class, plus lots of whitefish and wheelbarrow-loads of suckers. [T30N R17W S2]

STRAWBERRY CREEK. It flows due south from Badger Pass for 11½ miles, down a narrow, timbered canyon, to join with Bowl Creek at the headwaters of the Middle Fork of the Flathead River. There is considerable "traffic" up and down the trail that follows along its entire length—the trail is part of the National Scenic Trail system. The creek receives a moderate amount of fishing pressure, for good catches of 6- to 10-inch cutthroat. Watch for bull trout here, too. [T26N R11W S20]

TRAIL CREEK. A small stream that flows into Gateway Creek at the headwaters of the Middle Fork of the Flathead River. The lower 2½ miles are followed by trail through open park country and are seldom fished—which makes sense, because the fishing is poor, for 8- to 10-inch cutthroat trout. Big bull trout come up to spawn in the fall. [T26N R11W S16]

TRANQUIL BASIN LAKES. Two lakes, about ½ mile apart, in glacial cirques in Tranquil Basin. From Nimrod, take the Edna Creek trail up the Middle Fork of the Flathead River, which will get you to within ½ mile of the lakes. The upper lake is about 10 acres in area, the lower is 8 acres; both are deep. They're seldom fished, but are sometimes good for 2- to 3-pound cutthroat. [T28N R15W S4]

TUNNEL CREEK. A small stream, flowing to the north down a narrow, timbered canyon to the Middle Fork of the Flathead River, 8 miles above the Nyack Ranger Station. Crossed at the mouth by US 2, Tunnel Creek is followed upstream by trail for about 3 miles of fair fishing for 7- to 8-inch cutthroat. Bull trout are common visitors in the lower reaches. [T30N R16W S7]

TWENTYFIVE MILE CREEK. Only 7 miles long, it's followed pretty much the whole way down its steep-walled canyon by a trail to the Middle Fork of the Flathead River, 12 miles below the Schafer Ranger Station. It is reportedly fair fishing for 8- to 12-inch cutthroat. This stream dries up in places. [T28N R15W S36]

North Fork of the Flathead River, looking downstream. —Courtesy U.S. Forest Service

The North Fork of the Flathead—
A Float Fisher's Dream

The North Fork of the Flathead River originates in the rugged mountains of British Columbia, 50 miles north of the Canadian border. After entering Montana, it gently flows 58 miles to its confluence with the Middle Fork. The river is the physical boundary separating Glacier National Park on the east from the intermixed private and public lands of Flathead National Forest on the west.

The waters of the upper river system are derived from melting snowpack, which is generally clean and aesthetically spectacular. However, due to the rock formation of the North Fork drainage, such waters contain only small amounts of the primary nutrients that afford good fish growth, as compared to nutrient levels in the state's top-rated trout streams. Because the North Fork is primarily dependent upon migratory fish from Flathead Lake, as opposed to most other streams in the state, which contain fish populations that reside in the stream year-round, the fishing here is different. Fish found in the North Fork may travel 50 to 113 miles in the course of their spawning runs from Flathead Lake. Fishing for these migrants is seldom predictable, depending on seasonal weather and water conditions. However, for the angler fortunate enough to select the proper time, place, and lure, the results are worth the effort.

The westslope cutthroat trout, bull trout, and mountain whitefish are the migrants most often encountered in the North Fork by anglers. The cutthroat range from 8 inches to a respectable 18 inches, generally present in the North Fork from April until August. Bull trout migrants begin their movement from Flathead Lake in late spring, and may be found in the North Fork from July until October. However, due to declining bull trout numbers in the Flathead River drainage and threats of extinction over their range, the Flathead River is presently closed to fishing for bull trout. All bull trout incidentally caught by anglers must immediately be released unharmed. The mountain whitefish is a semiresident species that is finding increased acceptance by the serious fisher. Anglers should pay close attention to the fishing regulations.

The North Fork was classified in 1976 as a Scenic River under the National Wild and Scenic River Act. With its panoramic backdrop of

Glacier Park and its clear blue green water, it has become known as a floater's delight for persons of average ability. However, spring high water and logjams present boating concerns. Access is afforded at Forest Service easements along the gravel road that runs the entire length of the river. As with any outdoor activity, floaters must respect private land, which is interspersed with public lands along the river and road.

As relatively untouched as the North Fork may appear to be to the visitor, the entire drainage is undergoing rapid changes. Changes in the Flathead Lake food web, possible development of coal mines in areas of British Columbia, timber harvest in both British Columbia and Montana, and oil and gas exploration threaten the relatively pristine waters and native fish assemblages of the North Fork. However, these activities, if properly directed, hopefully will allow the North Fork River to continue to display itself in dramatic splendor for fishermen and women now and in generations to follow.

Mark Deleray
Fisheries Biologist
Montana Fish, Wildlife and Parks

NOTE: Since the above information was written, there have been substantial changes in fishing regulations. Please check current regulations for limits and other important information.

BAILEY LAKE. It's just off the North Fork road, 9 miles north of Columbia Falls. Maybe 20 acres in area, it's surrounded mostly by private land. Bailey was rehabilitated in 1963 and has been stocked regularly in recent years. It is good for 10- to 12-inch cutthroat, along with bass, perch, and sunfish of various sorts. [T31N R20W S10]

BIG CREEK. A fair-size stream in brushy, timbered mountains, crossed at the mouth by the North Fork road at the old Big Creek Ranger Station, 19 miles north of Columbia Falls. Big Creek and all its tributaries are closed to fishing the entire year, to protect the declining population of bull trout there. Also, you should know that there's no fishing within a 100-yard radius of the stream mouth (or as otherwise posted) from June 1 through August 30. [T33N R20W S22]

CANYON CREEK. A small stream in a steep-walled, brushed up, timbered canyon. It empties into the North Fork of the Flathead, 3½ miles above that river's junction with the Middle Fork. It's crossed at the mouth by the North Fork road and followed upstream by logging road to its headwaters in the Whitefish Range. Canyon Creek's not much for fishing—some small cutts hang out, but that's about it. [T32N R20W S27]

CHAIN (or TRIPLE) LAKES. Three nice little lakes (and a fourth that hardly qualifies) in subalpine country a mile northeast of Link Lake, or a mile north of and 1,200 feet above the Red Meadow Creek road. The trailhead is clearly signed. Lake Number 1 (at the top of the string) is 5 acres in area and 50-plus feet deep; it was stocked in 1989 and 1993. Number 3 is 23 acres and more than 100 feet deep, and Number 4 (at the bottom of the string) is 17 acres and only 14 feet at maximum depth. None of the three lakes (1, 3, and 4) is as good fishing as it once was, for 7- to 16-inch cutthroat. [T35N R23W S21]

COAL CREEK. About 20 miles long, in a narrow, timbered canyon on the eastern flanks of the Whitefish Range, Coal Creek empties to the North Fork of the Flathead River, 7½ miles north of the old Big Creek Ranger Station. It is crossed at the mouth by the North Fork road and followed upstream by logging road. Coal Creek and all its tributaries are closed to fishing the entire year. Bull trout are in trouble, and they need some of their best habitat set aside for them to use undisturbed. Coal Creek is also good cutthroat habitat. Be aware that there's no fishing within a 100-yard radius of the stream mouth (or as posted) from June 1 through August 30. [T34N R20W S20]

COAL CREEK, South Fork. A small stream that is reached at the mouth by the Coal Creek road and followed upstream by a logging road. Only the very bottom end of the logging road is accessible by vehicle, and the creek is brushy as all get out—but that's OK, since all the streams in the Coal Creek drainage are closed to fishing. [T34N R21W S30]

CYCLONE LAKE. At 4,100 feet above sea level, Cyclone is about 120 acres and mostly less than 20 feet deep. It sits in a timbered mountain pocket and is reached by logging road off the Coal Creek road, about 9 miles north of the old Big Creek Ranger Station. You can't quite drive right up to the lake, since it's so brushy and muddy around the edges, but you can get close enough to haul in a canoe or the like. Cyclone is

Fishing the North Fork of the Flathead.
—Courtesy John Fraley

fished more and more these days—like lots of spots in the North Fork drainage—and it can be good for 10-inch cutthroat trout. It was also planted with grayling in 1966 and 1967, but there probably aren't any more of those left. There are lots of suckers, if that makes you feel any better, and there might be some bull trout hanging around. [T34N R21W S16]

DIAMOND LAKE. It's 6 acres in area with a 16-foot maximum depth, in timber all around. It's been planted with cutthroat for years, most recently in '94 and '95, and they've made out well. If you care to look, you can get there on foot, about a mile from the end of the Coal Creek road—the trail that runs along the south side of the creek is open July 1 to September 1, and the last couple of miles might be a little rough. There are 12- to 14-inch cutthroat here. [T34N R23W S23]

ELELEHUM LAKE. A barren lake, 11 acres in area, and 25 feet at its deepest. Elelehum Lake was stocked with cutthroat in 1971 and 1976, but none made it. Apparently there hasn't been enough water in some years to support fish. Just in case you want to see for yourself, the lake is reached by foot trail, a very short hike above the end of the Elelehum Creek road (which takes off from the Big Creek road, about 6 miles north of the old Big Creek Ranger Station). The Elelehum Creek road is open from July 1 to September 1. [T33N R21W S10]

FROZEN LAKE. A long, narrow, 200-acre lake that straddles the Canada-U.S. border. It can be reached from the U.S. side by a trail 1 mile from the end of the Frozen Lake road, east of the Weasel Guard Station (in the Kootenai drainage). On your drive, you'll be treated to clear-cut after clear-cut after clear-cut, and when you look across the border to Canada, there's more of the same, only bigger. Near Frozen Lake, the Canada-U.S. boundary line runs right through a clear-cut—what one local calls "a good example of international cooperation." Frozen is pretty good fishing for cutts that thrive in the cold waters. [T37N R24W S2]

HAY CREEK. A small stream with about 13 miles of fishing, followed by a logging road down its timbered, brushy valley on the eastern slopes of the Whitefish Range to its mouth on the North Fork of the Flathead River, 13½ miles above the old Big Creek Ranger Station. It is hard to fish but good for 6- to 9-inch cutthroat, especially in the beaver ponds about a mile above the mouth and in the 5 miles below the bridge (1 mile downstream from Hay Lake). Now and then a bull trout might show up. [T34N R21W S12]

HAY LAKE. A small lake in a swampy meadow near the Whitefish divide, between Link Mountain and Diamond Peak. The Hay Creek logging road is gated about 4 miles from the lake. This one was not too popular even when the road was open, but it's fair fishing for 10- to 12-inch cutthroat. [T34N R23W S11]

HUNTSBERGER (or HUNCHBERGER, or HUNSBERGER) LAKE. Take the Whale Creek road about 17 miles upstream to a USFS foot trail, which bears off to the left (south) for a little better than 3 miles to the shore of this lake. Huntsberger is 5 acres, deep, in burned-over, mountainous country west of Huntsberger Peak, on the Whitefish divide. It's seldom fished, but it's reported to be fair for 8- to 10-inch cutthroat. [T35N R24W S11]

LINK (or LYNX) LAKE. Head west from the North Fork of the Flathead to the end of the Red Meadow road, and cross over the Whitefish divide to the trailhead access road—or come at it up the Swift Creek-Upper Whitefish Lake road on the west side of the Whitefish divide. About a mile of USFS trail takes you on in to the shore. The lake is 15 acres, 25 to 30 feet deep, and irregularly shaped, with small rocky islands here and there; it's ringed by steep subalpine mountains all around, about a mile northwest of Red Meadow Lake. Link is hot and cold fishing—more cold than hot these days, due to its tremendous popularity. The trail and campsites around the lake show signs of overuse. The lake is periodically stocked with westslope cutts. [T35N R23W S28]

MOOSE CREEK. A small tributary of the North Fork of the Flathead River, flowing 3 miles south of the Ford Guard Station. It's crossed near the mouth by the North Fork road, followed upstream by 5 miles of logging road and 5 miles of trail to headwaters at Nasukoin Lake. The dense brush and timber might have something to do with why this stream is not often fished. But there are plenty of small cutthroat here. [T36N R21W S31]

MOOSE LAKE. A shallow, 17-acre lake in a timbered valley below Moose Peak—mud-bottomed, weedy, and marshy at the west end. From the old Big Creek Ranger Station, take the Big Creek road 13 miles west, then the Hallowat Creek road 4½ miles north, and finally the Kletomas Creek road north for another 5 miles. Wow! In spite of the long trek, Moose Lake is moderately popular, maybe because there's a Forest Service campground at the lake. The fishing is fair for cutthroat trout, if you don't mind catching lots of small fish. It's planted every so often. [T33N R22W S14]

MORAN CREEK. This small stream is reached by logging road off the Hay Creek road. It is good fishing for 6- to 8-inch cutthroat. [T34N R21W S11]

MUD LAKE. This lake once covered about 15 shallow acres, in a timbered valley below and west of Glacier View Mountain. To reach it, take the Coal Creek road 3 miles north from the Big Creek campground. Mud Lake was used by the state, once upon a time, as a hatchery lake, and it used to be good fishing for cutts. Now the dam at the outlet has been breached, and the lake is weed-choked and filling in. You're more likely to find moose here than fish. [T33N R20W S17]

NASUKOIN LAKE. To reach this lake, continue west from the end of the Moose Creek road along the trail (old logging road) for 5 miles. The lake covers about 6½ acres and has a 27-foot maximum depth. It's planted periodically, last in 1994, and it supports lots of smallish cutts. [T35N R23W S15]

NINEMILE LAKE. See Spoon Lake.

NINKO CREEK. A steep, brushy, headwaters tributary of Whale Creek—and since it's below Whale Creek Falls, it's closed to fishing the entire year. It is crossed at the mouth by the Whale Creek road, 12 miles above the Ford Guard Station; if you're looking for exercise rather than fish, follow the trail from there for 3 miles to headwaters. There's a Forest Service recreational cabin back here that's available during the winter months, if you're up for skiing or snowmobiling back in. [T36N R23W S29]

RED MEADOW CREEK. A small, brushy stream about 13 miles long, in a narrow, timbered canyon, flowing eastward to the North Fork of the Flathead River. It's crossed at the mouth by the North Fork road, about 20 miles north of the Big Creek Ranger Station, and is followed upstream by a logging road past the headwaters. Red Meadow is hard to fish because of the dense brush, but it's fair in the many beaver ponds along its length for 6- to 10-inch cutthroat. You might also hook into grayling right below Red Meadow Lake, or whitefish in the lower reaches. There's a small and declining population of bull trout that uses Red Meadow Creek for spawning. [T35N R21W S8]

RED MEADOW LAKE. A beautiful 19-acre (but shallow) lake, its south side is real brushy (from an old snow slide), beneath high, rocky peaks. The north side is timbered and the lake is skirted to the west by the Red Meadow Creek road, 12 miles west of the North Fork road and 6 miles north of Upper Whitefish Lake (in the Flathead drainage). Heavily used campsites at the lake attest to Red Meadow's popularity. It's fair fishing for 8- to 14-inch cutthroat trout and lots of small grayling. Fish, Wildlife and Parks stocks grayling occasionally, last in 1992. [T34N R23W S33]

Westslope cutthroat, North Fork of the Flathead. —Courtesy John Fraley

SHORTY CREEK. From the North Fork road, follow the Whale Creek road about 12 miles west. Like all Whale Creek tributaries downstream from the falls, Shorty's closed to fishing, to help out the declining bull trout population. There are cutts in Shorty Creek, too. [T36N R23W S29]

SHORTY CREEK LAKE. See Stoney Basin Lake.

SOUTH FORK COAL CREEK. See Coal Creek, South Fork.

SPOON (or NINEMILE) LAKE. A 70-acre lake, about 30 feet deep in spots, mostly brushy around the shore and marshy on the south end. It's pretty much surrounded by private land with quite a few homes. The public fishing access on Spoon Lake is easily reached, 9 miles north of Columbia Falls, just off the North Fork road. The lake was rehabilitated in 1963 and is planted yearly with cutts. There are also bass, brookies, perch, and sunfish in the lake. The fishing is notoriously not so good—on one trip there, a lakeside cabin owner was overheard to say, "They must be nuts to fish here!" [T31N R20W S3]

STONEY BASIN (or SHORTY CREEK) LAKE. A small lake just northwest of Lake Mountain, its outlet drains into the South Fork of Shorty Creek. The best way to get there is from just below Link Lake, off the trail that winds around Lake Mountain. Stoney Basin Lake, about 15 feet deep, is stocked on occasion with cutthroat, most recently in 1993. [T35N R23W S20]

TEPEE LAKE. A very shallow lake near the Ford Ranger Station, in the Tepee Creek drainage. You can drive right to it from the main North Fork road near Trail Creek, on 2 miles of logging road. But be aware that the southeast side of the lake is private land. There are a few large cutthroat in the lake, but it winter-kills frequently. [T36N R22W S3]

TRAIL CREEK. A real pretty stream, it's crossed near the mouth by the North Fork of the Flathead road, about 4 miles north of the Ford Guard Station. Trail Creek and all its tributaries downstream from Thoma Creek are closed to fishing. Bull trout spawn here in the fall. [T37N R22W S36]

TRIPLE LAKES. See Chain Lakes.

TUCHUCK CREEK. It flows 4½ miles from Tuchuck Mountain, down a real steep canyon above, and across a couple of miles of relatively flat timberland below, to Yakinikak Creek. It is crossed at the mouth by the Yakinikak road and followed to headwaters by a USFS trail. Tuchuck is good fishing in the lower reaches for pan-size cutthroat, especially so in some brushy beaver ponds about 1½ miles above its mouth. There's a public campground at the mouth of the creek, 9 miles west of the North Fork road. [T37N R23W S33]

TUCHUCK LAKE. This is a nice little lake, about 8 acres in size with a 20-foot maximum depth. To get there from the end of the Thoma Creek road, hike ¼ mile north of the Tuchuck Mountain trail; it's about 2 miles south of the Canadian line and a couple of miles east of the mountain. Tuchuck is planted with cutthroat periodically, last in 1993. They are reportedly doing real well.[T37N R23W S18]

WHALE CREEK. About 20 miles long in a fairly wide, timbered valley, it's followed by a logging road from the North Fork road, 10 miles above Polebridge, nearly to its headwaters. A trail takes you the last 5 miles or so to Whale Lake. Whale Creek and its tributaries below Whale Creek Falls are closed to fishing, to protect bull trout that spawn and spend their younger days there. Above the falls, which are some 15 miles back, there are enough cutts to hold your interest—some of them hybrids of the native westslope cutts and Yellowstone cutts that were once planted in Whale Lake. [T36N R21W S30]

WHALE LAKE. A shallow, rock- and mud-bottomed lake of about 20 acres, in timbered mountains. Follow the Whale Creek road, 20 miles west of the North Fork of the Flathead River, to within 5 miles of the lake. A trail takes you the rest of the way. There are several large springs in Whale Lake that keep it from freezing out, and it's fair (though spotty) fishing for 10- to 14-inch cutthroat trout. [T35N R24W S9]

YAKINIKAK CREEK. In the north country of the North Fork of the Flathead, this stream is followed by logging road west of Trail Creek (North Fork drainage), or over from Grave Creek (Kootenai drainage). The upper reaches are steep and brushy, in a narrow, timbered canyon, and there's a USFS campground along the creek just below the canyon section. Yakinikak is good fishing for 7- to 12-inch cutthroat. This stream joins Thoma Creek, goes underground for 2 miles, and resurfaces to form Trail Creek. [T37N R23W S36]

The South Fork of the Flathead—
A Wilderness Paradise

There are few places where an angler can experience fishing as it was at the turn of the century. The South Fork of the Flathead is unique in that, with few exceptions, it supports an intact native fish assemblage. So forget those imported browns and rainbows, and come prepared to battle a native Montanan, the westslope cutthroat trout, in the solitude of the Bob Marshall Wilderness. The pristine setting, special fishing regulations, and native fish combine to make the South Fork an increasingly rare resource in the west.

The South Fork originates at the confluence of Danaher and Youngs creeks and flows north for 57 miles into Hungry Horse Reservoir. The construction of the Hungry Horse Dam in 1952 isolated migratory fish populations from the Flathead River and Lake. The upper 50 miles of the South Fork, from the headwaters to the Spotted Bear River, is classified as a Wild River under the 1976 Wild and Scenic Rivers Act. It is here that the best fishing is to be found, but expect to work for it. The virtues of wilderness demand work.

The primary access is by horseback and backpack. About 890 miles of trail navigate you around the "Bob," as it is affectionately called by locals. The headwaters can be accessed by trailheads near the community of Seeley Lake to the west, or from the south near Ovando. Those coming in from the north will have to endure a 55-mile drive on dirt roads to the Spotted Bear Ranger Station. Another option is to pack in a raft (or have an outfitter pack one in) to Big Prairie, which is a large, picturesque prairie graced with century-old ponderosa pines. Float trips usually last three to four days, taking time out to explore the surrounding country. The take-out is above Meadow Creek Gorge, the gorge being impassable to rafts. Special regulations have been enacted on the South Fork above the dam since 1982. Anglers can possess three cutthroat, all under 12 inches. The only complaint, if one can call it that, is that you can't find any fish under 12 inches for eating. How can one be so unlucky?

A side note here about bull trout should be mentioned. Bull trout populations appear to be stable in the South Fork while declining in

South Fork of the Flathead River near Woodfir Creek. —Courtesy U.S. Forest Service

most other places across their range. Managers hope to protect this population, so an emergency closure was placed on bull trout within the South Fork in 1993. Managers are working on solutions with diverse interest groups to recover bull trout across their range.

The South Fork below the Meadow Creek Gorge downstream to the reservoir offers good fishing for the roadside angler. Angling pressure is higher here than in the wilderness, but for those with limited time, this stretch offers a good alternative. Anglers should check the regulations and note that catch-and-release fishing with artificial lures only applies from the Meadow Creek bridge to the Spotted Bear footbridge.

Anglers with boats will want to try Hungry Horse Reservoir. There's access via eleven boat ramps. Abbott Bay has a ramp that extends to 130 feet below full pool and offers the best access when the reservoir is drawn down. When the reservoir is near full pool, Lost Johnny Point is a popular option, which has a ramp 45 feet below full pool. There are ten campgrounds around the reservoir. Angling pressure on the reservoir is light, with about 5,000 to 10,000 angler days each year. (An angler day is counted as one angler experiencing one day of fishing on a body of water or in a particular drainage.) Catch rates are less than boastful, but May and June can be profitable for large cutthroats. The most popular lake fishing can be found in the high mountain lakes that dot the landscape. Beautiful azure waters beckon you not only to wet a line but to dabble your toes in the refreshing cold water. Only two lakes, Big Salmon and Doctor, are believed to have endemic fish populations. Fish have been stocked in forty-five other lakes, primarily outside the wilderness, to create recreational opportunities. Some lakes were stocked in the early days with non-native rainbows and Yellowstone cutthroat trout. Managers are now trying to remove these exotics by overplanting with westslope cutthroat trout, thereby maintaining native fisheries. This technique is known as "genetic swamping" and is designed to replace non-native fish genetic material with native westslope cutthroat trout genetic material.

One last thing, don't forget the whitefish. You can always count on this overlooked fish for some action. A Montana Nymph or a Bitch Creek works well along the bottom, where the stoneflies lie. Reservoir tributary fishing is best in October and November, when whitefish ascend streams to spawn. This is the time to be in the stream, as most sportsmen put down their rods for their guns.

Before you go, please be cognizant of the rare resources the "Bob" has to offer up from its bounty. This is grizzly bear country—hanging your food in a tree while you're not attending your camp is a requirement, and don't leave fish entrails along the lakeshore. If using pack animals, certified weed-free hay is required, and always practice no-trace camping. Cherish and respect these resources, so future generations can experience the same opportunities that make memories.

Pat Van Eimeran
Fisheries Biologist
Flathead National Forest

NOTE: Since the above introduction was written there have been substantial changes in fishing regulations. Also, special regulations apply to all waters in the South Fork drainage from Hungry Horse Dam to the wilderness boundary, and all waters within the boundaries of the Bob Marshall, Great Bear, and Scapegoat Wilderness Areas. Please check current regulations for limits and other important information.

South Fork Drainage

ADDITION CREEK. A nice little stream followed by a road (that's closed to motorized vehicles partway up) for 6 miles down its steep, timbered canyon to the South Fork of the Flathead River at the Spotted Bear Ranger Station. The lower 4 miles are occasionally fished for good catches of 7- to 9-inch cutthroat trout. [T25N R15W S20]

AENEAS CREEK. A small tributary to Graves Creek, flowing through a steep, V-shaped, timbered canyon. Take the Hungry Horse Reservoir's westside road 22 miles south of the dam, then follow a poor logging road—which may or may not be passable—upstream, for 3 miles of poor to fair fishing for pan-size cutthroats and rainbow-cutt hybrids. [T27N R18W S1]

AENEAS LAKE. It's about 2 acres and fairly deep, in a cirque near timberline ½ mile east and over the ridge from Birch Lake (which is in the Swan River drainage). It is reported to have had fish in years gone by, but it's now too shallow to support fish life. [T27N R18W S5]

AYRES (or ARRES) CREEK. Reached at the mouth by the Danaher Creek trail, 1½ miles south of the Basin Creek landing field. Ayres is only a couple of miles long, but the lower reaches contain fair numbers of small cutthroat and, in the fall, some not-so-small bull trout spawners. Since this stream is so darn small, it's almost never fished. [T19N R12W S23]

BABCOCK CREEK. A seldom visited, steep, timbered mountain stream, crossed at the mouth by the Youngs Creek trail and followed by trail for most of its length. The lower 3 miles are good fishing for 8- to 10-inch cutthroat. Bull trout spawn here in the fall. [T19N R13W S33]

BALL LAKE. A deep, 3-acre lake on a rock ledge in timbered country, reached by trail 1½ miles from the end of the Posy Creek road, on the Quintonkon drainage. Ball is lightly fished but good for 10- to 14-inch cutthroat trout. [T26N R17W S30]

BARTLETT CREEK. A nice-size tributary of the South Fork of the Flathead River, crossed at the mouth by the South Fork trail, 2 miles north of the Big Prairie Ranger Station, then followed upstream by trail. There are about 5 miles of fair fishing for 8- to 10-inch cutthroat. If it was any place else, Bartlett would be heavily fished, but here it is seldom bothered. [T20N R13W S5]

BASIN CREEK. It heads in Grizzly Basin, and it's followed by a trail for 6 miles, through a steep canyon above and relatively flat country below,

271

Big Hawk Lake. —Courtesy James Pelland

to Danaher Creek at the Basin Creek airfield. The lower reaches (which are on the main trail to Benchmark) are good fishing for small cutthroat, plus a few bull trout and whitefish in the fall. [T19N R12W S12]

BETA LAKE. This small lake is at the headwaters of Beta Creek, in the mountains that border the west side of Hungry Horse Reservoir. Take the west side road across the dam for approximately 2 miles. Turn west onto USFS road 895H, a switchbacky logging road, that takes you within easy walking distance of the lake. Beta Lake is stocked regularly with cutts, and it's fished hard. [T30N R19W S33]

BIG HAWK LAKES. Three small, subalpine lakes in beautiful Jewel Basin country. They lie between 5,800 and 6,300 feet above sea level at the head of Jones Creek. From the end of the Wheeler Creek road, take USFS trails west and north for 5 miles. The small upper lake is barren. The middle lake is 32 feet deep and covers 4 acres; the lower one is 35 feet deep and covers 30 acres. These lakes are stocked periodically with westslope cutts that grow a bit bigger here than they do in many mountain lakes. Be aware that only hikers are allowed: no motorbikes, snowmobiles, horses, or the like. [T27N R18W S15]

BIGLOW LAKE. See North Biglow Lake.

BIG SALMON CREEK. This stream is a nice size, with lots of good-looking water, too, on the main Holland Falls National Recreation Trail, going northeast from Holland Lake. The upper reaches, south of Barrier Falls, were once stocked with cutthroat, but now rainbows, once planted in the lakes upstream, have pretty much taken over. There are some cuts and a few hybrids, too. Below the falls, for 3½ miles north to Big Salmon Lake, rainbows and bull trout provide most of the action; north of the lake for 1 mile, to the South Fork of the Flathead River, you're likely to hook into 10- to 14-inch cutthroat. There is a campground at the mouth of the creek, another at the southern end of Big Salmon Lake, and yet another about 2 miles south. [T22N R14W S26]

BIG SALMON LAKE. A large, deep lake, about 4 miles long by ½ mile wide, in a fairly high-elevation (4,500 feet), timbered canyon in the Bob Marshall Wilderness. It's a ways back—19 miles from Holland Lake on a good USFS pack trail, or 20 miles from the Spotted Bear Ranger Station, at the end of the Hungry Horse Reservoir road. There's a trail all along the west side of Big Salmon and a campground at the southern end. It is hit by most everybody coming through, and provides good fishing for 12- to 17-inch cutthroat, bull trout in the middlin' to big range, plus a few rainbow-cutthroat hybrids (whose ancestors probably worked their way down from Woodward Lake) and whitefish, along with quite a few suckers. [T22N R14W S35]

BLACK BEAR CREEK. A fairly open stream in burned-over country, Black Bear is followed by a trail upstream for about 5 miles from its mouth, on the east side of the South Fork of the Flathead River, 2½ miles north of the Black Bear Guard Station. It is seldom fished but excellent for 6- to 10-inch cutthroat. [T23N R14W S22]

BLACK LAKE. A very scenic, 50-acre alpine lake in the Jewel Basin hiking area, fairly deep, with a small island in the middle, a steep drop-off at the upper end, and shallows near the outlet. There are cliffs and talus around the head of the lake, and timber below. The lake is drained by Graves Creek, and you can reach it by a trail 7 miles up that creek from the Hungry Horse Reservoir, or go 3 miles from the end of the Noisy Creek road (USFS road 5392), which leads to the Jewel Basin trailhead area, northeast of Bigfork. Black Lake is stocked regularly with cutthroat, and the fishing can be excellent for 8- to 10-inch cutthroat. [T28N R18W S29]

BLACKFOOT LAKE. A lightly fished lake, 16 acres and as much as 22 feet deep in spots, but with mostly a gradual drop-off, in a timbered pocket 5,500 feet above sea level on the headwaters of Graves Creek. Blackfoot can be reached by a good trail 6 miles east from the trailhead at the end of the Noisy Creek road in the Flathead drainage, or you can go about the same distance from the end of the Graves Creek road. The lake is planted regularly with cutthroat and can be fair enough fishing. The occasional rainbow or rainbow-cutt hybrid would be the result of earlier plantings of rainbow. You'd better plan on hiking in, because the Jewel Basin is closed to all other forms of transportation. There oughta be more places just like it. [T28N R18W S120]

BLUE LAKES. These two lakes sit right alongside the Spotted Bear River and are accessed by several miles of trail from the Beaver Creek campground. From July 1 through September 1, you can drive on past the campground to a trailhead at the end of the road, within 2 miles of the lakes. Stocking with westslope cutthroat started in 1989, and reports of how they're doing are sketchy. [T25N R13W S16]

BRUCE CREEK. A steep little stream that sometimes goes almost dry, but there are lots of small falls and some good holes. The lower 1½ miles are accessible by logging road to the confluence with Stony Creek. Another trail, going south toward Bruce Mountain, follows the rest of the stream, pretty much to headwaters, another 1½ miles or so. Bruce Creek is small, but there are a couple of miles of fishing for lots of 6- to 9-inch cutthroat and some whitefish. [T25N R15W S30]

BUNKER CREEK. A good-size stream, followed by a logging road from its mouth just about to headwaters below Thunderbolt Mountain. The road is gated a few miles upstream, just past the turnoff for the Gorge Creek trailhead. Bunker Creek flows eastward for 16 miles down a formerly heavily timbered, now heavily clear-cut, flat-bottomed valley to the South Fork of the Flathead River, 9 miles south of the Spotted Bear Ranger Station. It's tough telling what all the logging and formerly easy access (the road used to be open during the summers) did to the fishery here. The last Fish, Wildlife and Parks survey for cutthroat was in 1984, and it showed cutthroat to be plentiful, although the native westslope cutts have hybridized with Yellowstone cutts that were planted in Sunburst Lake, upstream. Chances are you'll still hook into a fair number of cutts, and if you fish in the fall you're likely to catch some spawning whitefish. There may be a few big bull trout spawning in the lower sections of the creek. [T24N R14W S20]

BUNKER CREEK, Middle Fork. See Middle Fork Creek.

BURNT CREEK. The outlet of Big Knife Lakes, Burnt Creek flows for 8 miles to the South Fork of the Flathead River, 5 miles north of the Big Prairie Ranger Station. It is crossed at the mouth by the South Fork trail and followed to headwaters by USFS horse trail. There are about 2 miles of good fishing for 8- to 10-inch cutthroat, but most people find the main river so much more attractive that this creek is seldom bothered. [T21N R13W S32]

CAMP CREEK. A small tributary of Danaher Creek, crossed at the mouth by a trail, 1 mile north of the Basin Creek airstrip, and followed upstream for 5 miles through its steep, narrow canyon to Camp Creek Pass. The lower reaches, fished a little by trail crews passing through, are fair for 8- to 12-inch cutthroat. [T19N R12W S10]

CANNON CREEK. This tributary of Stadium Creek is about 4 miles long, in timbered country on the eastern slopes of the Swan Range. It's reached at the mouth by following Stadium Creek a couple of miles upstream from its confluence with Gorge Creek. Cannon is followed upstream by trail for 5 miles of good 8- to 10-inch cutthroat fishing. [T23N R15W S27]

CLAYTON CREEK. The outlet of Clayton Lake, it's followed by trail from the lake for about 3 miles, then by road for 2 miles to its mouth on the Hungry Horse Reservoir. Clayton is real steep above, and it's poor fishing at best for pan-size cutthroat. [T29N R18W S35]

CLAYTON LAKE. A really beautiful lake in the Jewel Basin, in a scenic timbered pocket at 5,900 feet above sea level. It's about 4 miles west of the Hungry Horse Reservoir as the crow flies, easily reached from the end of the Clayton Creek road by trail, going south for 3 miles. Clayton is 61 acres, shallow at both ends but over 100 feet deep in the middle, and mostly brushy along the shores. It's stocked regularly with westslope cutthroat and can be good fishing, especially if you haul in something to float around on. You might catch a Yellowstone cutt or two—remnants of earlier plantings. [T28N R18W S16]

CLIFF LAKE. Hike 3 miles east on the Graves Creek trail from Black Lake, or 3 miles north on the Graves Creek trail from Handkerchief Lake, and then follow along the little drainage to the west for 1 long mile to Cliff Lake. The lake is 5,550 feet above sea level, 23 acres in area, and 74 feet deep with steep drop-offs, below talus on the west and southwest, with a little timber on the southeast rim. It's tough shore fishing, and there's only one real campsite at the lake. The Department of Fish, Wildlife and Parks stocks Cliff with cutthroat periodically, the last time in 1993. [T28N R18W S28]

CONNER CREEK. A short, small tributary of Sullivan Creek, in logged-over country. It's followed by a poor logging road for about 2 miles of fair fishing for small cutthroat. Conner Creek has been a source of westslope cutthroat brood stock for hatcheries. [T26N R16W S31]

CRATER LAKE. A 75-foot-deep, 23-acre cirque lake—real pretty, in the rocky alpine country of the Jewel Basin, 5,650 feet above sea level. Take the Noisy Creek Road (USFS road 5392), which heads east from Foothill Road, north of Bigfork, to the Jewel Basin trailhead. Crater Lake is reached by a trail 5 miles from the trailhead parking area. It was stocked with rainbow years ago, but they didn't make it, so stocking with cutthroat began in '68 and continues periodically. It's pretty standard mountain lake fishing, meaning on and off for fair-size fish. [T27N R18W S8]

CRIMSON CREEK. This short, steep, and rocky outlet of Crimson Lake starts up high, around 7,000 feet, and drops about 1,000 feet as it flows for 2 miles to Marshall Creek. There's no maintained trail here, which is probably fine by the small cutthroat that spend the better part of their energy trying to stay in one place in this riotous creek. [T18N R14W S23]

DAMNATION CREEK. It heads on Pagoda Mountain and flows down a very narrow, steep canyon to the South Fork of the Flathead River, 4½ miles south of the Black Bear Guard Station. This one is real brushy, with lots of downfalls, etc., and it's no joy to fish. However, the lower reaches are good, though seldom bothered for small cutthroat and an occasional bull trout in the fall. [T22N R13W S3]

Big cutthroat.
—Courtesy Pat Markert

DANAHER CREEK. A slow, meandering, beaver-dammed stream that looks more like eastern water than a high mountain creek. One of the headwaters streams of the South Fork of the Flathead River, it flows from the Dry Fork-Flathead divide through timbered canyons for 10 miles, and then for 6 miles across a broad mountain meadow, to its junction with Youngs Creek, 5 miles south of the Big Prairie Ranger Station. Danaher Creek, named for an old ranching family that made use of the meadows near its headwaters, is on one of the main trails to the Blackfoot country, heavily fished for decent catches of 10- to 14-inch cutthroat and an occasional whitefish or bull trout. [T20N R12W S31]

DEAN CREEK. A small, shallow stream with a series of falls 1½ miles above its mouth, flowing out of the southern end of the Great Bear Wilderness into the Spotted Bear River. It's crossed at the mouth by the Spotted Bear River trail and followed by trail 8½ miles to headwaters, on the flanks of Dean Ridge. Dean Creek is seldom fished, but it's fair below the falls for 8- to 10-inch cutts. [T25N R13W S36]

DOCTOR CREEK. A small, brushy stream that headwaters at the foot of a glacier field on the east slope of the Swan Range. It drains Doctor Lake and is followed by a trail for 2 miles from the lake to Gordon Creek. There's fair fishing in lots of small holes for 8- to 10-inch cutthroat and a few 2- to 3-pound bull trout. [T20N R14W S1]

DOCTOR LAKE. A real deep lake (almost 100 feet in places) of 80 acres, in a subalpine cirque on the east side of the Swan Range, at a 5,645-foot elevation. Reach it by following a dead-end USFS trail south for 4 miles from the Shaw Creek Guard Station, or go 11 miles southeast, over Gordon Pass, from Holland Lake. Doctor is rocky and brushy around the shore, and it can be good fishing for skinny, overpopulated 10- to 12-inch cutthroat. Snow hangs around in this country late into the summer most years. Like most other mountain lakes, Doctor has a fragile shoreline that is easily damaged by overuse. Please respect the USFS regulations that prohibit pack animals within 200 feet of the shore. [T19N R15W S14]

DORIS CREEK. A very small stream that is heavily fished for cutthroat and whitefish spawners from the Hungry Horse Reservoir in the fall. Doris is crossed at the mouth by the westside Hungry Horse road, 3 miles south of the dam, and is followed by a logging road for about 5 miles upstream. There are lots of blowdowns and brush in the canyon above, but the lower mile is fairly open and easy to fish. [T29N R19W S2]

DORIS LAKES. Three small lakes on the northeast flanks of Doris Mountain. Reach them by following a short trail from the end of the Alpha and

Beta Creek road, or get there from USFS trail 7, or by hiking 5 miles along the Fawn Creek drainage. Two of these lakes are stocked periodically with westslope cutts. [T29N R19W S6]

EMERY CREEK. Another small stream, which is followed by a good logging road for its full length of 5 miles, through timbered mountains, to Emery Bay, at the northeast end of the Hungry Horse Reservoir. There are some falls about 1½ miles above its mouth, but the fishing is fair both above and below for 6- to 7-inch cutthroat. Whitefish are common in the lower reaches. [T30N R18W S17]

FAWN LAKE. At the headwaters of Fawn Creek, this little lake sits just below the Swan Crest, north of Doris Mountain. The trail along the Fawn Creek drainage isn't maintained all the way to the lake, and some people prefer to drop in off USFS trail 7. Fawn has been planted occasionally with cutts, most recently in 1996. [T30N R19W S31]

FELIX CREEK. It flows for 5 miles from headwaters on the west slopes of Felix Peak, through rolling timbered country, to the east side of the Hungry Horse Reservoir, 4 miles south of the Betty Creek Guard Station. Logging roads in the drainage provide access to the lower reaches, and there is a trail for the last 1½ miles or so to headwaters, inside the Great Bear Wilderness. Felix was stocked with westslope cutthroat several years running in the late 1980s, in an effort to restore the cutthroat population. [T28N R17W S15]

GEORGE CREEK. This is the steep and rocky outlet of George Lake. The lower 3 miles are followed by a maintained trail, up a narrow, timbered canyon, from Gordon Creek at the Shaw Creek Guard Station. The lower ½ mile is fair fishing for 8- to 10-inch cutthroat, and bulls in the fall, but about the only one to fish it is the "Lone Ranger." [T19N R14W S7]

GEORGE LAKE. A real deep lake (over 200 feet), 128 acres, in an alpine setting right on the Clearwater-South Fork divide. It is hard to get to— but the best way in is reportedly by trail, from Holland Lake 10 miles east, over Gordon Pass, to the Shaw Creek Guard Station, then 3 miles south on the George Creek trail, and finally another mile south (plus over 1,000 feet vertically) cross-country to the lake. Don't make this hike too early in the year, unless you're geared up for ice fishing. George Lake usually stays frozen over until late July, and it freezes up again in early October. Long ago, it was spotty for fishing for big Yellowstone cutts, but more recently, it's been stocked annually with westslope cutthroat. [T19N R15W S26]

George Lake. —Courtesy John Fraley

GILL CREEK. It's about 4 miles long, with no trail, but it's accessible at the mouth by the Little Salmon Creek trail, 9 miles upstream from the South Fork of the Flathead River. It is steep, rocky, and poor fishing (near the mouth only) for small cutthroat. This one is seldom if ever fished. [T22N R15W S20]

GORDON CREEK. A beautiful, wide, easily fished stream that is reached at the headwaters by a trail over Gordon Pass, 8 steep miles southeast from Holland Lake. It's followed by a trail for 16 miles to its mouth on the South Fork of the Flathead River, 3 miles south of the Big Prairie Ranger Station. Since Gordon Creek is one of the main access routes to the South Fork, there's quite a bit of fishing pressure. There is a campground at Shirttail Park, just downstream from the Shaw Creek Guard Station. The stream is good fishing for 8- to 10-inch cutthroat, and fall-running bull trout in the lower reaches. Some of the native westslope cutts have hybridized with Yellowstone cutts that were once planted in lakes in the drainage. [T20N R13W S23]

GORGE CREEK. You can reach this stream at the headwaters by a long haul over Inspiration Pass (in the Swan Range), or at its mouth from the Bunker Creek road. Gorge Creek drains Sunburst, Olor, and Inspiration lakes. It's followed by good trail for 8 miles up its most spectacular, steep-walled gorge to its headwaters at the confluence of Inspiration Creek and the unnamed outlet stream of Sunburst Lake. It's good fast-water fishing for 8- to 10-inch cutthroat. [T24N R15W S26]

GRAVES CREEK. A clear mountain stream that's crossed at the mouth by the westside Hungry Horse Reservoir road, about 31 miles south of the dam. It is followed upstream by a logging road for 1 mile to Hand-kerchief Lake, from there another 1½ miles beyond, and from there by a trail to its headwaters, in the Jewel Basin. Graves is good fishing in late spring and early summer for spawning cutthroat at its mouth and up to

Graves Creek Falls. —Courtesy U.S. Forest Service

the waterfall just above the reservoir. Between the falls and Handkerchief Lake you can catch 9- to 12-inch cutthroat and some grayling. Another set of falls, about 1 mile above Handerkerchief Lake, plus many beaver dams are barriers to the grayling and cutthroat which inhabit the lake. Above these barriers you'll find mostly small cutts. [T27N R17W S6]

HANDKERCHIEF LAKE. A good-size lake (32 acres), in timber and brush. You can reach it within 300 yards by taking a road a little over a mile west from the west side of the Hungry Horse Reservoir road. This lake is heavily fished and fair for grayling and cutthroat, which are stocked there on a regular basis. Handkerchief boasts a series of state records for grayling. Don't forget that special regulations apply here, as they do in all waters in the South Fork drainage—check the regulations for creel limits. There are no beaches and no boat launching facilities, but there is a USFS campground, which keeps getting smaller and smaller due to trees blowing down on outhouses, picnic tables, and such. [T27N R18W S1]

HARRIS CREEK. A small inlet on the east side of the Hungry Horse Reservoir, crossed at the mouth by the eastside road 4 miles north of the Betty Creek Guard Station. It flows through a steep, timbered canyon above, but the lower 1½ miles are good fishing for small cutthroat. Harris was planted with cutts annually from 1988 to 1990, as part of the Hungry Horse Dam mitigation effort. [T28N R17W S10]

HARRISON CREEK. This stream is followed by a USFS trail, from the Meadow Creek campground along the South Fork of the Flathead for 5 miles, across the flat-bottomed river valley below and through a very narrow, steep-walled, timbered canyon above. Reach it at the mouth by the eastside trail, 8 miles south of the Spotted Bear Ranger Station. Harrison is occasionally fished for fair catches of 6- to 9-inch cutthroat trout. [T24N R14W S8]

HELEN CREEK. About 5 miles long and paralleled by one of the main "crossover" trails across the Bob Marshall Wilderness, Helen Creek flows from the flanks of Pagoda Mountain to the South Fork of the Flathead River just south of the Black Bear Guard Station. Lots of traffic goes by, but very few people stop to fish this stream for its goodly numbers of 7- to 9-inch cutthroat trout. [T23N R14W S34]

HELEN CREEK, North Fork. It's crossed at the mouth by the Helen Creek trail, but there's no maintained trail up its heavily timbered, steep-walled canyon. The lower reaches are good for small cutthroat, but are out of the way and very seldom fished. [T23N R13W S31]

HIGHROCK CREEK. A tiny, brushy tributary of the Little Salmon River, crossed at the mouth by a trail. It's poor fishing, for maybe ½ mile above, for small cutthroat in the fall. Highrock is very seldom fished, and it's just as well, too. [T22N R15W S22]

HODAG CREEK. A small, unimpressive tributary of the South Fork of the Flathead River, reached at the mouth by the eastside trail, 1 mile north of the Black Bear Guard Station. Hodag is seldom fished because it's so small, but the lower 2 miles are fair for little cuts and maybe a few spawning bull trout in the fall. [T23N R14W S22]

HOLBROOK CREEK. Holbrook flows northeast for 9 miles, down a steep, deep, V-shaped canyon in partly timber and partly burned-over country, to the South Fork of the Flathead at the old Holbrook Ranger Station. It is followed all the way to headwaters by a trail, and the lower 4 miles are good fishing for 8- to 10-inch cutthroat, plus a few bull trout late in the season. [T21N R13W S8]

HUNGRY CREEK. Reach this stream at the mouth by the westside trail along the South Fork of the Flathead River at the Black Bear Ranger Station. The trail follows the creek upstream for 4½ miles to headwaters, on the slopes of Marmot Mountain. It's seldom fished, but the lower couple of miles are good for 8- to 10-inch cutthroat and an occasional bull trout. [T23N R14W S34]

HUNGRY HORSE CREEK. This stream is about 6 miles long, on a timbered bench, flowing to the northeast end of the Hungry Horse Reservoir. It is paralleled by a logging road for most of its length, and it's easily fished (a real good kids' creek) for 6- to 10-inch cutthroat and some whitefish. [T30N R18W S21]

HUNGRY HORSE RESERVOIR. A large reservoir, 34 miles long by 1 to 4 miles wide, with many coves, headlands, and a most irregular shoreline, it's beautiful when it's full and abominable when it's drawn down, which is each fall and winter, and recently a lot of summers. Hungry Horse occupies the flooded-out valley of the South Fork of the Flathead River—once densely timbered but now grossly scarred with many clearcuts (courtesy of the U.S. Forest Service). It's accessible all the way around by roads that originate from US 2, a few miles south of Coram. There are two resorts at the upper end, and several public campgrounds all the way around. The fishing is fair to good for 10- to 14-inch cutthroat and 10- to 12-inch whitefish. Fishing for bull trout is illegal here, as it is in the rest of western Montana, except Swan Lake. If you catch one by accident, please release it carefully. Wilderness limits apply on the reservoir and on all of tributary streams—a total of three cutthroat, rainbow,

South Fork of the Flathead at Hungry Horse Creek. —Courtesy U.S. Forest Service

Hungry Horse Reservoir. —Courtesy U.S. Forest Service

and grayling, in any combination, daily and in possession. [T29N R18W S5]

JENNY CREEK. It heads near Youngs Pass and is followed by a trail down its narrow, timbered canyon for 5 miles to the head of Youngs Creek. The lower mile contains a few small cutthroat and some bull trout in the fall. It is very seldom fished, by stray passers-by. [T18N R13W S19]

JENNY LAKE. A shallow, 4-acre pond in brushy timber, just east of Blaine Mountain. It's most easily reached by a trail 1½ switchbacky miles from the end of the Doris Creek road. Jenny is occasionally visited by Boy Scouts, fished for small cutthroat that are planted there every 3 or 4 years. [T29N R19W S18]

JEWEL BASIN LAKES. Five little lakes in a beautiful, subalpine basin, about an hour's hike, by good trail, east from the Noisy Creek trailhead (in the Flathead drainage). The smaller lakes are barren, but the largest two are deep and support fish. North Jewel is about 7 acres, South Jewel about 4 acres; both are stocked with cutthroat, and the fishing is good. [T28N R18W S19]

KNIEFF CREEK. A very small stream in a heavily timbered, V-shaped canyon, crossed at the mouth by the westside Hungry Horse Reservoir road, about 20 miles south of the dam. Logging roads cross it in a few spots upstream, but only the lower ½ mile or so may be worth fishing, and even there the fishing is only poor to fair for pan-size cutthroat. [T28N R17W S7]

KOESSLER LAKE. A lovely, subalpine cirque lake with a little island in its southwest end. It's real deep, 45 acres, ½ mile northwest of Doctor Lake. There's no maintained trail, but there's enough traffic here to prompt the Forest Service to prohibit livestock in the fragile area around the lakeshore. Like many other lakes in the neighborhood, Koessler was planted earlier this century with non-native Yellowstone cutts. Now it's managed for native westslope cutts, which are planted there regularly. [T19N R15W S10]

LENA LAKE. This 84-acre lake is fairly deep with steep drop-offs, in high, timbered mountains in the Bob Marshall Wilderness. Lena is reached by a USFS trail at the head of Big Salmon Creek, but the trail can be tough on pack animals, because there are lots of boggy areas and some places where it's more of a scramble than a trail. The Forest Service is considering reconstructing or rerouting the trail higher up the walls of the drainage. Despite the challenges, plenty of folks make it back there, and there's some campsite revegetation under way. Lena was planted back in the '20s with rainbow trout, but since 1988 Fish, Wildlife and Parks managers have been inundating the lake with native westslope cutthroat. [T20N R15W S26]

LICK CREEK. The outlet of Lick Lake, Lick Creek flows through a narrow, timbered canyon for 4 miles to Gordon Creek. It's followed—at a distance of about ¼ mile—along the lower reaches by the Gordon Pass trail. It is a small, brushy stream that is hard to fish, but it's fair for pan-size cutthroat. [T19N R14W S1]

LICK LAKE. This gorgeous little lake sits high up in a rock-walled cirque to the northeast of Ptarmigan Mountain on the Swan Crest. There's no maintained trail, and there are definitely some hard ways to get up to this lake, enough people know the easy way for the Forest Service to prohibit livestock within 200 feet to protect the lakeshore. Lick was planted with westslope cutts from 1988 to 1994—if you get in there to fish, give us a report on how they're doing. [T19N R15W S9]

LION LAKE. A deep, 35-acre lake in timbered rolling country, right on the road from the town of Hungry Horse to the Hungry Horse Dam. It is very popular, and there are a USFS campground, a new picnic area, and a nice sandy swimming beach in the southwest corner. Lion Lake had been overtaken by northern pike, sunfish, bass, and who knows what else, so it was poisoned and stocked with cutthroat and rainbow. They're doing well, and Fish, Wildlife and Parks stocks often, so even though the lake gets a lot of pressure (through the ice in wintertime, too), the fishing is good enough to support a special limit of 10 trout daily. [T30N R19W S9]

LITTLE SALMON CREEK. A nice-size stream, about 18 miles long, followed the whole way down its narrow, steep-walled, heavily timbered valley by a good USFS trail to the South Fork of the Flathead River, 6 miles above the Black Bear Guard Station. Little Salmon is only lightly fished, but it's good fishing for real nice 12- to 15-inch cutthroat and some whitefish. And it's one of the best bull trout streams in the state. They're hard to catch here, and that's a good thing, because it's illegal to fish for them intentionally, and if you catch one you'd better release it in a hurry. But they're fun to watch in the clear water. [T22N R14W S23]

LOGAN (or NORTH FORK LOGAN) CREEK. This stream empties into the east side of the Hungry Horse Reservoir near the Betty Creek Guard Station. It's good fishing for mostly 4- to 7-inch cutthroat. About 3½ miles long in brush and timber, it's real steep above but followed closely by a logging road and trail to headwaters. There's a boat launch onto the reservoir right at its mouth. [T28N R17W S35]

LOST JOHNNY CREEK. A brushy, 6-mile-long stream that flows into the Hungry Horse Reservoir, it's crossed at the mouth by the reservoir's westside road 4 miles above the dam, and followed upstream by a logging road to headwaters. There are some falls about a mile above the mouth, and it's fair fishing above them for small resident cutthroat, and below them for good-size spawners (cutts and whitefish) from the reservoir. [T29N R19W S1]

LOST MARE CREEK. A real small tributary of Hungry Horse Creek, crossed about a mile above the mouth by the eastside Hungry Horse Reservoir road, 6 miles south of Emery. It is steep in the upper reaches but fair to good fishing in the lower for small cutthroat—8 inches is a biggie. [T30N R18W S23]

LOWER TWIN CREEK. An 11-mile stream in an old, brushy burn, Lower Twin flows to the South Fork of the Flathead River about 1 mile south of Hungry Horse Reservoir. It is crossed by the eastside Hungry Horse Reservoir road at its mouth, and it's followed (sort of) for 6 miles upstream by a USFS trail. It is not a pleasant stream to fish, but the lower 4 miles can produce good catches of 10- to 12-inch cutthroat. [T26N R16W S25]

MARGARET CREEK. A small tributary of Hungry Horse Creek, about 6 miles long, followed by a logging road for 4 miles of heavily fished, but good, water for 6- to 9- inch cutthroat. [T30N R18W S22]

MARGARET LAKE. A truly beautiful alpine lake, 5,575 feet above sea level, 46 acres and 75 feet deep, with talus slopes around the upper end and timber below. Take the westside Hungry Horse Reservoir road for about 25 miles south of the dam, then a logging road up Forest Creek (which has little or no fishing potential), and finally a couple of miles of trail to the lakeshore. This one is seldom visited, but it has a fair population of really nice 11- to 16-inch cutthroat (and some bigger ones reported) that are plenty hard to catch. [T27N R17W S19]

MARSHALL CREEK. A nice-looking, fairly open stream, the outlet of five unnamed lakes on Crescent Mountain. Marshall is crossed at the mouth by the Youngs Creek trail, then followed by a trail for 4 miles of fair cutthroat fishing. A rare bull trout might show up here in the fall. It is lightly to moderately fished, by hunters and dudes passing through. [T18N R13W S18]

MID CREEK. Rising on the steep, timbered slopes of Silvertip Mountain, it's followed by trail for 5½ miles to the South Fork of the Flathead River, 6 miles below the Black Bear Guard Station. It is very seldom fished, but it's pretty good for 7- to 10-inch cutthroat. [T23N R14W S4]

MIDDLE FORK (of BUNKER) CREEK. It heads on the Swan River-South Fork Flathead divide below Warrior Mountain and flows for 6 miles, down a steep canyon above and through fairly flat, timbered country below, to Bunker Creek. It is seldom fished, in part because the logging road that follows it is closed, and hoofing it all those miles is a big commitment to make for 7- to 9-inch cutthroat trout. [T24N R16W S24]

MURRAY CREEK. A real short, brushy stream that empties into the Hungry Horse Reservoir, crossed at the mouth by the reservoir's eastside road. Murray is only lightly fished, but the lower 2 miles are good for 6- to 9-inch cutthroat. [T29N R17W S19]

NANNY CREEK. Only about 3 miles long, in good deer and elk country, Nanny is reached at the mouth by the Twin Creek trail, northeast of Spotted Bear. Although small, the lower reaches are sometimes fished by hunters for fair catches of eating-size cutthroat. [T26N R15W S22]

NECKLACE LAKES. Six little lakes, ranging from 1 to 12 acres, in high, timbered country just east of the Swan Crest. They're drained by Smoky Creek to Big Salmon Creek; some of these lakes are also known as the Smoky Creek Lakes, but getting which is which straight gets downright confusing. Anyway, they're all easily reached by trail from Holland Lake east about 5 miles (plus a couple of thousand feet vertically). The most

Necklace Lakes. —Courtesy Michele Archie

direct route is up what is affectionately, in some circles, known as the switchback trail. The Necklace Lakes range in depth from 10 to 50 feet, and all are fair to good, but notoriously temperamental, fishing for 10- to 12-inch cutthroat. The lakes directly on the trail sustain the most fishing pressure, but the area is pretty popular with hikers and horse packers, so it's not unusual to share a lake with another party, not to mention about a bazillion mosquitoes. [T20N R15W S17]

NORTH BIGLOW (or BIGLOW) LAKE. A 33-foot-deep, 24-acre lake in heavy timber, 6,000 feet above sea level, at the head of Biglow Creek. It is most easily reached by a cross-country hike 2½ miles northeast from the end of the Quintonkin Creek logging road. You can also get close to the lake on a closed-off logging road that takes off to the south from the Wheeler Creek road. Biglow is seldom fished, but last rumor has it that there's a small population of 16- to 18-inch cutthroat trout. [T26N R18W S1]

NORTH CREEK. Small, short, and steep, this tributary of Twin Creek is crossed at the mouth by the Twin Creek trail and seldom if ever fished for the few small cutthroat it contains. [T26N R15W S32]

NORTH FORK HELEN CREEK. See Helen Creek, North Fork.

NORTH FORK LOGAN CREEK. See under Logan Creek.

OLOR (or OLAR) LAKES. Two lakes north of Swan Peak, near Sunburst Lake. They were planted with lots of cutthroat many years ago, but there don't seem to be any left. [T23N R16W S15]

PAINT CREEK. A fishing stream you can step across. It's about 4 miles long, in rolling, timbered country, and it empties into the east side of the Hungry Horse Reservoir 1½ miles north of the Betty Creek Guard Station. A seasonally open logging road provides some access to the middle reaches. Paint Creek is fair fishing for 6- to 8-inch cutthroat. [T28N R17W S27]

PENDANT LAKES. Three lakes in high, timbered country, just a couple of miles over the Swan divide from Upper Holland Lake (in the Swan drainage). From west to east, they measure 9 acres, a hair over 2 acres, and almost 1½ acres. The outlet drops over some high falls, so there is no fish migration. They were planted years ago, but no longer, so they may have a very small remnant of the former population of rainbow trout. They were never much better than poor to fair fishing anyway, and not many anglers stop by. But enough folks do visit so that, to protect the lakeshore, the Forest Service asks that you keep your livestock back at least 200 feet. [T20N R15W S21]

PILGRIM LAKES. Two subalpine lakes in a small cirque just south and below the summit of Three Eagle Mountain. They're real hard to get to: from the Noisy Creek trailhead, at the end of USFS road 5392 (Flathead drainage), go several miles into the Jewel Basin to the Alpine trail, then cross-country for 1½ miles. The upper lake is only 3 acres, but the lower one, which is 29 acres and a whopping 135 feet deep, is good fishing for 6- to 13-inch cutthroat trout. It's been planted a couple of times in recent years. You might find a very few big cutthroat in the upper lake, too, but it's probably not worth your while. [T27N R18W S15]

POSY CREEK. A little tributary of Quintonkon Creek, in a "blow-down" logged-over area, it's crossed at the mouth by the Quintonkon road. It's followed by road for a short distance upstream, and then by trail, for 2 miles of fair fishing for pan-size cutthroat. This one is seldom bothered. [T26N R17W S19]

PRISONER LAKE. A 4-acre, subalpine lake just below Shale Peak, at the northeast end of the Flathead Alps. It's reached by a steep, 1½-mile cross-country scramble west from the end of the South Fork White River trail. Prisoner Lake reportedly has a good population of 6- to 8-inch cutthroat although it's so shallow that it looks as though it should freeze out. [T21N R12W S32]

QUINTONKON CREEK. A small, fast-moving mountain stream flowing to Sullivan Creek, about a mile south of the Hungry Horse Reservoir. It's about 12 miles long, in a steep-walled, logged-over canyon, followed by a logging road for 10 miles of good summertime fishing for lots of small cutthroat and a few grayling, and fair fall and winter fishing for whitefish. Fall might find an occasional bull trout migrating through, and large-scale suckers (in case you're curious) are common spawners in the lower reaches. [T26N R17W S11]

RAPID CREEK. This stream heads on the western slopes of the Continental Divide, at Observation Pass. It is followed by a good USFS pack trail for 7 miles to Danaher Creek, 4 miles below the guard station. The lower 3 miles, between Sentinel Mountain and Ursus Hill, are good fishing for 8- to 10-inch cutthroat. In the fall, watch for an occasional bull trout spawner. Rapid Creek is seldom fished—in favor of Danaher. [T19N R11W S30]

RIVERSIDE CREEK. A small inlet of the Hungry Horse Reservoir, crossed near the mouth by the reservoir's eastside road, 12 miles north of the Betty Creek work station. It's pretty steep in the upper reaches, but the lower reaches are flatter, fair fishing for about 1½ miles. They contain mostly small cutthroat that average between 6 and 8 inches, plus an occasional lunker up from the reservoir. [T29N R17W S7]

SEVEN ACRES LAKES. Two lakes, the upper at 6 acres and 100-plus feet deep, the lower at 12 acres and 76 feet deep. They are ¼ mile apart in a brushy, subalpine cirque, southeast of Cliff Lake in the Jewel Basin hiking area, reached cross-country from whatever direction strikes you in this steep terrain. Both lakes are planted with cutthroat periodically and can be good fishing—for those few intrepid souls who make it in. Get a good topo map and have fun! [T28N R18W S28]

SHELF LAKE. A deep lake, about 15 acres, in timbered lowland. It's reached by a USFS road past the Beaver Creek campground (open from July 1 to September 1), just north of the Spotted Bear River and a couple of miles below Silvertip Cabin. Shelf was planted with cutthroat trout years ago and is good fishing for 10- to 16-inch cutthroat. It is restocked periodically. [T25N R13W S7]

SILVER TIP CREEK. A small stream followed by a trail for almost all of its 11-mile length, down a heavily timbered, flat-bottomed canyon to the Spotted Bear River, 12 miles south of the ranger station. It is not often fished, but it's good for 1 mile above the mouth (to the falls) for 10- to 12-inch cutthroat. Incidentally, the namesakes of this stream still abound in the near vicinity. [T25N R13W S16]

SLIDE CREEK. A very small tributary of Sullivan Creek, in logged-over country, paralleled by a closed road for a couple of miles of fair 6- to 8-inch cutthroat fishing. [T25N R16W S8]

SMOKY CREEK LAKES. See under Necklace Lakes.

SNOW CREEK. A short, small tributary of the South Fork of the Flathead River, crossed at the mouth by the westside trail, 1 mile south of the Black Bear Airfield. There's no maintained trail upstream, but the lower mile is the only part worth fishing anyway. It's fair for 7- to 9-inch cutts. [T23N R14W S34]

SOUTH CREEK. From the Spotted Bear River, 3 miles south of the ranger station, a trail up Bent Creek crosses this small tributary of Twin Creek about 1½ miles above the mouth. It is fair cutthroat fishing for the first mile (past an old abandoned beaver dam, "Web Lake"), but it's seldom bothered. [T26N R15W S27]

SOUTH FORK WHITE RIVER. See White River, South Fork.

SPOTTED BEAR LAKE. From the Spotted Bear Ranger Station, take the trail 1½ miles east to this lake. It is something like 9 acres, mud-bottomed, and relatively shallow but fairly deep in the middle. Marshy and hard to fish from the shore, it's lots of fun (believe it) to get a float tube into. Periodically planted, it's excellent fishing, heavily fished now, for 16- to 18-inch cutthroat trout. [T25N R15W S16]

SPOTTED BEAR RIVER. A good-size, easily fished, open stream, it's followed by a road (that is closed above Beaver Creek) for 11 miles above its mouth on the South Fork of the Flathead River, at the Spotted Bear Ranger Station, then by a good USFS horse trail for another 23 miles to headwaters. The fish above Dean Falls (19 miles upstream) do not get very big, but it is good to excellent fishing below for good-size cutthroat and whitefish. Squawfish are common, and bull trout use the lower reaches as a migration corridor. This is a good place to go for the dyed-in-the-wool fly fisher. [T25N R15W S17]

Mouth of the Spotted Bear River. —Courtesy U.S. Forest Service

SQUAW LAKE. Squaw covers 2-plus acres in barren, rocky alpine country. From the Noisy Creek trailhead (Flathead drainage), take a trail 3½ miles south. This lake is often passed by for Crater and other bigger lakes south of there, but it is planted periodically with cutthroat and can be good fishing. [T27N R18W S5]

STADIUM CREEK. A small tributary of Gorge Creek, it's followed partway upstream by trail, but it's seldom fished or even visited. Its 3 or 4 miles contain a good population of 7- to 9-inch cutthroat trout. [T23N R15W S10]

SULLIVAN CREEK. A nice-size stream, 15 miles long, in a narrow, timbered canyon. It's followed for 4½ miles by a road from its mouth on the Hungry Horse Reservoir. Although the road continues on for another few miles, it's gated near the confluence of Sullivan and Connor creeks. Sullivan is moderately popular and good summer fishing for small cutthroat, and fall and winter fishing for whitefish in the lower reaches. Spawning bull trout move through in the fall. [T26N R17W S1]

SUNBURST LAKE. A beautiful, very deep (over 200 feet), 142-acre, subalpine lake. Take a good USFS trail east along Gorge Creek for 9 miles. Well, the trail is good for the first 7 miles, but the last couple of miles are restricted to hikers, because pack animals chew up the boggy

Getting ready at Sunburst Lake. —Courtesy Michele Archie

trail so much. There's a good campsite where the trail branches off toward Sunburst, with room for your livestock. You could also come in over Inspiration Pass, east from the Swan River drainage. Sunburst lies below Swan Glacier and is seldom free of ice before July 1. But when it does open up, it is excellent fishing for cutts with some size to them. The lake's been stocked in the past with rainbows and Yellowstone cutts, but now westslope cutts are the fish of choice. You might catch some hybrids, too. [T23N R16W S23]

TANGO CREEK. This stream is 4 miles long, steep and rocky. It's crossed near the mouth by the Big Salmon Creek trail, 2 miles above Barrier Falls. It is followed by a trail for 1½ miles of fair 7- to 9-inch cutthroat fishing, and it isn't bothered once in a blue moon. [T21N R15W S27]

TENT CREEK. A small stream in heavily timbered country, Tent is real steep in the upper reaches, but it flattens out lower down for about 2 miles, before emptying into the northeast side of the Hungry Horse Reservoir. It is crossed at the headwaters by the reservoir's eastside road, and it's good fishing in the lower reaches for 10- to 12- inch cutthroat trout. [T29N R17W S7]

THREE EAGLES LAKES. Two lakes, at 6,175 feet and 5,500 feet above sea level, on the northern slopes of Three Eagles Mountain, in the Jewel Basin. From Pilgrim Lakes, which aren't very easy to get to themselves, it's a rugged cross-country mile over the hill and north. Both lakes are set in talus, with scrub timber around the outlets. With maximum depths of 78 and 82 feet, the lakes are stocked periodically with cutthroat. The cutts grow slowly but provide excellent fishing. [T27N R18W S10]

TIGER CREEK. This small, brushy tributary of Hungry Horse Creek is followed by an old logging road upstream for 1 mile, through timbered country, as far as the mouth of Turmoil Creek. It is lightly fished for a couple of miles for good catches of 6- to 8-inch cutthroat. [T30N R18W S23]

TIN CREEK. A small tributary of the South Fork of the Flathead River, crossed at the mouth by the westside Hungry Horse-Spotted Bear road, 1½ miles south of the reservoir and just north of the Spotted Bear Airstrip. There is no trail upstream, but the first mile is moderately popular and fair fishing for 6- to 9-inch cutthroat. [T26N R16W S36]

TOM TOM LAKE. A 33-foot-deep, 8-acre pothole at 5,700 feet above sea level in heavy timber. It's reached by a 1-mile cross-country hike south from the upper end of the Wheeler Creek road. For years, it was overstocked with skinny Yellowstone cutthroat trout, but since 1985, the Department of Fish, Wildlife and Parks has been trying to change that by planting native westslope cutts. [T27N R18W S27]

TRICKLE CREEK. This stream heads east of Oreamnos Peak in the Swan Range, and it's followed by a trail for 4 miles through steep, timbered mountains to Stadium Creek. This Trickle is almost never fished, but the lower couple of miles are good for 7- to 9- inch cutthroat. [T23N R15W S27]

TROUT LAKE. Less than a mile from the shores of Hungry Horse Reservoir, Trout Lake is right alongside the reservoir's eastside road. It's been stocked for the last few years with cutthroat, and there's a ramp and a fishing access for anglers with physical disabilities. [T28N R17W S21]

TWIN (or UPPER TWIN) CREEK. A heavily fished stream, especially during hunting season. It's crossed at the mouth by the South Fork of the Flathead road, a mile above Hungry Horse Reservoir, and is followed by a good USFS horse trail for 15 miles, almost to headwaters. Twin flows beneath a natural rock bridge 4 miles above its mouth (about ½ mile below the mouth of South Creek), and it's pretty well log-jammed in the lower reaches. It is good fishing for 8- to 12-inch cutthroat and whitefish. [T26N R16W S25]

Twin Lakes. —Courtesy Michele Archie

TWIN LAKES. These two beautiful little lakes sit side by side in the mountains of the Jewel Basin. Go north for a couple miles from the Noisy Creek trailhead (Flathead drainage). The lakes are stocked periodically with cutthroat, although they were barren in the not-too-distant past. [T28N R18W S19]

UPPER TWIN CREEK. See Twin Creek.

WHEELER CREEK. This stream is 8 miles long, in a steep-walled, timbered canyon, flowing to Hungry Horse Reservoir, 10 miles north of the reservoir's head. It's followed by a road from its mouth for 7 miles upstream—the road is open July 1 through December 1. Wheeler is lightly fished but good in the summer for small cutthroat, and in the fall and winter for whitefish in its lower reaches. A few bull trout spawn in the lower reaches in the fall. [T27N R17W S15]

WHITE RIVER. A wide, shallow stream flowing south and then west for 20 miles, down its flat-bottomed valley, to the South Fork of the Flathead River, 1 mile north of the Holbrook Guard Station. The White River is a principal thoroughfare for those going and coming from the Sun River country, and the stream is heavily fished, from its mouth upstream for 8 miles to Needle Falls, for good-size cutthroat. Bull trout use the lower reaches in the fall for spawning. Long stretches of this stream above the falls (which are quite high and act as a fish barrier) go dry in late summer, and the seldom-fished holes that remain are jammed with 7- to 10-inch cutthroat like sardines in a can. [T21N R13W S8]

WHITE RIVER, South Fork. This smallish stream is excellent fishing for small cutthroat trout, and bull trout run up here in the fall. It is followed by a trail for 5 miles almost to headwaters, and it's fished a fair amount by hunters and dudes on their way to and from White River Pass. [T21N R12W S7]

WILDCAT CREEK. This very small tributary of Wounded Buck Creek is reached at the mouth by the Wounded Buck road, then followed upstream by a logging road for about 1½ miles beyond a series of big falls. There are no fish above the falls, but it's fair fishing below for pan-size cutthroat. [T29N R18W S30]

WILDCAT LAKE. A real deep, 39-acre alpine lake with steep drop-offs, surrounded by talus, rocky cliffs, and trees right down to the shore. To find it, take a good USFS trail 3 miles north from the Noisy Creek trailhead (in the Flathead drainage). Wildcat was planted via packhorse many years ago, and the last plant was in 1992, although who knows what role the packhorse played this time around. The lake can be good fishing for

Wildcat Lake. —Courtesy Michele Archie

cutthroat that will average 12 to 14 inches, especially if you haul some kind of watercraft in. [T28N R19W S12]

WOODWARD LAKE. A fairly deep, 65-acre lake in high, timbered country just east of the Swan-South Fork divide, drained by Cataract Creek. Go cross-country—unless you know where to look for the informal trail— about a mile northwest from the Necklace Lakes. Woodward is fished quite a bit for a "way back" lake and it's fair to good for decent-size cutts, and rainbow trout that range to several pounds. The rainbows are apparently the result of long-ago plantings. Cutts have been stocked here the last several years. Bring a boat, and keep your livestock more than 200 feet from the lakeshore. [T20N R15W S18]

WOUNDED BUCK CREEK. A brushy little low-gradient stream, in a timbered but heavily logged, flat-bottomed valley. It's crossed ½ mile from the mouth by the westside Hungry Horse road, 7 miles south of the dam, then followed by a logging road for 4 miles upstream (to the mouth of Wildcat Creek). A trail leads to headwaters, on the flanks of

Strawberry Mountain. The middle reaches are good fishing for small cut-throat, and the lower reaches are one of the best cutthroat and whitefish spawning areas in the entire Hungry Horse drainage. [T29N R18W S17]

YOUNGS CREEK. A nice-size stream, flowing for about 22 miles, through a narrow, brushy canyon, to the South Fork of the Flathead, 6 miles south of the Big Prairie Ranger Station. It's followed by trail the whole way, from the South Fork to headwaters, near Marshall Mountain. It's good fishing for whitefish in the lower reaches, and for good-size cut-throat in beaver ponds along the middle reaches, near the Hahn Guard Station. Bull trout spawn here in the fall. [T20N R12W S31]

St. Mary Lake. —Courtesy Ravalli County Museum, Ernst Peterson Collection

Glacier National Park

Glacier National Park is an area of massive mountain ranges, magnificently fashioned by water and glaciers, with about fifty glistening glaciers and two hundred sparkling lakes. Its 1,584 square miles of picturesque landscape are enlivened by a profusion of wildflowers and abundant wildlife. Glacier National Park headwaters and lakes contribute to three major continental river drainages: the Columbia, Saskatchewan, and Missouri rivers.

Each year, the park sees over two million visitors, arriving mostly by car, camper, or motor home, from which they view vistas from scenic roads. Visitors generally spend a night or two at a hotel, lodge, or at one of the developed campgrounds, and rent boats, hire horses and guides, and hike trails to explore further the natural delight. Campfire programs and guided hikes offered by park naturalists are informative and popular. Magnificent trails lead the fisher and backpacker into the backcountry to use the sixty-two remote campgrounds.

Glacier Park has changed little over the years, and while scenes are essentially the same as two hundred years ago, subtle changes have taken place. Natural processes, like gradually retreating glaciers and evolving forests marked by fires continually change the landscape. Changing, too, are management policies such as those toward predators, once hunted and killed to protect the "good" animals; toward bears, once passively allowed to feed in garbage dumps; toward deer and other animals, fed hay to supplement their diets in the 1930s. Certain fires, those naturally caused and not threatening to park developments, might soon be allowed to burn themselves out: research shows lightning-caused fires can be a natural and necessary part of forest life.

Changing policies toward fish date from the late 1960s. For many decades Glacier National Park stocked fish, even exotic species, in many park lakes and streams. Today the practice is discontinued. Park fishing regulations are designed to protect the native species: cutthroat, lake trout, bull trout, and Arctic grayling. The Glacier National Park fishing regulations contain the most up-to-date daily catch and possession limits. This information is available at any entrance station or any park ranger station. A "fishing for fun" area has been established along Lower McDonald Creek, where only artificial flies or lures with a single hook may be used, and fish caught must be released immediately to the stream. The park now considers fish not so much for their sport value as for their place in the natural ecosystem.

Ecosystem is the key word, and today national parks such as Glacier are managed with ecology in mind. Ecology means the ways in which plants, animals, and the environment interact. There are many kinds of ecosystems—an example is an aquatic ecosystem, where water, plants, insects, fish, mink, bear, otter, osprey, and eagles all play a part.

Glacier National Park is a beautiful place to visit, to enjoy, and to see the natural processes continue to develop, shaping the scenery and maintaining the plant and animal community. Here it is easy to become a bit of a botanist, geologist, zoologist, meteorologist, ecologist, and philosopher.

For Your Safety

Consider yourself lucky to see a black or grizzly bear. But remember—the wilderness is their home. Please be a well-mannered guest. Bears are usually shy; make no attempt to approach or startle them. They have been known to attack without warning. Hikers and fishers are advised to make noise to avoid surprise encounters with bears—especially during windy and inclement weather and near noisy water courses. A common means of doing this is to use bear bells, sing, whistle, or talk with lots of volume. Never offer food to bears and never get between a sow and her cub.

Bears have an excellent sense of smell, so it is important to avoid odorous foods. Regulations require that food, cooking utensils, and food containers be suspended away from sleeping areas at least 10 feet above the ground and 4 feet from any trunk or limb. In the absence of trees, store food and cooking gear in airtight containers, away from sleeping areas. Where possible, cook away from your sleeping area and keep your clothes and sleeping bag clean. Please report all bear sightings to a ranger.

Steve Frye
Chief Ranger
Glacier National Park

NOTE: Check current Glacier Park fishing regulations before fishing. Also, it's a good idea to check for trail closures, bear activity, and other factors that may influence your decision about where to fish in the park. You'll need a permit if you wish to camp in the backcountry.

Black bear cubs. —Courtesy U.S. Forest Service

Mountain goat. —Couresty Glacier National Park

GLACIER PARK LAKES

Name	Rating	Accessibility	Species	Best season	Boat access
Akokala	G	6 miles by trail from Bowman Lake	cutthroat	July & Aug.	no
Arrow	G	4 steep miles on the West Lakes trail from Lake McDonald	cutthroat	June & July	no
Avalanche	F	2 easy miles by trail from Avalanche campground	cutthroat	June & July	no
Bowman	F	Gravel road, 5 miles north of Polebridge Ranger Station	lake trout, kokanee, cutthroat, bull trout, whitefish	early & fall	yes
Bullhead	G	4 fairly level miles from Many Glacier	brook trout	June & July	no
Camas	G	5.5 miles on the West Lakes trail from Lake McDonald	cutthroat	June & July	no
Cerulean	F	Above Quartz Lake, difficult bushwhacking in grizzly country	cutthroat, bull trout	July & Aug.	no
Cosley (or Crossley)	G	8 miles of good hard hiking from the Chief Mountain Customs Station	whitefish, lake trout, brook trout	early & fall	no
Elizabeth	G	9 miles by trail from the Chief Mountain Customs Station, or by way of Ptarmigan Tunnel from Many Glacier	grayling, rainbow	June & July	no
Ellen Wilson	E	10 miles up the Sperry Chalet trail from Lake MacDonald Lodge (2.5 miles past the chalet)	cutthroat, brook trout	July & Aug.	no
Evangeline	G	5.5 miles by trail to Camas Lake, then 1.5 miles past Camas, no trail	cutthroat	June & July	no
Fishercap	F/P	5 miles by trail from Swiftcurrent campground	brook trout	June & July	no
Francis	G	6 miles by trail from the head of Waterton Lake	rainbow	June & July	no
Glenns	G	11 miles by trail from Chief Mountain Customs Station	lake trout, whitefish, cutthroat	early & fall	no
Grace	E	12 trail miles up Logging Creek from the inside North Fork road	cutthroat	June & July	no
Grinnell	F	4 miles by trail from Many Glacier, or 1 mile from the Lake Josephine boat dock	brook trout, rainbow	July	no
Gunsight	G	6 easy miles by trail from the Going-to-the-Sun Road (Jackson Glacier overlook)	rainbow, cutthroat	June & July	no
Harrison	G	3 trail miles from US 2 if you can ford the Middle Fork. Or 11 miles by trail from West Glacier.	cutthroat, whitefish, bull trout	June & July	no
Hidden	F	3 miles by trail from Logan Pass, in good bear country	cutthroat	July	no
Howe	F	2 miles by trail from the inside North Fork road	cutthroat	early season	no
Isabel	G	17 miles by trail from Walton Ranger Station, or 12 miles from Two Medicine	cutthroat, bull trout	June & July	no
Josephine	F	1.5 miles by trail from Many Glacier	brook trout, kokanee	June & July	no
Kintla	F	By gravel road north of the Polebridge Ranger Station	cutthroat, lake trout, kokanee, whitefish, bull trout	early & fall	yes
Kootenai	F	2.5 miles by trail from the head of Waterton Lake	brook trout	June–Aug.	no

Lincoln	G	8 miles by trail from the Going-to-the-Sun Road along Lake McDonald	cutthroat	June & July	no
Logging	G	4.5 miles by trail from the inside North Fork road	cutthroat, bull trout	early & fall	no
Lower Quartz	G/E	4 miles by trail from Bowman Lake	cutthroat, whitefish, bull trout	early & fall	no
McDonald	F/P	By paved road	lake trout, cutthroat, bull trout	early & fall	yes
Medicine Grizzly	G	5.5 miles by trail from Cut Bank campground	cutthroat, rainbow	July	no
Middle Quartz	G/E	6 miles by trail from Bowman Lake	cutthroat, bull trout	early & fall	no
Mokowanis	G	15 miles by trail from the Chief Mountain Customs Station	brook trout	June & July	no
Old Man	G	7 miles by trail from Two Medicine campground	cutthroat	June & July	no
Otokomi	G	6 miles by trail from Rising Sun campground	elusive cutthroat	July	no
Poia	N	5 miles by trail from Sherburne Lake	previously stocked with grayling, now barren		no
Ptarmigan	G	5 hard miles by trail from Many Glacier	brook trout, cutthroat	July & Aug.	no
Quartz	G/E	6 miles by trail from Bowman Lake	cutthroat, bull trout	early & fall	no
Red Eagle	G	8 miles by trail from St. Mary	elusive cutthroat and rainbow– cutt hybrids	June & July	no
Redrock	F	3 miles by trail from Many Glacier	brook trout	June & July	no
Rogers	P	4.5 miles by trail from the inside North Fork road	cutthroat, whitefish	early season	no
St. Mary	F/P	By paved road	lake trout, whitefish, rainbow, cutthroat	early & fall	yes
Sherburne	P	By paved road	northern pike	Aug., when lake level drops	yes
Slide	F/G	5 miles by trail from Chief Mountain Customs Station	cutthroat	July & Aug.	no
Snyder	F	4.5 miles by trail from Lake McDonald Lodge	stunted cutthroat	early season	no
Swiftcurrent	F	By paved road	brook trout	June & July	yes
Trout	G	4 miles by the West Lakes trail from Lake McDonald (fly fishing only)	cutthroat	June & July	no
Two Medicine	G	By paved road	brook trout, rainbow	June & July	yes
Upper Kintla	P	8 miles by trail from Kintla campground	bull trout (protected)	———	no
Upper Two Medicine	G	5.5 miles by trail from Two Medicine campground, or 2 miles from boat landing at head of Two Medicine Lake	brook trout, rainbow	June & July	no
Waterton	F	By paved road	lake trout, whitefish, a few trout of other species	July	yes
Windmaker	F	4 miles by trail and 1 mile bushwhacking through bear country from Many Glacier	brook trout	June & July	no

GLACIER PARK STREAMS

Name	Rating	Accessibility	Species	Best season	Boat access
Akokala Creek	G	By trail from Bowman Lake or inside North Fork road	cutthroat	late June–Aug.	—
Anaconda Creek	F	By trail from the inside North Fork road	small cutthroat	late June–Aug.	—
Belly River	G	By trail from Chief Mountain Road	rainbow, grayling	early season	—
Bowman Creek	G	By gravel road below the lake, trail above	cutthroat	late June–Aug.	—
Camas Creek	F	Crossed by inside North Fork road, and access to mouth from outside North Fork road	cutthroat	late June–Aug.	—
Coal Creek	F/G	By trail from the Middle Fork of the Flathead River	brook trout, cutthroat, whitefish	closed	—
Cut Bank Creek	F	4 miles by secondary road from US 89, then trail	brook trout, rainbow, whitefish	early season	—
Kennedy Creek	F	By secondary road and trail from US 89, or trail access from Many Glacier	bull trout, whitefish, maybe some rainbow	June & July	—
Kintla Creek	F	Walk from the Kintla Lake access road below the lake, access by trail above the lake	cutthroat, bull trout	late June–Aug.	—
Logging Creek	F	By trail from the inside North Fork road	cutthroat, bull trout	late June–Aug.	—
Lower McDonald Creek	F	By good gravel road to Quarter Circle Bridge, or by canoe from Lake McDonald	cutthroat, whitefish, rainbow, brook trout	late June–Aug.	yes
Ole Creek	F/G	By trail from the Middle Fork of the Flathead River	cutthroat, whitefish, bull trout	closed	—
Park Creek	F	By trail from the Middle Fork of the Flathead River	cutthroat, whitefish, bull trout	closed	—
Quartz Creek	F	By trail from the inside North Fork road	cutthroat	late June–Aug.	—
Saint Mary River	F/P	By trail from the upper end of Saint Mary Lake	rainbow, cutthroat (whitefish below the lake)	early season	—
Swiftcurrent Creek	P	By paved road	small brook trout	early season	—
Upper McDonald Creek	P	By paved road	cutthroat, whitefish, rainbow, brook trout	early season	—
Waterton River	F/P	By trail from the head of Waterton Lake	whitefish	early season	—

Along the trail to Iceberg Lake. —Courtesy Glacier National Park

Bowman Lake. —Courtesy Glacier National Park

Kootenai Falls. —Courtesy U.S. Forest Service

The Kootenai River—Changed Forever

The Kootenai River rises in Canada, on the west slope of the Rockies, and flows south and west, through northwestern Montana and northern Idaho, before turning north again, flowing back into Canada to Kootenay Lake. The Kootenai, almost 485 miles long, is the second largest stream in Montana, with most of its water coming from the high, rugged, glaciated mountains of Canada. Prior to the completion of Libby Dam, this emerald green river and its tributary streams provided some of the best fishing for wild cutthroat, rainbow trout, and mountain whitefish in Montana. A float trip through the narrow valley, surrounded by rugged mountains with abundant game populations, was an exciting and memorable experience.

The impounding of the Kootenai River in 1972 by Libby Dam, located about 17 miles northeast of Libby, has changed 90 miles (48 in Montana and 42 in Canada) of this once beautiful and wild river into a fluctuating reservoir. Maximum drawdown can be 178 feet, which makes mud flats of the upper 50 miles of the 90-mile-long impoundment. Average drawdown from 1972 and 1980 was considerably less than the 178-foot maximum.

Fishing in the reservoir has changed dramatically since 1972. Rainbow and cutthroat trout up to 18 inches long have been supplanted by kokanee salmon in the 11- to 14-inch size. Kokanee, inadvertently released in Canada around 1978, have flourished. Since 1985, the Montana Department of Fish, Wildlife and Parks, along with the Fisheries Branch of British Columbia Ministry of Environment, Lands and Parks, have stocked Duncan and Gerrard (Kamloops) strains of rainbow trout in Koocanusa Lake, the benefits of which are just now being realized. Rainbows from 3 to 20 pounds are being caught by persistent anglers. Most angling is from boats, with typical kokanee or Kamloops rigging, although some shore angling is still available, mostly in the springtime. Burbot (ling), a freshwater codfish, are being caught in the winter from the upper end of the reservoir in Montana.

At the present time, the Kootenai River below Libby Dam (48 miles from the Idaho border) provides good fishing for 10- to 20-inch rainbow trout. There are some special regulations that apply to this section, so be sure to consult the Montana fishing regulations pamphlet. Large numbers of good-size mountain whitefish are available to the angler but are mostly ignored. There's a trophy fishery for large rainbow, in the 5- to 10-pound class, in the spring near the mouths of Callahan Creek and the Yaak River. The only population of white sturgeon in Montana is found in the river below Kootenai Falls. In 1978, numerous net sets, set-line fishing, and rod-and-reel fishing produced only three sturgeon. The season was closed in 1979, and there's fear that the sturgeon have changed their spawning habits and no longer migrate to Montana in significant numbers. In 1994, Kootenai River white sturgeon were listed as an endangered species.

Access to the river is generally good, and many people fish from the bank, but a float trip is the most enjoyable way to fish this large river. Whitetail deer and Rocky Mountain bighorn sheep are often observed by fishers floating the river. Floaters are cautioned to bypass Kootenai Falls, which would be deadly to anyone foolish enough to go over it in a raft or boat. Anglers should also be cautious about where they are fishing and where they park their vehicle due to sudden increases or decreases in river flow from Libby Dam Powerhouse operations. The most productive flies are the Renegade, Black Gnat, Royal and Grey Wolf, Green Wooley Worm, Small Yellow May (size 18 to 20), Royal Coachman, Weighted Bitch Creek, and Muddler Minnow. For lure fishing, the Thomas Cyclone, Mepps Spinner, and Red and White Daredevil are hard to beat.

Nearly all the tributaries provide good fishing for pan-size rainbow, cutthroat, and brook trout, with some of the large streams consistently producing fish in the 10- to 16-inch bracket. Numerous small and medium-size lakes in the drainage provide excellent fishing for rainbow, westslope cutthroat, and brook trout. Yellow perch and largemouth bass are also found in a few lakes.

Visitors to the area should bring their hiking shoes and plan to walk into some of the high mountain lakes in the Cabinet Mountain Wilderness Area. Good trails lead to these beautiful, high, cold lakes, which are in basins formed by glacier activity. Most of the lakes contain good populations of rainbow, cutthroat, and brook trout in the 8- to 12-inch range. The knowledgeable angler brings a skillet and a little butter, and cooks the freshly caught mountain trout on the spot: a real gourmet treat. A size 18 to 20 Black Gnat or Renegade will ensure in most instances that the essential ingredient of the cookout—trout—is not missing.

Mike Hensler
Fisheries Biologist
Montana Fish, Wildlife and Parks

ALKALI LAKE. About 107 acres and 35 feet deep, it's a real "homely" lake, with lots of drowned timber all around. Alkali sits in rolling, timbered country, 3 miles south of Eureka by road. As the name implies, the water is very alkaline and doesn't support fish very well. After a failed three-year experiment with planting bass, they are back to regularly stocking rainbow fingerlings. Who knows? [T35N R27W S1]

ALVORD LAKE. Covering 56 acres, about 40 feet deep in the middle, it's got shallow drop-offs and a mucky bottom, with lots of sunken logs, lilies, and rushes. Alvord lies in a timbered pocket in the hills just north of Troy; it's accessible by a poor road 2 miles from town. It's fair fishing for good-size yellow perch, the occasional largemouth bass, and small sunfish. See current regulations for special early-season limits. [T32N R34W S36]

AMERICAN CREEK. A small stream that heads on Canuck Peak and flows north for about 5 miles, through a narrow, timbered canyon, to Canada just east of the Idaho line. It is accessible by logging roads from Idaho, and it's lightly fished but excellent for small rainbow trout. [T37N R34W S3]

ANT CREEK. See Brimstone Creek.

ARBO LAKE. See Wee Lake.

BANANA LAKE. A small closed-basin lake that used to support all kinds of nongame fish, Banana was poisoned in 1988 and has been planted every other year since with rainbows. The trout seem to be doing fine, and the fishing pressure is light. It's located just north of US 2, 45 miles west of Kalispell; reach it by road in between the Pleasant Valley and McKillop Creek roads. [T27N R28W S23]

BAREE (or STANDARD) LAKE. A deep lake, 8½ acres, in a rocky cirque. It's accessible from the Silver Butte-Fisher River road by trail 2½ miles west up Baree Creek. It is seldom visited and poor fishing indeed for 6- to 12-inch cutthroat, which are planted periodically. [T26N R31W S36]

BARRON CREEK. This stream heads between Banfield and Blue mountains and flows east for 7 miles, down a brushy-bottomed, logged-over canyon, to Koocanusa Reservoir. From the dam, take paved highway 8 miles north. Barron Creek is followed to headwaters by a logging road.

You'll find plenty of small brookies and cutthroat, with the occasional larger cuts and whitefish coming up from the reservoir. [T32N R29W S27]

BASIN CREEK. This is a small, headwaters tributary of the East Fork of the Yaak River, followed for 5 fishable miles by a good logging road. Basin Creek is lightly fished, and it's fair to good for pan-size cutthroat and brook trout. [T37N R30W S27]

BEAN LAKE. See No Name Lake

BEAR CREEK. The middle reaches (2 miles) of this small, beaver-dammed tributary of Libby Creek are accessible by the Cherry Creek road, the upper reaches (2½ miles) by closed road. These areas are heavily used, while the lower reaches are quite steep and seldom fished. You'll find fair fishing throughout for a decent population of midsize cutts and rainbows, with some resident bull trout as well. [T28N R30W S18]

BEAR LAKES. Three lakes in a rocky cirque, with some brush around the shore. They're accessible from the Silver Butte-Fisher River road by the Iron Meadow Creek trail, 3½ miles north. Middle Bear is very small and subject to winter freezing. Lower Bear (10.6 acres and deep) is fair fishing for cutthroat trout that will average 17 inches. Not too many of them—but nice. Upper Bear was historically barren. Both the upper and lower lakes were recently stocked with cutthroat. [T26N R30W S31]

BEETLE CREEK. A very small tributary of Pete Creek, crossed at the mouth by the Pete Creek road and followed upstream for 1½ miles by a logging road. There are a few small cutthroat and brook trout right at the mouth. [T36N R33W S1]

BETTS LAKE. This 5-acre lake is shallow but has steep drop-offs from the bank. There's no trail; the only access is across posted, private land, ½ mile west of the Wolf Creek road and 1½ miles south of the Fairview Guard Station. Betts is good fishing for brook trout that average 8 to 10 inches, with maybe a few to 14 inches. [T30N R27W S28]

BIG CREEK. From the junction of its north and south forks at an old USFS cabin, Big Creek flows eastward for 8 miles, through a narrow, timbered canyon, to Lake Koocanusa, 7 miles south of the Big Bridge. The lower 3 miles flow through a steep gorge; the rest of the stream, accessible by a good gravel road, has been moderately popular and is good fishing for spawners in the springtime and pan-size cutthroat, rainbow, and hybrids. The north fork is very small with limited fishing opportunities, while the south fork offers good fishing for small cutts and 'bows. A trail follows the north fork and a road follows the south. [T34N R29W S3]

BIG CHERRY CREEK. A fair-size tributary of Libby Creek, it's accessible at the mouth by a paved road 2 miles south of Libby, then followed upstream by a good gravel road for 16 miles to headwaters in steep, timbered country. The lower reaches have been mined (the bends straightened out) and the best fishing is in the middle and upper reaches, which are fair for 9- to 10-inch rainbow, cutthroat, and some brook trout. [T30N R31W S14]

BIG HAWKINS LAKE. See under Hawkins Lakes.

BLUE SKY CREEK. A small tributary of Grave Creek, it empties in about 1 mile north of the Clarence Guard Station and is accessible for 5 miles by a closed logging road. Blue Sky is seldom fished, but it has been excellent for pan-size cutthroat, plus an occasional one up to a pound. It is open to fishing only from the third Saturday in May until July 15, because spawning cutthroat and bull trout use this stream from midsummer through the fall. As always, check regulations before setting out. [T36N R25W S12]

BLUEBIRD LAKE (or UPPER BLUEBIRD LAKE). To find this lake, in the Ten Lakes Scenic Area, hike 3 miles west from the trailhead just beyond Little Therriault Lake. Bluebird is small, very alpine, and susceptible to winterkills. It's planted every three or four years with cutts that rarely get a chance to grow large. More a nice spot than a fishing destination. [T37N R26W S25]

BOBTAIL CREEK. It's about 9 miles long, the upper 3 miles in a steep, timbered canyon, the lower reaches in farmland. Bobtail empties to the Kootenai River, 3½ miles west of Libby, and it's accessible for its full length by road. It is a narrow, meandering stream with some beaver ponds near the mouth, and good fishing for small trout, especially in the meadows about 3 miles above the mouth. [T31N R31W S30]

BOOTJACK LAKE. An 11-acre pond, about 30 feet deep, situated mostly on Plum Creek timberland right beside US 2, at the south end of Pleasant Valley. Much of this lake is shoal, with lots of logs and much brush around the margins. It freezes out during long winters, and it's planted with cutthroat and rainbow every couple of years. Illegally planted pumpkinseeds are a problem here, but the trout are holding on and can be caught in the 15- to 18-inch range, with smaller trout common. [T27N R28W S24]

BORDER LAKE. See Burke Lake.

BOULDER CREEK. The outlet of Boulder Lakes, followed to the east by a logging road for 8 miles to Lake Koocanusa, 1 mile south of the Big

Bridge. It's steep and seldom fished in the lower canyon reaches, but the upper reaches are available by logging roads, and the entire stream is fair fishing for 6- to 12-inch cutthroat. [T35N R29W S1]

BOULDER LAKES. Big Boulder (about 20 acres) and Little Boulder (4 acres), at the head of Boulder Creek. A good USFS road, 13½ miles in from the west end of the Lake Koocanusa Big Bridge, 8 miles south of Rexford, takes you to within 1½ miles of Little Boulder, and then it's a steep, hard climb another ½ mile to Big Boulder. The smaller lake, in timber all around, is fairly shallow, with lots of submerged logs around the edges, and it's good fishing for 6- to 12-inch cutthroat. The larger lake lies below rocky cliffs and talus, except on the timbered north side. It freezes out and remains barren. [T36N R30W S35]

BRAMLET LAKES. Found 1½ miles by trail from the end of Bramlet Creek road, Lower Bramlet Lake covers about 40 acres in a barren, rocky cirque. Upper Bramlet is barren, but Lower can be fair to good fishing for midsize rainbows, and it doesn't get fished that much. [T26N R31W S11]

BRIMSTONE (or ANT) CREEK. A small tributary of Fortine Creek, accessible at the mouth by road 1 mile south of Fortine, then followed upstream by road for 4 miles through meadow and scattered timber. About 2 miles are easily fished, fair to good for 5- to 10-inch brook trout. [T34N R25W S17]

BRIMSTONE LAKE. Take USFS road 36 south of Trego to the Lime Creek road (USFS road 3780), then find USFS road 3781 on your left. It's closed, but you can walk the last mile to the lake. It's a small, 2- to 3-acre lake, about 22 feet deep, that gets fairly regular cutthroat plantings. Few people fish this lake, but there are some 12- to 14- inch cutthroat here. [T33N R25W S5]

BRISTOW CREEK. A small stream that heads below Lost Soul Mountain. It's followed by a logging road eastward, down its partly logged, brushy valley, to the Koocanusa Reservoir, 10½ miles north of the dam by the reservoir's westside highway. There are about 6 miles of fair water here, for pan-size cutthroat and brook trout. [T32N R29W S14]

BULL LAKE. A big lake (5 miles long by ½ mile wide, with a 64-foot maximum depth) in a timbered valley. About 15 miles south of Troy, the lake is followed along the east shore by a paved road. The west shore is quite steep, but the east shore is a gentle slope, on which are about two dozen cottages, a resort, and a couple of USFS campgrounds. Bull is only fair summertime fishing for 12- to 14-inch kokanee. It's fished somewhat in the winter, too, through the ice, for small catches of rainbow.

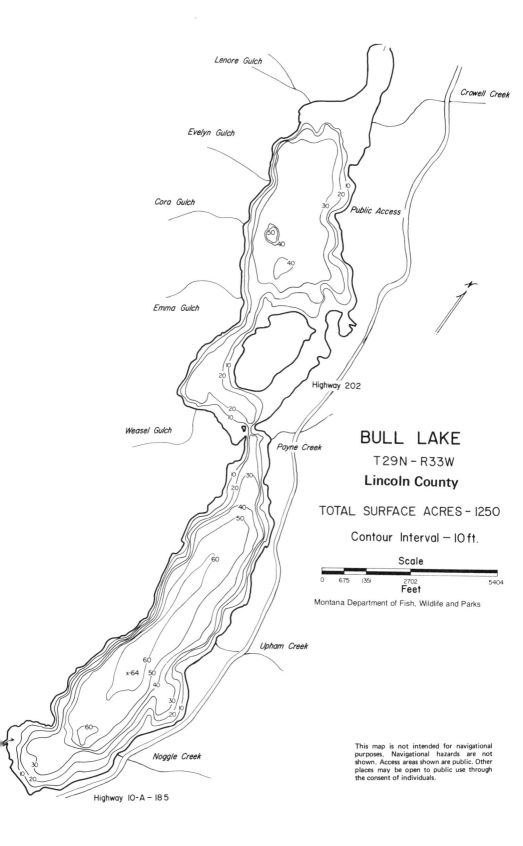

Lenore Gulch

Crowell Creek

Evelyn Gulch

Cora Gulch

10
20
30

Public Access

50
40

40

Emma Gulch

10
20

Highway 202

20
10

Weasel Gulch

Payne Creek

BULL LAKE

T 29N – R33W

Lincoln County

TOTAL SURFACE ACRES – 1250

Contour Interval – 10 ft.

10   30
20
40
50

60

Scale

| 0 | 675 | 1351 | 2702 | | 5404 |

Feet

Montana Department of Fish, Wildlife and Parks

Upham Creek

60
x-64   50
40
30   10
20

60

This map is not intended for navigational purposes. Navigational hazards are not shown. Access areas shown are public. Other places may be open to public use through the consent of individuals.

30
10   20

Noggle Creek

Highway 10-A – 18 5

The lower end is good fishing for 1- to 2-pound largemouth bass, along with lots of trash fish. The consistent plantings of kokanee and Kamloops rainbows done in the past few years may come to improve this fishery. [T29N R33W S20]

BURKE (or BORDER) LAKE. It's about 40 acres, maybe 40 feet deep, in timbered country. From the Hawkins Creek road, a mile above Hawkins Lake, go cross-country a mile north. The lake used to be barren, but it's now excellent fishing for small brook trout. It's overpopulated and seldom fished, probably because no one can find it. [T37N R33W S7]

BURNT CREEK. A small stream flowing for 8 miles, through a narrow, timbered canyon, to the Yaak River. It's accessible by road for 6 miles of fishing. It is heavily fished near the mouth for good catches of 8- to 12-inch rainbow, cutthroat, and brook trout; it's fair upstream for 6- to 8-inchers. [T34N R33W S9]

CABLE CREEK. A real small tributary of Bear Creek, in the old 1910 burn. It's accessible from mouth to headwaters, 3 miles on a jeep road, in a narrow, steep-walled canyon. Cable is only occasionally fished, but it's good for 6- to 8-inch rainbow. [T28N R31W S22]

CAD LAKE. It's pretty small, only 3.7 acres, and 30 feet deep in one place. In woods, it's reached by a road 1½ miles east of Horseshoe Lake. It is stocked every two years with rainbow trout, and in 1996 received a stocking of westslope cutthroats. It's now good fishing for 10- to 12-inchers, with fish up to 18 inches not uncommon. It's not named on many maps, but it's on the south side of the road, just east of Cibid Lake. [T27N R28W S24]

CALLAHAN CREEK. A fair-size stream flowing to the Kootenai River at Troy. The lower reaches are in a real rough canyon, but it is crossed by a road a couple of times above the falls (about 4½ miles up from the mouth). Below the falls, and difficult at best to approach, it's fair fishing for 8- to 10-inch rainbow, with the occasional spawner thrown in. A healthy population of Columbia Basin redband trout in the 4- to 8-inch range lives above the falls. This is one of the very few streams in Montana with these native rainbow trout. Both the north and the south forks offer a mile or two of similar fishing. [T31N R34W S13]

CARIBOU CREEK. A real small headwaters tributary of the East Fork Yaak River in a steep, timbered canyon. It's accessible at the mouth by the East Fork road, then followed upstream for a stretch of poor fishing for pan-size cutthroat. There's a campground at the mouth. [T37N R30W S28]

CARPENTER LAKE. See Tetrault Lake.

CEDAR CREEK. It drains Cedar Lakes, for 9 miles, through a steep canyon to the Kootenai River, 4½ miles west of Libby. The lower 2 miles are accessible by road, then you can take a good USFS trail on in to the lakes. This stream is seldom fished, but it's good for camp-fare trout. [T31N R32W S24]

CEDAR LAKES. Upper and Lower Cedar are in an alpine cirque right below Dome Mountain, in the Cabinet Range. A 5-mile hike up the Cedar Creek trail, west of Libby, gets you there. Upper Cedar is about 54 acres and 300 feet deep, while Lower Cedar is about 21 acres and deep enough to keep from freezing out. Both are good fishing for 8- to 12-inch rainbow trout. [T30N R32W S7]

CIBID LAKE. This one sits a few hundred yards away from Cad Lake, just a short bit east of Horseshoe Lake, in the Thompson Chain of Lakes area. It is 11 acres, 60 feet deep, and surrounded by trees. Cibid is planted regularly with rainbow, and it's pretty good fishing now for 8- to 14-inch trout, plus a few largemouth bass and many pumpkinseeds (both illegally planted prior to 1973). [T27N R28W S24]

Cedar Lakes. —Courtesy U.S. Forest Service

CLARENCE CREEK. A tiny headwater tributary of Grave creek. It's accessible at the mouth by the Grave Creek road at the Clarence Ranger Station, then followed upstream through a narrow, timbered canyon for 2 miles of fair fishing for cutthroat of 6- to 8-inches. It's open only from the third Saturday of May through July 15, to protect cutthroat and bull trout spawning activity. [T36N R25W S11]

CLAY CREEK. This little tributary of the South Fork of the Yaak River is crossed at the mouth by the South Fork road, then followed to headwaters by a logging road. The lower mile is in ranchland; the upper reaches (4 miles) are in a timbered canyon. The lower 2½ miles are poor fishing for 6- to 8-inch brook trout. [T35N R31W S30]

CODY LAKES. Three little lakes in timbered country at the head of (barren) Cody Creek. From the Fisher River road 5 miles south of the Kootenai River, take the Cody Creek road 8 miles east. Upper Cody is barren. Middle Cody is about 10 acres and supports a small population of 16- to 20-inch cutthroat. Lower Cody is about 8 acres and contains a similar population of brook trout. Neither are too well known and both are seldom fished. [T29N R28W S6]

CONTACT CREEK. This tiny outlet of Wishbone Lake flows to Granite Creek and is accessible at the mouth by the Granite Creek trail. It is only about 2 miles long, in real rough, brushy alpine country, and is almost never fished, although it reportedly has small trout. [T29N R32W S10]

COPPER CREEK. A very small tributary of Keeler Creek, accessible at the mouth by the Keeler Creek road 8 miles from Troy, crossed here and there by the Lake Creek and Iron Creek roads. The lower mile is poor fishing for 4- to 7-inch brook and cutthroat trout, but it's very seldom bothered. [T30N R33W S18]

COSTICH LAKE. A fairly shallow, privately owned 60-acre reservoir in open meadow. From Eureka, go a couple of miles east on a county road to within ¼ mile of it. It is lightly fished by a few local folks, for largemouth bass that average around 1 to 1¼ pounds and a few good-size rainbow and brook trout. It partly winter-kills, and summer-kills, too. In fact, it did better when it was a bass lake . . . period. [T36N R26W S18]

CRIPPLE HORSE CREEK. It's 12 miles long, flowing to Lake Koocanusa 7 miles north of the dam, where it's crossed by the lake's eastside highway. It's accessible by road to headwaters. Small fish in small numbers but in great variety are found here, ranging from cutthroat to suckers and whitefish. [T31N R29W S2]

Crystal Lake. —Courtesy U.S. Forest Service

CRYSTAL LAKE. A real deep lake (143 feet), 176 acres in size, right behind Happy's Inn on US 2, about 40 miles southeast of Libby at the northwest end of Thompson Lakes. Crystal is planted regularly with rainbow trout and kokanee salmon, and it's good fishing now for these (average size about 15 inches), along with lots of yellow perch and a few largemouth bass. [T27N R28W S24]

CRYSTAL LAKE. A very private pond located on a very private golf course northeast of Fortine. It's reported to be excellent fishing for good-size cutts and rainbows. [T35N R25W S19]

CURLEY CREEK. This stream drains Perkins Lake for 5 miles through Idaho, then 1½ miles in Montana, and finally another 3 miles to the Kootenai River in Idaho again. Reach it by road 4½ miles north of Leonia; it contains small rainbow trout. [T34N R34W S32]

CYCLONE CREEK. A really small stream that empties into the Yaak River 2½ miles above the Sylvanite Ranger Station. It's crossed at the mouth by the Yaak River road and followed upstream by USFS trail. Moderately popular for such a small stream, it's fair fishing for 6- to 8-inch rainbow and cutthroat. [T35N R33W S32]

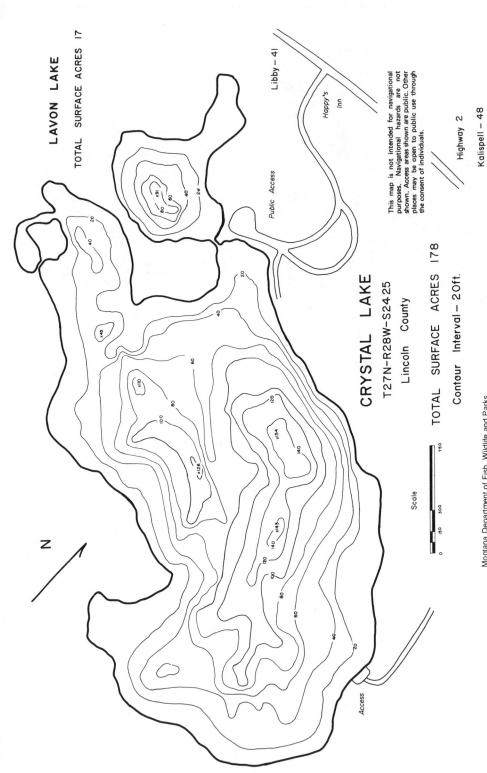

LAVON LAKE

TOTAL SURFACE ACRES 17

N

CRYSTAL LAKE

T27N-R28W-S24·25

Lincoln County

TOTAL SURFACE ACRES 178

Contour Interval – 20ft.

Scale

0   150   300   750

Public Access

Happy's Inn

Libby – 41

This map is not intended for navigational purposes. Navigational hazards are not shown. Access areas shown are public. Other places may be open to public use through the consent of individuals.

Highway 2

Kalispell – 48

Access

Montana Department of Fish, Wildlife and Parks

DAHL LAKE. About 165 acres and 10 feet or less deep, this aging lake has lots of marsh that floods in the spring but is dry by fall. There are a lot of pumpkinseeds and perhaps a few largemouth bass. Mostly on private land, Dahl is seldom fished. It's accessible by gravel road from the Raven Ranger Station, but you can skip this one because it's not even good for ducks—it freezes up early. [T28N R25W S30]

DAHL LAKE FORK OF PLEASANT VALLEY CREEK. A small stream, about 3½ miles long above Dahl Lake and 3½ miles below, to its juncture with Pleasant Valley Creek. It flows through mostly posted meadowland; it's accessible by road below (northwest of) the lake and by a trail above (southeast of) it. This stream is easily, although not often, fished for 6- to 10-inch brook trout, plus now and then a good one. [T28N R26W S17]

DAVIS CREEK. A wee-small headwaters tributary of Fortine Creek, reached at the mouth near the Twin Meadows Guard Station by the Fortine road, then followed upstream by a logging road for ½ mile of tough fishing for small brook trout. [T32N R26W S20]

DAVIS LAKE. A small lake just south of Northwest Peak, in the heart of the Northwest Peak Scenic Area. It's unnamed on the Kootenai National Forest map, and the same map indicates that to get there you must either: take your bike, horse, or feet 6 miles past the last gate to get to the trailhead, or find a logging road from Canada to get within a mile of the trailhead. If you really want to go there, talk to someone at the ranger station in Troy first. It's been planted every four years since '83 with cutthroat, with unknown results. Good luck! [T37N R34W S24]

DEEP CREEK. The lower 3 miles of this small stream flow through mostly posted private land, but the upper 4 miles can be accessed by USFS road. Head east from Fortine to find decent fishing for small brookies, cutts, and rainbows, with the occasional spawner passing through. [T35N R26W S25]

DEEP LAKE. This 6½-acre lake has shallow, marshy shores, but gets deep out a-ways (to better than 50 feet). It's about ½ mile south of Marl Lake, in wooded hills. Deep Lake is private, with no fishing for the public, and probably has a lot of sunfish. [T34N R26W S3]

DICKEY CREEK. A small stream that flows for 2 miles through Ant Flat from Dickey Lake to Murphy Lake. Accessible by a truck trail, it's easily fished for 8- to 10-inch brook and some rainbow trout. The first ½ mile out of Dickey Lake is private land. [T34N R25W S8]

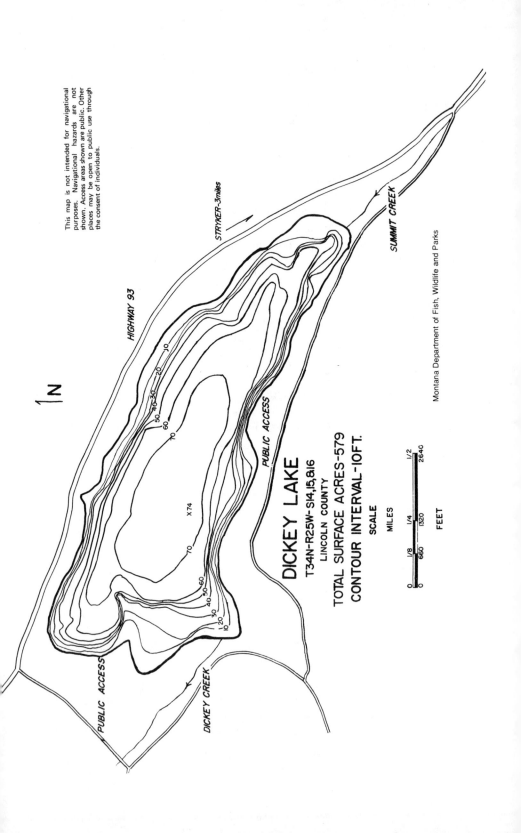

N

HIGHWAY 93

STRYKER-3miles

SUMMIT CREEK

PUBLIC ACCESS

PUBLIC ACCESS

DICKEY CREEK

X74

70

70

60

50 40 30

20

10

50 40 30 20 10

60

70

DICKEY LAKE

T34N-R25W-SI4,I5,8I6
LINCOLN COUNTY

TOTAL SURFACE ACRES-579
CONTOUR INTERVAL-I0FT.

SCALE

MILES

0   1/8   1/4   1/2
     660   1320   2640

FEET

Montana Department of Fish, Wildlife and Parks

DICKEY LAKE. A real deep, 579-acre lake in timbered country, with US 93 running along the east side and a county road down the west. Dickey is only poor to fair fishing for mostly a pound or so rainbow, plus 8- to 10-inch kokanee salmon, brook trout, cutthroat, northern pike, and the occasional largemouth bass. Kamloops rainbow and kokanee have been planted the last few years—we'll see how that goes. The lake is more popular for water sports, and there are about a dozen private cabins and a couple of campgrounds here. [T34N R25W S15]

DODGE CREEK. Seven miles long from the junction of its north and south forks, its upper reaches run through a canyon and the lower reaches are beaver-dammed, in rolling, timbered country and logged-over land. Dodge empties into Lake Koocanusa 8 miles north of the Big Bridge, and it's accessible by a double-lane road for 4 miles of tough fishing. It's not very popular, but it's fair fishing for 4- to 8-inch brook and a few cutthroat trout. Shadow Falls are located here, 2 miles above the creek's mouth, and there are more falls about 6 miles upstream. [T37N R28W S36]

DOUBLE LAKE. Two alpine lakes, North and South, about 50 feet apart and connected by a 10-foot channel. There is a little island in the North Lake; the South Lake is filling up with talus. Both together total about 12 acres and are bordered by brush and scrub timber. To reach them, take the Granite Creek trail 3 miles from the end of the road, and then

Dickey Lake.
—Courtesy U.S.
Forest Service

fight your way up Contact Creek for 2 miles, through a jungle of "devil's claws," to the shore. Once there, you'll be all alone and will find the lakes to be excellent fishing for an overpopulation of skinny, 6- to 10-inch brook trout. [T29N R32W S20]

DOUBLE N LAKE. This private 100-acre lake, 15 to 30 feet deep, is a long and narrow, half-moon-shaped flooded meadow, with aspens on the north and evergreens around. You'll find it ½ mile west off US 2, about 10 miles south of Libby. The Double N is really a "family playground," but permission to fish is usually granted, and it's truly fabulous for mostly 14- to 16-inch rainbow, plus an occasional cutthroat that will average around 10 inches but sometimes run up to as much as 5 pounds. [T29N R31W S24]

DUDLEY CREEK. A tiny tributary of Edna Creek, reached at the mouth and for a mile upstream by road. Seldom fished, it's fair for small brook trout in beaver ponds here and there along the way. [T34N R26W S33]

DUDLEY SLOUGH. About 5 acres, in a private meadow, reached by a road 2½ miles west of Trego. Dudley is good fishing for 8- to 12-inch brook trout. [T34N R26W S14]

DUNN CREEK. A small, westward-flowing tributary of the Kootenai River, which it joins ½ mile below the dam. Dunn Creek flows for 14 miles, down a narrow, timbered canyon. It's followed by a logging road along the north side for 8 miles. The fishing is fair in early spring for 8- to 10-inch cutthroat in the lower reaches, and 6- to 8-inchers above. The lower end may dry up in late summer. [T30N R29W S9]

EAST FISHER CREEK (or RIVER). A fair-size stream in a timbered valley, about 40 miles south of Libby on US 2. It drains Sylvan and Miller lakes, and it's followed for its full length of 12 miles by a good county road. It passes through some private land, so ask first. East Fisher is moderately popular, fair fishing for 5- to 10-inch brook and some cutts. [T26N R29W S30]

EDNA CREEK. A small stream about 10 miles long, accessible all the way by a logging road to its junction with Fortine Creek, 9 miles south of Fortine. It flows through a mix of public and private lands. Edna is brushy, beaver-dammed, and hard to fish, but it's good fishing for about 6 miles upstream for 6- to 8-inch cutthroat, brook, and some rainbow trout. A sizable spawning run of kokanee salmon has developed here in the last 15 years or so, as well. [T33N R26W S2]

ELK CREEK. A small tributary of the Pleasant Valley Fisher River, flowing through brush and timber to its mouth, across the highway from the

Raven Ranger Station. There are about 6 miles of fair fishing here for small rainbow, cutthroat, and brook trout. It's all accessible by road. [T26N R29W S1]

FALLS CREEK. A tiny stream that heads in the Cabinet Mountains Wilderness and flows through a steep, timbered canyon. It's reached at the mouth by the Lake Creek road, 14 miles south of Troy. A moderately popular early-season stream, it is fair fishing for mostly 6- to 10-inch brook and cutthroat trout, plus a few big spawners. Private land becomes an issue in the lower stretches, where the fishing is better. [T31N R33W S32]

FALLS CREEK LAKES. Two cirque lakes, at about 7,000 feet in elevation, in rocky alpine country on the side of Dome Mountain, at the head of Falls Creek. They're located 3½ miles from, and 4,500 feet higher than, the end of the road. There's no trail. The upper lake is about 2 acres, the lower 8 acres, and both reportedly contain cutthroat trout. [T30N R33W S12]

FISH LAKES (near Eureka). See Therriault Lakes.

FISH LAKES. Of these five little alpine lakes, in a steep, rocky canyon at the head of the Vinal and Windy Creek drainages near Yaak, North, Middle, and South are the only ones with fish. You can reach them from the Vinal–Mount Henry–Boulder National Recreation Trail. North Fish Lake is 6.9 acres and 33 feet deep; Middle Fish Lake is only 2.6 acres and 16 feet deep; and South Fish Lake is 14.7 acres and 40 feet deep. North and Middle are stocked periodically with cutthroat, and they're good fishing now. South has been stocked with brook trout as well as cutthroat, and there might be some rainbows there as well. Fishing pressure is fairly light due to the hike, which really isn't that demanding. [T36N R31W S23]

FISHER RIVER. A small river or a good-size creek, it flows for 30 miles from the junction of the East and Silver Butte Fisher rivers to the Kootenai River, 14 miles east of Libby, and it's followed by good roads all the way. The lower reaches flow through a narrow, steep-walled canyon, the middle and upper reaches through a flat-bottomed, timbered valley. Migrating and resident mountain whitefish are abundant, with some small rainbow thrown in. For the most part, this river looks better than it fishes. The Fisher has an extended whitefish season——check current regulations. [T30N R29W S17]

FIVEMILE CREEK. It flows for 10 miles through steep, timbered mountains to the east side of Lake Koocanusa, a dozen miles north of the dam, where it's crossed by Montana 37. There are about 3 miles of good early-season fishing here for 10- to 12- inch brook trout (especially in a passel of beaver ponds, about 1½ miles upstream from the mouth), plus rainbow and cutthroat trout throughout the stream. The lower 1½ miles were stocked with migratory cutthroat, and there is some decent spring-time fishing for spawners. There is a good road for the full length of this creek, so it's readily accessible. [T32N R28W S17]

FLATTAIL CREEK. This small stream is crossed at the mouth by the Seventeenmile Creek road, but it's pretty hard to get to otherwise. Flattail is reported to be good fishing for 10- to 12-inch rainbow—in beaver ponds 2½ miles above the mouth. It's very seldom bothered. [T33N R32W S15]

FLOWER CREEK. The outlet of Sky Lakes, Flower flows through steep, timbered mountains for 21 miles, to the Kootenai River at Libby, and it's the municipal water supply. It's all closed, except for the lakes at head-waters. There is a good road along the lower reaches and a trail above to the lakes. [T31N R31W S33]

FLOWER LAKE. Located on Flower Creek, 3 miles above Flower Creek Reservoir (which is closed to fishing), the lake sits in a closed, timbered basin, but it's open around the shores. It is only 1.6 acres and maybe 25 feet deep; it was last stocked in 1989 with cutthroat, and it's good fishing. With neither inlet nor outlet, it's a closed system. [T30N R32W S24]

Lower Fisher River—before and after channelization. —Courtesy R. Konizeski

FORTINE CREEK. A good, easily fished tributary of the Tobacco River, reached at the mouth by a road 3 miles north of Fortine, then followed south by truck roads through rolling, glaciated country for most of its 28-mile length. It contains 8- to 10-inch cutthroat, rainbow, and brook trout. This is also a spawning tributary for Koocanusa Reservoir. [T35N R26W S15]

FOUNDATION CREEK. The smallish outlet of a small, barren lake on Mount Wam, it flows for 2 miles to Grave Creek. It's reached at the mouth by the Grave Creek road, 4 miles north of the Clarence Guard Station. The lower mile is fair fishing for pan-size cutthroat, but the stream is too small to stand much pressure. [T37N R24W S32]

FOURTH OF JULY CREEK. A tiny stream in a narrow canyon, followed by a logging road for the first 2 miles, then crossed at the mouth by the Yaak River road, 1½ miles south of the Sylvanite Ranger Station. The fishing is fair to good for 6- to 8-inch cutthroat trout. [T34N R33W S21]

FRANK (or LITTLE DUCK) LAKE. Covering 137 acres and 40 feet deep on the north end, it lies in timbered hills about 6 miles south of Eureka. You can reach it by a poor, rutted, muddy road through swampland to the south end of the lake, or along an old railroad grade and then a poor road to the north end. Frank is known locally as Little Duck Lake, and it's excellent fishing for 12- to 16-inch rainbow planted as recently as 1996. The fishing pressure is correspondingly heavy for this part of the country, especially in the winter. [T35N R26W S18]

FRENCH CREEK. This little tributary of the West Fork of the Yaak River is reached at the mouth by the West Fork road, then followed upstream by a logging road for about a mile of poor fishing for small rainbow, cutthroat, and a very few brook trout. It is not recommended. [T37N R32W S36]

FROZEN LAKE. A long, narrow, 200-acre lake that straddles the Canadian line. It's reached from the U.S. side by a trail, going 1 mile from the end of the Frozen Lake road, east of Weasel Cabin, way up Grave Creek road. It is fair fishing (on the U.S. side) for cutts up to 20 inches. There are no facilities on the U.S. side, but there's a good campsite in Canada. Americans are welcome. [T37N R24W S2]

GARVER CREEK. A very small tributary of the West Fork of the Yaak River, reached at the mouth by a trail 1 mile from the upper end of the Pete Creek road, then followed upstream by an unmaintained foot trail for about 1 mile of poor fishing. It contains small cutthroat trout but it's seldom fished. [T37N R32W S7]

GEIGER LAKES. Two high lakes about a mile apart, in rocky country just east of the Cabinet Divide. They are accessible by a couple miles of good USFS horse trail that takes off from the Lake Creek road, a mile west of the Lake Creek campground. Lower Geiger is 35 acres and deep, in scattered timber and rock with some brush around the shore. Upper Geiger is 15 acres, deep, and perhaps 200 feet higher in elevation than Lower Geiger. Both lakes are fair fishing for rainbow and rainbow-cutthroat hybrids that average around 8 to 12 inches. They'll average maybe a little bigger in Upper Geiger. These are fairly popular lakes due to the horse trail. [T26N R31W S13]

GLEN LAKE. A dammed lake with about 8 to 9 feet of water-level fluctuation and a maximum area of around 300 acres, set in hilly, timbered country. It's accessible by road 6 miles east of Eureka. There is a day-use area on the northwest side of the lake, with a few homes as well. A fairly popular spot with the locals, it has been planted regularly with rainbow and kokanee. Lots of suckers here as well. [T36N R26W S21]

Lower Geiger Lake. —Courtesy Michele Archie

326

Glen Lake. —Courtesy U.S. Forest Service

GOOD CREEK. A small mountain stream flowing through a narrow, rocky canyon south to Big Creek, a mile south of the Big Creek Cabin. It is crossed at the mouth by the Big Creek road, and it's paralleled for 3 miles by a USFS trail. Or you can take a long drive on the Boulder Creek road and find the upper section. The lower reaches are good fishing for pan-size rainbow, or would be, if anybody bothered. [T35N R30W S35]

GRANITE CREEK. This stream is 9½ miles long, in a steep, timbered canyon above and rolling hills below. The lower 5 miles are followed by the Bull Canyon road, starting 6 miles south of Libby; access the upper reaches by trail. This stream is mostly shallow, but there are some nice pools in the middle reaches that are good fishing for small rainbow. It is a nice safe place to take the kids. [T29N R31W S2]

GRANITE LAKE. A deep, 55- to 60-acre lake in rocky country, reached by 6 miles of easy trail from the end of the Granite Creek road. The fishing here is usually good to excellent for small cutthroat, with now and then a lunker to maybe 16 inches or so. [T29N R32W S27]

GRAVE CREEK. A fair-size tributary of the Tobacco River, reached at the mouth by road, 8 miles south of Eureka, and followed upstream by a county road for 10 miles of fishing, some of which is on private land. Grave Creek is mostly fished by locals, and it has been good for 9- to 10-inch rainbow, plus a few that went to 2 pounds or so. There are also bull trout, an occasional brook and cutthroat trout, and whitefish. There's spring spawning for 10- to 18-inch cutthroat, while bulls and whitefish spawn in the fall. [T35N R26W S15]

GRIMMS MEADOWS LAKES. Two private lakes at the head of Lake Creek; the lower one is just a beaver pond, the upper one is maybe a couple of acres, and it's good and deep. In a swampy mountain park, these lakes are reached by the Lake Creek-Fortine road, about 35 miles south of Eureka. They are not often fished, but they're fair to good for cutthroat and brook trout that average around 7 to 9 inches, with a few lunkers to a couple of pounds. [T32N R27W S9]

GROB LAKE. From Eureka, take US 93 one for 1¼ miles north, then turn left (west) on Montana 37 for 2¾ miles, then right (north) on a county road for a mile, where you jog left around the Iowa Flats School and continue on for ¾ mile to a jeep road on your left, which takes you to within 150 yards of the shore. After all that, you'd best get the owner's permission to fish for all the sunfish living here. No trout as far as anyone knows. [T37N R27W S32]

GROUSE LAKE. It covers 7 acres, with a gradual drop-off and lots of marsh around the edges, on Grouse Mountain. It's reached by trail, a mile north from the Keeler Creek road. It's planted with brook trout every third year, and the fishing potential varies from fair to good to real good. [T30N R34W S12]

HANGING VALLEY LAKES. Two little alpine lakes, about a mile apart at the head of Hanging Valley Creek. You can reach the first lake by trail, hiking 2 miles west from the end of Flower Creek road to the trail junction, and from there it's another mile to the other one. These lakes are not fished much, but they're fair for skinny 9- to 12- inch rainbow. [T30N R32W S34]

HAWKINS CREEK. This stream drains Hawkins Lakes, flowing for 2½ miles through a steep, timbered canyon to Canada. It's accessible, for 1 ½ miles of poor fishing for small cutthroat, by a logging road from the head of Pete Creek. This road may be gated at times—check with the Forest Service for current information. [T37N R33W S5]

HAWKINS LAKES. Two beautiful alpine lakes about ½ mile apart. The lower lake (Big Hawkins) is 12.9 acres in area and 38 feet deep; the other is 4.2 acres and 20 feet deep. Big Hawkins is reached to within ½ mile by

Upper Hawkins Lake. —Courtesy U.S. Forest Service

a logging road north from the headwaters of Pete Creek. Little Hawkins is (mostly) reached by trail a mile from the end of the same road. They are both good fishing for 8- to 14-inch cutthroat and are stocked periodically. There may be a closed gate on the Pete Creek road, so check with the folks in Troy before you head up there. [T37N R33W S18]

HELLROARING CREEK. A small, straight stream, in a narrow canyon, flowing to the Yaak River 5 miles north of the Sylvanite Ranger Station. It's crossed by the Yaak River road at the mouth, followed upstream by a logging road for 4 miles, then by closed road and finally by trail to the headwaters. This seldom-fished Hellroaring stream contains real small rainbow and cutthroat, including Columbia Basin redband and Yellowstone cutthroat. [T35N R33W S19]

HELMER LAKE. See Vinal Lake.

HIDDEN LAKE. In timber and brush in the old 1931 burn at the head of Spread Creek west of Yaak, this lake measures 8 acres (at most) in area and is 65 feet deep. It's seldom fished because it's not close to much of anything, lying close to the Idaho-Montana line southwest of the Northwest Peak Scenic Area. It's reachable though, by a couple of miles of trail heading south and west along the state line from the pass at the head of Spread Creek. Hidden Lake used to be barren, but it was planted with cutthroat in 1969 and again in 1982, and there may still be some of their progeny hanging around waiting for some company. The only way to find out is to go there and try it. [T36N R34W S8]

HIDDEN LAKE. This lake runs fairly deep and covers 10 acres in rolling, timbered hills near Stryker, 2½ miles south of Dickey Lake and 2 miles west of Bull Lake. It lies east of the Rattlebone Lake road, which is gated about 1 mile from the lake. The road's been in terrible shape for years, so parking at the gate and walking the rest of the way to the lake might turn out to be a favor to you and your vehicle. Hidden Lake is seldom fished, although it's reported to be fair for 6- to 10-inch cutthroat and brook trout. [T34N R25W S35]

HORSESHOE LAKE. It's located between Loon and Crystal Lakes in the Thompson Chain of Lakes area, off US 2 near Happy's Inn. Horseshoe is 159 acres in size, deep, and full of trash fish, along with a few whitefish and some largemouth bass. A 1990 planting of Kamloops rainbow was mostly unsuccessful, and current plans call for a non-chemical rehabilitation (the lake is too large to poison). Fisheries managers are considering a plan to plant the lake with sterile tiger muskies that may help reduce non-game fish populations enough for plantings of trout to establish a strong population. There is a campground here with a maximum three-day stay. [T27N R28W S23]

HOSKIN LAKES. Upper Hoskin is small, shallow, and either barren or close to it. Lower Hoskin, 33 acres and 30 feet deep, is not. In timbered country, they're reached by an easy ½ mile walk on a well-maintained USFS trail (162), not far from the town of Yaak. Lower Hoskin is good to excellent fishing for 12- to 14-inch cutthroat trout, stocked every two years. [T36N R31W S17]

HOWARD CREEK. The real small outlet of Howard Lake, it flows for 2 miles through heavily timbered mountains to Libby Creek, 2½ miles south of Old Town. Howard is not normally fished, but it's good for rainbow that average 6 to 8 inches, sometimes setting records of up to a pound. [T27N R31W S1]

HOWARD LAKE. A 34-acre lake with a 58-foot maximum depth, in heavy timber at the head of Howard Creek. Reach it via the Libby Creek road, about 30 miles south of Libby, and then the Howard Creek road upstream for 2 miles to a well-used public campground. It is excellent early spring and fall trolling, summer fly-fishing, and winter ice fishing for 6- to 16-inch rainbow, with the occasional lunker to keep up the interest. [T27N R31W S13]

HUDSON LAKE. A private, posted, 3-acre pothole, about 40 feet deep in the middle with shallow drop-offs, in open rangeland ½ mile west of Sophie Lake and 2½ miles south of Gateway. It's excellent fishing for 12- to 18-inch largemouth bass, and brook and rainbow trout. [T37N R27W S21]

INDIAN CREEK. This stream flows west, through a little timbered canyon to the open rolling hills of the Eureka Valley, and then southwest for about 4 miles to the Tobacco River, 1½ miles west of Eureka on the Great Northern Railroad tracks. It gets quite low in late summer, but the lower reaches are fair kids' fishing for 6- to 10-inch brook and cutthroat. [T36N R27W S9]

ISLAND LAKE. This is a warm-water lake with lots of weeds around the edges, in a wooded valley in partly open, logged-over country a few miles north of Pleasant Valley. It is 225 acres in area and 50 feet deep, and it's seldom fished because it supports mostly rough fish (suckers, squawfish, and pumpkinseed), along with an occasional largemouth bass. [T29N R26W S30]

IVOR CREEK. A very small (2 miles long) tributary of Edna Creek, crossed by a truck road at the mouth and followed upstream by a poor jeep road. It is real brushy and hard to fish, but it's fair for 7- to 8-inch brook trout. It's not often fished. [T33N R26W S2]

JACKSON CREEK. About 2 miles long, from the junction of its north and south forks to its mouth on Lake Koocanusa, where it is crossed by the westside road 4 miles north of the dam. Jackson flows through brushy, logged-over country and provides perhaps ½ mile of heavily fished water, for poor catches of small brook and cutthroat trout. [T31N R29W S9]

JUMBO LAKE. "Jumbo" is a misnomer for this series of beaver ponds of about 1.8 acres total area and 15-foot depth, in timber and brush near Hidden Lake. You can get to within ½ mile by following the old, washed-out Rattlebone Lake road a couple miles past the gate (a total of about 6 miles southeast of the town of Trego). Jumbo is lightly fished, but it's fair for 8- to 10-inch brook trout, along with zillions of suckers. [T34N R25W S35]

KEELER CREEK. It's crossed at the mouth by the Lake Creek road 8 miles south of Troy, then followed by a logging road for 10 miles to headwaters. The lower reaches are in what is more or less bottomland, the upper reaches in a steep-walled, heavily timbered canyon. Keeler provides fair fishing for mostly 6- to 8-inch cutthroat, and a few brook, rainbow, and bull trout. It is open only from the third Saturday in May through July 15, to protect those spawning bull trout. [T30N R33W S17]

KILBRENNAN CREEK. It flows 3½ miles down a timbered canyon to the Yaak River, 3 miles north of the Kootenai River, and it's reached near the mouth and also at the lake by logging roads, 10 miles north from Troy. Kilbrennan goes dry in the middle reaches, but it's fair fishing for 6- to 10-inch brook trout in big beaver ponds above and below, some rainbow, and, unfortunately, black bullheads that were put in by some idiot. [T33N R33W S30]

KILBRENNAN LAKE. Covering 59 acres, it's about 50 feet deep, with a shallow drop-off at each end. Reach it via a logging road, 10 miles north from Troy. It's fairly popular with locals and has a public campground and boat ramp. This lake is excellent fishing for brook and a very few rainbow trout, and large numbers of black bullheads. It was most recently stocked in 1988, with a fairly small number of westslope cutts, which didn't do all that well. [T33N R33W S29]

KLATAWA LAKE. About 30 acres in area, this lake sits in a timbered pocket at the head of the West Fork of Granite Creek. Take trail 136 a steep 5 miles west, then go 2½ miles north and west along the West Fork of Granite Creek, where there used to be a trail, but now it's pretty much a bushwack. Klatawa is seldom fished and do you know why? Because there is nothing in it! [T29N R32W S8]

LAFOE LAKE. An old broken-out beaver pond on LaFoe Creek, 1 mile north of Loon Lake. It is good fishing, but seldom bothered, for small cutthroat. Reach it by a minor logging road off of the Seventeenmile Creek road, near the mouth of Lost Fork Creek. [T33N R32W S13]

LAKE CREEK. A 5-mile-long tributary of Swamp Creek, followed by a logging road from its mouth upstream past headwaters to the Fivemile Creek drainage, southwest of Trego. This is a brushy stream that is hard to fish, but it's fair for the usual mix of small cutthroat, brookies, and rainbow. [T33N R27W S25]

LAKE CREEK. A brushy little stream that flows for 4 miles through heavy timber to West Fisher Creek, east of Noxon. It is crossed at the mouth by the West Fisher road, then followed along the lower reaches by an old logging road. It is seldom fished for the few 6- to 10-inch cutthroat it contains. [T26N R30W S4]

LAKE CREEK. One of the very few bottomland streams in the Kootenai drainage, Lake Creek flows northward from Bull Lake for 15 miles down its wide, open valley to the main river at Troy. It is easily accessible by good roads all the way. It provides excellent fishing for midsize rainbow and cutthroat, plenty o' whitefish, and a few brookies to boot. This is one of the best creeks in the area. [T31N R33W S18]

LAKE GENEVA. This one's up the westside road on Lake Koocanusa, above the bridge. Take a left on USFS road 470, right on 7220, then left on 7202 to the trailhead. You've got only a 1½ mile hike to the lake. Don't know much about it, except that it was planted with cutthroat in 1989 and 1993. Give it a try and let us know! [T37N R29W S8]

LAKE KOOCANUSA. See introduction, p.307–8.

LAVON LAKE. Seventeen acres in area, 91 feet deep, Lavon connects to Crystal Lake at the west end of Pleasant Valley. See Crystal Lake for more information. [T27N R28W S22]

LEIGH CREEK. The outlet of Leigh Lake, it flows for about 5 miles down a steep, glaciated canyon to Big Cherry Creek. It's followed all the way by logging road and trail. It is excellent fishing for 8- to 10-inch brook and some rainbow trout, especially in pools across a big flat just below the lake. [T28N R31W S3]

LEIGH LAKE. A pretty, deep, 133-acre lake in a cirque. Take the logging road that goes up the north side of Big Cherry Creek to the Leigh Creek horse trail, then take that 3 miles west. The lake is reported to be real spotty but sometimes very good for 10- to 11-inch brook and rainbow trout, and the occasional lurking lunker. The outlet just below the lake is also good. [T28N R32W S1]

LEON LAKE. A deep lake, 18½ acres in area, in the Thompson Lakes area, a couple of hundred yards south of Loon Lake, off US 2 (near Happy's Inn). Rehabilitated in 1969, Leon is planted every two years with rainbow and is still mediocre fishing. Recent gill-net surveys turned up yellow perch and crayfish, though trout do live here. [T27N R28W S22]

LIBBY CREEK. A little stream followed by road for 15 miles, through rolling timberland, to the Kootenai River at Libby. This creek has been badly messed up by mining operations. It's fair fishing for small rainbow and cutthroat, and as many whitefish as you can handle. Bull trout use this stream as well. It is a stream highly susceptible to flooding—every seven years or so. There's an extended whitefish season here—check your regulations. [T30N R31W S3]

LICK LAKE. It covers 15 acres and is 40 feet deep, with logs around the shores, open meadows to the east, and the rest in timber. From Eureka, take a county road 7 miles east; Lick Lake is ½ mile east of Glen Lake. It is a private lake with good fishing for a mix of trout. It can't hurt to ask! [T36N R26W S26]

LILLY PAD LAKE. A small lake just west of Bootjack Lake, in the Thompson Chain of Lakes area, off US 2, near Happy's Inn. Very appropriately named for its vegetation, Lilly Pad offers limited fishing opportunities

Leigh Creek Falls.
—Courtesy U.S. Forest Service

for brook trout, and less-limited opportunities for largemouth bass. [T27N R28W S24]

LIME CREEK. This brushy little stream flows through rolling timberland 4 miles south of Trego, east of the Fortine road. It provides about 2 miles of lightly fished water, for fair catches of pan-size cutthroat. [T34N R26W S36]

LITTLE CHERRY CREEK. Reach this stream at the mouth by the Libby Creek road, 19 miles south of Libby. There are a couple of miles of fair fishing here, for 6- to 8-inch cutthroat. It flows through private land and there is no trail. [T28N R30W S19]

LITTLE CREEK. Proceed north on the Yaak River road a couple of miles beyond the Sylvanite Ranger Station, then ford the river to the mouth of Little Creek. There is no trail, and it's seldom fished, but the first ½ mile is fair for 6- to 8-inch rainbow and cutthroat trout. It's as small as its name implies. [T34N R33W S32]

LITTLE HAWKINS LAKE. See under Hawkins Lakes.

LITTLE LOON LAKE. This shallow, 10-acre lake is really the beginning of the Fisher River. Reach it from US 2 near Loon Lake; it's full of rough fish and quite a few nice (3- to 6-pound) largemouth bass (some small-mouth, too), and some 12- to 14-inch rainbow trout. [T27N R28W S22]

LITTLE NORTH FORK BIG (or LITTLE NORTH FORK) CREEK. It joins Big Creek a mile above its mouth at Lake Koocanusa, and it can be followed by trail 3 miles upstream. There are some nice falls not too far from the trailhead, which are pretty much the highlight of this stream. Fishing is fair for small cutts and rainbows, especially below the falls. [T35N R29W S32]

LITTLE SPAR LAKE. An alpine lake in barren, rocky country at the head of Spar Creek, reached by a poor trail going southwest for 4 miles from Spar Lake. Little Spar is 50.6 acres in area, over 90 feet deep, brushy around the shores, and good fishing for 8- to 10-inch, big-headed, snaky brook trout. The lake was replanted with westslope cutthroat, and the fishing is fair for lots of 6- to 8-inchers. It could stand a lot of fishing but, for one thing, it is often iced in until mid-July. [T28N R34W S5]

LONG LAKE. A 48-acre lake with shallow drop-offs and lots of water-killed trees around the edges, in rolling hills between Lost Lake and Rock Lake. It is reached to within a few hundred yards by road, going 5 miles south from Eureka. It was planted with cutthroat in 1972 and was good fishing for awhile. However, it went kaput—too much alkali because of decreasing water level. Now they're trying rainbow—we'll see. [T35N R26W S5]

LOON CREEK. A heavily fished stream, closely followed by a logging road for 5 miles, from its mouth on Pipe Creek (just south of Turner Mountain), up a narrow gorge through the old burn, to Loon Lake. It's fair fishing for 10- to 12-inch brook and rainbow trout in beaver ponds along the lower mile. [T33N R31W S28]

LOON LAKE. This lake covers 238 acres, and it's fairly deep, but with shallow drop-offs. It's located ¼ mile west of Horseshoe Lake, in the Thompson Lakes area, just off US 2 near Happy's Inn. This lake is full of trash fish, plus a few sunfish and brookies, fair populations of both large- and smallmouth bass, and a good population of 10- to 15-inch rainbow trout. Loon Lake is closed to spearing. [T27N R28W S22]

LOON LAKE. A long, narrow lake, 25.7 acres, deep in the middle but with shallow drop-offs, in a timbered valley. Reach it via the Loon Lake road, off the Pipe Creek road north of Libby. This is a real spotty lake for 10- to 12-inch (and a few to 20 inches) brook and a few cutthroat trout. Rainbows have been planted regularly since 1987, in an attempt to provide consistent catches. It's good ice fishing and there is a public campground. [T33N R32W S25]

LOON LAKE. This 33-acre lake has some deep holes, but it's mostly shallow with marshy shores. On private land 1 mile east of Mud Lake, it's reached by a poor road, 3 miles southwest of Fortine. It's not very popular, but it's good for 1-pound brookies and some cutthroat. [T34N R26W S11]

LOST FORK CREEK. This stream offers 2½ miles of fishing, down a narrow, timbered canyon. Reach the mouth by going 9 miles east on a logging road that follows Seventeen Mile Creek. Lost Fork is not very popular, but it has quite a few nice holes that are good fishing for small cutthroat trout. [T33N R31W S23]

LOST LAKE. Located 4 miles south of Eureka in hilly timberland, it's followed all around the shore by a poor road. This marshy, 16.2-acre lake was most recently planted in 1991, '93, and '94 with rainbows, in a continuing battle with low, alkaline water. Some brook trout call this lake home as well. [T35N R26W S6]

LOST LAKE. A 4-acre lake with shallow drop-offs and mostly marshy shores, in logged-over hill country near Happy's Inn. Reach it from a logging road 2 miles north of Middle Thompson Lake, off US 2. It is populated by suckers, small yellow perch, and a few small brookies. [T27N R27W S26]

LOUIS LAKE. From Stryker, take the Sunday Creek road 7 miles south, to the Louis Creek road, then 4 more miles west to the lake. It's a small lake with marshy edges. Recent plantings of rainbow and cutthroat allow decent angling opportunities for pan-size and better trout. [T33N R25W S15]

MARL LAKE. From Fortine, take the Meadow Creek road 3 miles west, then turn south for 1¼ miles to this roughly subcircular, 106-acre lake in rolling, timbered hills. This is a very good spot to get lost, and most of the surrounding land is private, so access can be tricky. Marl Lake is planted annually with rainbow, and it's fair fishing now for 12- to 14-inchers. Pike, perch, and sunfish also call this lake home. [T34N R26W S3]

MARTIN LAKE. This one is accessed by Laughing Waters Road, just north of the Murphy Lake Ranger Station, near Fortine. The road ends and a trail takes you the last ¼ mile to this shallow, 15-acre lake. Martin isn't fished much, but it's fair to good for 8- to 10-inch brook trout and it has recently been planted with westslope cutthroat. [T35N R25W S4]

MARTIN LAKE. An alpine lake at the head of Big Cherry Creek, south of Libby. From the end of the Big Cherry road, take the trail 2½ miles to the end. From there, it's a steep, 2½-mile scramble cross-country to the lake. Here is a lake that is seldom fished, but it's reportedly good for small cutthroat, rainbow, and brook trout. [T28N R32W S14]

MARY RENNELS LAKE. See Rene Lake.

MCGINNIS CREEK. There are about 5 miles of brush and meadowland fishing in this small tributary of Elk Creek. You can reach it at the mouth by USFS road 516, just east of the Raven Ranger Station; you can follow this road all the way upstream to headwaters. McGinnis is lightly fished, but it's fair for 6- to 10-inch brook trout. Much of the stream is on private land—ask first! [T26N R28W S5]

MCGUIRE CREEK. This small, steep stream is followed by a trail through its rocky canyon to Lake Koocanusa, between Peck Gulch and Rocky Gorge campgrounds. There isn't much fishing here except right near the mouth in early season, for 7- to 10-inch cutthroat and brook trout. [T34N R29W S23]

MEADOW CREEK. It's less than a mile long from the junction of its North and South forks to its mouth on the Yaak River, 5 miles above the Sylvanite Ranger Station, north of Troy. Followed along its entire length by a logging road, it's fair fishing for 4- to 7-inch cutthroat and brook trout. Same story for the forks, though you might run into a gate on the road a ways up there. [T35N R33W S19]

MEADOW CREEK. A small, brushy, hard-to-fish stream that is accessible by logging roads for most of its 8½ mile length, from headwaters to its mouth on Fortine Creek, 1¼ miles west of the town of Fortine. There are lots of beaver ponds along the lower 3 or 4 miles, and they're fair fishing for 8- to 10-inch brook trout and a few rainbow. [T35N R26W S22]

MIDAS LAKE. See Standard Lake.

MIDDLE FISH LAKE. See under Fish Lakes (near Yaak).

MILNOR LAKE. This 29-acre, 60-foot-deep lake is located within 100 yards of the Bull Lake road, about 5 miles south of Troy and ⅛ mile from Savage Lake. This is a private, warm-water lake that supports largemouth bass and a few northern pike, and probably some sunfish as well. [T31N R33W S28]

MINOR LAKE. A deep, 20-acre lake in an alpine cirque, reached by pack trail up Parmenter Creek and its south fork, about 10 miles southwest of Libby. Here is a moderately popular "dude" lake that is good July, August, and September fishing for 10- to 14-inch cutthroat, with some fish topping 20 inches. [T30N R32W S20]

MORAN LAKE. A shallow, 39-acre lake set mostly in private timberland ½ mile east of Sophie Lake. The south end of the lake takes up the better part of an isolated chunk of Forest Service land, and access is through a stile, over the fence, and across this land. It might help to ask around a bit. Moran is stocked regularly with brookies, 'bows and cutts, all of which can be caught consistently if you can get there. [T37N R27W S22]

MOUNT HENRY LAKE. This lake covers 8 acres and is 30 feet deep, set in a cirque just east of the summit of Mount Henry. Reach it by a good USFS trail, 2 miles east from the end of the Vinal Lake road, along the Vinal–Mount Henry–Boulder National Recreation Trail. There's a campsite with a fire ring and picnic table, and the trail is often used by horse packers and riders. This lake is good fishing for 10- to 12-inch cutthroat and, as usual, it has a few lunkers cruising its waters. It is stocked periodically. [T36N R30W S17]

MUD LAKE. A shallow, 12-acre lake with marshy shores, about ½ mile south of Marl Lake. Take a road 7 miles west and south from Fortine. Mud Lake is on private land so it isn't bothered much, but it's fair fishing for 8- to 11-inch brook trout and whitefish. [T34N R26W S10]

MURPHY CREEK. It flows from Murphy Lake for 2 miles to Fortine Creek, about 1 mile south of Fortine. It's easily accessible by road. A swampy meadow and beaver-ponded stream, it is hard to fish with any

Mount Henry Lake. —Courtesy Bill Archie

luck, but it does contain a good population of 8- to 10-inch rainbow and brook trout, as well as some suckers. [T35N R26W S36]

MURPHY LAKE. A 163-acre lake in timbered hills found right by US 93, about 3 miles south of Fortine. Murphy is deep at the north end, mostly marshy around the shore, and it's real good fishing for 10- to 14-inch (and a few reported to 8 or 9 pounds) largemouth bass, lots of perch, some northern pike, and a few rainbows. This is a popular lake with families and summer campers. It's closed to spearing. [T34N R25W S5]

MYRON LAKE. It's located in the Thompson Lakes area, on land owned by Plum Creek. You get there by going north on the McKillop road and taking the second right. You might need a 4x4 vehicle for this road, and a good map to find it. Myron is 5 acres in area and 30 feet deep. It is stocked every two years with rainbow or cutthroat, and it's one of the very few lakes in the region that has not been illegally stocked with un-desirable fish species. Fishing is good for 8- to 14-inch trout, and some that run larger. [T27N R28W S15]

NORTH FISH LAKE. See under Fish Lakes (near Yaak).

NORTH FORK BIG CREEK. See under Big Creek.

NO NAME (or BEAN) LAKE. It's located just east of Rainbow Lake in the Ten Lakes Scenic Area, northwest of Eureka. Drive about as far as you can on the Grave Creek road system to find USFS trail 89, which will take you pretty close to the lake. It's planted every two years with cutthroat and, barring freeze-out, should be decent fishing. [T37N R25W S8]

OBERMAYER LAKE (or OVERDALE LODGE POND). This private 5-acre pond on Lang Creek is reached by road, just south of the town of Yaak. Last we heard, it had been stocked with rainbow and was good fishing for 8- to 16-inchers. [T35N R32W S10]

O'BRIEN CREEK. A little mountain stream that serves as the municipal water supply for Troy. The entire stream, including the North Fork, is accessible by road, for several miles of fishing for 6- to 10-inch cutthroat, brook trout, and rainbow. O'Brien is closed year-round from the Troy city water intake to a point ¼ mile upstream, as posted. It's also closed to fishing within a 100-yard radius of the mouth. [T31N R33W S18]

OKAGA (or PHILLIP) LAKE. It's a private hatchery, about 1 mile long by ¼ mile wide, at the mouth of Windy Creek, maybe 5 miles or so east of the old guard station at the Upper Ford. You can pay to fish here for trout of unknown size or species (probably rainbow). Boats and cabins are available. [T37N R31W S25]

OTHORP(E) LAKE. Accessible by the Baker Lake road, going southwest from Eureka, this long, L-shaped lake lies partly on private and partly on Forest Service land. It was stocked in the '60s with rainbow, and then with largemouth bass. After a 20-year respite, it's been planted with rainbow every year since about 1992. [T36N R27W S28]

OVERDALE LODGE POND. See Obermayer Lake.

OWAISA LAKES. See Sky Lakes.

PARMENTER LAKE. Take a good USFS trail (number 140) for 7½ miles west from the trailhead along the Parmenter Creek road west of Libby. Then continue west along the North Fork trail 1¼ miles until the trail leaves the stream and heads north toward Cedar Lakes. Leave the trail at this point and continue to follow the North Fork drainage southwest for the last mile to the lake. There is another small lake on the way that may or may not hold fish. As for Parmenter itself, it's not often fished (due mainly to the approach), but it's reported to contain trout. [T30N R32W S18]

PETE CREEK. A little stream in timbered mountains, it flows for about 1 mile through numerous beaver ponds in the Pete Creek meadows, then for 2 miles through a narrow canyon, another ½ mile of beaver ponds, and finally about 6 miles down a little flat-bottomed valley, where it splits, comes together, and resplits into several channels before finally emptying to the Yaak River, about 3 miles west of the town of Yaak. The Yaak River road crosses this stream at its mouth, and a logging road follows it to headwaters. Moderately popular, it's fair fishing for 8- to 10-inch brook, and some cutthroat, trout. [T35N R32W S5]

PHILIP (or PHILLIP) LAKE. See Okaga Lake.

PHILLIPS CREEK. A small, meandering stream that rises in Canada and flows for about 3 miles through U.S. farmland to Sophie Lake, and eventually to the Koocanusa Reservoir, 2 miles south of Gateway. The lower reaches dry up in summer, but the upper reaches contain a few small brook and cutthroat trout. It's seldom fished. [T37N R27W S2]

PHILLS LAKE. Covering 16½ acres but shallow, it can be found in timbered country midway between the Big Bridge and Rexford, reached by a jeep road off Melvin Drive. Phills was last planted in 1986 with cutthroat, and there may be some left, along with some bullheads that were illegally introduced a long time ago. [T36N R28W S27]

PINE CREEK. A little stream flowing from Windy Pass on Cross Mountain, down a narrow, flat-bottomed valley, for 14 miles to the Kootenai River, 10 miles north of Troy. Pine is accessible for most of its length by road. The lower reaches (about 5 miles) are fair early-season fishing for pan-size brook trout. Quite a few local fishermen hit this one. [T33N R34W S27]

PINKHAM CREEK. This stream, 20 miles long, is followed by county roads westward through timbered hills, from headwaters to its mouth on the Koocanusa Reservoir, a mile north of the Big Bridge. Pinkham is lightly fished, and there are lots of logjams, beaver dams, and cover. From the falls down to the mouth (about 5 miles), it is cutthroat and rainbow water, and there are a few nice fish. There are lots of smallish (4 to 7 inches) rainbow and brookies, plus a few cutthroat too, above the falls. Some sections go dry in summer. [T35N R28W S5]

PIPE CREEK. It's followed for 21 miles by a good oiled USFS road, from its headwaters in steep mountains, through timbered hills, to its mouth on the Kootenai River, 3 miles west of Libby. It is one of the most popular streams in the entire Libby area, inasmuch as it is readily available, easily fished, and good for pan-size rainbow, 8- to 12-inch cutthroat, and a few brook trout. The best fishing is in beaver ponds and timbered areas away from the road. [T31N R31W S30]

PIPE CREEK, East Fork. Small and about 8 miles long, it flows through a steep, rocky canyon in the middle reaches. It is crossed at the mouth by the Pipe Creek road near Turner Mountain, and followed by a logging road to headwaters. The East Fork is only lightly fished, but it's good for 5- to 12-inch rainbow and cutthroat. Note: The middle reaches look like they wouldn't have any fish—but they're there. [T33N R31W S10]

PLEASANT VALLEY CREEK. It flows from headwaters just west of Little Bitterroot Lake into and out of Dahl Lake, then through timber and ranchland for 12 miles to the Pleasant Valley Fisher River. Pleasant Valley Creek is easily accessible by road, although there is some posted land, but that's no great loss because this creek is poor fishing at best for small rainbow and maybe a few cutthroat and brookies. [T28N R27W S27]

PLEASANT VALLEY FISHER RIVER. The upper reaches of this 40-mile river are mostly on posted ranchland in Pleasant Valley; the lower 11 miles are followed by US 2, the middle 12 miles by a good logging road. This is a moderately popular, easily fished stream that produces catches of 9- to 11-inch or so rainbow and brook trout, plus a few good-size ones. You'll probably find some whitefish as well. [T29N R29W S34]

POORMAN CREEK. It flows from Ramsey Lake for 5½ miles, down a steep canyon above and a narrow valley below, through the old 1910 burn to Libby Creek at Old Town. It is easily accessible, by a logging road in the lower reaches and by trail up to the headwaters, and it's good fishing for small rainbow. [T28N R31W S25]

QUARTZ CREEK. A small stream in a steep, timbered canyon, followed by road for its entire length, from its mouth on the Kootenai River, 5 miles west of Libby. Quartz Creek is only fair fishing for pan-size cutthroat, but it's valued as excellent bull trout spawning habitat. It is open only from the third Saturday in May through July 15, to protect the decreasing spawning runs. [T31N R32W S24]

QUARTZ CREEK, West Fork. Take a left off the Quartz Creek road onto USFS road 399, and go on up to the Skyline National Recreational Trail 13. The trail follows the West Fork for 4 miles to the headwaters area, and then climbs up and out of the drainage. Fishing on this fork is similar to that of the main fork—decent fishing for small cutts. And just like the main stream, the West Fork is open only from the third Saturday in May through July 15, to protect spawning bull trout. [T31N R32W S2]

Rainbow Lake. —Courtesy Anne Archie

RAINBOW LAKE. Just west of the Pipe Creek road, a good 22 miles north of Libby, Rainbow Lake covers about 35 acres. It's planted every other year, ironically enough, with cutthroat trout. Because of its proximity to Libby and to a main travel corridor through the Kootenai National Forest, Rainbow sees a fair amount of fishing pressure. [T33N R31W S7]

RAINBOW LAKE. This fairly deep, 20-acre lake lies between Upper Thompson Lake and US 2, near Happy's Inn. It is lightly fished for the abundant yellow perch and the rainbow planters. The perch compete with and prey on the 'bows, and they seem to be winning the battle. Largemouth bass have been reported in great numbers in the past, but recent gill-net surveys failed to turn them up. They're probably still there. Rumor has it that, due to recent land sales by the Plum Creek timber company, the lake is now private. So be on the alert for "No Trespassing" signs if you decide to fish it. [T27N R27W S30]

RAINBOW LAKE. Located in the Ten Lakes Scenic Area northeast of Eureka, this lake is reached in a rather roundabout way. Take the Grave Creek road until it becomes USFS road 319; follow it all the way around to USFS road 7086, then take 7086 to 7090; follow 7090 to the end, where you pick up trail 89. A 2-mile hike on trail 89 will get you close, then it's cross-country down to the lake. With a good population of small to midsize cutts, Rainbow gets fished fairly hard for a backcountry lake.

The northern exposure ensures that there's snow well into the summer. [T37N R25W S8]

RAMSEY CREEK. A popular little stream, crossed at the mouth by the Libby Creek road, about 7 miles south of where that road meets US 2. Ramsey is followed by a logging road and trail for about 3 miles of fishing. It used to be real good but is now poor to fair for small rainbow. [T28N R31W S36]

RATTLEBONE LAKE. It's about 15 acres in area, with a maximum depth of 35 feet, set in rolling timberland at the head of Cripple Creek. You can at least get close by driving up Cripple Creek, on a road that might require a 4x4 vehicle, about 2 miles southeast from the Ant Flat Ranger Station. Rattlebone is a good largemouth bass lake that produces lots of ½- to ¾-pounders and a few that will go to 8 pounds or better, plus too many sunfish. [T34N R25W S22]

RED TOP CREEK. It flows for 5 miles, through a steep, timbered canyon, to the Yaak River, 4 miles above the Sylvanite Ranger Station. It's crossed at the mouth by the Yaak River road, where there is a Forest Service campground. A logging road loops around and intersects the stream about 3 miles upstream, but the lower reaches are more difficult to get to. Red Top offers fair fishing for 6- to 8-inch rainbow and cutthroat. [T35N R33W S30]

RENE (or MARY RENNELS) LAKE. A private, fairly shallow, 100-acre lake on Clay Creek, about 6 miles south of Yaak. It is not available to the public, but it's stocked, and good fishing for 8- to 14-inch cutthroat. [T34N R31W S2]

ROCK LAKE. It's 5 miles southeast of Eureka by crowflight, fairly deep, about 34 acres in area, with 30-foot cliffs around the east side and timber on around. There is a poor road to the south end and a better one to the campground on the north end. Rock was planted in the early '60s and was good fishing for 1-pound rainbow trout. It had become too alkaline and too shallow to support fish for a time, but there have been rainbow plantings there the last few years. [T35N R26W S6]

ROSS CREEK. It flows east for 8 miles from its headwaters, down a fairly flat, timbered valley, to the south end of Bull Lake. The middle reaches go low, but there are about 5 miles of fishing water above and below. You can reach it via 3 miles of road and then a fair trail. It is lightly fished but fair for small cutthroat, and some brook trout right near the lake; the reach from the falls down to the lake offers the best fishing. There is a nice campground at the end of the road, near the Ross

Creek Cedars Scenic Area (very impressive) and a mile past the falls. This stream offers better scenery than fishing. [T28N R33W S4]

SAVAGE LAKE. It covers 73 acres, about 30 in aquatic vegetation, and is over 60 feet deep. Go about 5 miles southeast of Troy on US 2, then take the Bull Lake road a couple of miles south. Savage is a popular summer-home lake, with three dozen or so cottages, as well as public access areas. There are a few brook trout and numerous perch and sunfish. There may be a few bass as well. [T31N R33W S28]

SCHOOL HOUSE LAKE. A private lake, about 14 acres in area and 30 feet deep, 4 miles south of Troy off the Lake Creek road. It has been taken over by sunfish, so don't even bother asking permission—unless, of course, sunfishing is your game. [T31N R33W S29]

SCHRIEBER CREEK. It flows to Schrieber Lake and out again for 1½ miles down a canyon, where it is followed by US 2 to near its junction with the Fisher River. It is lightly fished by local kids for a few small brookies. [T27N R29W S17]

SCHRIEBER LAKE. A shallow, marshy, 20-acre lake in timberland close to US 2, a couple of miles north of the West Fisher Creek road. It's seldom fished but has a few brook trout in it, average size 8- to 10-inches, and maximum maybe up to 12. [T27N R30W S13]

SEVENTEENMILE CREEK. Reach it at the mouth by the Yaak River road, 3 miles above the Sylvanite Ranger Station. It's followed by a logging road upstream, through a flat-bottomed canyon, for its entire length. The lower reaches provide good early-season fishing for 7- to 12-inch cutthroat (including some spawners up from the Yaak River) and rainbow trout. The upper stretches hold brook trout, as well as some hybridized versions of Columbia Basin redband trout. [T34N R33W S27]

SHANNON LAKE. A shade under 2 acres in size, it sits in a rocky canyon (there are no trees around the lake). It's a short ½ mile, going south and straight up, from Old Highway 2, 6 miles east of Troy. Shannon used to be good fishing for brookies, but had been ruined by an overpopulation of sunfish. Rehabilitated and restocked with brook trout, last in 1989, the lake now offers decent fishing for small brookies. [T31N R33W S23]

SILVER BUTTE FISHER RIVER. A brushy stream, 7½ miles long, followed by a good USFS road down a valley to its junction with East Fisher, 4 miles south of US 2. There are about 5 miles of fair fishing here for 6- to 9-inch brook, rainbow, and cutthroat trout. [T26N R29W S9]

SINCLAIR CREEK. A very small, lightly fished tributary of the Tobacco River, crossed at the mouth by US 93, 1 mile southeast of Eureka. It's followed by a county road for 5 miles of fair fishing for pan-size cutthroat, rainbow, and brook trout. [T36N R27W S14]

SKY (or OWAISA) LAKES. Upper Sky (4.2 acres) and Lower Sky (24 acres) are ½ mile apart in steep, timbered mountains, just south of Sugarloaf Mountain in the Cabinet Mountains Wilderness. Take USFS trail 137 southwest for 5 miles from the end of the Flower Creek (or Flower Lake) logging road. Both lakes used to be fair fishing for goldens, but there was no reproduction and none are left. These lakes are currently planted with cutthroat, and the lower one is now good fishing for 10- to 14-inch trout, and some up to 18 inches. [T30N R32W S32]

SLEE LAKE. A private, 16-acre lake, reached by road, 2 miles northeast of Troy. At last report, it was very good fishing for largemouth bass, yellow perch, and sunfish. Who knows what's going on there now? [T31N R33W S6]

SNOWSHOE CREEK. A tiny tributary of Big Cherry Creek, followed by a jeep road and then by a trail for 4 miles, from its mouth to some beaver ponds at the headwaters. It is seldom fished, but the ponds are fair for 10- to 12-inch rainbow. [T28N R31W S3]

SOPHIE LAKE. It covers 232 acres and has a maximum depth of around 60 feet, with shallow drop-offs, in rolling grassland. Find it via an oiled county road, 6 miles north from Eureka. Sophie is planted regularly with cutthroat and Kamloops rainbow. You might also find largemouth bass and various kinds of trash fish here, maybe even a bull trout or two. [T37N R27W S15]

SPAR LAKE. It's over 200 feet deep with steep drop-offs all around, covering 392 acres, with no outlet and a lot of water-level fluctuation. Spar lies in a wooded pocket among steep mountains, reached by the Lake Creek road, 25 miles south from Troy. The lake is moderately popular; there's a campground, and the fishing is fair to good for kokanee salmon that occasionally run up to 2½ pounds, along with 10- to 20-inch lake trout (some to 20 pounds) and a scattering of large brookies. [T29N R34W S21]

SPREAD CREEK. A nice little stream (the outlet of Hidden Lake) in a narrow, timbered valley. It's easily reached from its mouth on the Yaak River, 11 miles north of the Sylvanite Ranger Station, along a logging road that follows it for 6 miles. Moderately popular, it's fair to good fishing for small cutthroat, eastern brook, and rainbow trout. You'll probably find a few whitefish here as well. [T35N R33W S3]

SOUTH FISH LAKE. See under Fish Lakes.

SOUTH FORK BIG CREEK. See under Big Creek.

ST. CLAIR LAKE. A mile southwest of Big Therriault Lake beneath St. Clair Peak, it's reached by bushwhack up the drainage from Big T. Lake. It is only 3.2 acres in size with 17 feet maximum depth, and it's planted periodically with cutthroat. There is fair fishing here. [T37N R25W S31]

STAHL CREEK. A tiny, relatively open stream in a steep valley. You find it by taking the Grave Creek road northeast from US 93 to Clarence Creek. USFS road 7021 follows Stahl upstream for a couple miles to a trailhead. Like Clarence and Grave creeks, this one should provide some good spring fishing for nice-size cutthroat spawners, plus lots of little ones. To protect spawning bull trout, Stahl Creek is open only the third Saturday of May through July 15. [T36N R25W S11]

STANDARD CREEK. Very small, it flows for 3 miles to West Fisher Creek, 2½ miles north of the old guard station. It is reached at the mouth by the West Fisher road and followed by logging road and trail to head-waters. Standard is chock-full of crisscrossed logs, and it's very good fishing in spots for 9- to 11-inch brookies, plus an occasional cutthroat. [T27N R30W S31]

STANDARD LAKE. See Baree Lake.

STANDARD (or MIDAS) LAKE. It's about 10 acres, shallow, and marshy around the shore, in the Standard Creek drainage. You reach it by a 1-mile cross-country hike through the timber from the old Midas mine, 4 miles north of the old West Fisher Guard Station. It's fair fishing for camp-fare cutthroat and brook trout. [T27N R31W S24]

STAR CREEK. This one empties to the Kootenai River, 11 miles north of Troy. It is followed for nearly its entire length by logging roads. Not surprisingly, siltation has become a problem in Star Creek and habitat is poor. This stream is seldom bothered, and it's only poor fishing for small rainbow. [T32N R34W S8]

STEWART CREEK. This stream has about 2 miles of fishable water. It's crossed at the mouth by the Fortine Creek road and followed upstream for 4 miles through logged hills. Stewart is quite brushy, but it's fair fishing for 4- to 8-inch brook, and some cutthroat, trout. [T33N R26W S11]

SULLIVAN CREEK. About 6 miles long, it's accessible near the mouth by road, 3 miles north of the Big Bridge on Lake Koocanusa. It's followed its full length by a good USFS road. It can be good fishing in the lower stretch for nice cutthroat, and above for the little ones. [T36N R28W S21]

SUMMIT CREEK. A tiny, brushy stream, followed by US 93 for 2 miles, to the east end of Dickey Lake. It's not fished much, but the lower reaches are fairly open and contain a few 6- to 8-inch brookies. [T34N R25W S23]

SUTTON CREEK. This stream is 10 miles long, and the lower 5 are followed by a good logging road, going westward down a narrow timbered canyon, to Lake Koocanusa opposite Cliff Point. Sutton is seldom bothered, but it's fair early-season fishing for rainbow and cutthroat in the lower 4 miles, down to Fourmile Falls, and for small brook trout near the mouth. [T35N R28W S30]

SWAMP CREEK. Reach this stream at the mouth by the Fortine Creek road (USFS road 36), 8 miles south of Trego. It's followed upstream by a logging road for about 5 miles of fishing. Some sections are brushy, others are posted, but as a whole it is fair fishing for little trout—brook, rainbow, and a few cutthroat. [T33N R26W S21]

SWAMP CREEK. A slow, meandering stream flowing through private ranch and timber land for 6 miles, beside US 2, to Libby Creek, 14 miles south of the town of Libby. It is heavily fished, mostly by summer people, for 6- to 8-inch brook, and a scattering of rainbow and cutthroat, trout. Keep in mind the private land. [T29N R30W S32]

SWISHER LAKE. This is a small lake sandwiched between Sophie Lake and Lake Koocanusa, a few miles northwest of Eureka. It comes equipped with a four-unit USFS campground, with toilets and picnic tables and all that good stuff. Swisher has been planted with Kamloops rainbow, eastern brook, and westslope cutthroat in recent years, so it should offer a good opportunity to catch some nice trout. [T37N R27W S17]

TETRAULT (or CARPENTER) LAKE. It covers 115 acres, the east end deep and the west end shallow. It's reached by a good county road, 7 miles north from Eureka. Tetrault had been stocked with westslope cutthroat, but someone illegally planted largemouth bass, which are clobbering the cutthroat. Kamloops rainbow have been planted recently, because they compete better with the bass, along with plants of cutthroat and Arlee rainbow. You'll find a few trout, more bass, and lots o' bluegills, though this equation could turn around in the future. Check current trout regulations. [T37N R27W S28]

THERRIAULT CREEK. A 9-mile-long stream that flows from the west side of Therriault Pass down to its meeting with the Tobacco River, 4 miles southeast of Eureka. The lower reaches flow almost exclusively through private land—ask first. The upper sections are followed by USFS road 756, and then by trail up to the headwaters. There are brook trout downstream, and rainbow and cutthroat scattered throughout. [T36N R26W S33]

THERRIAULT (or FISH) LAKES. Two lakes—Big and Little—in timbered mountains at 5,000 feet in elevation, 9 miles east of Eureka by crowflight. Take the Grave Creek road (114), to the Weasel-Wigwam road (319) and follow it right to the lakes. Both lakes have public campgrounds and trails around them, and Little Therriault has handicapped access and docks. Big Therriault is 55 acres, over 65 feet deep, and it offers fair fishing for 10-inch cutthroat. Little Therriault is 26.9 acres, 60 feet deep, and very scenic. Little T. is fair fishing for 10- to 12-inch cutthroat—they run maybe a little larger here. Both are stocked regularly. [T37N R25W S32]

Big Therriault Lake.
—Courtesy Bill Archie

THROOPS LAKE. A very pretty little 40-acre private lake in some rock ledges on the north side of US 2, a few miles east of the junction with Montana 22 (east of Troy). There are quite a few lilies here, and the water is real black, and deep in spots. It's reported to be excellent fishing for ¾- to 1-pound largemouth bass, plus an occasional 8- to 10-inch brook trout. [T31N R33W S16]

TIMBER LAKE. It's 27.5 acres, with a maximum depth of 40 feet, set in timbered hills but open around the shore. You get there on a poor road out of the Rock Lake campground, 5 miles south from Eureka. It is planted periodically with rainbow and is good fishing for trout that will average around a pound. [T35N R26W S7]

TOBACCO RIVER. A nice open stream, flowing through mostly private meadow and timber for 16 miles, past Eureka, to Lake Koocanusa, ½ mile east of Rexford. Crossed by roads along its course, it's good fishing for small cutthroat (10- to 18-inch spawners in the spring), rainbow, and whitefish. Bull trout pass through from late July on. There's a boat launching ramp (and sometimes water) at the mouth. An extended whitefish season begins December 1—check your regulations. [T36N R27W S8]

TOM POOLE LAKE. From Libby, take the Yaak River road 15 miles north, to about a mile south of the old Turner Guard Station, then take a good but steep trail for a couple of hundred yards. This marshy lake is 6.8 acres in area and 15 feet deep, in dense timber and brush, and full of freshwater shrimp. It has provided some of the very best fishing in the district (at times) for 12- to 16-inch cutthroat. At other times, it is a good place to go—to get skunked. It is planted periodically. [T33N R31W S28]

TOPLESS LAKE. It's located in the Thompson Chain of Lakes area, just east of Horseshoe Lake and across the road from Cibid and Cad lakes. It's about 15 acres and 25 feet deep, and it used to be good fishing for 10- to 14-inch cutthroat. Illegal plantings of bullheads and pumpkinseeds have severely impaired the trout fishery, though rainbow are still regularly planted. There are many stories about how the lake was named, and one of them might even be true. [T27N R28W S24]

TRACK LAKE. A small lake covering about 10 acres, Track Lake lies ¼ mile northeast of the Rattlebone Lake road (3755), about 5 miles south of the town of Trego, just west of Dickey Lake. It's in the chain of lakes that includes Hidden and Jumbo lakes, and the road's that same, washed-out excuse for a road that's gated about a mile from the lakes. Track is not easy to locate, especially since it's not named on most maps, but it's worth finding since it's stocked just about every year with Kamloops rainbow. [T34N R25W S35]

TRAIL CREEK. A very small, seldom fished tributary of West Fisher Creek, it is crossed at the mouth by the West Fisher road at the old guard station, then followed upstream by a trail, for a couple of miles of fair fishing for small cutthroat. [T26N R30W S3]

UPPER BLUEBIRD LAKE. See Bluebird Lake.

VIMY LAKES. Two little mountaintop potholes (3 acres total), a couple of hundred yards apart. They're almost impossible to get to but they're reached once in a blue moon. To try it, hike from Double Lake ½ mile south, and 600 feet up, cross-country; the lakes sit in rocks and scrub timber north of Vimy Ridge. They support a population of rainbow, but they can freeze out very easily. [T29N R32W S20]

VINAL CREEK. It flows through a flat-bottomed canyon, and it's followed by a trail for 4 miles, from ½ mile above its mouth on the Yaak River upstream to some 50-foot falls. There are no fish above the falls, but it's good fishing below the falls and in a series of potholes below Fish Lakes, on the north branch of the creek. [T36N R31W S30]

VINAL (or HELMER) LAKE. This lake is 18½ acres in area and over 40 feet deep in some places, with mostly shallow drop-offs, and it's open around the shore. To reach it, take a ½-mile walk down a well-maintained trail off the Vinal Lake road (USFS road), near the town of Yaak. It

Vinal Lake.
—Courtesy Bill Archie

is planted regularly with cutthroat and is good fishing for 10- to 14-inchers. [T36N R31W S30]

WEASEL CREEK. The outlet of Weasel Lake, it's followed north by the Graves Creek logging road for 4 miles, down its timbered canyon to Canada. Seldom fished, it's poor at best for very small cutthroat trout. [T37N R24W S6]

WEASEL LAKE. A 10-acre, fairly shallow lake in a spruce-timbered basin. It can be reached via USFS road 7108, off the Grave Creek road. The Forest Service has developed this lake, and a lot of families take advantage of these improvements, including fishing docks at the access. Weasel provides adequate fishing for small cutthroat trout. [T37N R24W S28]

WEE (or ARBO) LAKE. A 27-foot-deep, 5-acre alpine lake in timber, brush and talus. From the head of Seventeenmile Creek, take the Hemlock Creek road south to the end, then hike a mile west cross-country. You can also get in from the Eastside Yaak River road: take it 10 miles north from Troy, then take the Arbo Creek road east 3½ miles. Wee Lake, planted years ago, is now good fishing for rainbow and cutts that will average 14 inches and range up to 20. [T33N R33W S13]

WEST FISHER CREEK (or RIVER). It flows for 12 miles through a narrow valley, and it's crossed at the mouth by US 2, 30 miles south of Libby. West Fisher Creek road follows it upstream for 8 miles, until the roads are gated. The stream is easily fished, but it's only fair for small cutthroat, rainbow, and a few brook trout. [T27N R29W S29]

WIGWAM RIVER. More of a creek than a river with its 5-mile length, it is paralleled by USFS road 319 for most of this stretch. It's not very popular, but it's fair for 6- to 8-inch cutthroat. Anglers must use only artificial lures and release all catches. [T37N R25W S1]

WILLIAMS CREEK. It flows down a narrow, steep canyon to Grave Creek, 2 miles south of Clarence Creek. From the Grave Creek road, USFS road 7019 takes off near the campground and goes up to the trailhead on the stream. From there, it's a 5-mile hike up to the headwaters, near Mount Locke. Williams is quite small and practically never fished, but it's fair for 7- to 8-inch cutthroat below the falls, at the lower end of the canyon. In the upper canyon area, there are only small resident bull trout. [T36N R25W S27]

WINDY CREEK. A very small stream flowing north to the East Fork Yaak River, through Okaga Lake, about 5 miles northeast of the old Upper Ford Guard Station. The lower 2 miles, including the lake, are private, while the upper reaches can be approached from Fish Lakes to

Wigwam River. —Courtesy Bill Archie

the south. The stream isn't worth bothering with, so your best fishing bet is to pay the folks at Okaga Lake. [T37N R31W S35]

WISHBONE LAKE. It's 18 acres and fairly deep, in rocky cliff, talus, and scrub timber on the north side of Vimy Ridge, at the head of the East Fork of Contact Creek. Wishbone is reached cross-country, basically following Contact Creek from the Granite Lake trail. Very seldom fished, it's overpopulated with 6- to 16-inch brook trout. [T29N R32W S21]

WOLF CREEK. It's 36 miles long, rocky upstream and slow, meandering, and brushy below. It is followed its entire length by a paved road (USFS road 36), to its junction with the Fisher River, near Lightning Peak. This stream is easily fished, but it's no more than fair for small cutthroat, a few whitefish and rainbow and brook trout, and some suckers. [T29N R29W S34]

WOLVERINE LAKES. Three lakes, ⅛ mile apart in subalpine, timbered country. Take a USFS trail 2½ miles from the end of the Wigwam Creek road. Upper Wolverine is about 15 acres in area and 30 feet deep; Middle Wolverine is about 25 acres and 30 feet deep; and Lower Wolverine covers only about 4 acres and is maybe 7 to 8 feet deep. All three are good fishing for 9- to 11-inch cutthroat, but they've been better in years gone

Wolverine Lakes. —Courtesy U.S. Forest Service

by. Upper Wolverine has the best chance of producing larger fish. These lakes are fished pretty heavily. [T37N R26W S13]

WOODS RANCH POND. It straddles private and Forest Service land a couple of miles southeast of Roosville, a mile south of the border. It has been stocked the last few years with cutthroat, and in 1994 with brood-stock rainbow. It is likely very good fishing now. Follow USFS road 1001 off US 93, 3 miles north of Eureka. [T37N R26W S8]

YAAK RIVER. It flows from within a few miles of the Canadian line for 53 miles south, to the Kootenai River, a few miles east of the Idaho line. It's followed by a good road all the way. It is a good-size stream, mostly in a flat-bottomed valley upstream and a narrow, steep-walled canyon below. The lower 8 miles (below Yaak Falls) are fairly fast, heavily fished for good catches of 10- to 12-inch rainbow, plus a few cutthroat, brook trout (these reported to 27 inches), and whitefish. Most anglers walk from one of the campgrounds to access this stretch. The stream is much

Yaak Falls. —Courtesy U.S. Forest Service

slower above the falls, with lots of still, deep water that is good fishing for 8- to 10-inch rainbow, quite a few brookies, and an occasional cutthroat. [T32N R34W S5]

YAAK RIVER, East Fork. You can reach the mouth from the Yaak River road, 4 miles east of the old Upper Ford Guard Station, which follows it upstream past the falls, 1½ miles east of the mouth. You'll find a total of 5 miles of good fishing water in timbered country, just this side of Canada. This stream is moderately popular for 8- to 12-inch rainbow, some cutthroat, and a few brook trout that average around 10 inches and range up to 20. Logging activity has contributed to a siltation problem, and the fishery is declining. [T37N R31W S22]

YAAK RIVER, North Fork. It's paralleled by road, mostly through private land, for a couple of miles, until a gate 1 mile south of the border. You'll find brookies, Columbia Basin redband trout, whitefish, suckers,

355

squawfish, and some migrating kokanee. The North Fork is another fishery in decline, unfortunately. [T32N R34W S5]

YAAK RIVER, South Fork. The lower reaches of this stream flow through a steep, inaccessible canyon, while the middle reaches (about 5 miles) open out into a flat-bottomed valley, easily accessible by road. There is some private land here. The canyon is best fished by going up the road for a couple of miles to the stream's head, and then fishing down. The South Fork is moderately popular and as a whole fair fishing for 5- to 9-inch cutthroat, rainbow, and brook trout. {T36N R32W S35]

YAAK RIVER, West Fork. This fork flows from its headwaters on the high, alpine slopes of Rock Candy Mountain, down a fairly wide canyon for 8 miles to Canada, then many miles beyond, before it eventually recrosses into the States, flowing for another 10 miles, through a steep-walled canyon above and a wide, timbered valley below, to the main river, 2½ miles north of the old Upper Ford Guard Station. The upper reaches can be accessed from the Pete Creek road, and they're followed all the way by logging road and trail. There you'll find fair fishing for 6-inch cutthroat. The lower reaches are followed by a logging road for 3 miles, and then by trail to the border. They're very good fishing for 8- to 10-inch cutthroat and rainbow, especially below the falls, which are 3 miles upstream from the mouth. [T37N R31W S32]

YOUNG CREEK. This stream heads just this side of Canada and flows southeastward for 11 miles down a narrow valley, then for about a mile along the south side of some private open meadows (northwest of Alkali Lake), and finally down a tight, brushy little draw to the reservoir, 10½ miles north of the Big Bridge. It's accessible at the mouth, then about a mile upstream (near the Tooley Lake School), and again from the meadow reaches on up, by jeep and logging roads. This stream has been rehabilitated with migratory cutthroat, which should provide good year-round fishing for small (6- to 7-inch) trout, and early spring fishing for 10- to 18-inch spawners. Bull trout sometimes wander up Young Creek on feeding runs as well. [T37N R28W S24]

YOUNG CREEK, South Fork. It flows to Young Creek about 8 miles west of Young Creek's mouth. This small tributary is seldom bothered, but it has pan-size cutthroat in the lower ¾ mile. [T37N R29W S14]

The Swan River—
Gateway to Wilderness

The Swan River is located in northwestern Montana, immediately west of the Continental Divide. Crystal and Gray Wolf lakes form its headwaters, in the Mission Mountains Tribal Wilderness. The river flows north for approximately 66 miles before it discharges into Flathead Lake, at the town of Bigfork. Fifty-three major tributaries enter the river, primarily from the east and west.

The Swan drainage encompasses nearly 700 square miles, flowing through a heavily forested and glaciated valley; it's 3 to 6 miles in width. The majority of the drainage is owned and managed for timber harvest by the U.S. Forest Service, the state of Montana, and Plum Creek Timber Company. The river's immediate corridor is primarily under private ownership.

Three relatively large, oligitrophic lakes on the valley floor are linked directly to the Swan River system. The southernmost is Lindbergh Lake (726 acres), which receives headwater flow from the upper Swan River. Nearly 5 miles downstream, Holland Creek enters the river from the east, after flowing through Holland Lake (408 acres). The Swan River then flows uninterrupted for nearly 35 miles, where it enters Swan Lake, the largest within the drainage, covering 2,680 surface acres. The river then flows nearly 13 miles below Swan Lake, to where it is impounded by Bigfork Dam, a 12-foot-high, run-of-the-river hydroelectric facility. Below the dam, the river cascades through a 1-mile high-gradient section that's popular with whitewater enthusiasts, then it enters Flathead Lake.

The mean annual flow of the Swan River is 1,300 cubic feet per second (cfs), measured immediately below Swan Lake. Peak flows, in excess of 5,000 cfs, typically occur in June and are determined by the amount and rate of snowmelt in the mountainous watershed.

Fishing opportunities in Lindbergh and Holland lakes center primarily on westslope cutthroat and kokanee, provided through natural reproduction and supplemental stocking. Large bull trout are also present, however current regulations prevent taking them or intentionally fishing for them. Swan Lake is the only water where bull trout can be

The Swan River below Lindbergh Lake. —Courtesy U.S. Forest Service

harvested—at one per day. A trophy bull from Swan Lake will go 15-plus pounds. Cutthroat and rainbow are frequently caught as well, but kokanee and northern pike receive the greatest pressure and harvest.

Within the Swan Valley floor are twenty-five lakes that are managed for fisheries. These lakes range in size from 2 to 275 acres. Half of these lakes provide an environment for warmwater fish, such as bass and perch, whereas the remainder are managed for trout, primarily by stocking. Additional lakes within the drainage do not contain viable fisheries. Nearly eighty high mountain lakes lie in the mountainous cirques above the valley floor, found within the Swan Range to the east and Mission Mountains Tribal Wilderness to the west. Westslope cutthroat trout are the primary trout species in these lakes, and where there are not self-sustaining populations they are customarily maintained through rotational stocking.

Historically, the Swan drainage was home to only two native trout species—the westslope cutthroat trout and the bull trout. Seasonal migrations of bull and cutthroat trout and kokanee ascended the Swan River from Flathead Lake for spawning until construction of Bigfork Dam in 1902. A fish ladder was subsequently built, but fish passage was minimal. The ladder was recently closed, to block upstream migration of additional non-native species, including lake trout and lake whitefish from Flathead Lake. Non-native species now compromise a major portion of the fishery throughout the drainage. Brook trout inhabit many of the lower-gradient tributary reaches, and brook and rainbow trout predominate in the Swan River above Swan Lake. The river between Swan Lake and Bigfork Dam contains northern pike, largemouth bass, yellow perch, and limited numbers of rainbow, brook, and cutthroat trout.

Fish species distribution and abundance in tributaries to the Swan River are strongly influenced by channel gradient. In the steeper headwater sections, resident cutthroat trout prevail in the majority of streams. As gradient decreases, brook trout begin to dominate and cutthroat numbers generally decline. Rainbows are found in a few tributary streams but tend to be in low numbers. Bull trout from Swan Lake spawn in a number of the larger tributaries in the Swan. Their numbers have been steadily increasing due to favorable forage in Swan Lake, but they're still protected by regulation.

The distribution of fish species within the Swan River varies with habitat types and temperature conditions. The upper river portion, below Lindbergh Lake, is relatively shallow, containing numerous riffles and pools, and it substantially warms during summer months, influencing trout distribution. Wading is favorable during summer, and logjams become more numerous as you progress downstream. Water volumes are fairly low, and rainbow and brook trout, generally under 12 inches, prevail. The middle section, located midway between Swan and Lindbergh lakes, is characterized by increased flows, improved channel diversity, and much pool development from log debris. Rainbows are more numerous, followed by brook trout and cutthroat. Recent electrofishing surveys indicate there are nearly 1,000 rainbow trout, greater than four inches per mile, in the midsection. Floating can be dangerous, due to numerous logjams, which shift annually.

The lower section of the river, above Swan Lake, roughly begins at the Fatty Creek Bridge. Flows are increased due to tributary inflow and the channel becomes more diverse in depth, cover, and water volume. Rainbow trout are the most abundant species, and average densities are similar to those in the middle section, at 1,000 per mile. A large rainbow from the middle and lower sections will be 20-plus inches and weigh about 3 pounds. Floating is more common on this lower section, but the main channel is constantly shifting, creating hazards.

After flowing through Swan Lake, the river maintains a riffle-run complex until its confluence with Bear Creek. Rainbow and brook trout numbers are very low, due to warm summer temperatures from the Swan Lake outflow. Below Bear Creek, to Bigfork Dam, the gradient is reduced, depths are increased, and warm-water fish predominate, including northern pike, largemouth bass, and yellow perch. The 1-mile section ("Wild Mile") from Bigfork Dam to Flathead Lake has an extremely high gradient, containing numerous boulder cascades, forming pools and runs. The fishery is primarily for rainbow and cutthroat, but lake trout and lake whitefish from Flathead Lake frequently occupy the section.

Scott Rumsey
Fisheries Biologist
Montana Fish, Wildlife and Parks

BARBER CREEK. Flows from the junction of its north and south forks (a couple of miles north of Holland Lake) for 3 miles west, through rolling timber and pasture land in the Swan Valley, to the river, where it is crossed near the mouth by Montana 83. There's limited road access to the lower reaches, which are fair fishing for pan-size brook trout. Below the forks, the stream is accessed by a couple of miles of road and supports a few cutthroat. [T20N R16W S19]

BEAVER CREEK. This stream flows northeast for 12 miles, through heavily timbered mountains along the Swan-Clearwater drainage divide, to the Swan River, 2½ miles east of Lindbergh Lake. Its middle reaches are followed by several miles of good logging road, west off Montana 83, just north of Summit Lake. The lower 8 miles are good brook trout water for fish 6 to 14 inches. The upper reaches support a good population of small cutts. [T19N R16W S8]

BEAVER LAKE. This 25-acre lake sits at an elevation of 5,700 feet, just west of the Swan-Clearwater divide in the Beaver Creek drainage. You can come at it from logging roads in the Beaver Creek drainage, or over the divide from the Uhler Creek drainage: either way, you'll have to walk the last mile or so on a Forest Service trail. Beaver Lake is stocked every few years with westslope cutts, and fishing can be good for cutts to 14 inches. You might want to haul back a boat or float tube to give yourself a little casting room. [T18N R16W S5]

BIRCH LAKE. A 29-acre alpine lake, 105 feet deep with steep drop-offs, in a cirque near the top of the Swan Range, at 6,000 feet above sea level. Take good county roads north and east from Bigfork, past Echo Lake. Follow the signs to the Jewel Basin hiking area, at the end of the steep and sometimes washboarded Noisy Creek road. From the trailhead, it's 2½ miles around the west side of Mount Aeneas to the shore. The Jewel Basin is a hikers-only area, and Birch is among its most popular lakes. It's stocked periodically and offers fair fishing for small cutthroat and some rainbow-cutthroat hybrids that range from 7 to 14 inches. [T28N R18W S32]

BOND CREEK. It drains Bond Lake for 5½ miles west, to the south end of Swan Lake. Crossed near the mouth by Montana 83, it's followed to headwaters by a good USFS trail that takes off from the highway near the Swan Lake Ranger Station. This is a pretty small creek, the upper reaches running through a steep, timbered canyon, but the lower mile is fairly flat, swampy in spots, accessible by road, and fair fishing for 6- to 8-inch brook, and some cutthroat, trout. [T25N R18W S23]

BOND LAKE. Almost 5 acres and fairly deep, it sits in a timbered pocket on the northern slopes of Spring Slide Mountain, about 6 miles east as the crow flies from the town of Swan Lake. It's accessible by 5 miles of good USFS trail up Bond Creek. This lake is fair fishing for cutthroat trout that will average around 10 inches and range up to 14. [T25N R17W S10]

BUCK CREEK. A small, westward-flowing stream, about 6 miles long from its headwaters on the steep western slopes of the Swan Range to its mouth on the Swan River. It's crossed near the mouth by Montana 83, 4 ½ miles south of the Condon Ranger Station. There is limited access on logging roads, and Buck Creek is crossed by USFS trail 192 from Holland Lake. The lower reaches are fair fishing for small brook trout, with a few cutthroat joining the brookies in the middle reaches. [T20N R16W S18]

BUNYAN LAKE. A 9-acre lake, deep in spots but mostly shallow, marshy at the east end, Bunyan lies in wooded country a mile west of the southern end of Lindbergh Lake. It's reached by a logging road 7 miles from the northern end of Lindbergh Lake, but unless you have a high-clearance truck and don't mind some "Montana pinstriping" from the brush that's overgrowing the road, you might want to park above the lake and walk the last ¼ mile. Bunyan is moderately popular and can be good fishing for 6- to 13-inch cutthroat trout. [T19N R17W S34]

CAT LAKE. This lake lies in steep, mountainous terrain at the head of the Cat Creek drainage, a mile south of Pony Lake. There's no maintained trail, and it's tough going to get to this 14-acre, 50-foot-deep lake, which is stocked periodically with cutthroat and is now good fishing for 10- to 14-inchers. [T22N R16W S33]

CEDAR CREEK. The outlet of Cedar Lake, it flows for 10 miles down the east side of the Mission Range, eventually spreading out into a swamp adjacent to the Swan River, near the Goat Creek Guard Station, 15 miles south of Swan Lake. Logging roads provide some access to the lower reaches, which are fair fishing (it used to be excellent) for little brook trout and an occasional bull trout spawner up from the main river. There's no maintained trail along the upper reaches, which are home to some small cutts. [T23N R17W S18]

CEDAR LAKE. A 46-acre alpine lake that is good and deep, with mostly gradual drop-offs. Take a trail south for 4 miles from the end of the Fatty

Creek road, near the crest of the Mission Range in the Mission Mountains Wilderness. Moderately popular, Cedar is good fishing for cutts that average 10 to 12 inches and put up a good fight. [T22N R18W S17]

CILLY CREEK. A little stream flowing west for 6 miles through steep, timbered mountains to the Swan River. It's crossed near the mouth by Montana 83, 4½ miles south of Swan Lake, and it's accessible by logging road along much of its length. The lower mile is fair fishing for pan-size brookies. [T24N R18W S12]

COLD CREEK. It flows some 13 miles from its headwaters near the crest of the Mission Mountains to the Swan River, 3 miles north of Condon. It's moderately popular fishing, especially in the lower reaches, where there's fair fishing for small brookies and cutthroat, with the possibility of spawning bull trout up from the river in the fall. [T21N R17W S15]

COLD CREEK, North Fork. A small stream, about 3½ miles long, the outlet of Cold Lakes. Reach the mouth by a logging road 5 miles west from Montana 83 near the Condon Ranger Station. The lower reaches are available by road and are fair fishing for small cutthroat and brook trout, and a few bulls in the fall, water permitting—Cold Creek itself gets real low at times. [T21N R17W S20]

COLD LAKES. Two lakes in the Mission Mountains Wilderness, each about 80 acres and deep, ¼ mile apart in high alpine country. It's rocky above but heavily timbered around the outlets. The lower lake is reached by a good USFS trail, 2 miles from the end of the Cold Lakes road. Both are good fishing for cutthroat ranging to 16 inches, with better fishing and better casting spots at the upper lake (also known as Frigid Lake). Maybe because getting around the lower lake can be tough going, some folks just don't seem to get around to fishing the upper lake. The best time to visit these aptly named lakes is in late July, August, and September. Because of overuse, the Forest Service has designated Cold Lakes for day use only, with no overnight camping within ¼ mile of either lake. If you keep any fish from these lakes, remember that you are in grizzly country—your best bet for minimizing problems with bears is to pack your fish out whole and clean them at home. [T21N R18W S22]

CONDON CREEK. This small stream heads at the crest of the Swan Range and flows for 8 miles westward, through steep, timbered mountains, to the Swan River, where it is crossed by Montana 83, 1½ miles south of the Condon Ranger Station. Condon Creek is crossed by logging roads in a few places, but otherwise it's not very accessible by road or trail. The lower 3 miles are fair fishing for camp-fare brook trout; the headwaters are good for cutts and brookies. [T21N R17W S3]

COOLEY CREEK. Just a trickle between Rumble Creek and Buck Creek—it's not even named on maps. Cooley Creek dries up in late summer, but a few beaver dams in the headwaters are good fishing for small cutthroat trout. You gotta walk, and the fish aren't bothered but once in a blue moon. The land is private, so make sure you have permission to fish. [T21N R16W S7]

COONEY CREEK. A little stream flowing for 5½ miles west, from the Swan Range to the river. It's crossed ½ mile upstream of its confluence by Montana 83, near the Condon Airfield. Cooney Creek gets quite low in late summer, but the short stretch between the road and the river is fair fishing for small cutthroat. This is all private land, but chances are you'll get permission if you ask. There are some "lost" beaver dams in the headwaters that might also be worth checking out, but you'll have to work hard to find them. [T20N R17W S1]

CRAZY HORSE CREEK. A high mountain stream flowing southeast-ward to Glacier Creek, about 1 mile east of Glacier Lake. Crossed at its mouth by the trail up Glacier Creek, it has no maintained trail of its own. Crazy Horse is seldom fished, but it contains a few small cutthroat trout in the lower mile. [T19N R17W S29]

CRESCENT LAKE. You can reach it by trail going 3 miles west past the Glacier Lake trailhead. In late summer, loads of huckleberries can help take your mind off the switchbacks. Crescent is 24 acres with a 35-foot maximum depth, in rugged, rocky alpine country, above 6,000 feet in elevation, on the eastern slopes of the Mission Range. It used to be barren, but it was planted with golden trout in the early '60s and was excellent fishing for a while. Now stocked periodically with cutthroat, it sometimes offers fast fishing for small fish. Crescent Lake sees a lot of pressure, so be light on the landscape and respect occasional campsite closures. [T19N R18W S24]

CRYSTAL LAKE. A deep lake, about 186 acres, in heavily timbered mountains. Take the trail from the southern end of Lindbergh Lake, west for 2 ½ miles, or take USFS trail 351 from the end of the Beaver Creek road, going west about 4 miles. There is a nice camping spot on the north side of the lake's eastern end. Crystal is moderately fished for good catches of 9- to 10-inch cutthroat trout. [T18N R17W S8]

DEER CREEK. The upper reaches of this small inlet of Mud Lake are on the western slopes of the Swan Range, too steep for fish; but the lower reaches, beaver-dammed about ½ mile above the lake, are fair fishing for pan-size brookies. To reach it, go 3 miles north from Bigfork, then 3 miles east to the lake, following the road around the lake's south end to the creek. There is some gravel-road access to the lower reaches. [T27N R19W S15]

DOG CREEK. Seven miles long in heavy timber, it empties from the east to the Swan River. It's crossed near the mouth by Montana 83, about 6 miles north of the Condon Ranger Station. A short gravel road provides access to the lower mile, and the upper reaches are partly accessible from logging roads. The lower 3 miles are occasionally fished for fair catches of 6- to 10-inch brook trout. Cutthroat take over in the upper reaches. [T21N R17W S3]

DUCHARME (or UPPER PIPER) LAKE. It's about ⅛ mile up the drainage from Piper Lake, (¼ mile southwest by trail). It's 16 acres in area, 6,462 feet in elevation, in an alpine cirque just east of the Swan-Flathead divide. It hasn't been stocked since 1966 and fishing reports are scarce, but in the past the lake has been good at times for cutthroat in the 14- to 18-inch class. [T22N R18W S32]

EAST LAKE. See Lost Lake.

ELK CREEK. This stream is such high-quality bull trout habitat that it's closed the entire year, to give the fish a place to spawn in peace. [T21N R17W S35]

ELK LAKE. A seldom-visited alpine lake in barren country near the crest of the Mission Range, in the Mission Mountains Wilderness. Elk Lake can be reached by bushwhacking a few miles west from the end of an old pack trail up the Elk Creek Ridge, or by way of an unmaintained trail that starts a couple of miles south of Mollman Lakes. This lake, about 80 acres in area and deep, is poor to fair fishing for good-size cutthroat and rainbow trout. [T20N R18W S29]

FATTY CREEK. It heads near Cedar Peak in the Mission Mountains Wilderness, flowing for several miles, through heavily timbered mountains, to Cedar Creek. It is followed by logging road and trail for most of its length. The lower reaches contain a few small cutthroat trout. [T22N R18W S1]

FATTY LAKE. An alpine lake, about 21 acres and fairly deep, with a mud bottom and brushy shores. You can reach it via a poor hunters' trail, going 1½ miles northeast from its starting point, near the end of the Fatty Creek road. The lake, though lightly fished, is planted periodically with cutthroat, last in 1995. It's good fishing for 10- to 12- inchers.

This one can be a lot of fun, especially if you've packed in a boat or float tube to avoid the brush and the muck! [T22N R18W S5]

FISH LAKES. Two lakes, ¹/₂ mile apart in subalpine country, in the North Fork of Cedar Creek drainage. To get to the upper lake, take a short foot trail going southeast from Cedar Lake. Upper Fish Lake is about 7 acres, with brushy, rocky shores. It's planted occasionally with cutts, and they provide good fishing in the small to midsize category. To reach Lower Fish Lake, take a cross-country hike downstream, going ³/₄ mile southeast from the upper lake. The lower lake, which covers about 20 acres, doesn't get fished much; rumor has it that it can be excellent for 6- to 14-inch cutthroat trout. [T22N R18W S20]

FRANCIS (or FRAN) LAKE. The second of three small, undrained lakes off the Cold Creek road, west of Montana 83. The access road has a kelly hump about ¹/₈ mile from the lake. Fran, at 8.8 acres, is stocked with rainbow and cutthroat trout. The rainbows grow big, but are elusive, and there are times when a person would swear there are no fish in this lake. Other times, fishing can be fun for cutts in the 12- to 15-inch range. The lower lake in this chain is barren, while Russell Lake, right around the bend from Fran, is a popular fishing hole among locals. [T21N R17W S21]

FRIGID LAKE. See under Cold Lakes.

GILDART (or GILBERT) CREEK. A small stream that flows for about a mile down a steep canyon on the eastern slopes of the Mission Range, then meanders across the timbered bottomland in the Swan River Valley, ultimately joining with the river about 2 miles south of Swan Lake. Gilbert, accessible by logging road for about ¹/₂ mile above the mouth, is fair fishing for cutthroat, rainbow, and brook trout. [T25N R18W S34]

GLACIER CREEK. A clear, snow-fed tributary of the Swan River. It's reached here and there by a logging road in the lower reaches, then followed by trail for a couple of miles below Glacier Lake. Glacier Creek is moderately popular, but it offers generally poor fishing, unless you're after brook trout in the sloughs in the middle section. Between Crazy Horse Creek and Glacier Lake, the fishing picks up a bit, and you might catch cutts, rainbow, brook trout, an occasional bull trout, and maybe even a golden trout, whose ancestors were planted in the drainage. [T21N R17W S36]

GLACIER LAKE. A deep, 104-acre lake in heavily timbered mountains, 4 miles due west of Lindbergh Lake. Take a trail a quick 2 miles west from the end of the Glacier Creek road. It is heavily fished in summer and good, too, for mostly 9- to 12-inch cutthroat trout (plus a few lunkers). Because the shoreline was getting so hammered, the lake has been designated a day-use-only area by the USFS, and there's no camping. [T19N R17W S30]

GLACIER SLOUGHS. See Notlimah Lake.

GOAT CREEK. A small stream flowing for 9½ miles, down a steep canyon above and through timbered hills below, to the Swan River, about 14 miles south of Swan Lake. Crossed at the mouth by Montana 83, it's followed upstream to headwaters by a logging road. It's popular with bull trout of all shapes and sizes, so it's closed to fishing, to give these native fish a better chance of survival. [T23N R17W S18]

GRAY WOLF LAKE. A deep, 300-plus-acre alpine lake in barren, rocky country (with some scrub timber), below Gray Wolf Glacier, near the crest of the Mission Range. To get to Gray Wolf, take a trail 10 steep miles southwest from a logging road in the Beaver Creek drainage, or

Waterfall on Glacier Creek above Glacier Lake. —Courtesy U.S. Forest Service

Gray Wolf Lake. —Courtesy U.S. Forest Service

take a trail about 6 miles northwest from the Jocko River middle access road. This lake is not exactly overrun with fishermen. It was last planted in the 1950s, with cutthroat trout, and it's fair fishing—but only at times—for 12- to 18-inchers. A short stretch of the trail crosses over tribal land on the Flathead Reservation, so make sure to buy a tribal recreation permit before you do this hike. [T18N R17W S30]

GROOM CREEK. This 4-mile stream flows into Swan Lake at the town of Swan Lake. The trail to Hall Lake runs along this creek for about a mile in the middle section; otherwise, you're bushwhacking to get to some fair to good fishing for small cutthroat. This fishery has seen its ups and downs, and in the early 80s it received plantings of cutthroat to restore the fishery. It's all right now, but releasing cutts never hurts. [T25N R18W S14]

HALL LAKE. A deep, 12-acre subalpine lake with lots of brush and talus around the north end. Take a good USFS trail 7 miles northwest (which includes a 3,000-foot vertical gain) from the town of Swan Lake. It is good fishing for mostly cutthroat that average about 12 inches. Hall is stocked regularly. [T26N R17W S31]

HEART (or HART) LAKE. Reach it by trail, in alpine country, ½ mile west of Crescent Lake. It's 13 acres in area and 55 feet deep, with mostly steep drop-offs, and it was originally barren. In the early '60s, Heart was planted with golden trout, and fishing was red hot for awhile—but you won't be catching any of those nowadays. This was the best of the Crescent-Heart-Island Lakes chain, and it was fished accordingly. The lake is now planted with cutts, and fishing pressure is still heavy for those little buggers. The few good campsites at Heart Lake see lots of use, so please tread lightly. [T19N R18W S25]

HEMLOCK LAKE. It lies at the head of Hemlock Creek, in the timbered mountains of the Mission Mountains Wilderness. There is trail access from two directions, both trails picking up from USFS road 566. The shorter of the two hikes—about 4 miles northwest from the end of the Red Butte Creek road—is also the steeper. Hemlock is about 30 acres and deep, and it's moderately popular for good catches of 10- to 12-inch cutthroat trout. [T19N R18W S1]

HIGH PARK LAKE. A deep, 220-acre alpine lake on the east side of the Mission Range, at a 6,377-foot elevation, just beneath Goat Mountain. High Park is hard to get to, so it's not often fished. Hike in to Crystal Lake, then head southwest up the drainage from there—cliffs can make the going tough. There's an old trail partway there, if you can find it. If you do reach the lake, you might find very good fishing—especially when the winds are calm—for 9- to 14-inch cutthroat trout. The scenery alone is worth the trip. [T18N R18W S13]

HOLLAND CREEK. It heads in Upper Holland Lake and flows for 4 miles, down a steep, timbered canyon (crossed occasionally by a heavily used USFS trail), to the main Holland Lake. Below that, there are another 4 miles of stream, flowing through timbered bottomland to the Swan River, just north of the Clearwater-Swan drainage divide. The lower reaches are somewhat accessible by road, and they're fair fishing for 6- to 8-inch rainbow, with lesser numbers of brook trout, along with too many trash fish. The waterfall above Holland Lake forms a barrier to fish migration, so you'll find only cutts—some with size to them—in those few places where there's holding water along the steep drop. [T20N R16W S32]

HOLLAND LAKE. A nice, big (416 acres) recreational and summer-home lake, at the foot of the Swan Range. You can reach it by road a couple of miles east from Montana 83, just a few miles north of the drainage divide. Holland used to be fabulous fishing in the late 1800s, for whopping big trout. It now contains rainbow trout, kokanee, cutthroat trout,

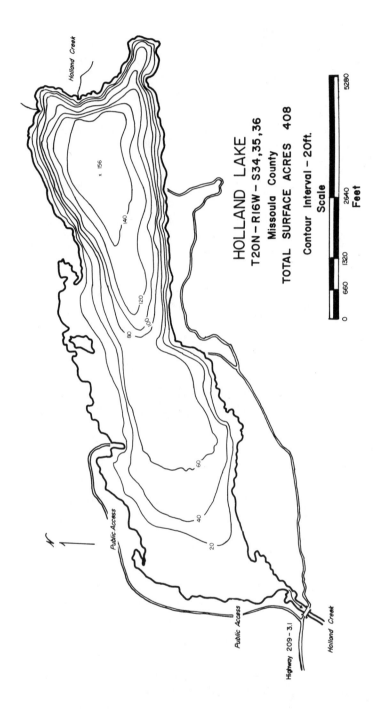

HOLLAND LAKE
T20N−R16W−S34,35,36
Missoula County
TOTAL SURFACE ACRES 408

Contour Interval − 20ft.

Scale

| 0 | 660 | 1320 | 2640 | 5280 |

Feet

Holland Creek

x 156

140

120

100

80

60

40

20

Public Access

Public Access

Highway 209 − 3.1

Holland Creek

N

Montana Department of Fish, Wildlife and Parks

and a few nice-size bull trout, plus lots of whitefish and increasing numbers of trash fish. There are both public and private campgrounds, as well as a lodge, on the north side of the lake. [T20N R16W S35]

HORSESHOE LAKE. This is one of the few lakes in Montana with smallmouth bass. It covers about 50 acres, and it's marshy and swampy in spots, with lots of lilies along the south shore. Horseshoe Lake sits in timbered private land on the south side of the Loon Lake road, about ½ mile west of the north end of Swan Lake, 9 miles east of Bigfork. Quite a few people fish it now for fair catches of 1- to 4-pound bass and lots of sunfish. Horseshoe is closed to spearing, and special bass limits apply, so

Holland Lake. —Courtesy U.S. Forest Service

check current regulations. Access to the lake had been no problem when the Plum Creek Timber Company owned the land surrounding the lake, but now that they've sold the land to a private party, access is a question mark. [T26N R19W S15]

ISLAND LAKE. The uppermost of the Crescent-Heart-Island lakes chain, with an elevation of 6,570 feet, in alpine country about a mile west of Heart Lake. It's 22 acres with a 40-foot maximum depth, and there's a big rock island at the southeast end. Island Lake used to be barren, then it was planted with golden trout in the early '60s. Fishing was good for a while, but not many are left now. Today you'll find mostly small cutts and hybrids. [T19N R18W S26]

JIM CREEK. It drains the Jim Lakes Basin and flows eastward for 9½ miles to the Swan River, just west of the Condon Ranger Station. The lower 4 miles, right down in lodgepole bottomland in the Swan Valley, are accessible here and there by logging roads and trails. There's fair fishing there for brook trout, some bull trout in the fall, and a few cut-throat and rainbow trout. [T19N R18W S26]

JIM (or JIM CREEK) LAKES. Now hear this! If you've got a summer to spend just exploring one set of mountain lakes, this is the place. You've just got to get past the clear-cuts to do it. Taking USFS roads west from Montana 83, a few miles north of Condon, you can drive right up to the main Jim Lake, which is in what used to be beautifully timbered country. The lake covers about 20 acres, and it's full of freshwater shrimp. Planted with cutthroat and rainbow trout in years past, it can be good early-season fishing for cutts in the 12-inch range. If you scramble around in the drainage (there's no trail) you'll find lots of lakes—most of them in timber and brush, some in rocky cirques. Depending on what counts as a lake in your book, there are something like 20 lakes here for you to explore. And a handful of them even have fish! This is good bear coun-try, so be careful with your food and fish. Fishing for cutthroat in these lakes is not a bad way to spend a summer, or two or three. [T21N R18W S14]

JOHNSON CREEK. A small stream that flows west, through timbered bottomland, across Montana 83, then empties into the Swan River just above the north end of the lake. The lower 3 miles or so are accessible by logging road. Johnson Creek contains mostly 7- to 10-inch brook trout and whitefish in the lower reaches, and brookies in the few beaver ponds above. It's fair fishing. [T26N R19W S14]

KELLY (or WYMAN CREEK) RESERVOIR. The quickest way to get to Kelly Reservoir might be to float or swim across Swan Lake to the mouth of Wyman Creek, which flows into the lake about halfway down its west shore. (Wyman Creek is too small to fish.) Taking a more conventional approach, you could hoof it along gated logging roads on the west side of Swan Lake. Kelly Reservoir was built away-back when Kelly was one of the "copper kings" in Butte. The reservoir covers 19 acres, in timber all around; it has the remains of an old dam (with water wheel) at the outlet, lots of moss on the bottom, and springs too. It's loaded with small brook trout. This is a private lake; not many people fish it, but there are no signs telling you not to. [T25N R18W S5]

KRAFT CREEK. A small stream, crossed at headwaters by the Kraft Creek (Glacier Lake) road, 7 miles south of Montana 83. It's accessible by that road along much of its 5-mile course to Glacier Creek. It contains a few small cutthroat, and brook trout in the lower reaches, for the few folks who try it. [T20N R17W S27]

LACE LAKE. It's about 18 acres in area and 6,330 feet in elevation, in rocky scrub-timber country near the crest of the Mission Range in the Mission Mountains Wilderness. You can reach it by trail 3 miles south of Glacier Lake. Turquoise Lake lies 100 yards up the inlet to the west, and drains to Lace. Nearby Jewel and Lagoon Lakes are barren. Moderately popular in late summer, Lace is good fishing for 9- to 14-inch cutthroat trout. [T19N R18W S36]

LILY LAKE. A shallow, 7-acre lake, ¼ mile above the west side of Swan Lake, near the mouth of the Swan River. It's a short walk on a good gravel road to get there. It was stocked with grayling in 1970, but they didn't make it. Since 1982, Lily Lake has been stocked with cutthroat every few years. [T25N R18W S9]

LINDBERGH LAKE. A long (4 miles), deep (125 feet), narrow (⅛ to ½ mile), summer-home lake, with a USFS campground on the north end. Take Lindbergh Lake road, which is 3 miles north of the Swan-Clearwater drainage divide on Montana 83, and follow it 3½ miles southwest. Lindbergh is stocked regularly with cutthroat and kokanee, but the lack of food and the intense competition from trash fish keep their numbers in check. Lindbergh can be fair summer fishing for 12-inch cutts and kokanee, and you might hook into a bull trout in the spring. Of course, you might also spend your time taking suckers and squawfish off your line. In its favor, though, Lindbergh is a good jumping-off place for quite a few good fishing lakes and creeks in the high-up and away-back country. [T19N R17W S14]

LION CREEK. A fair-size stream, loosely followed by a trail from headwaters, below Lion Creek Pass at the crest of the Swan Range, westward

Lindbergh Lake. —Courtesy U.S. Forest Service

for 8 steep miles down the slopes of the range. The stream continues—but not the trail—for 6 more miles, across the flat timbered bottoms of the Swan Valley, to the river, south of the Goat Creek work station. Lion Creek supports brookies, cutts, and importantly, bull trout. It's such good habitat that the entire stream is closed to fishing. [T22N R17W S8]

LOON LAKE. This 44-acre lake is 50 feet deep with mostly steep drop-offs, marshy on one end, in hilly timber, meadow, and marsh country. It's located ½ mile west of the northern end of Swan Lake, just north of Horseshoe Lake. Take a gravel road 1½ miles west from Montana 83. There's a public fishing access. Rehabilitated in 1959, Loon now supports a population of rainbows and a few cutts courtesy of the hatchery folks and offers good fishing for largemouth and smallmouth bass in the 3- to 5-pound range. The lake is closed to spearing. [T26N R19W S10]

LOST CREEK. This is really two creeks, North Fork and South Fork, that join west of Montana 83, about 3 miles south of Swan Lake. The lower reaches sometimes sink about ¼ mile above Swan River. The South Fork is followed by a logging road and trail for 4 miles of fair fishing; the North Fork by 5 miles of logging road, but only about 3 miles of it is decent fishing. Both forks contain small cutthroat and bull trout, plus some big bull spawners up from the river (but remember that it's illegal to fish for them). Below the confluence, Lost Creek contains resident populations of 6- to 7-inch brook trout and a very few cutthroat. [T24N R18W S1]

LOST (or EAST) LAKE. A deep, 109-acre alpine lake in scrub timber and talus between Goat and Daughter of the Sun mountains, near the crest of the Mission Range. There is no maintained trail, but you might be able to pick up a poor hunters' trail at Crystal Lake and follow it west for 1½ miles to Lost Lake. The questionable trail and an elevation gain of 1,500 feet mean that this lake is almost never visited, but the few who do get there find it to be good fishing at times for wild westslope and Yellowstone cutts that run 9 to 18 inches and may go up to 3 pounds. [T18N R18W S12]

LOWER PIPER LAKE. See Piper Lake.

MEADOW LAKE. A shallow, marshy, 14.7-acre lake, ¾ mile south from Bunyan Lake. The logging road is gated a short distance from the lake, so you'll need to walk in and find your way through the bog to the lake. It is lightly fished but very good for 10- to 12-inch cutthroat trout. [T18N R17W S4]

METCALF LAKE. It covers 13 acres in timbered bottomland of the Swan Valley, right on the edge of the mountains. Take a rough road a few miles from the Fatty Creek turnoff, just south of the Goat Creek work station on Montana 83. You'll do best with a high-clearance vehicle, especially on the last ½ mile or so. Metcalf used to be a bass lake, but is much more popular in its current incarnation as a trophy trout lake. The rainbows here can run better than 25 inches and can be fun fishing if you can figure out what they're eating. Otherwise, it's fun to watch them cruise the clear waters in obvious disdain of your offering. Metcalf is open to fishing from April 1 through November 30. There's a special limit aimed at making sure there are plenty of big fish to go around—only one trout daily and in possession, and it's got to be over 22 inches. And to make it even more challenging, you must use artificial flies and lures. [T23N R18W S13]

MOLLMAN LAKES. Two really "high up" alpine lakes and a pothole, right at the top of the Mission Range, in barren, rocky country. You can get there from the end of a logging road right past the north end of the Kicking Horse Reservoir in the Flathead Valley, then take a good but steep trail 5 miles or so over the crest of the Missions. Otherwise, you could be in for an adventure, heading up an old trail that has a tendency to get lost, from the South Fork Cold Creek drainage. It's gorgeous country,

Mollman Lake. —Courtesy Pat Markert

though, and worth the effort if you know how to use a map and compass. All three of the Mollman Lakes have populations of cutthroat that run from 10- to 16-inches. There are plenty of camping spots around the lakes. [T20N R18W S19]

MOORE LAKE. This lake is 10 acres in area and deep, in timbered mountains at the edge of the Mission Mountains Wilderness. There's no trail, but you can get to within 1 mile east of the lake on a logging road that goes partway up the Moore Creek drainage, southwest of Montana 83. There used to be all kinds of trail access, but the lack of maintenance is telling—Moore is believed to be barren. [T22N R18W S34]

MUD LAKE. From Bigfork take the Echo Lake road 3 miles north and then 3¼ miles east to the lake. Mud Lake covers about 150 acres, mostly in farmland but with timber on the east side. It's real shallow, with such a soupy, muddy bottom that you need a boat to fish it. It provides, however, some fair to good morning and late evening fishing (and in wintertime through the ice), for 6-inch to 2-pound yellow perch, some largemouth bass, 8- to 12-inch brook trout, and some northern pike. None of the cutts that were planted here in 1942 seem to be around any more. [T27N R19W S15]

NORTH FORK COLD CREEK. See Cold Creek, North Fork.

NORTH HEMLOCK LAKE. It's about 10 acres and deep, in scrub timber and talus. Reach it via a trail that heads 5 miles west from the Kraft Creek–Glacier Lake road at Hemlock Creek. This lake was planted years ago, and it's good fishing now for 10- to 12-inch cutthroat trout. [T20N R18W S36]

NOTLIMAH LAKE (or GLACIER SLOUGHS). Although they are named separately on the map, Notlimah Lake and the Glacier Sloughs are really part of the same big slough (swamp?), which is about 1¼ miles long by about 100 yards wide, in heavy timber on Glacier Creek. It's reached cross-country—wear your rubber boots—from the switchbacks on the Kraft Creek–Glacier Lake road, or by a couple of miles of trail heading west from the Lindbergh Lake road. Moderately popular, it's fair fishing for 6- to 12-inch cutthroat and brook trout in all seasons of the year. [T19N R17W S16]

PECK LAKE. You can drive to within a couple of hundred yards of this shallow, marshy lake just off USFS road 888, which parallels Montana 83, connecting the Cold Creek and Piper Creek roads. The shoreline is

Peck Lake. —Courtesy Michele Archie

very boggy, and you'll need a canoe or shallow-draft boat to get to any of the rainbows that are stocked in this lake. [T22N R17W S32]

PIERCE LAKE. A 29-acre lake with a mucky bottom and many drowned trees around the shore. In rolling timbered country, it's reached by a road a mile east from Montana 83, just north of the Swan-Clearwater drainage divide. This summer-home lake is poor fishing for 10- to 12-inch cutthroat trout—the locals say there are bigger cutts here, but fortune has to smile on you if you're going to catch one. It is stocked periodically, last in 1992. [T19N R16W S22]

PIPER CREEK. It heads up in the Mission Mountains Wilderness near Piper Crow Pass, flowing to the Swan River several miles north of Salmon Prairie. The lower reaches are loosely followed by logging roads; the upper reaches are followed by trail to Piper Lake. The lower reaches offer good fishing for brook trout, bulls, and an occasional cutthroat. Up higher, cutthroat and brookies make up most of the action. [T22N R17W S8]

PIPER (or LOWER PIPER) LAKE. A beautiful, deep, 83-acre subalpine lake in rock, scrub timber country. Take a USFS trail 6 miles from the Piper Creek road. Piper is not too heavily fished, but it can be good for 9- to 12-inch wild westslope cutthroats. [T22N R18W S32]

PONY CREEK. The small outlet of Pony Lake flowing westward across the Swan Valley to Swan River near Salmon Prairie. It's crossed by logging road in a couple of spots up above, but you'll probably want to stick to the lower mile, which offers fair fishing for pan-size brook trout. [T22N R17W S33]

PONY LAKE. A deep, 17-acre alpine lake on the western slopes of the Swan Range. To reach it, take a 2½ mile cross-country hike east from where Pony Creek is crossed by a logging road. It sustains a light to moderate fishing pressure, is stocked periodically, and is reportedly fair for 8- to 16-inch cutthroat trout and an occasional lunker (1 to 3 pounds or so). Cat Lake is a mile to the south. [T22N R16W S29]

RAINBOW LAKE. It's about 8 acres and 25 or so feet deep, with an island in the middle, in rock, brush, and scrub timber near the crest of the Mission Range. There's no maintained trail, so your best bet is to bushwhack west from the trail to Cedar Lake. Rainbow Lake lies about 1 ½ miles north of Cedar Lake, as the crow flies. It was planted with cutts in 1952, but they didn't survive. The lake was barren for some time, but the Fish, Wildlife and Parks Department planted rainbow there in 1992. You might want to go check it out. [T22N R18W S7]

Lower Rumble Creek Lake. —Courtesy Michele Archie

RED BUTTE CREEK. This tributary to Kraft Creek flows from the northern flanks of Red Butte in the Mission Mountains Wilderness. A logging road that takes off to the west from the Kraft Creek–Glacier Lake road provides access to a couple of miles of fair fishing for small cutts in the lower reaches. [T19N R17W S4]

RUMBLE CREEK. A small stream that heads up near Holland Peak, at the crest of the Swan Range; its South Fork drains the Rumble Creek Lakes. The lower reaches flow westward, across the timbered bottoms of the Swan Valley, to the river, about 2½ miles south of the Condon work station. Rumble Creek is crossed by gravel road a couple of times in the lower reaches, which provide good fishing for small brookies. Both forks are crossed by the foothills trail from Cooney Lookout, and both can be good fishing for pan-size cutthroat, if you can find the flatter spots. [T20N R16W S7]

RUMBLE CREEK LAKES. Two lakes in alpine country just beneath and west of Holland Peak, at the crest of the Swan Range. They are visited mostly by folks climbing Holland Peak, and by people who know where

Upper Rumble Creek Lake.
—Courtesy Michele Archie

to find the locals' trail that leads up—sometimes pretty much straight up, since locals don't believe in switchbacks—to the lower lake. The trail to the upper lake runs along steep talus slopes, ending up with a tough scramble alongside a section of the waterfall that drops 900 feet between the lakes. The upper lake is just a shade over 27 acres and 5 feet deep; it's stocked with cutthroat periodically and is good fishing, especially in early season (but early season can be any time, even into July). The lower lake is only about 11 acres, but it's real deep (over 95 feet) and is good fishing for 8- to 12-inch cutthroat trout. [T21N R16W S36]

RUSSELL (or RUSS) LAKE. The uppermost in a string of pothole lakes off the Cold Creek road, west of Montana 83 near Condon. A gravel access road that leads back to some private property passes right by Russ Lake. There are two small pullouts, one of which provides easy canoe access. Russ Lake is 10 acres in area and deep in spots, with a mud bottom and lots of aquatic vegetation. It's stocked often and can be fun

Russell Lake. —Courtesy Michele Archie

fishing for cutts and rainbows in the midsize range. It's a popular ice fishing spot. [T21N R17W S21]

SAPPHIRE LAKE. A gem of a lake, set in a rocky basin on a shelf, northwest of Upper Holland Lake. Sapphire, at about 15 acres, is about 1½ miles west by trail from Upper Holland, or 6 miles northeast on what is affectionately—and accurately—known as the switchback trail from Holland Lake. At the edge of the Bob Marshall Wilderness, Sapphire is a popular spot, with several good campsites around the lake, lots of open areas for shore fishing, and a bunch of overzealous 6- to 10-inch cutts. [T20N R15W S29]

SHAY LAKE. Surrounded by timber, Shay covers 17 acres and is moderately deep. The road to Shay takes off to the south from the Fatty Creek logging road, about a mile west of its junction with Montana 83. It's a rough road—enough to make you thankful for every inch of clearance your truck has. There's some private land along the road, and after the turnoff from the Fatty Creek road, there are no signs, so be careful to stay on the main road. Shay is a good but temperamental winter lake that is moderately popular for 10- to 14-inch rainbow, grayling, and a few cutthroat. It is stocked periodically, mostly with rainbow and grayling. [T22N R17W S6]

SIMPSON CREEK. This creek drains the west slope of the Swan Range, flowing 3½ miles into Condon Creek, where it crosses under Condon

Sapphire Lake. —Courtesy Michele Archie

Road. The mouth is accessible by road, and the upper reaches are crossed by logging road here and there. Fishing's OK for little cutts and brook trout, but not much more than that. [T21N R17W S11]

SKYLARK LAKE. A 6½-acre pond, reached to within 1½ miles by the road to Bunyan and Meadow lakes. You might be able to pick up an old trail off the end of the gated road. This one is pretty shallow and could freeze out, but it has (up to now) supported a very few cutthroat trout. [T19N R17W S32]

SMITH CREEK. A small stream with lots of beaver dams, it flows from the crest of the Swan Range near Cooney Mountain. Its lower reaches flow through swampy meadow and timberland to Condon Creek. There is some access to the middle reaches by logging road and by a short stretch of the trail that leads into the Bob Marshall Wilderness over Smith Creek Pass. It is heavily fished downstream for early-season catches of 6- to 9-inch brook trout. The upper reaches support a very few cut-throat. [T21N R17W S11]

SNOW LAKE. Really a part of the swampland at the head of Carney Creek, Snow is about 2 acres in area and shallow, on private land. You can get to within a couple of hundred yards of the shore by a road going 5 miles east and south from Bigfork. Snow was rehabilitated a long time ago, and it's good fishing for 8- to 12-inch cutthroat trout. [T26N R19W S10]

SOUP CREEK. A pretty small stream flowing west from the Swan Range to Swan Valley, and crossed by Montana 83 a mile above its mouth. Soup Creek is followed upstream by a logging road for nearly its entire length, including a couple of miles of fair fishing for cutthroat trout. Soup Creek is a cutthroat recovery stream: the brookies were poisoned in the early 1990s, and the stream was planted with westslope cutthroat. There may be a rare resident or spawning bull trout, too. [T24N R18W S13]

SOUTH FORK COLD CREEK LAKES. There are 13 in all, ranging in size from 3 to 20 acres and from fairly shallow to deep. They sit in an old burn mostly, although there is some nice timber too. These lakes, in the Mission Mountains Wilderness, are not named on the maps. The easternmost one is reached to within a mile or so by the South Fork road. The rest—including the bigger lakes—just string out for about 3 miles up the canyon and north over the ridge in real rough country, with no trail to connect them. They're very seldom fished, but the first three you come to of any size (5, 13, and 7.3 acres, a couple of hundred yards apart) have fish. These lakes support nice populations of naturally reproducing rainbow and cutthroat, which tend to increase in size as you go west. Past these lakes another ½ mile (and past a little 1-acre pothole), you will arrive at the last fishing lake in the chain, which lies just east of a big swamp. [T20N R18W S10]

SOUTH FORK LION CREEK LAKE. There's no maintained trail, so just head south up the South Fork drainage from a point about 4 to 5 miles from the Lion Creek trailhead. South Fork Lake is not on the main stem of the South Fork, so pass on by the lake that's just over a mile upstream from the main stem of Lion Creek. Find South Fork Lake by heading another mile or so upstream, then following a small tributary of the South Fork about ¼ mile to the west and uphill. This lake was planted with cutts in 1991, and when you find out how the fishing is now, let us know. Be warned: This lake is not on most maps. [T22N R16W S22]

SOUTH HEMLOCK LAKE. It's just ½ mile downstream from North Hemlock Lake, on the North Fork of Hemlock Creek. South Hemlock Lake has a population of wild westslope cutts. [T20N R18W S36]

SOUTH WOODWARD (or SOUTH WOODWARD CREEK) LAKES. The upper two of these lakes sit ½ mile apart as the crow flies, in the headwaters of South Woodward Creek. The third lake is a couple of miles east, down the drainage. All three of these lakes are reached to within ¼ mile or so by rough logging road that heads east from the Fatty Creek road, about 4 miles back from Montana 83. The upper two lakes are easily fished from shore, but that's not the case for the lower lake, which is surrounded by beautiful, peaceful, and thick cedar forest. Since the late 1980s, they have been planted periodically with cutts. [T13N R18W S29 and 34]

SPRUCE LAKE. A 5-acre alpine lake that's not named on most maps. Take a short cross-country hike southwest from Cedar Lake. It's very seldom fished, but it's reported to be fair for 12- to 14-inch cutthroat trout. [T22N R18W S19]

SQUARE LAKE. This was the site of the Fred Wagner plane crash many years ago, on the headwaters of the Fatty Creek drainage. Your best bet is to bushwhack west from the trail to Cedar Lake. Square Lake covers about 12 acres and runs 25 feet deep; it was planted by airdrop with cutthroat trout way back in 1952. It hasn't been fished a dozen times since, but the trout are reported to be plentiful, running mostly from 10 to 16 inches. [T22N R18W S8]

SQUEEZER CREEK. There's not much road access to this tributary of Goat Creek, which is fine, since it's closed to fishing. Squeezer Creek is incredible bull trout habitat, and also supports a healthy population of brookies that could pose problems for the bulls. [T23N R17W S17]

SQUEEZER LAKE. This lake—not named on the maps—is way up on the west flank of Swan Peak, accessible to within about a mile by trail up Squeezer Creek. If you're gung ho enough to get there, you'll find some incredible country and some good fishing for cutts, which are airdropped into the lake—the last plant was in 1992. [T23N R16W S28]

STONER LAKE. A 31-acre pothole with about 20 acres in vegetation. It has a maximum depth of 15 feet and gradual drop-offs. In dense timber just north of Loon Lake, it is reached by a logging road going east off the Kraft Creek–Glacier Lake road. Stoner used to be good trout fishing, but it winter-killed and now has only yellow perch. [T20N R17W S23]

SWAN LAKE. A big and exceptionally beautiful lake, about 10 miles long by 1 mile wide. It's followed along its east side by a good blacktop highway down the flat-bottomed, heavily timbered Swan Valley. Swan Lake is a moderately popular resort area; there is a USFS campground just north of the town of Swan Lake, quite a few summer homes, and several resorts. There's a little bit of everything in this lake, notably

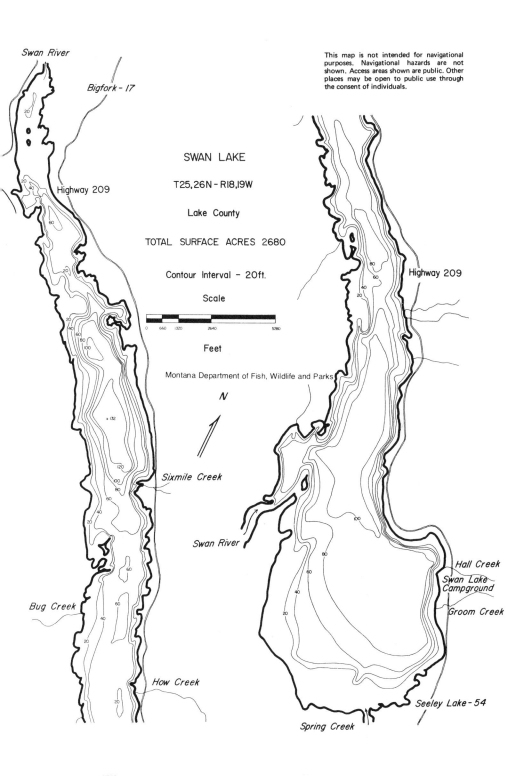

Swan River

Bigfork - 17

Highway 209

Swan River

SWAN LAKE

T25, 26N - R18,19W

Lake County

TOTAL SURFACE ACRES 2680

Contour Interval - 20ft.

Scale

| 0 | 660 | 1320 | 2640 | | 5280 |

Feet

Montana Department of Fish, Wildlife and Parks

N

Highway 209

Sixmile Creek

Swan River

Hall Creek

Swan Lake Campground

Groom Creek

Bug Creek

How Creek

Seeley Lake - 54

Spring Creek

rainbow, cutthroat, brookies, kokanee, yellow perch, and northern pike (which did in the bass that used to share the lake). There are big bulls in the spring and summer, and the Department of Fish, Wildlife and Parks has had some success establishing cutthroat spawning runs in some of the tributaries. It's a good trolling lake—the only public boat launch is located near the USFS campground. If you're fishing for kokanee, you should know that the limit is 50 per day and 100 in possession. It's closed to spear fishing. And it's the only place in western Montana where you can keep a bull trout—only one per day and in possession. Since it's unlawful to possess a live bull trout, you must immediately release or kill the bulls you catch here. [T25N R18W S11]

TRINKUS LAKE. Trinkus is really two subalpine lakes about 75 yards apart. Take the Bond Creek trail east from the town of Swan Lake, go 5 easy miles to Bond Lake, then 1 steep mile north to Trinkus. You can also drop down into the Trinkus Lakes from USFS trail 7, which follows the Swan Crest. The upper lake is barren; the lower, about 12 acres and maybe 65 feet deep, is fair fishing for 9- to 14-inch cutthroat trout. This is good elk country, and the lake is fished mostly by hunters. [T25N R17W S9]

TURQUOISE LAKE. A 184-acre alpine lake located just beneath and east of Glacier Peaks at the crest of the Mission Range, a few hundred yards above Lace Lake. Go about 5 miles past the Glacier Lake trailhead, heading southeast. Turquoise used to be good cutthroat fishing, but reproduction is limited and Turquoise is not so hot any more, with only a few picky trout in evidence. Pretty tough! [T19N R18W S35]

Turquoise Lake.
—Courtesy U.S. Forest Service

UNNAMED LAKES AT THE HEAD OF FATTY CREEK. There are four of them, ranging in size from ½ to 3 acres, sitting close together in alpine country on the eastern slopes of the Mission Range. Two are near the trail to Cedar Lake. The others can be reached only by cross-country hikes of up to a mile. All four of these little ponds were once fast fishing for skinny 6- to 8-inch cutthroat; they might be worth visiting, if you're up for some exploring and don't mind questionable fishing results. [T22N R18W S8]

UPPER HOLLAND LAKE. This one is good and deep, about 50 acres, in subalpine country below the crest of the Swan Range. Take the USFS trail above Holland Lake 6 miles east. The trail is steep and switchbacky in places, and it's very popular with hikers and horse packers out for day hikes or heading into the Bob Marshall Wilderness. Horse packers use the Owl Creek trailhead south of Holland Lake, while hikers use the northside trailhead near the lodge. At Upper Holland, there is one big

Upper Holland Lake. —Courtesy Michele Archie

campsite and a horse hitching area along the north side. The lake contains a goodly number of 6- to 12-inch cutthroat trout—and some bigger—but they can be real temperamental, and more anglers get skunked than not. This lake is stocked periodically. [T20N R15W S29]

UPPER PIPER LAKE. See Ducharme Lake.

VAN LAKE. Take Montana 83 from Swan Lake south for 15 miles, then follow a signed logging road several miles east to Van Lake. In mountainous, timbered country, the last ½ mile or so can get pretty rough, and you might want to park and walk unless your rig has high clearance. Van is a popular lake, with several informal but obvious campsites along the south shore. Covering 58 acres, it's about 40 feet deep in the middle, with gradual drop-offs and some marsh around the shore. Take a cue from the Van Lake regulars and bring a boat or a float tube to get to the best fishing. The lake has been managed sometimes for cutts and sometimes for rainbows. Since the early 1980s, Van has gotten yearly plantings of rainbows, some of them in the 20-inches-plus range. Regardless of all that effort, Van Lake is only fair fishing—in part because of competition from a large red-side shiner population. [T22N R17W S3]

WHELP LAKE. It's on the Swan drainage a few hundred yards east of Gray Wolf Lake. Covering about 5 acres, it's fair to middling fishing for 10- to 16-inch cutthroat trout.[T18N R17W S31]

WOLF CREEK. This real small stream flows out of the Swan Range near Crater Mountain for 7 miles, to its confluence with the Swan River, northeast of Bigfork. It's crossed by Montana 83 about 1½ miles up from its mouth. Wolf Creek used to be excellent fishing for small cutthroat above and brook trout in the lower end, but now it's only fair in the lower end, and good above. [T27N R19W S22]

WOODWARD CREEK. This stream empties into the Swan River 10 miles south of the lake, and it's more or less accessible by logging road for about 1½ miles of fishing. Head west off the Fatty Creek logging road about 4 miles past its junction with Montana 83. Woodward Creek is moderately popular for fair catches of 9- to 12-inch brook trout, plus some large bull trout up from the lake. [T23N R18W S1]

WYMAN CREEK RESERVOIR. See Kelly Reservoir.

Index of Listed Waters

Bear Creek (Middle Fork Flathead drainage), 247
Bear (or Bear Creek) Lake (Bitterroot drainage), 22
Bear Lakes (Kootenai drainage), 310
Bearmouth Access Pond, 155
Bear Run Creek, 23
Beartrap Creek Reservoir, 71
Beatrice Creek, 108
Beaver Creek (Bitterroot drainage; south of Conner), 24
Beaver Creek (Bitterroot drainage; west of Stevensville), 23
Beaver Creek (Blackfoot drainage; near Lincoln), 72
Beaver Creek (Blackfoot drainage; near Seeley Lake), 72
Beaver Creek (lower Clark Fork drainage), 108
Beaver Creek (upper Clark Fork drainage), 155
Beaver Creek (Swan drainage), 361
Beaver Lake (Flathead drainage), 201
Beaver Lake (Swan drainage), 361
Beavertail Creek, 24
Beavertail (or Beavertail Hill) Pond, 155
Beefstraight Creek, 155
Beetle Creek, 310
Belly River, 304
Belmont Creek, 72
Bergsicker Creek, 247
Bergsicker Lake, 247
Bertha Creek, 72
Bertha Lake, 81
Beta Lake, 272
Betts Lake, 310
Big Altoona Lake, 153
Big Ashley Lake, 201
Big Barker Lake, 154
Big Beaver Creek, 108; South Branch, 108
Big Beaver Lake, 201
Big Cherry Creek, 310
Big Creek (Bitterroot drainage), 24; South Fork, 24
Big Creek (lower Clark Fork drainage), 108
Big Creek (Kootenai drainage), 311; Little North Fork, 335
Big Creek (North Fork Flathead drainage), 259
Big Creek Lakes, 25
Big Hawkins Lake, 328
Big Hawk Lakes, 272

Big Hogback Creek, 173
Bighorn Lake, 72
Big Lake, 108
Big Lost Creek, 203
Biglow Lake, 288
Big Pozega Lake, 155
Big Rock Creek, 109
Big Salmon Creek, 272
Big Salmon Lake, 273
Big Sky Lake, 86
Big Spring Creek, 156
Big Terrace Lake, 145
Big Thornton Lake, 192
Birch Lake, 361
Bison Creek Reservoir, 154
Bitterroot Irrigation Ditch, 25
Bitterroot River, 19; Burnt Fork, 26; East Fork, 26; Nez Perce Fork, 27; West Fork, 27
Black Bear Creek, 273
Blackfoot River, 69; Dry Fork of the North Fork, 72; East Fork of the North Fork, 73; Landers Fork, 73; North Fork, 74
Black Lake (Blackfoot drainage), 85
Black Lake (South Fork Flathead drainage), 273
Blackfoot Lake, 273
Blacktail Creek, 156
Blaine, Lake, 212
Blanchard Creek, 75; North Fork, 75
Blanchard Lake (Blackfoot drainage), 75
Blanchard Lake (Flathead drainage), 203
Blast Lake, 203
Blind Canyon Creek, 76
Blodgett Creek, 28
Blodgett Lake, 28
Blossom Lakes, 109
Bluebird Lake, 311
Blue Creek, 109
Blue Joint Creek, 29
Blue Lake (Flathead drainage; north of Bigfork), 203
Blue (or Green) Lake (Flathead drainage; near Stryker), 203
Blue Lakes (South Fork Flathead drainage), 274
Blue Sky Creek, 311
Blum Creek, 156
Bobtail Creek, 311
Bock Lake, 204
Bohn Lake, 156
Boiling Springs Creek, 109

Boles Creek, 76
Bonanza Lakes, 109
Bond Creek, 361
Bond Lake, 362
Bootjack Lake (Flathead drainage), 204
Bootjack Lake (Kootenai drainage), 311
Border Lake, 314
Boulder Creek (Bitterroot drainage), 29
Boulder Creek (upper Clark Fork drainage), 156; South, 156
Boulder Creek (Kootenai drainage), 311
Boulder Lake (Bitterroot drainage), 29
Boulder Lake (Blackfoot drainage), 76
Boulder Lakes (upper Clark Fork drainage), 157
Boulder Lakes (Kootenai drainage), 312
Bowl Creek, 248
Bowles Creek, 157
Bowman Creek, 304
Bowman Lake (Glacier Park), 302
Bowman Lakes (upper Clark Fork drainage), 157
Bowser Lake, 204
Boyle Lake, 204
Bradley Lake, 248
Bramlet Lakes, 312
Brewster Creek, 157; East Fork, 157
Brimstone Creek, 312
Brimstone Lake, 312
Bristow Creek, 312
Brown's Gulch, 157
Brown's Lake, 77
Bruce Creek, 274
Bryan Creek, 158
Bryan Lake, 29
Buck Creek (Bitterroot drainage), 29
Buck Creek (Swan drainage), 362
Buck Lake, 110
Buford Pond. See Twomile Creek.
Bull Creek, 77
Bullhead Lake, 302
Bull Lake (Flathead drainage), 204
Bull Lake (Kootenai drainage), 312
Bull River, 110; East Fork, 110; Middle Fork, 110; North Fork, 110; North Fork of the East Fork, 111; South Fork, 111
Bunker Creek, 274; Middle Fork Creek, 287
Bunyan Lake, 362
Burdette Creek, 111
Burgess Lake, 231
Burke Lake, 314

Burns Slough, 158
Burnt Creek (Kootenai drainage), 314
Burnt Creek (South Fork Flathead drainage), 274
Burnt Fork Bitterroot River, 26
Burnt Fork Lake, 30
Burnt Lake, 204
Butler Creek, 111
Butte Cabin Creek, 158
Butte Creek, West Fork, 66
Butterfly Creek, 30

Cabin Creek, 77
Cabinet Gorge Reservoir, 112
Cabin Lake (lower Clark Fork drainage), 112
Cabin Lake (Flathead drainage), 204
Cable Creek (upper Clark Fork drainage), 158
Cable Creek (Kootenai drainage), 314
Cache Creek, 113
Cad Lake, 314
Calbick Creek, 248
Calf Creek, 30
Callahan Creek, 314
Camas Creek (Bitterroot drainage), 30
Camas Creek (Blackfoot drainage), 77
Camas Creek (Glacier Park), 304
Camas Lake (Glacier Park), 302
Camas Lakes, 30
Cameron Creek, 30
Camp Creek (Bitterroot drainage), 31; East Fork, 31; West Fork, 31
Camp Creek (Blackfoot drainage), 77
Camp Creek (South Fork Flathead drainage), 275
Camp Lake, 77
Cannon Creek, 275
Canyon Creek (Bitterroot drainage), 31
Canyon Creek (Blackfoot drainage), 79
Canyon Creek (lower Clark Fork drainage), 113
Canyon Creek (North Fork Flathead drainage), 259
Canyon Lake (Blackfoot drainage), 79
Canyon Lake(s) (Flathead drainage), 210
Canyon Lakes (Bitterroot drainage), 32
Capitan Lake, 32
Capri Lake, 32
Caribou Creek, 314
Carlton Creek, 32
Carlton Lake, 33
Carpenter Creek, 158

Lang Creek, 125
Lappi Lake, 44
Larry Creek, 44
Lavene Creek, 45
Lavon Lake, 333
Lawn Lake, 125
Lazy Creek, 214
LeBeau Creek, 214
Legend Lake, 42
Leigh Creek, 333
Leigh Lake, 333
Lena Lake, 284
Lenore Lake, 125
Leon Lake, 333
Libby Creek, 334
Lick Creek, 285
Lick Lake (Kootenai drainage), 334
Lick Lake (South Fork Flathead drainage), 285
Lilly Pad Lake, 335
Lily Lake, 373
Lime Creek, 335
Lincoln Gulch, 90
Lincoln Lake, 303
Lindbergh Lake, 373
Link Lake, 262
Lion Creek, 373
Lion Lake, 285
Little Altoona Lake, 153
Little Barker Lake, 154
Little Beaver Creek, 125
Little Beaver Lake, 214
Little Bitterroot Lake, 215
Little Bitterroot River, 235
Little Blackfoot River, 176
Little Blackfoot Spring Creek, 176
Little Blue Joint Creek, 45
Little Boulder Creek, 46
Little Burnt Fork Creek, 46
Little Cherry Creek, 335
Little Creek, 335
Little Duck Lake, 325
Little Fish Lake, 176
Little Hawkins Lake, 328
Little Hogback Creek, 177
Little Joe Creek, 126
Little Lake, 126
Little Loon Lake, 335
Little McGregor Lake, 126
Little Ninemile Creek, 123
Little North Fork Big (or Little North Fork) Creek, 335
Little Pozega Lake, 177

Little Racetrack Lake, 177
Little Rock Creek (Bitterroot drainage), 46
Little Rock Creek (lower Clark Fork drainage), 126
Little Rock Creek Lake, 46
Little Salmon Creek, 285
Little Spar Lake, 335
Little Thompson River, 126; North Fork, 126
Little Thornton Lake, 177
Little Trout Creek, 127
Little West Fork (of Bitterroot) Creek, 46
Liverpool Creek, 90
Lockwood Lake, 46
Lodgepole Creek (Blackfoot drainage), 90
Lodgepole Creek (Middle Fork Flathead drainage), 252
Logan Creek (Flathead drainage), 215
Logan (or North Fork Logan) Creek (South Fork Flathead drainage), 285
Logging Creek, 304
Logging Lake, 303
Lolo Creek, 46; East Fork, 47; South Fork, 47; West Fork, 47
Lone Lake, 215
Lone Pine Reservoirs, 232
Long Creek, 252
Long Lake (Flathead Reservation) . See Summit Lake.
Long Lake (Kootenai drainage), 335
Loon Creek, 336
Loon Lake (Kootenai drainage; near Fortine), 336
Loon Lake (Kootenai drainage; near Happy's Inn), 336
Loon Lake (Kootenai drainage; north of Libby), 336
Loon Lake (Swan drainage), 374
Lore Lake, 215
Lost Creek (lower Clark Fork drainage), 127
Lost Creek (upper Clark Fork drainage), 177
Lost Creek (Flathead drainage), 217
Lost Creek (Swan drainage), 374
Lost Fork Creek, 336
Lost Horse Creek, 48; North, 48; South, 48
Lost Horse Lake, 49
Lost Johnny Creek, 286

Middle Fork (of Landers Fork) Creek, 92
Middle Fork Flathead River, 245
Middle Kootenai Lake, 50
Middle Quartz Lake, 303
Middle Thompson Lake, 130
Middle Trio Lake, 147
Mike Renig Gulch, 180
Mill Creek (Bitterroot drainage; near Lolo), 50
Mill Creek (Bitterroot drainage; near Woodside), 50
Mill Creek (lower Clark Fork drainage), 130
Mill Creek (upper Clark Fork drainage), 180; South Fork, 180
Mill Creek Lake, 181
Miller Creek, 51
Miller Lake, 181
Miller's Lake. See Hoover Creek.
Mill Lake, 50
Milnor Lake, 338
Mine Creek, 51
Miner Creek, 253
Minesinger Creek, 238
Minnesota Gulch, 181
Minor Lake, 338
Mission Creek, 238
Mission Reservoir, 238
Missoula Gulch, 132
Missoula Lake, 132
Modesty Creek, 181
Mokowanis Lake, 303
Mollman Lakes, 375
Monarch Creek, 181
Monroe, Lake, 214
Montana Creek, 132
Monture Creek, 92
Moon Lake. See Summit Lake.
Moon Slough, 208
Moore Lake (lower Clark Fork drainage), 132
Moore Lake (Swan drainage), 375
Moose Creek (Bitterroot drainage), 51
Moose Creek (Blackfoot drainage), 92
Moose Creek (North Fork Flathead drainage), 262
Moose Lake (upper Clark Fork drainage), 181
Moose Lake (Middle Fork Flathead drainage), 253
Moose Lake (North Fork Flathead drainage), 262

Moose Meadow (or Moose) Creek (upper Clark Fork drainage), 181
Moran Basin Lakes, 132
Moran Creek, 262
Moran Lake, 338
Morigeau Lakes, 236
Morrell Creek, 92
Morrell Lake, 93
Morrison Creek, 253
Mosquito Creek, 132
Mosquito Lake, 181
Mountain Ben Lake, 182
Mountain Creek, 93
Mount Henry Lake, 338
Mount Powell Lake. See Elliot Lakes.
Mud Creek (Bitterroot drainage), 51
Mud Creek (Flathead Reservation), 238
Mud Lake (Blackfoot drainage), 93
Mud Lake (upper Clark Fork drainage; west of Deer Lodge), 182
Mud Lake (upper Clark Fork drainage; east of Hamilton), 183
Mud Lake (upper Clark Fork drainage; east of Phillipsburg), 182
Mud Lake (Flathead drainage), 219
Mud Lake (Kootenai drainage), 338
Mud Lake (North Fork Flathead drainage), 263
Mud Lake (Swan drainage), 375
Mud Lakes (Flathead Reservation), 238
Murphy Creek, 338
Murphy Lake, 339
Murray Creek, 287
Murray Lake, 219
Murr Creek, 132
Myron Lake, 339
Mystery Lake, 219

Nanny Creek, 287
Nasukoin Lake, 263
Necklace Lakes, 287
Nelson Lake, 51
Nemote Creek, 133
Nevada Creek, 93
Nevada (or Nevada Creek) Lake, 93
Nez Perce Fork Bitterroot River, 27
Ninemile Creek, 133
Ninemile Lake, 264
Ninepipe Reservoir, 239
Ninko Creek, 263
No Name Lake, 340
North Biglow Lake, 288

We encourage you to patronize your local bookstores. Most stores will order any title that they do not stock. You may also order directly from Mountain Press by mail, using the order form provided below or by calling our toll-free number and using your Visa or MasterCard. We will gladly send you a complete catalog upon request.

Mountain Press Titles to Complement Your Montana Fishing Trip:

_____Fly Fishing for the Compleat Idiot: A No-Nonsense Guide to Fly Casting	$15.00
_____Fly Tying: Adventures in Fur, Feathers, and Fun	$15.00
_____Packin' In on Mules and Horses	$15.00
_____Llamas on the Trail: A Packer's Guide	$15.00
_____Birds of the Northern Rockies	$12.00
_____Mammals of the Northern Rockies	$12.00
_____OWLS Whoo are they?	$12.00
_____Northwest Weeds: The Ugly and Beautiful Villains of Fields, Gardens, and Roadsides	$14.00
_____Edible and Medicinal Plants of the West	$21.00
_____Alpine Wildflowers of the Rocky Mountains	$14.00
_____Roadside Geology of Montana	$20.00
_____Northwest Exposures: A Geologic Story of the Northwest	$24.00
_____The Lochsa Story: Land Ethics in the Bitterroot Mountains	$20.00
_____Names on the Face of Montana	$12.00
_____Tough, Willing, and Able: Tales of a Montana Family	$12.00
_____The Journals of Patrick Gass: Member of the Lewis and Clark Expedition	$20.00
_____The Range	$14.00
_____The Ranch: A Modern History of the North American Cattle Industry	$14.00

Please include $3.00 per order to cover shipping and handling.

Send the books marked above. I enclose $_____

Name_____

Address_____

City_____State_____Zip_____

☐ Payment enclosed (check or money order in U.S. funds)
Bill my: ☐ VISA ☐ MasterCard Expiration Date:_____

Card No._____

Signature _____

Mountain Press Publishing Company

P.O. Box 2399 • Missoula, Montana 59806
E-mail: mtnpress@montana.com • Website: www.mtnpress.com
Order Toll Free 1-800-234-5308 • *Have your Visa or MasterCard ready*